Seventh Edition

THE PROFESSIONAL COUNSELOR

A PROCESS GUIDE TO HELPING

Harold L. Hackney

Syracuse University

Sherry Cormier

West Virginia University

Boston   Columbus   Indianapolis   New York   San Francisco   Upper Saddle River
Amsterdam   Cape Town   Dubai   London   Madrid   Milan   Munich   Paris   Montreal   Toronto
Delhi   Mexico City   São Paulo   Sydney   Hong Kong   Seoul   Singapore   Taipei   Tokyo

Vice President and Editorial Director: Jeffery W. Johnston
Senior Acquisitions Editor: Meredith D. Fossel
Vice President, Director of Marketing: Margaret Waples
Senior Marketing Manager: Chris Barry
Senior Managing Editor: Pamela Bennett
Senior Project Manager: Mary M. Irvin
Production Manager: Laura Messerly
Cover Designer: Jodi Notowitz
Project Coordination: Niraj Bhatt/Aptara®, Inc.
Composition: Aptara®, Inc.
Printer/Binder: Courier/Westford
Cover Printer: Courier/Moore Langen
Text Font: 10/12 Times

Every effort has been made to provide accurate and current Internet information in this book. However, the Internet and information posted on it are constantly changing, so it is inevitable that some of the Internet addresses listed in this textbook will change.

If you purchased this book within the United States or Canada you should be aware that it has been imported without the approval of the Publisher or the Author.

10 9 8 7 6 5 4 3 2 1

ISBN 10:   0-13-289931-0
ISBN 13: 978-0-13-289931-4

PREFACE

NEW TO THIS EDITION

With this seventh edition of *The Professional Counselor*, we set out to enhance and broaden the concepts inherent in the process of helping others. This process of counseling is a vibrant and evolving entity. It grows through the practice of skilled counselors, explorations of researchers, and musings of thoughtful scholars. One can recognize this evolution over the history of counseling, beginning with the earliest explorations of people like Carl Rogers, B. F. Skinner, Fritz Perls, and others. But the evolution is less obvious in the restricted timeframe of popular texts moving from one edition to the next. Nevertheless, with the helpful suggestions of independent reviewers, dedicated students, and colleagues, new areas for improvement do emerge. Specifically, this new edition is expanded in six areas:

- Identifying and targeting those Council for Accreditation of Counseling and Related Educational Programs (CACREP) Standards that are addressed in each of the chapters
- Revising and adding new case examples to illustrate how skills and competencies are applied to counseling cases
- Updating and expanding research and references that illustrate current practices
- Revising and expanding web-based video samples at the end of each chapter that illustrate skills and procedures discussed in the chapter
- Identifying ethical issues and relating them to the American Counseling Association (ACA) Ethical Code
- Providing Internet URLs for ten professional codes of ethics (Appendix C)

FEATURES OF THIS BOOK

This edition maintains a number of features that have long set this book apart from most other introductory counseling textbooks. These features include the following:

- Carrying a case through each of the intervention chapters, thus allowing students to visualize the same case with different treatments—and describing case illustrations that bring theory into the realm of authentic practice.
- A five-step model (used in the National Counseling Examination [NCE]) that provides students with a roadmap for assessing client progress, helps students plan for interventions, and encourages students to view counseling as an evolving process with an end in sight.
- Clear guidelines for assessing cases using five theoretical contexts—affective, cognitive, behavioral, systemic, and spiritual—that help students apply what they have learned in counseling theory courses to the practice of counseling.
- Identification of spiritual issues that provide an alternative way of working with clients.
- Separate chapters on client assessment and treatment planning that help students incorporate specific counseling interventions as they are learning them.
- Discussion of treatment planning that reflects the growing influence of managed care and the necessity of knowing how to plan treatments that will meet managed-care criteria.
- Helpful boxed material throughout the chapters that summarizes and illustrates skills.
- A series of forms and guides (Appendix B) that illustrate the management of counseling cases.

HOW THE BOOK IS ORGANIZED

Beginning with Chapter 1, we provide a context for counseling, including how to think about the profession and the process. We discuss the intimacy of the counseling relationship, conditions that facilitate positive relationships, considerations of what successful counseling is like, characteristics of effective counselors, and a case illustration of how to measure counseling outcomes.

In Chapter 2, we explore the language of counseling. What is it that counselors say that sets them apart from other caregivers? What special verbalizations do counselors use? What is their purpose in using this language? How does this language affect the client? And how does the counselor's language change, depending on a client's goals? We address this professional communication through basic nonverbal as well as verbal helping skills and advanced verbal skills.

Chapter 3 sets the format for the book by discussing the counseling process as a passage through five stages of development. We give students a way to conceptualize the process, beginning with establishing the relationship, following with assessing (understanding) the client's presenting problem, helping the client recognize what can be achieved (goals), structuring the sessions with the problem and goals firmly in mind, and helping the client complete the counseling relationship successfully. Chapters 4 through 7 address each of these specific stages with a discussion of skills that enhance each stage and with case illustrations to guide the beginner in the use of those skills. In each chapter, we help the student understand the how and the why of that particular stage and provide exercises and discussion questions to help students apply the skills. At the end of each chapter, we provide video illustrations of the skills that are available at MyCounselingLab. In Chapter 7, we also introduce the four ways to view client problems: problems as feeling states, problems as thought processes, problems as behavior patterns, and problems as interpersonal or environmental conditions.

Chapters 8 through 11 examine each of these four ways to view client problems and the validated counseling interventions that address each one. In each case, we connect the choice of intervention to specific client goals. These intervention chapters all include case illustrations of the more complex interventions so students can understand how the ideas are applied to real clients. In addition, each of these chapters contains exercises to help students explore and develop skills. These chapters also include video examples of how interventions are used.

Finally, in Chapter 12, we return to the final stage of counseling, termination, as a process in itself rather than an event. What are the ingredients of a successful termination? What ethical issues are raised in the termination process? Who decides when termination is appropriate? How is referral to another helping source part of the termination process?

Because counseling occurs in a real world composed of many cultures and backgrounds, we have included considerations based on cultural and age differences. Rather than devote a specific chapter to such client differences, we have infused multicultural and age discussions, based on the research and experience of specialists in the field in each chapter. We make a specific point of discussing how children relate differently to certain counseling interventions and which interventions prove less effective with children. We also discuss the impact that specific counseling approaches have on clients—for example, which clients tend to respond better to affective versus behavioral interventions.

Students will find a variety of forms commonly used in counseling practice in Appendix B. These forms may be copied and used by students as they practice their craft. A new appendix (Appendix C) contains websites for ten professional codes of ethics, which may be downloaded for continuing use as counselors advance in their training.

MyCounselingLab

Help your students bridge the gap between theory and practice with **MyCounselingLab**. **MyCounselingLab** connects your course content to video- and case-based real world scenarios, and provides:

- *Building Counseling Skills* exercises that offer opportunities for students to develop and practice skills critical to their success as professional helpers. Hints and feedback provide scaffolding and reinforce key concepts.
- *Assignments & Activities* that assess students' understanding of key concepts and skill development. Suggested responses are available to instructors, making grading easy.
- *Multiple-Choice Quizzes* that help students gauge their understanding of important topics and prepare for success on licensure examinations.

Access to **MyCounselingLab** can be packaged with this textbook or purchased standalone. To find out how to package student access to this website and gain access as an instructor, go to www.mycounselinglab.com, email us at counseling@pearson.com, or contact your Pearson sales representative.

ACKNOWLEGMENTS

Thinking about a new edition begins with the opinions of others. Specifically, the persons who serve as reviewers provide invaluable insights into how the user views a text, its strengths and its weaknesses. Insightful reviewers provide enormous value in this renewal process. We wish to thank Robert Colbert, University of Connecticut; Hugh Crethar, Oklahoma State University; Kenneth C. Hergenrather, George Washington University; Sue Stickel, Eastern Michigan University; Barbara J. Thompson, George Washington University; and Susan C. Whiston, Indiana University, for their generous and serious attention to this responsibility. Their comments have given us a real advantage in our effort. We also wish to thank the editorial staff at Pearson for their assistance. Meredith Fossel, our editor, was wonderful in her support, her ideas, and her follow-up; her editorial assistant, Nancy Holstein, responded to our needs and concerns with efficiency and accuracy; and Mary Irvin, senior project manager, gave us the material and good advice we needed as we moved through this process. Our sincere thanks to each of you.

H.H.
S.C.

ABOUT THE AUTHORS

Harold Hackney, Professor Emeritus of counseling at Syracuse University, is a national certified counselor, licensed professional counselor, approved clinical supervisor, and a Fellow of the American Counseling Association. Harold is past-president of the Association for Counselor Education and Supervision and former member of the ACA Governing Council, and has served on the Board of the Center for Credentialing in Education. His areas of expertise include counselor training, training of future counseling professors, research methodology, counseling processes, and counseling theory. Hackney's writings draw from his experiences as a school counselor, a marriage and family counselor, and his research on counseling processes and spirituality in counseling. Prior to his appointment at Syracuse University, Hackney was a professor at Purdue University and Fairfield University.

Sherry Cormier, Professor Emerita of counseling, rehabilitation counseling, and counseling psychology at West Virginia University, is a licensed psychologist in the state of West Virginia and a long-standing member of the American Counseling Association. Her areas of expertise include counselor training, counseling interventions, cognitive-behavioral therapy, clinical supervision, and health and wellness. Currently she is affiliated with Transformational Practices, an endeavor in which she provides clinical and consultation services and training to a variety of individuals and organizations. Prior to her appointment at West Virginia University, she was a faculty member at the University of Tennessee.

BRIEF CONTENTS

CONTENTS

Conceptualizing Counseling

PURPOSE OF THIS CHAPTER

In this chapter, we introduce a number of concepts and conditions that are fundamental to the counseling process. In so doing, we provide a structure for the remainder of the book. Counseling must be viewed within a context. The factors that contribute to that context include philosophy, current theoretical premises, and culture—in other words, the social milieu. That milieu changes as a society changes. And, of course, it changes when one moves from one society or culture to another. In addition, we address helper qualities that are universal, crossing cultures and time. Our ultimate objective is to help you, the reader, begin to identify yourself within these parameters and to do some introspection regarding how your personal qualities match those of the professional counselor.

Considerations as You Read This Chapter

- As you read about the different theoretical approaches to client problems and change, which ones do you find most comfortable?

- How do you view life? Do you believe that most things that happen to people are unplanned and coincidental, or do you believe that life events tend to fit a "larger plan"?

- Is life's challenge a matter of analyzing situations and developing successful responses to those situations? Or is life's challenge to become the best person one can be, given the circumstances life presents?

- How do you describe your culture? From whom did you get that culture? Your parents? Your community? Your nation?

This is a book about the process of counseling. In the hands of a skilled and sensitive person, this process can be used to enhance the lives of people who are seeking to change their relationships, to develop self-understanding, or to learn how to anticipate and meet life's challenges. Although it is almost impossible to define precisely what the counseling experience will be for you, some general parameters of the counseling process will certainly be part of your experience. There are several ways to consider the counseling process, beginning with a clear sense of what the process is, how counseling is applied to human problems, how the client influences the process, and what constitutes successful counseling. In this chapter, we will examine these and other fundamental issues as they relate to the practice of counseling.

WHAT IS COUNSELING?

The process of counseling has a long history. Scholars have traced it to the Enlightenment, with connections to the incantations of ancient priest-healers in Mesopotamia, Persia, and Egypt. Even with that long history, counseling has proven to be a difficult concept to explain. The public's lack of clarity is due, in part, to the proliferation of modern-day practitioners who have adopted the counselor label. They range from credit counselors to investment counselors, and from camp counselors to retirement counselors. Although their services share the common ingredient of verbal communication and possibly the intention to be helpful, those services have little in common with the type of counseling this book addresses.

Professional counseling has emerged as the descriptor for the treatment of interpersonal and intrapersonal issues so common to U.S. culture. It takes the form of individual (one-to-one) and group (multiple clients) modes. The content of professional counseling tends to include both internal and relational concerns. Internal (intrapersonal) concerns can range from issues of self-concept to psychological disturbance. Relational (interpersonal) concerns can range from communication and perceptual problems between the client and others to issues of hostility, aggression, and criminal activity. These problems cross all age groups and developmental stages. It is important to note that these issues, even the "lesser" ones, are diagnostic in nature. That is, the problems must be understood both in their expression (as behaviors, feelings, or thoughts) and in the context in which they are supported (what keeps the problem alive).

The American Counseling Association (ACA) defines professional counseling as "the application of mental health, psychological, and human development principles through cognitive, affective, behavioral and systemic intervention strategies, that address wellness, personal growth, and career development, as well as pathology" (American Counseling Association, 1997). This definition embraces both problems that are considered "normal" and "developmental" and problems that are of a more serious psychological nature. However, that is not to suggest that a professional counselor might be a provider of services for any type of problem. Within the counseling profession are many specialties, including mental health counselors, marriage and family counselors, school counselors, rehabilitation counselors, pastoral counselors, creative arts counselors, geriatric counselors, and so on. Each specialty is based on specific therapeutic skills required by the clientele who would seek that specialty for assistance. Common across these specialties are the relationship, communication, conceptualization, diagnostic, and intervention skills that are covered in this book.

Why Counseling?

It may be necessary to remind some aspiring counselors that the problems of life can be solved in many ways, counseling being one of those ways. The vast majority of the human race has never experienced professional counseling. Does that mean that they are functioning at some sub-level of life? Of course not. Many people adapt to life's challenges by using personal resources, friends and family, or religious faith. But even with these resources, challenges can sometimes accumulate to the point that an unencumbered, skilled helper can facilitate the process of growth and adaptation to such challenges.

Viewed in this way, counseling can assume the function of change, prevention, or life enhancement. As change, counseling is concerned with situations that, for whatever reason, have become so disruptive that people are unable to continue through the normal passage of life without excess stress, dissatisfaction, or unhappiness. As prevention, counseling is able to take into account those predictable life events that produce stress; cause people to draw on their psychological resources; and, ultimately, demand adaptation to changing life forces. Finally, a third form of counseling, enhancement counseling, goes beyond life's challenges and predictabilities. As a counseling goal, enhancement attempts to open clients' experiences to new and deeper levels of understanding, appreciation, and wisdom about life's many potentialities.

THE PARAMETERS OF COUNSELING

Counselors can talk about counseling as change or growth. Or they can talk about counseling as a process or product. If counselors go very deeply into an examination of these alternatives, it also becomes apparent that they are beginning to talk about philosophical, cultural, and spiritual issues as well as psychological or interpersonal concerns. How counselors view these issues and concerns will determine what they do in the counseling interview. If I happen to hold an optimistic view of human beings and how they adapt to life's ups and downs, my view of what should happen in counseling will be quite different from that of the person who holds a cautious, or even pessimistic, view of human beings and how they adapt. If I have experienced life only in a sheltered or encapsulated culture, then I may view counseling as not involving cultural dimensions. If I solve my problems by careful examination and analysis of issues, decisions to be made, appropriateness of outcomes, and so on, then I might naturally assume that others should approach life problems in a similar fashion. Or if I see life as a multifaceted gestalt, then I might feel less urgency to identify, prescribe, and, thus, control the outcomes of counseling. These are just part of the counselor's context when she or he enters the process of counseling.

Occurring simultaneously with these issues, counseling addresses the personal concerns of the client. These concerns may have a strong basis in reality, or they may be self-generated by the client's discomfort. And it is also obvious that clients come as optimists or pessimists, bold or cautious. Whatever the case, the counselor must have a healthy appreciation of the very broad range of behaviors, attitudes, self-concepts, cultural agendas, and feelings that emerge as people develop. In other words, normal behavior, normal functioning, or normal feelings can include occasional flirtations with abnormal, a kind of testing the limits of one's self. It is best observed in the lives of adolescents, but it is found in people of all ages and stages of development. On the other hand, *normal* does not mean the same as *functional*. Functional behavior is that which facilitates growth, problem solving, and coping. People can behave in ways that are within the range of normal but still not be behaving functionally. When listening to the personal concerns of clients, counselors must seek to understand life as clients see it and the reasons they see life as they do. Only then can counselors begin to participate as helpers in the counseling relationship. Only then can clients begin to move toward more functional behavior. In a similar way, *dysfunctional* does not necessarily mean *abnormal*, which is why many people now refer to their families of origin as dysfunctional.

Finally, there is no way to understand human existence by separating it from the setting or environment in which existence occurs. Children cannot be fully understood separate from their families of origin, their neighborhoods, or their peer groups; adults cannot be understood separate from their families, careers, or ethnicities; and individuals cannot be dissected into intellectual selves, occupational selves, affective selves, or whatever. Each individual is an ecological existence within a cultural context, living with others in an ecological system. One's intrapersonal dimensions are interdependent with others who share one's life space. A keen understanding and appreciation of this interdependence will facilitate your understanding of yourself as a counselor, and of your clients as people seeking to recover, to grow, or to enhance their lives.

Counseling and Theory

Theory is another way to approach counseling. In its most generic sense, theory is a way of explaining that, which is not directly observable. Thus, counseling theory is an effort to explain the process by which a set of activities begins, develops, and ends. Personality theory, from which numerous counseling theories spring, is an effort to explain the various ways that the psyche emerges, evolves, and matures, both in terms of normal development and in terms of dysfunction. On the other hand, therapy is the application of principles adapted from theory. In the discussion of counseling theories, authors will often refer to person-centered *therapy*, behavioral *therapy*, and so on. These approaches refer to what the counselor is doing with the client, based on the counselor's theoretical orientation.

Within the context of counseling therapies, well over 400 approaches have been identified. Most of these approaches would be better labeled as variations on a much smaller number of theoretical themes. The four dominant themes are the psychodynamic, cognitive/behavioral, humanistic, and transpersonal approaches. To this list, we would add a fifth theme: the systemic approaches that have their origins not in personality theory but in cybernetic theory.

Counseling theories can serve a number of functions. They provide a set of guidelines to explain how human beings learn, change, and develop; they also propose a model for normal human functioning (and ways in which human dysfunction may be manifested); and they suggest what should transpire in the counseling process and what the outcomes of counseling could be. In short, a counseling theory offers a type of map of the counseling process and the route its participants should take to achieve certain goals. Rarely does a counseling theory prescribe what the specific goals of counseling should be. Because there is much room for alternative viewpoints on matters such as normal human functioning, how people change, and what is a desirable outcome, different theories have emerged to reflect these various viewpoints. On a more practical level, counselors use theories to organize information and observations, to explain or conceptualize client problems, and to order and implement particular interventions with clients.

One might think, or even believe, that some theories are more valid than others, but research does not support that belief. In a classic meta-analysis of the effects of over 400 psychotherapy outcome studies, Smith and Glass (1977) concluded that the

> results of research demonstrate the beneficial effects of counseling and psychotherapy. Despite volumes devoted to the theoretical differences among different schools of psychotherapy, the results of research demonstrated negligible differences in the effects produced by different therapy types. (p. 760)

So counseling does seem to help people in distress, but no particular counseling theory stands out as better than the rest. Counselors tend to identify with particular theories for a variety of reasons. Some counselors look for a theory that provides the most utilitarian explanation of the counseling process. Their quest is for a theory that provides concrete guidelines. Other counselors look for a theory that is compatible with their life perspective—that is, a theory that makes similar assumptions about human nature as their own private assumptions. Still other counselors seek a theory that best explains or conceptualizes the types of problems their clients will present. Of course, it is possible for a counselor to obtain all three objectives with the same theory, but this realization tends to emerge only as the counselor gains experience.

In recent years, the counseling profession has witnessed an increased convergence among theorists and a growing realization that no single theory can explain or fit all client challenges. The result is an emerging view that theory is meant to serve the user, and when no single theory totally fits the counselor's needs, then a blending of compatible theories is an acceptable practice. This is known as an eclectic or integrative approach. Prochaska and Norcross (2010) report that more than a third of practicing counselors prefer an eclectic approach (37%), followed by existential/humanistic theory (13%), cognitive theories (10%), person-centered therapy (8%), psychodynamic theories (8%), systemic theories (7%), and behavioral approaches (6%). The integrative approach to strategy selection draws from theories based on the characteristics of the client's presenting problems and outcome goals. This approach would rarely select strategies from a single counseling theory.

The following list presents seven elements about counseling that are operative for all of the major theoretical approaches:

1. Counseling involves responding to the feelings, thoughts, and actions of the client. Existing theoretical approaches tend to emphasize one of these to the exclusion of another. Some approaches (person-centered, existential) favor an emphasis on feelings; others (rational-emotive, reality therapy, cognitive-behavioral) emphasize the importance of behaviors and actions; an integrative approach recognizes the importance of being able to identify and respond appropriately to feeling states, behavior patterns, and relationship patterns.

2. Counseling involves a basic acceptance of the client's perceptions and feelings, regardless of outside evaluative standards. In other words, you must first acknowledge who the client is before you can begin to consider who the client might become. Clients need your understanding of their current reality and concerns before they can anticipate growth and change in a new direction.

3. Confidentiality and privacy constitute essential ingredients in the counseling setting. Physical facilities that preserve this quality are important.

4. Counseling is voluntary. Ordinarily, it is not effective when the client is required to participate. Regardless of how the client is referred, the counselor never uses coercion as a means of obtaining or continuing with a client.

5. Generally speaking, the counselor operates with a conservative bias against communicating to the client detailed information about his or her own life. Although there are times when counselor self-disclosure is appropriate, counselors generally do not complicate the relationship by focusing attention on themselves.

6. One skill underlying all systems of counseling is that of communication. Counselors and clients alike continually transmit and receive verbal and nonverbal messages during the interview process. Therefore, awareness of and sensitivity to the kinds of messages being communicated is an important prerequisite for counselor effectiveness.

7. Counseling is a cross-cultural—and probably a multicultural—experience.

Counseling and Philosophy

Few people consider themselves to be philosophers. And yet everyone has a philosophical outlook on life. Some people see life as a sequence of events and experiences over which they have little or no control. Others view life as a challenge to be analyzed, controlled, and directed. Some see achievement and self-improvement as the purpose of life. Others view life as a process to be experienced. Who is right? Everyone. Philosophical outlooks on life are varied, allowing each individual to choose or to identify with that outlook that seems to fit him or her best.

Counseling theory has drawn from four philosophical positions (Hansen, 2004; Wilks, 2003). The first of these, essentialism, assumes that human beings are rational by nature, that reason is the natural goal of education, and that the classical thinkers are the chief repository of reason. From this orientation come the problem solvers, the analyzers, those who search for patterns in life.

The second philosophical position, progressivism, is concerned with the fundamental question, What will work? Knowledge is based on experimental results, truth is identified through consequences, and values are relative rather than absolute. From this orientation come the persons who rely on data and research for their truths, who believe that pragmatic solutions do exist for human problems, and who are committed to the pursuit of logical and lawful relationships in life.

The third philosophical position, existentialism, holds that life's meaning is to be found in the individual, not in the environment or the event. Lawfulness (progressivism) and rational thinking (essentialism) are meaningless unless the individual gives them meaning. People who align with this view of life believe that values are real and individually determined, and that experiences are subjective rather than lawful or predictable. Individual responsibility is emphasized; human reactions are the result of choice or potential choice.

And the fourth philosophical position, postmodernism, raises the fundamental question, What is real? This question is particularly relevant in terms of the client's experience versus an external reality. Or more specifically, which reality is more important, the client's reality or an outside reality to which the client should adapt? Although there are some similarities between postmodernism and existentialism in this regard, the important point is that one can never know a reality outside oneself and, therefore, must focus on personal reality. From this orientation come persons who believe that reality can have only a personal meaning, that reality gains meaning through one's personal perceptions or explanations of experiences.

Obviously, all counselors enter the profession with some variation of these viewpoints. Each counselor's philosophical view will be reflected in how he or she reacts to client problems and how those problems are addressed. Similarly, clients enter counseling with some variation of these viewpoints, which will be reflected in how they view their problems and what they consider to be viable solutions.

Counseling and Culture

Increasingly, society is becoming aware of the complex role that culture plays in interpersonal relationships. An early advocate of multiculturalism, Pederson (1991) observed that:

> Before we were born, cultural patterns of thought and action were already prepared to guide our ideas, influence our decisions, and help us take control of our lives. We inherited these cultural patterns from our parents and teachers who taught us the "rules of the game." Only later and sometimes never, did we learn that our culture was one of the many possible patterns of thinking and acting from which we could choose. By that time, most of us had already come to believe that "our" culture was the best of all possible worlds. (p. 6)

By *culture*, Pederson included demographic variables (e.g., age, sex, place of residence), status variables (e.g., social, educational, economic), and affiliations (formal and informal), as well as ethnographic variables such as race, nationality, ethnicity, language, and religion. This definition is broader than that used by some authors who would limit cultural concepts to ethnic or racial criteria. Even a narrower definition of culture demands an understanding of the context from which a person of another culture functions—the assumptions about relationships; about authority, power, and privilege; about right and wrong, success and failure; and about values worth fighting to preserve.

If *multiculturalism* embraces variables such as gender, ethnicity, race, religion, and sexual orientation, then it is almost certain that every counseling relationship will cross at least one of these dimensions and probably several. Thus, all counseling is multicultural. Even if both counselor and client are Caucasian, one may be gay and the other straight, or one may be male and the other female, or one may be older and the other younger, or one may be privileged and the other poor. Crossing such multiple boundaries becomes a multicultural relationship with all the complexities inherent in multiple interactions of social variables.

The implications for counseling and for the counselor are quite clear. If understanding and acceptance of the client are to occur, then the counselor must understand the cultural factors that have shaped and continue to influence the client's worldview. Even before that can happen, the counselor must understand his or her own worldview and how it is shaped in ways similar to the client's experience even when the two worldviews are substantially different from one another. To do less is to flirt with what Wrenn (1962) termed *cultural encapsulation*. Cultural encapsulation involves defining reality according to one set of cultural assumptions and stereotypes, becoming insensitive to cultural variations among individuals, and assuming that one's personal view is the only real or legitimate one, thus embracing unreasoned assumptions that one accepts without proof. Clearly, successful counseling cannot go forward when the counselor is handicapped by cultural encapsulation.

Ivey, D'Andrea, Ivey, and Simek-Morgan (2007) identify three major abilities that are necessary in working with clients of different cultures:

1. Maximizing the amount of thoughts, words, and behaviors that allow communication within a given culture
2. Maximizing the amount of thoughts, words, and behaviors that allow communication across a variety of diverse groups and individuals
3. The ability to formulate plans and actions that respond to the many possibilities existing in a culture and then to evaluate those actions

COUNSELING CONDITIONS AND THEIR EFFECTS

Many clients find seeking counseling to be a major life decision. Apart from the fact that mainstream society associates personal problems with weakness or inadequacy, the process of finding a person who is trustworthy, confidence-inspiring, and competent is a daunting challenge. For the most part, clients are ill-informed about counseling. If the experience is new, they may be unprepared to appraise the situation, determine the counselor's personal qualities, and make the judgment to commit to the process. The counselor must also make an initial assessment of the situation, determine that his or her skills are appropriate to the client's presenting concerns, and that the interaction of personalities and personal values are a good match for counseling success. What conditions or events provide signals both to clients and counselors that the prospective relationship holds promise for success?

Clients feel encouraged by factors such as feeling support and understanding from another person, beginning to see a different and more hopeful perspective, or experiencing a more desirable level of relating to others. Similarly, counselors feel reinforced as they are able to establish those conditions that lead to successful counseling outcomes. Although different theoretical orientations emphasize somewhat different counseling outcomes, most practitioners agree on some rather basic outcomes. When counseling has been successful, clients often experience the following four types of outcomes:

1. *Clients begin to perceive their problems and issues from quite different contexts.* Many times, clients have formulated a set of explanations for their problems. Such explanations may reflect cultural factors, societal factors, or familial factors. In the Eurocentric context (reflecting a northern European cultural heritage), the issue might be one of helping clients to "own" their problems. *Owning* means that clients begin to accept responsibility for themselves, their problems, and solutions. However, there are other ways of viewing the source of client problems. It is generally agreed that many problems experienced by people of color can be traced to active or passive forms of racial discrimination. Similarly, for people with physical disabilities, many of the problems they face may be associated with societal insensitivities involving access, employment skills, or misinformation. Thus, many clients enter counseling inappropriately blaming their problems on others, whereas other clients may enter counseling inappropriately blaming their problems on themselves.

Example: DiShawn, a 19-year-old black male, seeks counseling for a recent bout with depression. Raised in an upper-middle-class home in an integrated suburban neighborhood, he has been a college student for about 18 months. During this time, DiShawn has found himself pulled between the majority white culture of his college and the sizeable body of minority students. He has started to question some of his earlier views about race and opportunity, particularly because he has come to know an increasing number of other black students—many more, in his words, than he ever knew in high school. He is beginning to move from the conformity stage to the integrative awareness stage of racial identity (Helms & Cook, 1999). Thus, it would be important for the counselor to determine whether DiShawn's depression is related to racial identity development or to pathological factors, or both.

2. *Clients develop a more useful understanding of problems and issues.* Once clients begin to view the sources of their problems more appropriately, they frequently develop greater understanding or insight into the problem. There are four aspects of problem awareness that understanding brings into client awareness: feelings and somatic reactions (affect) associated with the problem, thoughts (cognitions) related to how clients perceive or explain their problems, behavior patterns that may be associated or attributed to experiencing the problem, and interpersonal relationships that affect or are affected by the problem occurrence. Understanding these different dimensions of a problem helps clients to perceive their reality more clearly and to gain or experience more control over their reactions to an issue.

Example: Jim, a white college student, complains of being depressed since his girlfriend ended their relationship. He describes his situation as feeling down, hurt, lonely, and unlovable. He shows no clinical signs of depression (e.g., sleeplessness, weight loss, or isolation). Rather, he has taken on a "mopey" demeanor, looking for all the world like someone who needs to be taken care of. Through counseling, Jim begins to realize that his reaction is similar to how he would respond as a child when his mother would get on his case. Then, he reports, she would start to feel sorry for her effect on him and would try to repair the obviously damaged relationship. In other words, Jim began to understand that his style of dealing with stressful relationships was to manipulate the other person into repairing the damage. In so doing, Jim never had to assume any responsibility either for the initial issue or for the solution to the relationship problem. Thus, his reaction involved feelings, how he explained the problem to himself (as someone else's doing), his mopey appearance, and how he would manipulate relationships. Through counseling, Jim also began to understand the relationship between his problem resolution style and his resulting behaviors that reflected passivity and inertia. Finally, Jim came to understand that his interactional patterns with his mother were intruding and controlling his relationships with women.

3. *Clients acquire new responses to old issues.* Many counseling theorists now agree that, for most clients, insight or understanding of problems is not a sufficient counseling outcome. In addition to developing greater understanding of issues, clients also need to acquire more effective ways of responding, verbally and/or behaviorally, to problematic situations. Otherwise, they tend to repeat their ineffective interactional style and fail to make any connection between how they understand their problem and what they do when experiencing their problem.

Example: Maria and Juan see a counselor because of "poor communication" in their marriage. Gradually, they are realizing that part of the problem is that Juan is at work all day in a very intense environment and wants to come home to relax, to sit down with the TV or paper, and to be left alone. Maria, on the other hand, has been at home alone all day with a young child. She seeks out Juan for some adult conversation until he pushes her away. Maria retreats in tears. Although an understanding of the dynamics of this scenario may be useful to both Maria (she might be able to understand that it is not she, personally, whom Juan was rejecting) and to Juan (he, in turn, might realize that Maria had reasonable and understandable needs), it is unlikely that they will be able to alter or interrupt their reentry behavior patterns through understanding alone. They must also develop new behavioral patterns or interactions that will meet each person's unique end-of-the-day needs.

4. *Clients learn how to develop effective relationships.* For a significant number of people who end up in a counselor's office, adults and young people alike, effective and satisfying interpersonal interactions are nonexistent or rare. Because change is often created and enhanced by a social support network, it is essential for clients to begin to develop more adequate relationships with other people. Often, the counseling relationship is the initial vehicle by which this occurs.

Example: Renee comes to see a counselor because she wants to lose a significant amount of weight. In talking to her, the counselor realizes that Renee's obesity has also shielded her from having significant relationships with other people, particularly males. (Renee may have perceived this as having prevented her from having significant relationships.) It is unlikely that Renee will have much success in losing weight unless she also learns to feel more comfortable in initiating and developing a greater social support network.

To summarize, counseling usually results in more than one single, all-inclusive outcome for clients. Effective change is multifaceted and comprehensive, and includes keener understanding of the dynamics of problem sources and maintenance, new insights, different and more facilitative behavioral responses, and more effective interpersonal relationships.

CASE ILLUSTRATION OF POSSIBLE COUNSELING OUTCOMES

The Case of Janet

Janet is a 35-year-old single parent of two teenage girls. She has been employed as a bookkeeper for a local auto parts company for 12 years and is considered to be "the glue that holds the operation together" by her colleagues. Within her work context, Janet feels competent and comfortable. At home, her self-confidence disappears and she has overwhelming doubts about her parenting role and her relationship with neighbors "who see what a bad job I am doing." These doubts also invade her relationship with her parents, her ex-husband and in-laws, her church, and social relationships. The result is that she has been spending increasing amounts of time in her job, thus accentuating her feelings toward her nonwork world. These feelings seem locked into a downward spiral from which she cannot escape. Lately, she has been experiencing some physical symptoms involving her digestive system, inability to sleep more than four to five hours, and a nagging sense of despair.

Given an effective counseling experience, Janet might realistically expect to see some of the following kinds of change:

- Development of a more positive perception of herself as a parent and adult.
- Increased awareness of the relationship between her satisfying work setting and her overcommitment to time at work rather than at home.
- A more objective (and possibly enhanced) personal view of herself as a mother.
- A more realistic view of how others see her as a single parent and adult.
- Awareness that her physical symptoms might be related to her emotional reactions.
- A plan that would help her extract herself from these various "traps" she is experiencing at work, at home, in her neighborhood, in her church, and in her social relationships.

CHARACTERISTICS OF EFFECTIVE HELPERS

Research on the effectiveness of counseling does not provide clear evidence of the relative contributions of factors that influence counseling (Sexton, Whiston, Bleuer, & Walz, 1997). Nevertheless, the professional literature is consistent in its emphasis on counselor characteristics as important to the success of counseling. Among the characteristics that are considered important are

- Self-awareness and understanding
- Good psychological health
- Sensitivity to and understanding of racial, ethnic, and cultural factors in self and others
- Open-mindedness

- Objectivity
- Competence
- Trustworthiness
- Interpersonal attractiveness
- Ethical behavior

Other characteristics that have been identified include the ability to be empathic, genuine, and accepting (Neukrug, 2007); belief in the personal meaning of another person (Combs, 1986); power (Cormier, Nurius, & Osborn, 2009); and striving for internality (Neukrug, 2007).

Self-Awareness and Understanding

On the road to becoming an effective counselor, a good starting place for most counselors is a healthy degree of introspection and self-exploration. We suggest you might examine and seek to understand the following four specific areas:

1. Awareness of your needs (for example, need to give or to nurture, need to be critical, need to be loved, need to be respected, need to be liked, need to please others, need to receive approval from others, need to be right, need for control)
2. Awareness of your motivation for helping (for example, what do you get or take from helping others? How does helping make you feel good?)
3. Awareness of your feelings (for example, happiness, satisfaction, hurt, anger, sadness, disappointment, confusion, fear)
4. Awareness of your personal strengths, limitations, and coping skills (for example, things you do well or things about yourself that you like, things about yourself you need to work on, how you handle difficulties and stress)

Self-awareness and understanding are important in counseling for a variety of reasons. First, they help you see things more objectively and avoid "blind spots"—that is, difficulties that may arise because you do not understand some aspects of yourself, particularly in interpersonal interactions. One such difficulty is projection. Counselors who do not understand their needs and feelings may be more likely to project their feelings onto the client and not recognize their real source (for example, "I had a very angry client today" instead of "I felt angry today with my client"). Projection is one example of a process we discuss later in this chapter called counter-transference, or the emotional reactions of the counselor to the client.

Self-awareness and understanding also contribute to greater security and safety for both counselor and client. Lack of self-awareness and understanding may cause some counselors to personalize or overreact to client messages and respond with defensiveness. For example, a client questions whether counseling "will do her any good." The counselor's need to be respected and approved of are jeopardized or threatened, but the counselor is not aware of this. Instead of responding to the client's feelings of uncertainty, the counselor is likely to respond with personal feelings of insecurity and portray defensiveness in his or her voice or to portray other nonverbal behavior.

Good Psychological Health

Although no one expects counselors to be perfect, it stands to reason that counselors will be more helpful to clients when they are psychologically intact and not distracted by their own overwhelming problems. In a classic study of the psychological health of mental health providers, White and

Franzoni (1990) reported that studies of the psychological health of psychiatrists, psychologists, and psychotherapists in general reveal higher rates of depression, anxiety, and relationship problems than the general population. Even those counselors-in-training at the master's degree level showed evidence of higher levels of psychological disturbance than did the general public (White & Franzoni, 1990, p. 262).

Unfortunately, some counselors do not recognize when their own psychological health is marginal, or they realize it but continue to counsel anyway, often using counseling as a defense mechanism to reduce the anxiety they feel about their own issues. At selected times in their lives, counselors may need to refer clients with similar life problems to other counselors and/or seek out the services of a competent counselor for themselves.

Sensitivity to and Understanding of Racial, Ethnic, and Cultural Factors in Self and Others

Many clients live in two worlds, the world of their cultural and racial-ethnic heritage and the world of their reality. In recent years, the counseling profession has begun to act on this awareness and examine its implications for clients, counselors, and the counseling process. As society has become more multicultural, people have begun to understand the oversimplifications of earlier worldviews. Even counseling theory (e.g., Rogerian theory, psychodynamic theory, and cognitive-behavioral theory) tends to reflect an individual worldview with minimal attention to contextual issues (Ivey et al., 2007).

Where culture and ethnicity once were defined in terms of race, there is increasing emphasis on viewing ethnic variations within race and variations within ethnicity as shapers of one's reality. We have already noted that good psychological health allows the counselor to be more helpful to clients. It is just as true that awareness of one's own ethnic and cultural heritage and how that heritage shapes one's worldview contributes to one's effectiveness as a counselor.

There are two views of how counselors should be aware of their own and their clients' cultural and ethnic contexts. These are referred to as etic, or focused culture-specific, and emic, or universal, approaches. The focused culture-specific approach holds that all cultures are unique and must be understood for their uniqueness. The universal approach argues for a more subjective or inclusive understanding of how culture affects the counseling process by broadening the definition of *minority* to include all oppressed groups (Atkinson & Hackett, 1998). Concerns have been raised that the inclusivity of the universal approach (taking into account variables such as gender, sexual orientation, physical disabilities, etc.) could make the concept of multiculturalism less clear or even meaningless. Proponents of the universal approach believe that culture is defined by more than racial or ethnic factors alone. Others (Ivey et al., 2007) believe that both the universal and the focused cultural-specific approaches are important and can be found in the blended theory approach called multicultural counseling and therapy (MCT).

Open-Mindedness

Open-mindedness suggests freedom from fixed or preconceived ideas that, if allowed expression, could affect clients and counseling outcomes. Open-mindedness must include enlightenment and knowledge of the world outside the counselor's world. It must also include an acute understanding of one's inner world and how those internal standards, values, assumptions, perceptions, and myths can be projected on clients if the counselor is not vigilant.

Open-mindedness serves a number of significant functions in counseling. First, it allows counselors to accommodate clients' feelings, attitudes, and behaviors that may be different from their own. Second, it allows counselors to interact effectively with a wide range of clients, even those regarded by society at large as unacceptable or offensive. Finally, open-mindedness is a prerequisite for honest communication.

Objectivity

Objectivity refers to the ability to be involved with a client and, at the same time, stand back and see accurately what is happening with the client and in the relationship. It has also been described as a component of empathy—the ability to see the client's problem as if it were your own while maintaining personal distance (Rogers, 1957). It is extremely important to maintain objectivity for the client's benefit. Most clients are bombarded with views and advice from many well-meaning persons, such as friends and family, who are also part of the problem and thus are not objective. Counselor objectivity gives the client an additional set of eyes and ears that are needed to develop a greater understanding or a new perception of (or reframe) the issue.

Objectivity also helps the counselor avoid getting caught up in certain client behaviors or dysfunctional communication patterns. For example, clients sometimes try to manipulate the counselor to "rescue" them, using a variety of well-learned and sophisticated ploys. Counselors who remain objective are more likely to recognize client manipulation for what it is and respond with therapeutic appropriateness. It must sound like a contradiction to ask you to be both empathic and involved with your clients and, at the same time, be objective. Clearly, we are asking for an involved and caring objectivity.

Also, objectivity acts as a safeguard against developing inappropriate or even dysfunctional emotional feelings about or toward a client. Counselors must learn to recognize when countertransference develops in the relationship. As we mentioned earlier, countertransference involves either a counterproductive emotional reaction to a client (often based on projection) or the entanglement of the counselor's needs in the therapeutic relationship. Some of the more common ways in which countertransference may manifest itself include the need to please one's clients, overidentification with certain client problems, development of romantic or sexual feelings toward clients, need to give constant advice, and a desire to form friendships with clients (Corey, 2011). Astute counselors gradually learn to identify certain kinds of clients who consistently elicit strong positive or negative feelings on their part and also certain kinds of communication patterns that entice the counselor into giving a less objective and nonhelpful response.

Competence

Ethical standards of all mental health professions call for maintaining high standards of competence. According to Egan (2010), *competence* refers to whether the counselor has the necessary information, knowledge, and skills to be of help and is determined not by behaviors but by outcomes. The profession generally agrees that counseling competency includes knowledge in areas such as psychological processes, assessment, ethics, and other areas relevant to professional work, as well as clinical skills, technical skills, judgment, and personal effectiveness. And, of course, competence also includes multicultural competence, which we have already discussed.

Counselor competence is necessary to transmit and build confidence and hope in clients. Clients need to develop positive expectations about the potential usefulness to them of the counseling experience. Competent counselors are able to work with a greater variety of clients and a wider range of problems. They are more likely to be of benefit to their clients and to make inroads more quickly and efficiently. Sometimes referred to as expertness, competence is often associated with a model of counseling known as the social influence model. The two basic assumptions of this model are:

1. The helper must establish a power or a base of influence with the client through a relationship comprising three characteristics or relationship enhancers: competence (expertness), trustworthiness (credibility), and attractiveness (liking).
2. The helper must actively use this base of influence to effect opinion and behavior changes in the client.

An increasing amount of evidence on this model suggests that clients' respect for the counselor increases in direct proportion to their perceptions of the counselor's expertness or competence.

Trustworthiness

Counselor trustworthiness includes qualities such as reliability, responsibility, ethical standards, and predictability. Trust can be hard to establish, and it can be destroyed by a single action and in a brief moment. Counselors who are trustworthy safeguard their clients' communications, respond with energy and dynamism to client concerns, and never let their clients regret having shared information. The essence of trustworthiness can be summarized in one sentence: Do not promise more than you can do, and be sure you do exactly as you have promised. Trustworthiness is essential, not only in establishing a base of influence with clients, but also in encouraging clients to self-disclose and reveal often very private parts of their lives. Counselors cannot act trustworthy; they must *be* trustworthy.

Interpersonal Attractiveness

Clients perceive counselors as interpersonally attractive when they see them as similar to or compatible with themselves. Clients often make this assessment intuitively although it is probably based on selected dimensions of counselors' demeanor and attitude, particularly their likability and friendliness. In other words, it is helpful to be down to earth, friendly, and warm rather than formal, stuffy, aloof, or reserved. Interpersonal attractiveness can be influenced by race and gender factors, too. However, a counselor's worldview is probably of greater importance than either race or gender. Counselors who are perceived as interpersonally attractive become an important source of influence for clients and may also inspire greater confidence and trust in the counseling process.

Perhaps the most important point we should make about the qualities of effective helpers involves awareness and growth. Few beginning helpers will feel prepared, either technically or personally, to begin working with clients. In part, this is a matter of developing self-confidence in the new skills that have been learned. But it is also associated with their personal growth as human beings. Experienced counselors find that they learn much about themselves and about the process of living through their work with clients. We have certainly found that to be true in our own experience. Each new client introduces us to ourselves in another way. Very often, that experience reveals aspects of our own life adjustment that merit attention and exploration. When this happens, we become increasingly aware of both our strengths and our limitations. It is around those personal strengths that effective counselors build their approach to helping. And it is around those personal limitations that effective counselors attempt to structure growth experiences, with the expectation that the counselors will either reduce their limitations or will attempt to circumscribe their effect on clients and counseling practices.

Ethical Behavior

How the counselor performs under conflicting or challenging conditions affects all of the other conditions. But what determines ethical behavior? The American Counseling Association has established guidelines for ethical counselor performance in a variety of settings and under a broad spectrum of problem situations. Ethical behavior is primarily a self-determined adherence to these standards. However, there are conditions in which failure to perform ethically could lead to malpractice and lawsuits. The ACA Ethical Standards may be found and downloaded at the American Counseling Association's website: www.counseling.org.

THE DEVELOPMENTAL NATURE OF LEARNING TO COUNSEL

Over the years, counselor educators have participated in a recurring debate regarding the experience of learning to counsel. The two poles of this debate are (1) that potential counselors already possess the "skills" of counseling but must learn how to differentiate these skills and use them selectively with clients and (2) that the skills of counseling have been rather specifically defined and can be taught to potential counselors with a reasonably high degree of success, whether or not they possessed the skills initially. Obviously, most counselor preparation programs fall somewhere between these two poles. But regardless of the source of those skills, whether they are inherent in the candidate's personhood or are imbedded in the curriculum of the preparation program (or both), the process of bringing them into dominance is worthy of attention.

Almost everyone has known someone who was untrained and yet was a natural counselor. In getting to know such people, one often finds that they assumed the helper role as children. They may even have been identified by their families as the peacemaker, the facilitator, the understanding one, or the one to whom other family members could turn. Such a role emerges both from temperament and from expectations. Such helpers evolve into the role as their sensitivities, skills, and confidence grow over time. Similarly, students entering counselor preparation programs find that the process is a developmental experience. That is to say, early in the training, the focus tends to be on professional issues external to the person and the context for helping. Gradually, the focus of preparation turns to the personal qualities of helpers, and the process then becomes more personal. From this, attention turns to the skills of counseling— what effective counselors are doing and thinking as they work with clients. Finally, preparation begins to integrate these skills with the practical experience of counseling clients in professionally supervised settings.

Beyond these anticipated changes lie the personal changes that will take place within you. Counseling scholars have identified these changes as (1) personal issues that arise and must be addressed; (2) conflicts between personal values and professional role demands, which sometimes are resolved by deciding not to become a counselor; (3) being in constant change during the learning process; and (4) becoming viewed differently by your circle of friends as you take on the identity of professional helper.

Summary

In this chapter, our aim has been to describe the various parameters of the counseling process; to relate the process to counseling theory, philosophy, and culture; to illustrate the purposes of effective counseling; and to highlight the major personal characteristics of effective counselors. The counseling relationship has certain features that set it apart from other professional or social relationships or even friendships. One of the most significant features of the counseling relationship is that the counselor is a trained professional capable of providing assistance in a competent and trustworthy manner.

In Chapter 2 we will examine the skills of counseling. These include the basic skills of communication that occur intentionally or unintentionally between counselor and client, and the more advanced verbal and nonverbal skills that the counselor uses as interventions into the process and the client's experience.

Then, in Chapter 3, we take a more focused look at the landscape of the counseling process. Subsequent chapters examine portions of this landscape in greater detail. The larger intentions of this book are to provide the skills dimension of the learning process and to offer some structure for the implicit and explicit interactional nature of these skills. Each chapter will conclude with suggested exercises as well as discussion questions to assist your integration of the content. A list of additional resources will allow you to explore certain topics in greater depth.

Exercises

I. Purposes and Goals of Counseling

Two client case descriptions are presented in this activity. Based on the case description for each client, identify possible counseling outcomes that also appear feasible and realistic. You may wish to share your responses with your instructor or another student.

A. Ben is in his early fifties. He has been fairly happily married for 25 years and has two grown children. Ben has run a successful business for the past 20 years; however, his business took a nosedive due to the 2008 recession. He had to lay off several employees and take a 50% reduction in his own salary. Going to work each morning has become a punishing experience because each day seems to bring only more bad news. Ben is very nervous about his ability to hold on to the company and his marriage during this stressful time.

B. Margaret is an older woman (in her late seventies). Her hearing has begun to deteriorate and she finds that often she must ask people to repeat themselves when they speak to her. She has also had a couple of bad falls in the past year, one of which resulted in a severe back sprain. Margaret lives alone in a two-room apartment and receives only a Social Security check. She has no means of transportation other than public transportation. She often complains of loneliness and boredom.

II. Qualities of Effective Counselors

Listed here are the eight qualities of effective counselors described in this chapter. With a partner or in a small group, discuss what you believe is your present status with respect to each quality. For example, how open-minded are you? What makes it easy (or difficult) for you to be open-minded and relatively tolerant of different values and ideas? Then identify several areas that you may need to work on during your development as a counselor. Refer to the case description about Margaret in I.B. above. Which factors do you believe would have the greatest impact on Margaret's psychological health?

A. Self-awareness and understanding
B. Good psychological health
C. Sensitivity to and understanding of racial, ethnic, and cultural factors in self and others
D. Open-mindedness
E. Objectivity
F. Competence
G. Trustworthiness
H. Interpersonal attractiveness

Discussion Questions

1. Counseling has been described by some as a "purchase of friendship." Do you agree with this statement? How do you believe counseling differs from a close friendship?

2. Do you know someone who possesses the qualities to be an effective counselor? What are some of this person's qualities? How do you suppose these qualities were acquired?

3. Considering your age, background, racial/ethnic heritage, and life experiences, what do you think you have to offer to clients that is different from what they would receive from their friends or family members?

4. What are the most important reasons why you want to be a counselor? How might a typical client react to your reasons for choosing counseling as a career?

5. How likely are you to see a counselor yourself? In what ways do you think counseling could help you in your own development as a person and as a counselor? For which reasons might you resist getting involved in this experience?

2

The Language of Counseling

PURPOSE OF THIS CHAPTER

What do counselors do? And how do they do it? We listen. And we talk. And then we listen some more. The simplicity of that answer belies the complexity of the process. Otherwise, why would so many beginning counselors panic at the thought of meeting that first real client? And why would national standards for training exist?

Counseling does begin with talking. There is a language of helping that counselors acquire as they learn how to counsel. To some extent the media has given us a stereotype of that language, including head nods, "uh-huhs," "I see," "How do you feel?" and other minimally representative expressions. In fact, the language of counseling is both broad and effective when used intentionally. In this chapter, we introduce a wide range of verbal and nonverbal skills that have demonstrated their importance and usefulness with clients. Following chapters will discuss when and how to use these communication skills.

Considerations as You Read This Chapter

- How do different counselor responses change the discussion?
- How does silence affect the client? How does silence affect you?
- What is it that you are doing when you listen to someone? ("Just sitting there" is not the right answer!)
- What communication challenges might exist among persons of different cultures, genders, and age groups?

Counseling is not for everyone who might want to be a helper. Not everyone is a good listener. Not everyone can help people share their innermost thoughts and feelings. Not everyone can keep the discussion going for 30 minutes, or 40 minutes, or (heaven forbid!) 50 minutes. And it isn't because some people are "born" counselors although a few are. Rather, the skilled counselor has learned helping skills that lead clients to explore and take risks, to confront old beliefs and generate new ones. Helping skills incorporate basic communication skills and advanced therapeutic skills, all within the context of an environment of relationship and safety for the client. These skills have been part of the counselor's repertoire for decades and have been studied for their effect on client behavior.

COMMUNICATION IN COUNSELING

Before going further, we must attempt to define communication and how it occurs. In the human dyad, communication occurs when messages are encoded (by communicators) and decoded (by receivers). The skill of encoding and the accuracy of decoding are obvious concerns. Both you and your clients encode and decode continuously. Not all encoded messages are intentional. Nor are they always recognized by receivers. Consequently, miscommunication can occur due to either inaccurately composed messages or by unrecognized or misperceived messages.

Communication in counseling is both verbal and nonverbal. From the moment you and your client first meet, messages are sent and meanings are inferred. Counselors communicate self to others through physical appearance, initial behaviors or gestures, the comfort or awkwardness of the first moments, the use of verbal expressions, and the appearance of nervousness or comfort. In the early moments of a first meeting, a story begins, often vague and of uncertain meaning, but significant and to be remembered by both this point, you begin to work, by deciphering (decoding) the client's messages, facilitating the client's comfort, and encouraging the client to enter into a "helping world."

From your client's perspective, this entry is somewhat different. The client's focus is twofold: how to read and interpret your meanings and how to monitor his or her own. It is too early to trust and too soon to hope, and your client is too exposed to discard caution. Your sensitivity to what messages you are sending, the messages your client is sending, and how both are being received and decoded is critical in this initial period of the relationship.

NONVERBAL SKILLS OF COUNSELING

Much research has been conducted on how our nonverbal behavior affects communication, particularly in intimate settings. Early studies examined the impact of space and distance (e.g., how near or distant two persons are), arrangement of furniture (e.g., seating around a table in a restaurant, at a bar, or in a living room), appearance of the room (professional or casual), psychological warmth, physical appearance (how one is dressed), cultural effects, and conversational distance. One pioneer in the field of communication concluded that nearly two-thirds of the meaning in any social situation is derived from nonverbal cues (Birdwhistell, 1970).

So what aspects of nonverbal communication are particularly important in the counseling office? Research suggests that we should be sensitive to placement and comfort of furniture, including its movability; whether the room suggests confidentiality and professionalism; facial expressions and eye contact; and vocal cues (paralanguage) such as verbal rhythm and tempo, loudness or softness, and use of minimal verbalizations such as *umm*, *uh-huh*, *huh-uh*, or *oh*.

Physical Conditions

In real terms, perhaps the most important consideration is how you physically position yourself in relation to your client in the counseling setting. Placing furniture between yourself and a client introduces a psychological barrier; having nothing between your chair and your client can induce discomfort or vulnerability. Professional counseling offices typically are arranged so the counselor and client either sit adjacent to but not fully separated by a table, or sit across from each other with no separating piece of furniture.

Body Language

How we sit or stand communicates our comfort with the setting. Our physical movements, head nods, and facial expressions all have a place and convey a meaning in the counseling room. For example, sitting back in one's chair and leaning away from the client can imply escape. Sitting forward and leaning toward the client can imply intensity. Sitting with arms or legs crossed can imply guardedness or disengagement. Sitting with an open, relaxed posture communicates comfort with the process. Visible tension in the counselor's body can suggest nervousness, self-doubt, and discomfort with the process.

One of the more common nonverbal behaviors of counseling is the head nod. When used selectively, it communicates an acceptance or understanding of the client's message. Like most counseling skills, however, it can be overused and can thus lose its power to communicate; its overuse can even cross the line from effective to annoying. Similarly, an appropriate smile (not a grin) can communicate warmth and acceptance, but a smile can also be overused.

Silence

Intentional silence is one of the most important skills a counselor can employ. It doesn't need to be said that without silence, your client won't have space to talk. However, silence is more than a convenience that provides the client with talk time. It is also a tool in the counselor's repertoire. Used judiciously, silence can communicate counselor expectation to the client; the message is, "I want you to talk." Silence can also induce mild anxiety in the client, and overly long silences can have the undesirable effect of inducing extreme self-consciousness and anxiety in a client. It is probably better to think of silences as 5- to 10-second pauses in conversation. Such pauses have several potential effects:

1. They can give the client an opportunity to think about and integrate a newly discovered insight or awareness.
2. They can be an invitation to continue a line of discussion or exploration.
3. They can communicate to the client the importance of taking some responsibility in the counseling relationship.
4. They can encourage the client to focus on self-exploration. (See Exercise I, Exploring Silence, at the end of this chapter.)

Cultural Factors

Researchers have also been interested in the multiple effects of nonverbal communication across cultures. The contribution that culture makes to nonverbal behavior is mixed. In the 1970s, much research was conducted on the meaning of nonverbal communication across cultures. Ekman (1973) concluded that there is a universality of facial expressions across cultures, but later work by Knapp (1978) reported that the meanings attached to specific nonverbal gestures was, in fact, culturally determined and not universal in nature. This would suggest that counselors must be concerned with their nonverbal messages when counseling in a multicultural relationship.

How different cultures respond to conditions of communication in intimate settings is another matter that has been widely studied. Early studies suggested that cultures could be differentiated as either contact cultures, in which tactile and smell modes of communication were primary communicators, or noncontact cultures, which relied primarily on visual communication cues. More recent studies have dismissed this classification as too simplistic, suggesting that cultural differences tend to be defined by comfort levels related to physical closeness and touch when communicating. Generally speaking, North American, northern European, and Australian communicators prefer greater interaction distances (3 to 5 feet) and less touch than many Latino, Middle Eastern, southern European, and Asian cultures, who are more comfortable with closer physical distances and physical touch (Barnland, 1975; Klopf, Thompson, Ishii, & Sallinen-Kuparinen, 1991; Sussman & Rosenfeld, 1982). (See Exercise II, Personal Space/Personal Comfort, at the end of this chapter.)

Summary

Now that we may have made you completely self-conscious, let's look at how all of this nonverbal insight plays out in the counseling session. First, awareness of and insight into the effect of nonverbal communication is crucial. Much is at play in those early moments of a counseling relationship when silence, gestures, postures, and facial expressions are part of the client's hypersensitive awareness. Much that is communicated risks misinterpretation or miscommunication. Consequently, the counselor's messages need to be intentional and clear. Second, it is important to realize that nonverbal communication is your friend, not your enemy. It is a useful component in your creation of a comfortable, safe, and workable environment.

BASIC VERBAL SKILLS OF COUNSELING

Verbal behavior of counselors was an important area of study during the 1960s and 1970s. Using a variety of methodologies, researchers identified some 15 different types of counselor responses that were present in therapy sessions across different counseling theories (Hackney, 1974; Tepper & Haase, 1978; Zimmer & Anderson, 1968; Zimmer & Park, 1967; Zimmer, Wightman, & McArthur, 1970). Their effect was measured for impact on client verbal participation, degree of perceived counselor empathy, level of topic exploration, and other relevant counseling effects. Today, these counselor responses are still seen as essential counselor communication skills (Cormier & Hackney, 2012; Hill, 2009; Ivey, d'Andrea, Ivey, & Simek-Morgan, 2007; Neukrug & Schwitzer, 2006; Okun & Kantrowitz, 2008; Young, 2009). Each counselor response has an intended outcome in the interaction between counselor and client. A number of counselor verbal responses can be classified as facilitating. These responses—

minimal response, reflection, paraphrase, and clarification—act to return the topic focus to the client, much as the tennis player returns the ball to the opponent's side of the court. The result is to keep the focus on clients, their stories, and their reactions.

Minimal Responses

Counselors communicate their involvement in a client's story in many ways, ranging from attentive expressions to brief statements, including the familiar *OK*, *mmm*, and similar minimal expressions. All serve to communicate the counselor's attentiveness or interest in what the client is saying. When used intermittently, they encourage the client to continue talking. But if they are overused, they become distracters. For example, in the following excerpt from a counseling session, the client is describing a discussion he had with his employer. The counselor listens and occasionally responds with a minimal response (noted in bold print).

> CLIENT: I guess Mike was just having a bad day yesterday. As soon as I got to work he started in on me, **[mmm]** how I hadn't finished the material the day before, and how I was slowing up the project. **[oh?]** Yeah, and I had done everything he had told me to do. I don't know what was going on, but he got over it later and apologized to me for his tantrum.

Reflection

The reflection, or repeating a phrase or thought uttered by the client, is the simplest response to the content of a client's message.

> CLIENT: I don't know what I would do if he stopped trying.
>
> COUNSELOR: You don't know what you would do.

It serves to emphasize a thought, to bring the client's attention to the statement, and perhaps even to challenge the client to reconsider what was just said. The reflection is particularly effective in response to an exaggerated or foreclosing statement by the client.

Consider the following statement:

> CLIENT: No matter how hard I try, I will never be happy with him.

What are some possible reflections you could make that would either mirror the client's hopelessness or would challenge the client's conclusion?

Reflection 1: No matter how hard you try.

Reflection 2: You'll never be happy.

Reflection 1 encourages the client to continue talking about her effort; reflection 2 invites the client to consider her predetermined future unhappiness.

Paraphrase

Rephrasing the client's response using the counselor's own choice of words is called a paraphrase or a restatement (Hill, 2009). This rephrasing of the client's message neither adds to nor detracts from the client's meaning. Its effect is quite similar to the reflection except that it uses the counselor's vocabulary. As a result, it communicates that the message has been (accurately) received but avoids parroting what the client said. For example:

> CLIENT: It's going to be a little tricky to leave work early tomorrow in order to go to the interview.
>
> COUNSELOR: You're not sure about leaving work in order to try to get a new job.

The paraphrase has many of the same qualities as the reflection. It focuses attention on some aspect of the client's message and communicates that the counselor understands. If the counselor misunderstands, it allows the client to modify the message, an equally important outcome. But it also allows the client to hear his or her own message as someone else has heard it, and that often adds to the client's perspective.

As we have already noted, communication occurs only when the message has been accurately perceived. Otherwise, it is miscommunication. Consequently, the counselor must sometimes seek confirmation from the client that what the counselor is hearing (decoding) is what the client is trying to communicate (encode).

Typically, the first hurdle in counseling involves helping the client reach a minimal level of comfort with the setting and with the counselor. Once that has occurred, the client is able to begin a process of sharing those issues and concerns that led the client to seek counseling. This is often referred to as "the client's narrative." Typically, that narrative also contains gaps of missing information and meanings. Counselors can use a number of effective verbal responses to help clients fill in those gaps, including the question, the summary, the clarification, and the challenge.

The Question

The question is a statement beginning with who, what, how, when, or where. There are two types of questions in the counselor's repertoire: the closed question, and the open-ended question. Questions (sometimes referred to as probes) achieve different results and are used in different situations.

CLOSED QUESTIONS.   Closed questions ask the client to respond with a minimal statement, usually yes or no, or a bit of information. It is the most overused and underproductive of all responses made by beginning counselors and is the primary reason why they can't get their clients to talk freely. After all, a closed question, such as "Do you beat your wife?" doesn't require elaboration. Consequently, when clients are peppered with closed questions, their tendency is to give a minimal response and wait for the counselor to come up with another question. This shifts complete responsibility to the counselor to make the session flow. However, the closed question is valuable in an intake interview where specific information about the client is required. And occasionally, the counselor needs a specific bit of information to understand the client's narrative, in which case the closed question is also appropriate. (See Exercise III, "Recognizing Different Counselor Responses," at the end of this chapter.) Following are examples of closed questions typically used in a counseling session or intake interview (note the boldface probe in each question).

- **How long** have you been married?
- **When** did you and your husband separate?

- **Who** was your other counselor?
- **What** would be a good time to meet next week?
- **Do you** have difficulty sleeping?

OPEN-ENDED QUESTIONS.   Open-ended questions seek elaboration without specifying precisely what information is being sought. These questions cannot be answered with a simple yes or no response. Counselors use open-ended questions to understand how the client perceives the problem, relationships, conditions, and so on. Examples of open-ended questions include:

- What happens when you say that to her?
- How would you like him to react to you?
- What are you doing when you get this feeling?
- How does the conversation change when she gets involved?

Clarification

The clarification is a counselor response that seeks confirmation of what the counselor is hearing the client say. Clarifications seem like restatements, but their intention is more than communication of understanding and interest. Instead, they are phrased to solicit a confirmation or correction. The clarification often is initiated with a statement of the counselor's intent. For example, the counselor might say, "Let me see if I am following you accurately," "If I'm hearing you correctly, . . . ," or "I want to be sure I understand." Notice that the counselor is being careful not to assume the client's intent and is offering the response tentatively so the client would be comfortable making a correction if necessary.

> COUNSELOR: Before we go further, let me just be sure I am understanding. You want to say to Danielle that she should back off and give you some space, but if you do that, she may take it wrong, and you'd rather not say anything than to risk the relationship. Is that right?

SUMMARY.   Basic verbal skills are the most frequently used components of the counselor's repertoire. They allow the counselor to establish rapport, communicate empathy and positive regard, and begin building a working alliance with the client. While they are heavily used in the early sessions, they continue to be useful over the full course of the counseling relationship.

ADVANCED VERBAL SKILLS OF COUNSELING

Advanced skills involve intentionality beyond that of facilitating discussion or soliciting information. These skills nudge the client toward self-exploration, gaining new insights, considering alternative perspectives, setting goals, and planning for change. In other words, they reflect the counselor's counseling plan as well as the client's immediate issues. The first of these counselor responses is the summary statement.

The Summary Statement

The summary statement typically follows a client discussion of events or circumstances. It may include content that the client has been discussing for 5 minutes or an entire session. The obvious effect of the summary statement is confirmation that the counselor is following the client's narrative, but it also has more subtle effects. It can pull together aspects of the client's narrative that reveal contradictions in the client's thinking, feelings, or assessments. Or it can wrap up a discussion, permitting a transition to a new topic or concern. The summary is always selective; that is, the counselor is not trying to collect all details of the discussion. Rather, it focuses on, or highlights, aspects of the client's narrative.

SUMMARY OF FEELINGS.   The summary of feelings brings together aspects of the client's shared feelings and can lead the client to deeper exploration or even a sense of completion (catharsis). The counselor presents the summary as a reporter or observer might and excludes all judgmental references.

> COUNSELOR: You've been describing a lot of reactions to your meeting with your professor. At first, you were afraid to approach him. Then you made the appointment and felt some resentment because he didn't seem to think it was necessary. When you did meet with him, it made you mad that he didn't have any suggestions for how you could do a better job. Finally, after the meeting, you felt like it hadn't achieved anything and you were mad at yourself for hoping. [At this point the counselor stops to let the client consider the implications of the emotional trip the client has put herself through.]

SUMMARY OF CONTENT.   The summary of content is different only in focus. The purpose of the content summary is to collect the details, facts, or events related to the client's narrative, thereby revealing the total picture. Often when this is done, the client can make observations or note connections that are slightly or even dramatically different from the original assessment. Consequently, the summary of content moves the client toward insight, reassessment, or revision of events or conditions. The counselor does not add his or her personal assessments to the summary.

> COUNSELOR: Let's go over the events you have been describing, Bob. When you first got together with Marissa, you would watch a movie together, maybe cook a dinner or order in, and you would spend a lot of time just talking. But lately, when she comes over, she says she can't stay long and the conversations aren't the same. Instead, she seems to be preoccupied with her work. When that happens, you think the relationship is starting to change, and you have no idea where it's going or even why it's changing. So when you see that starting to happen, you end up cutting off the contact.

Note that the counselor's response contains no reference to feelings even though feelings could be present. Instead, the counselor makes reference to actions, activities, opinions, and conclusions.

The Encouraging Response

This response is meant to be supportive, to suggest that the client has the skill or potential to do something, to feel a particular way, or to think in a different way. What makes this a more sophisticated verbal response by the counselor is how and when it is used. The most critical element is timing. A counselor would not want to suggest that the client could be different in some way when, in fact, the client is not prepared to be different. That would only set the client up for disappointment or failure. So knowing that the client is ready or able to respond in a particular way is crucial. A second consideration is knowing that, if the client responds in the way the encouragement suggests, that suggestion would make a positive difference for the client. So it is important for you to know both that the client is ready and able to respond as the encouragement suggests, and that the suggestion would make a difference.

Encouraging responses are typically phrased as statements that imply or suggest that the client has the ability or potential to act in a different way. Here are some examples:

- You could ask her to accompany you to the play.
- I think you could manage that by yourself.
- Of course, you could consider changing your schedule.
- You are probably ready to take on some new responsibilities now.

In the following exchange the client is considering a plan of action but reflects some uncertainty. The counselor offers encouragement in response.

CLIENT: I've been thinking about looking for a different job but then I worry if I will like it. Or if I will like the people as well. Or what if I take a new job, and they don't like me?

COUNSELOR: You could deal with this if you had a pretty good idea of what jobs best fit your skills and interests.

The Confrontation or Challenge

Beginning counselors tend to avoid confronting a client, fearing that doing so might damage the relationship. If confrontation occurs too early in an emerging relationship, the effect can be negative. But once the counselor has established a sense of trust and acceptance, clients are able to receive confrontation as a necessary part of the process. In fact, when a confrontation is rooted in a condition the client can recognize as true, it is often welcomed by the client.

The confrontation is effective in those instances when the client is experiencing but not acknowledging a condition, belief, or feeling that is part of the presenting problem. In other words, like everyone else, clients have blind spots in their thinking and experiencing. Those blind spots can become troublesome when they support or maintain dysfunctional thoughts and behavior. Blind spots can be recognized in the client's narrative through contradictions, missing logic, or lack of awareness. When a client speaks of her shyness but describes it to you in an unshy manner, the moment for confrontation is present. If a client presents himself as unlikable but is surrounded by a support group, that confrontation moment becomes appropriate.

Often, the confrontation addresses the client's misinterpretation of others' behaviors or feelings. One of the most obvious opportunities for the counselor to confront is when the client is immobilized by a problem or doesn't see how to address a problem.

CLIENT: I'm really frustrated with my math class. The teacher goes too fast. She assumes that everyone is keeping up, and I'm not. She has this group of smart kids who are getting it and if they get it, then everyone must be getting it. Not!

COUNSELOR: Perhaps you need to tell her that you can't move as fast as this other group of kids. Maybe she needs to hear that you really want to learn, but it doesn't come as easy for you.

The Interpretation Response

The interpretation response proposes or assigns meaning to an event, condition, reaction, or feeling that the client is experiencing. The meaning might be suggested by the counselor (Hill, 2009), or the counselor can ask the client to interpret the meaning. In using interpretation responses or requests, the counselor's intent is to take the client's awareness or understanding of a situation, person, or process and move it in a different direction or level. This is considered an advanced communication response because it requires the counselor to reconceptualize the condition while at the same time remaining consistent with the details of the client's narrative, a demanding task. When the interpretation is counselor-initiated, it is framed as a possible meaning or a speculation that the client can either accept or modify. Interpretation responses can be framed as questions or statements, for example:

CLIENT: When I try to talk to Nancy [daughter] she immediately flares up and pushes me away. It's so frustrating.

Possible Counselor-Initiated Interpretations:

- Is it possible that Nancy thinks it's timeto become more independent?
- Perhaps Nancy is trying to be responsible and figure it out herself.
- Is it possible that you are coming on too strong because you are anticipating Nancy's reaction?

When the counselor asks the client to assign meaning, it is made in the form of a question.

CLIENT: When I try to talk to Nancy, she immediately flares up and verbally pushes me away. It's so frustrating.

COUNSELOR: What do you think is going on with Nancy when you initiate and she pushes away? What does it mean?

Clients may not be able to assign meaning at first, but as the topic is explored further, the counselor can again ask what meaning the client might read into the interaction.

Generally speaking, the interpretation response has four qualities or conditions that must be met:

1. It must be as logical an explanation as one that the client has rendered.
2. It must be potentially true.
3. It must change the perspective from a negative valence to a positive valence.
4. It must provide the client with a way of responding to the problem in a manner that effectively eliminates the problem.

The Directive Response

Directive responses involve assignments to do or to think in a specified manner. The most frequent use of the directive response is when the counselor uses a homework assignment designed to help the client develop or strengthen a particular skill or thought response. It carries an instructional message, usually with a plan for implementing the instruction. Examples of the directive response include the following:

- Between now and our next session, I would like you to keep a record of when and where you are each time you start feeling discouraged and down.
- This week, when you start feeling isolated and lonely, I want you to get away from your computer and go for a walk where other people are, maybe the library, or the park, or the grocery store.
- When you start to feel your anxiety rise, I want you to find a quiet place and use the relaxation exercises on the tape we recorded.

The Informative Response

The informative response is used primarily when information is missing that the client requires in order to act or to think in a particular way. It is also instructional in nature, but it is not advice-giving. For example, the counselor may wish to suggest alternatives regarding relationships, actions, or plans. It may involve information about referrals for services, sources for self-help materials, career information, and so on. The informative response is not frequently used in counseling because it sets the counselor up as an authority. Examples of informative responses include the following:

- If you do a computer search for "hypertension," you probably could get some good information on reasonable activities.
- I can take you through a relaxation exercise that you should use whenever you begin to feel this high anxiety.
- There are several websites that provide good information on different medications.

Summary

The nonverbal and verbal messages of counseling are a step beyond mere conversation. They reflect intentionality or purpose on the counselor's part. That purpose is determined by what the counselor believes is the client's current need(s) or by the goal or objective currently being addressed. Nonverbal counselor messages can either facilitate or inhibit the counseling atmosphere. Verbal responses have a more intentional role. Basic verbal responses are most common—heavily used early in the process—but they continue to be useful throughout the counseling relationship. Advanced verbal responses are tied to specific interventions or purposes and require greater skill in use, are heavily dependent

on timing, and require good clinical judgment about when they are appropriate.

Table 2.1 summarizes the 12 responses described in this chapter and indicates how they relate to content of different topic domains in the counseling process. For example, the open-ended question, which is a basic verbal counseling skill, is useful in several ways. It can invite the client to explore feelings, thought processes, behavior patterns, or interpersonal relationships. The danger is that open-ended questions can be overused, so it is important that the counselor vary his or her responses. All 12 response categories will be discussed in greater detail as we proceed through the chapters on counseling stages and interventions.

TABLE 2.1 Verbal Responses in Counseling Domains

Counselor Response	Affective Domain	Cognitive Domain	Behavioral Domain	Interpersonal Domain	Cautions
Basic Verbal Skills of Counseling					
Minimal Reinforcers	Encourage client discussion	Encourage client discussion	Encourage client discussion	Encourage client discussion	Can be overused
Open-Ended Questions	Explore feelings	Explore client thinking processes	Explore client behavior patterns	Explore client relationships	Can be overused
Closed Questions	Not as helpful with feeling domain	Obtain specific thought statements	Obtain specific behaviors/reactions	Obtain specific relationship data	Can be overused; shift responsibility
Clarification Responses	Seek to verify client feelings	Seek to verify client thinking	Seek to verify client actions/behaviors	Seek to verify client relationships	Must listen for client corrections
Reflection Responses	Bring focus to client feeling reactions	Bring focus to client thought processes	Bring focus to client behaviors/reactions	Bring focus to client relationship patterns	Can sound like parroting if overused
Paraphrases	Let client hear feelings differently	Let client hear thinking differently	Let client hear behaviors differently	Let client hear systems differently	Can be overused
Advanced Verbal Skills of Counseling					
Summary Responses	Help client connect feeling statements	Help client connect thoughts	Help client identify behavior patterns	Help client identify interpersonal patterns	Can have important missing elements
Encouraging Responses	Point out potential for feeling differently	Point out potential for thinking differently	Point out potential for acting differently	Point out potential for changing relationship	Can be unrealistic
Informative Responses	Suggest possible feeling choices	Suggest possible thinking choices	Suggest possible behavioral choices	Suggest possible interpersonal choices	Can miss if situation is misunderstood
Confrontation Responses	Point out competing feelings	Point out competing thoughts	Point out self-defeating behaviors	Point out ineffective interaction patterns	Can be introduced too soon
Interpretation Responses	Provide alternative meaning	Provide alternative meaning	Provide alternative meaning	Provide alternative meaning	Be sure alternative is plausible
Directive Responses	Modify feeling reactions	Modify thought patterns	Modify behavior or assign homework	Modify interaction patterns	Client must be ready to change

Exercises

I. Exploring Silence

As a way to explore and expand your comfort with silence, have a conversation with a member of your class or a colleague. Discuss whatever you wish for about 10 minutes. The only ground rule is that each of you wait 5 to 15 seconds before responding to the other.

II. Personal Space/Personal Comfort

With a colleague, determine your personal space requirements. Begin a conversation standing (or sitting) about 10 feet apart. Move closer and continue talking. Move closer again. Keep moving closer until either of you becomes uncomfortable with the distance. Then find the optimum space that accommodates personal comfort for both of you. Discuss the implications of this exercise with each other. Do you think your preferences are cultural? Gender-related? Age-related?

III. Recognizing Different Counselor Responses

In the list of counseling responses below, label each response using the following categories:

O-E = Open-ended question	E = Encouraging
CL = Closed question	I = Informative
C-R = Clarifying response	C = Confrontation
R = Reflection	INT = Interpretation
P = Paraphrase	D = Directive
S = Summary	

_____ 1. How would you respond if she asked....?

_____ 2. Let me be sure I understand. You would like to change jobs, right?

_____ 3. You really wouldn't want to move to another city.

_____ 4. You could look up the cost-of-living index for Seattle.

_____ 5. I have a friend who lives in Bellingham and she says that it isn't expensive.

_____ 6. How much would they pay you?

_____ 7. You say you want to move, but you aren't doing anything to make it happen.

_____ 8. Tonight, I want you to go to the library and look up Places Rated Almanac.

_____ 9. You seem to walk right up to the edge of making a decision and then you back off. Can you help me understand why that is?

Share your responses with a class member and resolve any differences you might have with your ratings.

IV. The Counseling Session Typescript

Record a 10-minute counseling role-play with another class member. Transfer all comments made by both you and the client to a typescript of the session. Then label each of your responses according to the type of response it is. Note the effect that different responses have on the client's response.

Feedback for Exercise III, Recognizing Different Counselor Responses

III. Recognizing Different Counselor Responses

1. O-E
2. C-R
3. R
4. E
5. I

6. CL
7. C
8. D
9. INT

Discussion Questions

1. Discuss the conditions that make a difference between miscommunication and successful communication.

2. This chapter is devoted to counselor responses. Discuss what you believe would constitute client communication responses.

3. Some counselor responses ask the client to elaborate, whereas others lead the client to a deeper level of exploration. Identify two responses that would do both.

4. Below is a client narrative from a counseling session. At each point where the typescript has an asterisk [*], provide a counselor response and identify what type of response it is.

   When I went back home last weekend, my parents told me that they had decided to separate and maybe divorce [*] and it really threw me. [*] Then they watched me *the entire weekend, I guess to see how I was reacting to them. [*] Anyhow, I just pulled in and didn't give them anything to react to. I couldn't. I didn't know what to say. [*] I mean, I knew that they had been having some trouble, but I never expected this. So they just unloaded and what was I to do with that? [*] What would you do? [*] By Saturday night, I had to get out, get away from the house because all I was doing was staying in my room and crying, [*] so I called a friend and we went out and really hung one on. I haven't been so*

drunk in a long time. [*] Then Sunday morning, I was, like, really feeling it, and that's when they chose to try to have a conversation with me about their reasons for deciding to separate. I mean, I just couldn't hack it and so I packed up and left early to come back to school.[*]

Discuss your choice of responses with a class member. Together, consider what other responses might have been appropriate and how the discussion might change if different responses were used.

MyCounselingLab Assignment

Go to the Video Resource Library on the MyCounselingLab site for your text and search for the following clips:

- **Gina: Individual Childhood Experiences**
- **Youth: Empathy, Unconditional Regard, Congruence**

- **Exploring the Problem**

View and listen to these video clips. How many different verbal responses can you identify and label?

Stages and Skills of Counseling

PURPOSE OF THIS CHAPTER

The overall objective of this chapter is to present the structure of the counseling process and how that structure helps you determine what the counselor should be doing. The beginning point of counseling is a time when you and your client must decide, both independently and mutually, whether this particular pairing of persons and personalities offers the potential for growth and change. Beyond that decision, you must reach agreement on what the problem is; how counseling might assist in changing problematic circumstances; what counseling activities would help produce that change; and, finally, when the helping effort should conclude. Then the chapter examines this process from the client's perspective, which will be different from your own.

Considerations as You Read This Chapter

▪ How do you approach new relationships? Do they make you nervous? Offer excitement?

▪ What do you suppose other people observe in you when you are beginning a new relationship?

▪ What do you think it would be like if you were a minority seeking help from someone of a majority culture (or vice versa)? What kinds of thoughts would go through your mind? How do you think you might view the other (helping) person?

▪ How much structure do you prefer in most situations? What type of structure do you need in relationships? What kinds of structure would make you comfortable in the counseling relationship? How would you accommodate your client's needs for structure if they were different from your own?

For many years, counseling was viewed as a process that did not lend itself to concrete behavioral analysis. For this reason, some people began to think of counseling as having indefinable, almost mystical, qualities. In the 1970s, through the work of Robert Carkhuff, Allen Ivey, Stanley Strong, and others, this mystical character began to disintegrate and to be replaced by more specific definitions. In recent years, counseling has taken on a much more defined character.

In this chapter, we shall examine the helping process from the counselor's perspective and from the client's experience. We shall consider how two persons meet and begin to establish understandings that gradually evolve into a meaningful and productive relationship. These instrumental stages and the counseling skills indigenous to them are presented as a conceptual base for the chapters that follow.

THE COUNSELING PROCESS

Counseling is often described as a process. The implicit meaning of this label is a progressive movement toward an ultimate conclusion, that conclusion being the resolution of whatever precipitated the need for help. This movement may be described as a series of stages through which the counselor and client move, including:

Stage 1   Establishing the working relationship

Stage 2   Assessing or defining the presenting problem

Stage 3   Identifying and setting goals

Stage 4   Choosing and initiating interventions

Stage 5   Planning and introducing termination and follow-up

Each of these stages leads logically to the next subsequent stage; that is, one must establish a minimal relationship with the client before an assessment can occur, and assessment should occur before counseling goals are established. The process is not totally linear, however. It is not uncommon to have to retrace one's steps to a prior stage when new material emerges that affects the previous stage.

Once initiated, each of these stages becomes a permanent part of the process (see Figure 3.1). In other words, establishing rapport and a relationship becomes a continuing agenda for the counselor and client, even after a good relationship has been initiated. Likewise, assessment (stage 2) continues to be a matter of interest as the counselor and client better understand the nature of the presenting problem. Each remaining stage follows and continues to be a presence in the process, up to and including termination.

Establishing the Relationship

The term *relationship* has many meanings, including the ties between two people in love, kinship within a family, the bond between close friends, and the understanding that can develop between humans and animals. In the counseling setting, relationship takes on a more specific meaning. When the counselor establishes rapport with a client, the relationship includes factors such as respect, trust, psychological comfort, and shared purpose. Rapport refers to the psychological climate that emerges from the interpersonal contact between you and your client. Consequently, good rapport sets the stage for positive psychological growth, whereas poor rapport leads to undesirable or even counterproductive outcomes. The dimension of relationship

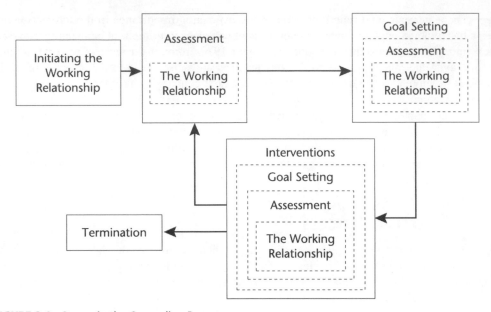

FIGURE 3.1 Stages in the Counseling Process

that moves beyond most relationship experiences is the shared purpose. This has been variously described in the professional literature as a therapeutic alliance between the counselor and the client, or as a working alliance, suggesting a participatory involvement by both parties toward therapeutic goals and outcomes. (See Section A, The Counseling Relationship, ACA Code of Ethics, 2005, www.counseling.org.)

Obviously, this psychological climate will be affected by several factors, including your personal and professional qualifications and the client's interpersonal history and anxiety state. In other words, even the best-trained, best-adjusted counselor still faces a variety of challenges when meeting a new client. Many of these preexisting conditions can be anticipated. For example, few people like the prospect of asking others for assistance. Thus, when people are forced to admit to themselves that they need help, they approach the situation with two sets of feelings: (1) "I know I need help and will feel better when I get it" and (2) "I wish I weren't here." This conflict is quite common in the early stages of counseling and is particularly evident in the rapport-building stage.

Other preexisting client conditions relate to the client's previous experience with sharing personal information or interacting with authority figures, with older persons, with the opposite sex, and with people of a different cultural background. Some of these conditions are affected by the client's ethnic and/or cultural background as well. In Chapter 1, we referred to some of these factors within the context of interpersonal attraction, trustworthiness, competence, and sensitivity to and understanding of cultural factors in oneself and others. The culturally sensitive client will read your nonverbal and verbal messages and make inferences about these qualities. These first impressions influence rapport building and may need to be reexamined later when you and your client have reached a more comfortable level with each other (Helms & Cook, 1999, Chap. 9).

These interpersonal reactions can assume overriding importance in the interaction and begin to influence or even control the process of counseling. When this happens, professionals refer to the psychological dynamic as *transference* or *countertransference*. Transference occurs when the client associates certain qualities with the counselor. For example, if the counselor's demeanor reminds the client of his or her nurturing mother, demanding boss, or prejudiced colleague, the client may decide that the counselor is like that person, or, in extreme cases of transference, is that person. Transference can be either positive (favorable comparison) or negative (unfavorable comparison). Countertransference, which we referred to in Chapter 1, describes the same psychological condition, except it is the counselor who is associating imagined qualities with the client. This might seem less likely, but in fact it is not uncommon.

Although we have suggested that relationship building is a critical stage in the counseling process, we do not mean to imply that once the counselor has established a relationship with the client, the issue is put to rest. On the contrary, the relationship is a continuous condition. Impressions made in the early stages of counseling change and mature as the counselor and client work together. Often, the early impressions are revisited and reexamined, and each person grows in understanding. The critical determinant in this maturing process is the counselor's ability to recognize psychological dynamics, interpersonal assumptions, and the subterranean emotions that are part of the relationship.

Skillful counselors develop a self-congruent style for meeting clients—a style that reflects both the counselor's personal qualities and counseling experience. Even though there is no set formula for establishing rapport, some guidelines and skills are associated with this stage of counseling.

The relationship begins with adequate social skills. Introduce yourself. Hear the client's name and remember it. Invite the client to sit down and see to it that he or she is reasonably comfortable. Address the client by name. If he or she appears highly anxious, initiate some social conversation and watch to see if the anxiety begins to dissipate. Notice nonverbal behavior and use it to try to understand the client's emotional state. Invite the client to describe his or her reason for coming to talk to you. Allow the client time to respond. This behavior is often described as attending or active listening. It communicates to the client that you are interested in the person and in what she or he has to say, and that you will try to understand both the spoken and the unspoken message in the communication.

The working relationship is not established in a single contact. During early sessions clients become comfortable with you and begin to accept you into their more private world of thoughts and feelings. This condition represents the initial phase of therapeutic relationship building. During these several sessions, consistency is an important quality. Your behaviors, your attitudes and opinions, your promptness and attentiveness to detail, and your acknowledgment of the client's personal and cultural realities—all may be noted by the client. If you vary from session to session in these details, the client will find you less predictable and will find it more difficult to become comfortable with you. Equally important is your sensitivity to cultural similarities and dissimilarities in this process. It is a time for you to be hypersensitive to the many legitimate ways people can be different from you.

Beyond this initial phase of relationship building lies the broader landscape of genuine alliance with another person. While this, too, is part of a relationship and rapport, it reflects the accumulation of experience that only a longer relationship can achieve. Thus, in the model shown in Figure 3.1, rapport and relationship building are shown at the beginning (initial phase), but they also continue throughout the remaining stages.

Although it is not the same as friendship, the counseling relationship shares some qualities with good friendships, and this may prove confusing to some clients. Sometimes the counselor will also find this aspect of relationship to be problematic. This is primarily a boundary issue and a balancing act. If you place too much emphasis on being professional, you may find that the role doesn't fit what you feel about yourself or about your client, and thus lacks authenticity. At the other end of the spectrum is the temptation to be yourself fully and compromise the professional character of the relationship that is so important in facilitating client change. Finding a balance on this continuum is one of the early challenges in building a therapeutic alliance.

Assessing the Problem

Even as you and your client are in the process of establishing a relationship, a second process is under way. That process involves the collection and classification of information related to the client's life situation and reasons for seeking counseling. This is commonly called assessment although it might also be thought of as the problem identification process. In this context, you can think of assessment in three ways. First, assessment depends on the counselor's theoretical and philosophical view of human problems. Second, assessment depends on the conditions present in the client's situation and the counselor's understanding of those conditions. And third, assessment depends on the client's cultural frame of reference and the conditions that frame of reference imposes on the client's worldview. (See Section E, Evaluation, Assessment and Interpretation, ACA Code of Ethics, 2005, www.counseling.org.)

Likewise, client problems may be conceptualized in different ways: as needs ("Something is missing in my life and its absence is disturbing the natural flow of life forces"); stressors ("Something unpleasant has entered my life and its presence is producing distress and distraction"); life conditions ("Conditions outside my control are limiting my potential happiness and success in life"); misinterpretations ("The way I am thinking about my life limits my alternatives"); dysfunctional social patterns ("I am a worse person with some people than I am with others and that is a source of distress and unhappiness"); or, more likely, a combination of these factors. Counseling theories tend to classify these client conditions as either affective, behavioral, cognitive, or systemic in origin. In other words, the client's problems emerge from emotional sources, undesirable behavioral contingencies, cognitive misrepresentations of reality, or systemic/contextual contingencies.

Seligman (2004) proposes that the assessment process should be a way of recognizing the importance and uniqueness of each person, a way of saying to the person, "You are special and I want to get to know you and understand why you are the way you are." In actual practice, it is important to assess problems in more than one way to avoid the constraints of personal bias or theoretical encapsulation. This also includes thinking of the problem in the client's social context and in a theoretical context as a way of manifesting Seligman's advice. Although the source of the client's problem(s) may be conceptualized as emotion-based (affective), behavior-based (behavioral), thought-based (cognitive), relationship-based (systemic), or milieu-based (cultural), the impact or consequences of the problem may be manifested as feelings, worries, undesirable consequences, fear, missing or unsatisfactory interpersonal relationships, or unfair discrimination (see Chapter 5).

At first, assessment is an information-collecting time. You will want to open all of your communication channels to receive information that the client is communicating. Initially, you may see no patterns, no meaning to the information. As you continue to work with the client, however, patterns will emerge, and you will begin to understand how the client perceives and tries to affect reality. You will also begin to see your client in the larger context of his or her environment, social setting, or world of relationships. And as the subtleties become increasingly obvious, either by their repetition or by their inconsistencies, you will begin to recognize how you can help your client.

Many views exist about how assessment should be conducted. Our view is that you should have some blueprint to follow. Otherwise, the amount of detail will begin to overwhelm the process, and you will either overlook important information to solicit and consider or you will become distracted from your purpose, which is to determine just what the problem is before you begin to provide solutions. In Chapter 5, we offer an approach to problem assessment that is widely used in clinical settings.

The process of clinical assessment involves several specific skills, including observation, inquiry, making associations among facts, recording information, and forming hypotheses or clinical hunches. Observation includes:

- Taking notice of the client's general state of anxiety or discomfort
- Establishing some sense of the client's cultural context
- Noting gestures or movements that suggest either emotional or physical dysfunctions
- Hearing the manner in which the client frames or alludes to his or her problems (for example, some tend to diminish whereas others inflate aspects of a problem)
- Noting verbal and nonverbal patterns

What may appear to be an insignificant detail at the moment can prove to be part of a significant pattern over time. Thus, observation—mental attentiveness to the persona of the client—is a significant component of the assessment process.

Inquiry is equally important. Beginning counselors have a tendency to ask a lot of initial questions but few follow-up questions, whereas experienced counselors pursue certain topics in great detail. Issues related to health, medication, feelings of despair or depression, self-destructive thoughts, and even interpersonal conflicts are examples of such topics. Inquiry is the skill of asking for the finer points, the details behind the event, or the information that provides the meaning to an event or condition. Open-ended questions explore processes; closed questions provide specifics. Both of these important inquiry tools were discussed in Chapter 2.

Collected information must somehow be organized and recorded. Some counselors take notes as they acquire information. Others record sessions on CDs or DVDs. Some do neither but allow time immediately following the session to write down observations and impressions. The recording of information is a disciplined process. If recording is not done systematically and promptly, information is lost and, therefore, useless. It is a common counselor lament that information previously given is unavailable because it was not recorded promptly.

When the counselor utilizes observation and inquiry to collect information related to the client's presenting problem, the result is a huge quantity of material. The more observant the counselor, the greater the amount of data. Somehow this information must be synthesized so it is usable. This synthesis is conducted within a context. The context may be a counseling theory, or it may simply be the counselor's view of life. Whatever the case, the process involves associating facts and events, constructing possible explanations for events, and making educated (or intuitive) guesses. This assimilation process condenses a large quantity of information into a more usable form. These hypotheses, hunches, and educated guesses become the foundation for the next stage—identifying and setting counseling goals. At this time, it is vital that you incorporate multicultural perspectives into your assessment. Pederson (1991) cautions, "Behavior [or feelings, or cognitions, or social systems are] not data until and unless [they are] understood in the context of the person's culturally learned expectations" (p. 9). You might ask the client, What do you think the problem is? This simple question often elicits the most important information, the most accurate insights of the entire process. It is surprising that counselors often fail to ask this straightforward question.

Setting Goals

Setting goals is extremely important to the success of counseling. And yet some clients and even some counselors are resistant to this stage of the process. The act of setting a goal involves making a commitment to a set of conditions, a course of action, or an outcome. Sometimes the highly stressed client or the disoriented client may find goal setting difficult to do. Even in this situation, the goal ultimately becomes one of setting goals.

Why are goals so important? The best answer is a simple one. Goals are set in order to know how well counseling is working and when counseling should be concluded. Isn't it enough to let the client decide these questions? Yes and no. The client is an important source of information and reaction to counseling. However, because counseling can generate dependent relationships, the immediate desire to hold on to a rewarding relationship may overshadow the more appropriate objectives of counseling. As will be evident later, the kinds of things that are done in counseling are often determined by the counseling goal.

The process of setting goals is mutually defined by the counselor and client. The counselor has the advantage of greater objectivity, training in normal and abnormal behavior, and experience in the process. The client has the advantage of intensive experience with the problem and its history, potential insights, and awareness of personal investment in change. Thus, the client needs to be involved in the thinking as well as the decisions about what should happen.

The skills involved in goal setting can be divided into three classes. First are the counselor's inferential skills. A counselor must be able to listen to a client's vague descriptions of existing and desired conditions and read between the lines of those messages. Rarely are clients able to describe crisply and concisely what they would like to accomplish through counseling. On the contrary, most clients describe their reasons for seeking help in generalities. The typical client is more likely to conceptualize concerns as "I don't want to feel this way any longer," rather than "I want to start feeling that way." Given this condition, the counselor must be able to think of alternative behaviors and attitudes even as he or she listens to clients describe their concerns.

The second skill involves differentiation between ultimate goals, intermediate goals, and immediate goals. Most people think in terms of ultimate goals (e.g., when I grow up . . ., when I graduate from college . . ., when I get that promotion . . ., when my boat comes in . . ., etc.). But if a person is to accomplish ultimate goals, he or she must be able to think in terms of intermediate goals (in the next six months, I plan to . . .) and immediate goals (I will do the following things tomorrow . . .). Intermediate and immediate goals provide the strategies necessary to accomplish ultimate goals and are the real vehicle for change in counseling.

The third skill of the goal-setting process involves teaching clients how to think realistically in intermediate and immediate terms. In other words, the counselor may need to teach clients how to set goals that are attainable. In Chapter 6, we discuss ways in which you can use these three sets of skills to help clients set realistic goals for counseling.

Finally, it should be emphasized that counseling goals are never chiseled in stone. Goals can be altered when new information or new insights into a problem call for change. Sometimes a goal is identified inappropriately and must be dropped. It is important to remember that the major function of goals is to provide direction to the counselor and the client.

Initiating Interventions

There are different points of view concerning what a good counselor should do with clients. These viewpoints are, by and large, related to different counseling theories. As you are aware from Chapter 1, there are a variety of counseling theories, each of which can be used by counselors to organize information, define problems, and select intervention strategies. For example, a person-centered orientation suggests that the counselor involves rather than intervenes by placing emphasis on the relationship. The existential counselor views intervention as encouraging clients to recognize and assume personal responsibility for their choices. The behavioral counselor seeks to initiate activities that help clients alter and manage personal contingencies, both in the counseling session and in the clients' real world. The cognitive counselor intervenes by introducing conditions that invite cognitive dissonance or disrupt static cognitive states. The systemic counselor intervenes by challenging interpersonal "rules" or interrupting systemic sequences. The multicultural counselor uses the total spectrum of approaches and intervenes by understanding the client's cultural milieu and helping the client take charge of his or her life within that milieu (Ivey, D'Andrea, Ivey, & Simek-Morgan, 2007). In short, all counselors, regardless of theoretical orientation, have a therapeutic plan that they follow, a plan that is related to the assessment of the presenting problem, to their view of human nature and change processes, and to the resulting goals that have been agreed on. ([See Section A.5.d, The Counseling Relationship (Potentially Beneficial Interactions), ACA Code of Ethics, 2005, www.counseling.org.)

The real issue in talking about interventions is change and how it occurs. The whole object of counseling is to initiate and facilitate desirable change. Thus, when you and your client are able to identify desirable goals or outcomes, the next logical question is, How shall we accomplish these goals? In Chapters 8 through 11, we shall discuss specific types of interventions used in counseling. For the moment, let us consider briefly the process a counselor goes through in identifying counseling interventions based on the assessment process.

Having defined the "problem," the first thing you should do is ask clients what solutions or remedies they have already tried. Most of the time, clients will be able to describe one or more things they have done that were not productive or only minimally successful in alleviating the problem. This information not only saves you from suggesting alternatives that will be rejected, it also gives you a sense of the clients' past efforts to remedy difficulties and the clients' resourcefulness as problem solvers. Occasionally, clients will report that something they attempted did work but for one reason or another, they discontinued the remedy. Client-induced interventions that were temporarily effective can sometimes be modified and made more effective. Such answers might also broaden your definition of the problem to include the clients' inability to stay with a solution until it succeeded.

Assuming all client-induced interventions have been ineffective, the next step is to relate problems to interventions, depending on the character of the problem. Problems that appear to be a result of how a client is viewing a life situation may be defined as cognitively determined problems. This would suggest that interventions directed toward cognitive change should be considered. If the problem appears to be related to the client's social environment (family, work, friends, community), then interventions designed to alter interdependent social systems should be considered. If the problem appears to be couched in terms such as hurt, sadness, or anger, then it may be affectively based, in which case interventions that facilitate affective disclosure and exploration should be included. Or if the problem's character appears related to the client's actions or efforts to affect others, the problem may be behaviorally based. Then the most effective interventions may be designed to help clients achieve more successful behaviors. The intervention strategies described in Chapters 8 through 11 are grouped around these dimensions of client problems. Chapter 8 examines affective strategies, Chapter 9 presents cognitive strategies, Chapter 10 addresses strategies for behavioral change, and Chapter 11 explores strategies and interventions designed to bring about system change.

At this point in the counseling process, your own theoretical preferences begin to emerge. We all tend to have a preferred lens for viewing life. One person might emphasize the importance of feelings. Another may view life as a behavioral to-do list. And yet another may see life as a set of challenges to be thought out and planned for. Though these do not appear to be theoretical, they are. We have consistently found that students who favor the feelings world also identify with humanistic theories; those who identify with thinking out problems prefer the cognitive theories. There is nothing wrong with this, except that problems are rarely confined to a specific theory. Rather, a problem usually can be assessed through several theoretical lenses. Similarly, clients have a habitual perspective for dealing with their problems, which may be why their solutions can consistently miss the mark.

Choosing the right intervention is often a process of adaptation. Not all interventions work with all clients, or as well as one might predict. Sometimes the "perfect" intervention turns out to be perfectly awful. It is important that you approach selection of interventions judiciously and be prepared to change strategies when the intervention of choice is not working. This process is similar to the treatment of medical problems. When one treatment does not produce the desired response, the practitioner should have an alternative treatment in reserve or reevaluate how the problem is defined.

The four skills related to initiating interventions are (1) competency in using a specific intervention, (2) knowledge of appropriate uses of a specific intervention, (3) knowledge of typical responses to that type of intervention, and (4) observational skills related to the client's response to the intervention. Developing the skills necessary to use different interventions requires that the counselor be able to practice in safe surroundings under expert supervision. Typically, this kind of practice occurs in a counseling practice or supervised clinical field practice. Counselors who try interventions on clients without the benefit of supervised practice are fooling themselves about their potential harmful effect on clients or about their ability to recover from destructive situations.

The counselor also needs to know how clients normally react to a specific intervention. Usually, this is expressed in terms of a range of typical reactions. The object is to recognize the abnormal reaction, the unpredictable response, the result of which might intensify the problem rather than alleviate it. For example, the "empty chair" (discussed in Chapter 8) is a gestalt technique often used to help clients recognize and expand their awareness of alternative feelings or reactions. It is a powerful technique, one that sometimes provides access to hidden and possibly frightening feelings. Occasionally, this technique will unlock an overwhelming amount of emotion for the client. In this case, the counselor must be able to recognize that the client's reaction is more than the typical response to this treatment. Related to this awareness of potential effects are the counselor's observational skills. It matters little that the counselor knows the warning signs if he or she does not see them flashing. These three characteristics—skill with a specific intervention, knowledge of its effects, and ability to "read" client reactions—constitute the skills inherent in effective counseling interventions.

Planning Termination and Follow-Up

It is difficult for beginning counselors to think of termination. They are so much more concerned with how to begin counseling that ending the process seems a distant problem. However, all counseling has as its ultimate aim the successful termination of the client. With this in mind, let us consider the significance and subtleties of the termination process.

Counseling, and especially good counseling, becomes a highly significant event for most clients. The relationship to the counselor may be the most important relationship in the client's life at that moment. Thus, it is imperative that the counselor acknowledge how important he or she is to most clients and how much his or her actions affect them. Some counselors will find this flattering. Others may find it uncomfortable. Some will find it incomprehensible that they could become so important to a stranger in so short a time. However, the fact that the relationship is important does not negate the fact that the relationship must eventually end. (See Section C, Professional Responsibility, ACA Code of Ethics, 2005, www.counseling.org.)

How does a counselor terminate a counseling relationship without destroying the gains that have been accomplished? It must be done with sensitivity, with intentionality and forethought, and by degree. As the client begins to accomplish the goals that have been set, it becomes apparent that a void is being created. The temptation is to set new goals, create new activity, and continue the counseling process. However, even this may not succeed in filling the void. Eventually, the client begins to realize that the original purpose for seeking counseling no longer supports the process. At this point, a creative crisis occurs for the client.

Long before the client reaches this awareness, the counselor should be recognizing the signs, anticipating the creative crisis, and laying the groundwork for a successful termination. As a general rule, the counselor should devote as many sessions to the active terminating process as were devoted to the rapport-building process. This is what is meant by termination by degree. When it is apparent that the counseling relationship may not last more than four to six more sessions, it is time for the counselor to acknowledge that the relationship will eventually end. This can be done simply by saying, "I think we are soon going to be finished with our work."

However, the process can be somewhat different when working with children because children may not have a sense of endings, or if they do have a sense of endings, it may be traumatic. Consequently, it is important that you ease the child toward completion (not termination) while emphasizing that this does not mean ending the relationship. Periodic reconnection with a child, either through a note, visit to the child's classroom, or telephone or e-mail contact, will help the child adjust to the transition.

It is not uncommon for an early acknowledgment of termination to provoke a denial or even a temporary crisis. Up to this point, the client may not have been thinking about facing his or her problems alone. If the client denies, allow it. The denial is part of the recovery process and will dissipate. On the other hand, if the counselor resists the denial by assuring the client that he or she is much stronger, it may only intensify the crisis. It is important to remember that the client must get used to this new thought. In succeeding sessions, the opportunity may arise to introduce the thought again. Gradually, the client will come around, will begin to let self-resourcefulness fill the void, and ultimately will "decide" that counseling can end soon.

Occasionally, clients need a bit of security to take with them even though they feel ready to terminate. This can be accomplished by making a follow-up appointment 6 weeks, 3 months, or even 6 months in advance. It may be a good idea to ask clients to decide whether they feel the need to keep the appointment as the date approaches. If they do not, they can call and cancel and let the counselor know that they are doing well. On the other hand, it is also important to communicate to clients that if new counseling needs arise, they should feel free to call before the appointment date. (See Section A.11, Termination and Referral, ACA Code of Ethics, 2005, www.counseling.org.) In Chapter 12, we discuss in greater depth the skills and concepts associated with termination and follow-up.

Using the Stages to Plan for Counseling

Counseling begins with building a relationship and then moves to assessment, and from assessment to goal setting, and so on. The fact that one begins assessment before completing the rapport-building stage does not negate this progression. Perhaps the best use of stages is to provide a blueprint for the beginning counselor. For example, as you begin working with a client, you may expect to devote the early sessions to developing a helping relationship. This is very important time. When the client begins accepting and trusting the counseling experience (and thus, you), this may be a signal to move fully to the assessment stage. However, you will soon realize that relationship and rapport building continue to be issues that need be addressed, even as you move into the subsequent stages. As you and your client study the problem, comments will be made and wishes will be visualized that point directly toward potential counseling outcomes. The process begins to seem like a natural flow. With experience, this blueprint becomes second nature, until it is no longer necessary to think in terms of stages. However, even experienced counselors find occasionally that cases are not progressing well. It is not uncommon for a case to stall or for a sense of lack of movement to take over. When that happens, it is a good idea to return to the blueprint, analyze the progress of the case in terms of stages, and redirect the counseling process where appropriate.

THE CLIENT'S EXPERIENCE IN COUNSELING

Most people have been in a position at some point in their lives when it would have been useful to seek counseling. Perhaps you can identify such a time in your life. Did you enter into a counseling relationship as a client? Whether you did or not, it is helpful to consider all of the factors that were involved in your situation. As noted earlier, asking for help is often experienced as a sign of personal weakness in the U.S. culture. When one's life situation clearly calls for some kind of professional assistance, the competing pressure to "go it alone" mobilizes and a personal dilemma is imposed. To go with the tendency not to seek counseling lets the individual off the hook temporarily. And, of course, one can muddle along for long periods of time in a state of disequilibrium. On the other hand, if one chooses to seek professional assistance, it means giving up that sense of isolation and failure in exchange for finding a hopeful solution. Acknowledging one's vulnerability as a price for gaining hope that life could be better is a difficult choice. Such is the situation for most people who decide to enter counseling.

The dilemma itself plays out as the counseling process unfolds. Carl Rogers first described how the client experiences positive change in psychotherapy. This description became formalized as the Process Scale (Rogers & Rablen, 1958) and was used for many years to study client change. The scale describes seven kinds of client reactions as change occurs. Typically, the client begins counseling by talking about externals (work, relatives, etc.). This is probably the client's way of controlling his or her commitment to an as-yet-uncertain venture. Next, discussion gradually changes to include references to feelings, albeit past feelings or those that are external to the client—again a careful step toward commitment. In the third stage, the client elaborates on feelings, but these are historical in nature rather than current feelings (e.g., "I was really hurt by her comment"). At the fourth level, the client begins to talk about present feelings and acknowledges ownership of those feelings (e.g., "I'm still upset with her for what she said to me!"). The fifth stage is one in which the client allows him- or herself to experience current feelings in the presence of the counselor (e.g., "Every time I think about it, I get the same rush of emotion" [begins weeping]). In the final two stages, the client begins to (1) experience previously denied feelings and (2) be accepting and comfortable with those feelings. Rogers never forced this development. Rather, he allowed the client to move at whatever speed was comfortable through this developmental process.

The client's experience can be similarly described within the context of the five stages of counseling. As we noted earlier, most clients approach counseling with mixed feelings. They want to improve their life situation, and yet they are reluctant to become involved in the counseling process. This is the first obstacle for many clients to overcome. In the following sections, we discuss some typical responses clients have during these five stages of counseling.

Rapport and the Client's Experience

Inexperienced clients enter counseling without knowing exactly what to expect or what will be expected of them. Because of this information deficit, they may feel uncertain, vulnerable, or guarded and doubtful. When the counseling relationship crosses cultural boundaries, this sense of vulnerability is even more pronounced. In addition to an information deficit, the client who is culturally different from the counselor may have concerns that are directly related to the person of the counselor (e.g., Will he or she understand how life is for me? Will he or she be sympathetic to the special problems I may face in life? Will the counselor expect me to conform to the values and standards of his or her own cultural background? Will we be able to negotiate our differences and find a common ground of understanding and acceptance?).

The counselor can do several things to ease this type of client anxiety. A helpful word of direction—whether it be a suggestion of where to sit, how long the session will be, or a description of what takes place when people are counseled—will be welcomed. When the relationship involves multicultural dimensions, it is appropriate to acknowledge those factors, and communicate your respect and acceptance for your client's worldview. If you don't know the client's worldview, it is appropriate to learn what it is. Sue (1992, p. 6) argued that traditional counseling that fails to acknowledge cultural worldviews can actually harm minorities and women because it may transmit a set of individualistic cultural values that maintain the status quo and, as such, represent a political statement. His identification of traditional counseling includes those approaches that fail to acknowledge multicultural factors in the counseling process.

Not all clients will react tentatively to the newness of the situation or with reservations that are culturally determined. Some task-oriented clients begin as though it were already the third session and give little indication that they are anxious or uncertain. This, too, does not mean that rapport has been established. The issues of trust, respect, and safety have been suspended temporarily as the client rushes into the process. Those issues may arise later as the client begins to look to the counselor for reactions.

By the end of the first session, many clients have begun to relax and take in the environment of the counseling setting. They may notice and comment on details such as furniture, pictures, and room arrangement. The client is taking mental pictures and forming first impressions. Between the first and second session, these mental pictures have a significant role. They are the bridge between sessions. If the mental pictures are inaccurate, as is often the case, the client will enter the second counseling session with erroneous perceptions that will lead, once again, to heightened anxiety.

Usually, the second session begins on a somewhat better footing than did the first. At the least, the client understands some of the conditions surrounding the counseling process (e.g., time limits, responsibility, etc.). But the client must also check out the impressions recalled from the first session and, of course, discover what direction the second session will take. As a result, the second session might be another nervous experience. If you are still attending to relationship issues, the client will become reassured once again, and the focus of the session will gradually shift to substantive issues. This same development will be repeated for several sessions. But as you and the client become better acquainted and more comfortable with one another, the progression from relationship to substantive issues takes less and less time.

Assessment and the Client's Experience

Most clients expect assessment to take place, but their expectations are often quite different from what actually happens. It is not uncommon for clients to ask for some form of verification of the nature and intensity of their problem(s). This expectation probably is fostered by the medical model. One goes to the family physician with a fever, swollen glands, and aching joints, and expects to leave with a prescription for medication and some advice on how to treat the symptoms. A more analogous situation would be one in which the patient undergoes lab tests to determine the source of a problem as well as the appropriate treatment. In fact, neither analogy adequately describes the assessment process in counseling. For that reason, it is a good idea to explain the process early in counseling, thereby informing the client as well as soliciting the client's assistance.

Clients also have a strong interest in determining what or who "caused" their problems. Very often, this question is pursued with such vigor that one might expect the answer to be the solution. In fact, the cause of most human concerns is rarely the solution to the problem. There are exceptions to this, of course. An example might be the feminist therapist's view that environmental conditions affecting women may be as much the problem as a particular female client's depression. It would be critical to help this woman develop awareness of how society's expectations of her gender relate to her depression, thus achieving a balance of self and environment. Similar perspectives are appropriate with people of color who suffer from societal oppression, or with physically challenged clients whose struggle with the environment is a major part of their problems.

Knowing why a set of conditions exists will not make them go away. But this knowledge may have implications for some of the goals of counseling. Counselors cannot assume that all human problems are internal—that is, determined by how the client thinks, feels, or behaves. Some problems include an external dimension. Family therapy has helped therapists recognize this fact. It is also true that society and culture can be part of the problem for women, for the gay community, for the physically challenged, and for the culturally different. When this is recognized, the assessment process must account for these external factors as well as the more traditional internal factors.

For whatever reason, clients tend to approach assessment with mixed feelings. Although the solution to their problem may be found in the process, so might the cause, and that may prove to be intractable. What if the problem is unsolvable? This process of assessment leads the counselor and client to the next stage: setting goals to deal with the client's unique situation.

Goal Setting and the Client's Experience

As counseling progresses, both client and counselor grow in their understanding of one another and of the dynamics and interrelationships that are part of the client's problems. As this happens, appropriate solutions or outcomes often begin to appear that may seem unreachable without the counselor's help. Thus, the client will look to the counselor for assistance in identifying interventions or strategies that will lead to the desirable outcome. Although this involves a certain amount of trust in the counselor's ability to assist, it may also be accompanied by some suspicion. The client probably does not intend to be suspicious of the counselor. Rather, the suspicion grows from the fear that the problem cannot be solved, the situation cannot or will not change, or the prospect of change is too threatening to contemplate. This latter resistance is described in Chapter 11 as homeostasis, a tendency to maintain the status quo. Thus, some clients will resist setting goals. It is as though their mantra is "Nothing ventured, nothing lost." Only as they experience some success in counseling will these reservations begin to dissipate, but that takes both time and wise direction by the counselor.

Will the client accept your assistance and direction? One criterion that clients use in determining this is the extent to which you appear to understand them or their problems. A client may express this condition as, "She understands my problem in the same way I understand it," or "He really understands what makes me tick." Thus, goal setting is intimately connected to the process of assessment. And, of course, goal setting is intimately connected to action.

Interventions and the Client's Experience

Many clients enter counseling vacillating between hope and doubt. Having already failed at solving their problems, they find it difficult to imagine that someone else could find the magic key. On the other hand, the need to find relief demands that they continue their search. In this context, the counselor begins to suggest, assign, challenge, encourage, empathize, and monitor. Many clients have an early rush of hopefulness as positive rapport is established and assessment begins. Soon, however, they begin to look for change and may become discouraged if none is apparent. There are many ways to help clients through this period. Some counselors begin by cautioning their clients that a lull sometimes occurs before change. Other counselors handle this phenomenon by carefully planning goals and objectives to ensure some level of early success. Another approach would view this as a natural crisis in the counseling process, one in which the client is beginning to address the issues of personal responsibility for change.

Change is a vulnerable process. People do not let go of old ways until they have new ways to put in their place. When the new is forced on individuals, they often resist or retreat until they can make the necessary personal adaptations. It is not uncommon for clients to react enthusiastically to interventions, to make major strides, and then to regress to old patterns. Typically, the regression is less than the original progress and is temporary. Nevertheless, as clients observe first their progress and then their regression, they can begin to doubt the process or, more accurately, their prospects for change through counseling.

As they recover from these temporary setbacks, clients regain their confidence and new patterns become more stable. By this time, some clients can begin to anticipate a new kind of crisis—the crisis of termination. They are feeling better about themselves, about their ability to handle problems, and about the counseling process. A cognitive dissonance emerges, which may be conceptualized as:

Through counseling I am stronger, more satisfied, more in control. Thus, I soon may need to end that which has proven so helpful. But I'm not sure I would be as strong, as satisfied, as in control without counseling. On the other hand, I will never know if counseling is propping me up or if I have really changed unless I leave counseling.

The resolution of this conflict is critical to the success of the counseling process. Only when the client decides to take the risk of ending counseling can it ever be established that counseling helped. It is critical at two levels. First, counseling gains must be supported and maintained in the client's real environment. Second, the client must be able to view him- or herself as a changed person.

Termination and the Client's Experience

Counseling is no more permanent than any other life condition. When termination occurs as a result of successful counseling, the process is one of both accomplishment and regret. Feeling self-confident, more integrated, and forward-looking, the client experiences a sense of optimism about the future. At the same time, the client is saying good-bye to a significant relationship, unique in that it allowed the client to be the center of attention, concern, and effort. One does not give up such relationships easily. Thus, there is also a sense of loss blended into the termination. These two emotional undercurrents will surface as the client and counselor discuss the ramifications of terminating. Some clients may even be confused by these seemingly contradictory feelings. Under these circumstances, they probably are misinterpreting the loss reaction as weakness or nonreadiness to terminate.

When termination occurs as a result of unsuccessful counseling, the critical factor is who initiated the termination. If the counselor initiates it, either because he or she lacked the requisite skills or because the relationship between counselor and client was counterproductive, then ethical and personal issues must be acknowledged. The ethical issues relate to professional responsibility for the client's well-being. Usually, this is handled by making an appropriate and successful referral. Personal issues are those that deal with client interpretations of why referral is necessary. As was noted earlier, clients are quite vulnerable when they seek counseling. If the experience turns out unsuccessfully, some clients are likely to turn on themselves as having failed again. Others may conclude that counseling will not work, just as they had feared. The counselor must acknowledge and help the client work through these reactions as part of the termination process.

On the other hand, if the client initiates termination, a different set of dynamics arises. In this situation, both the client and the counselor are vulnerable. The counselor's responsibilities are no less real, however, and include referral considerations and, if possible, personal considerations.

Perhaps the most difficult of termination situations is that in which counseling has been partially successful but cannot be continued. This might occur as a result of the counselor or client changing residence, as a result of client decisions to discontinue or postpone counseling, or as a result of the counselor's conviction that the client should begin working with another counselor. In this case, the client experiences loss even more intensely than when counseling was successful. That loss may be justifiable. The anger is a means of adapting to the new circumstances. But the fear is a potentially debilitating condition and must be addressed for successful termination to occur.

Whatever the reason for termination, you are professionally obliged to extend a helping relationship to the client until you are replaced by another helping professional. (See PAR. A.11.a, ACA Code of Ethics, 2005, www.counseling.org.) This may take the form of providing an opportunity to make future appointments, calling the client at a future date to check in, finding a mental health professional who would be an appropriate reference and who would be willing to accept the referral, or collaborating with the professional to whom the client has been referred.

DEPENDENCE AND GROWTH

Throughout the counseling process, psychological dynamics are present and affect the development of the relationship, the progress toward goals, and ultimately the outcome. We have already discussed issues such as trust, respect, and psychological comfort in this context. Another dynamic that should be addressed is client dependence.

As you and your client begin to understand one another and the counseling relationship unfolds, a state of client dependence often develops quite appropriately. At this time, some obstacles to the relationship will become factors. If cultural differences between you and your client have not been accommodated, client dependence is far less likely to occur.

Typically, client dependency begins at a low level, while the client is deciding whether to become involved in the counseling relationship. As confidence in you grows, so does the dependency on both you and the process. Through the relationship-building and assessment stages, this dynamic is particularly noticeable. Even in the goal-setting stage, many clients will lean as much as possible on the counselor to make the decisions and to point out the direction counseling will take. However, an important transition occurs during this stage as clients begin to realize that the decisions they are making and the goals they are setting are very important personal commitments. At this time, dependency begins to shift from the counselor toward self-responsibility. This transition becomes increasingly obvious in the intervention phase as the client assumes more and more responsibility for changes in behavior, attitudes, and emotions. The final accomplishment in this evolution from dependence to independence is reflected in the client's decision to terminate. Even as the client wrestles with the conflicting desires to keep the relationship or to let it go, there is an underlying awareness that success means termination, cutting the bonds, and becoming self-managing.

Summary

All relationships have structure. That structure may take the form of roles that the participants play, rules that they follow as they interact with one another, or concepts about what different types of relationship are like. Until an individual understands the structure of a relationship, he or she will find it difficult to understand how to be part of that relationship. In this chapter, we have provided a structure for viewing the counseling relationship. Beginning with building the helping relationship, the counselor then moves on to assessment; goal setting; planning and initiating interventions; and, finally, termination and follow-up. These stages are never accomplished without the participation of the client. Within each stage, there is much to be considered. Often, two stages overlap. Occasionally, the counselor and client need to take stock and move back to an earlier stage. Throughout these stages, evaluation is an important activity, whether it be considering how well the relationship seems to be developing; whether the problem has been correctly identified; whether the goals that have been identified are appropriate (or achievable); how well the interventions seem to be working; and, of course, what needs are part of the process of ending the relationship.

Finally, we considered the client's part in this experience. How does the typical client react to this passage from initiation to termination? What are normal expectations? These many facets of the counseling experience are important but often intangible. Thus, while you attend to the progress of counseling, it is also important that you attend to the client's experience, listening for the intangible, the unique, the nonconforming aspects of each client's passage.

Exercises

I. Stages of the Counseling Process

Select a partner and role-play a counseling relationship. Determine in advance which of the five stages you will illustrate in the role-play (relationship building, assessment, goal setting, interventions, termination). Have other class members observe and then identify the stage. Continue this exercise until you have illustrated all five stages. Then discuss the following question: Are the counselor's verbal behaviors the same across all stages or do they change? Describe any changes you would expect to see.

II. Cultural Identity of Client

Using the same partner, develop a role-play in which the relationship-building stage is enacted. One of you should assume the identity of a person of a distinctly different culture than the other. After the enactment, discuss what dynamics you experienced in the role-play. What insights did you gain? What problems did each of you experience? What implications for learning did you discover? Share your experience with minority members of your class and ask them if they can offer additional insights.

III. Termination of Counseling

Select a partner and determine who will be the counselor and who will be the client. Then enact the following role-play:

You and your client have been working for 5 months and have reached a plateau. Most of the client's presenting problems at the outset of counseling have been resolved. In your judgment, based on the client's report, the client is functioning well and could terminate counseling at this time. The client both agrees and disagrees with this assessment. He or she has no new problems to address but deeply regrets (and perhaps fears) to see counseling end. You have no desire to terminate prematurely, but your concern is that the client realize and accept that he or she is functioning well and is not in need of further counseling.

Following the role-play, discuss among yourselves the dynamics that seemed to arise during the session. What were your feelings? The client's feelings? Were you able to stay on task? Could you see the client's ambivalence? Could you help the client with that ambivalence? Where do you think the relationship was heading? What does the ACA Code of Ethics say about this dilemma?

Discussion Questions

1. How is assessment different from goal setting? What counseling activities are part of assessment but not part of goal setting? What activities are common to both?
2. Discuss the ramifications of the relationship-building stage. How does it affect assessment? Goal setting? Intervention? Termination?
3. If counseling interventions do not seem to be working, what might be the problem? How would you know?
4. What do you think is the most important stage of the counseling relationship? Why? How does your choice reflect your theoretical biases? Your own cultural ethnic background and values? Your gender? Would you consider yourself more attuned to what people do, to what people think, or to how people feel? How much of people's reactions can be attributed to their personal qualities? How much to their environment?
5. How does one know when counseling should terminate? Is there more than one way of knowing? Explain.

Building a Working Relationship

PURPOSE OF THIS CHAPTER

This chapter examines the first of the five stages in the counseling process: establishing rapport and a positive therapeutic relationship. Counselor qualities and behaviors and client qualities and input that are associated with therapeutic relationships are discussed. The increased likelihood that counseling will be a multicultural experience is recognized as an important factor in forming the relationship. The chapter addresses relationship issues that will likely be part of that multicultural counseling experience, including the counselor's responsibility for the client's cultural identity and sensitivity as well as his or her own.

Considerations as You Read This Chapter

- You have known many relationships. What have your relationship experiences been like? Which ones were supportive, helpful, or meaningful to you? What personal needs did they satisfy in you?

- Which of your relationships have had the same effect on the other person? What is it about you, or the things you do in a relationship, that would prove supportive, helpful, or meaningful to another person?

- How well do you know yourself as a person? Where did you get your eccentricities? Your values? Your ways of viewing yourself and others?

- What were the values of your family? Did your family value closeness or separateness? Organization or disorganization? Confronting or avoiding? Touching or distance? Inclusiveness or exclusiveness?

- With what social, cultural, or ethnic group did your family identify?

C lients "need to feel cared for, attended to, understood, and genuinely worked with if successful therapy is to continue" (Deffenbacher, 1985, p. 262). The actions that lead to these conditions are subsumed under rapport and relationship, heavily used concepts within the context of professional counseling. Each has acquired an impressive array of meanings and importance. *Rapport* refers to conditions of "mutual trust or emotional affinity" within the relationship (*American Heritage Dictionary of the English Language*, 2006). Rapport is the entry point into a therapeutic relationship; that is, it must be minimally present before the therapeutic relationship can take form. It might also be conceptualized as the synoptic root of relationship.

Therapeutic relationship is a broader concept than rapport. Gelso and Carter (1994) conceptualize it as three dimensions: the working alliance, the transference configuration, and the real relationship. By working alliance, they refer to the "joining of the client's 'reasonable' self and the therapist's analyzing or 'therapizing' self for the purpose of work" (p. 297). The authors define the second component, transference configuration, as "distortion," thus separating it from the real relationship. This distortion refers to a perception that only partly reflects reality. They define the real relationship somewhat sparingly, describing it as "having two defining features: genuineness and realistic perceptions" (p. 297).

In this chapter, we shall address only the "real" relationship component of the therapeutic relationship construct. Working alliance will be examined in greater detail in later chapters; the complexity of the transference configuration is a topic beyond the scope of this text.

CHARACTERISTICS OF THE REAL RELATIONSHIP

Carl Rogers was among the first American therapists to provide the conditions of a humanistic therapeutic relationship. Early in his career, he proposed six counseling conditions that he considered both necessary and sufficient to produce constructive client personality change (Rogers, 1957). Those conditions included two persons in psychological contact, one of whom was in a state of incongruence (the client) and the other of whom was congruent or integrated in the relationship (the counselor). Beyond these primary states, the relationship also required that the counselor experience unconditional positive regard and empathic understanding for the client, and that these two conditions be communicated to and perceived by the client.

Conditions that have been identified as important in the establishment of an effective counselor-client relationship include accurate empathy, counselor genuineness, and an unconditional caring or positive regard for the client. Proponents of diverse theoretical orientations tend to join on this one issue: Effective counselors are personally integrated and self-aware, value the client as a unique person, and are able to understand how and what the client is experiencing.

A constructive counselor-client relationship, what Gelso and Carter call the "real" relationship, serves both to increase the opportunity for clients to achieve their goals and as a potential model of a healthy interpersonal relationship, one that clients can use to improve the quality of their relationships outside the counseling setting. It is a condition that is generally accepted by most theories of counseling as an important component of therapy.

Empathy

Rogers (1989) noted that accurately experienced empathy means

> the therapist senses accurately that the client is experiencing and communicates this acceptant
> understanding to the client. When functioning best, the therapist is so much inside the private
> world of the other that he or she can clarify not only the meanings of which the client is aware

but even those just below the level of awareness. Listening, of this very special active kind, is one of the most potent forces of change that I know. (p. 136)

The emphasis on communicating empathy has introduced the concept of the *language* of empathy. Welch and Gonzalez (1999) propose that this requires that counselors communicate on two levels. First, counselors must demonstrate that they understand "the narrative—the situations, events, and people in the story [and] the sequence, the connections, and the themes apparent in clients' life stories. This is the content of the narrative" (p. 141). Beyond understanding content, empathic counselors must also understand the meanings clients attach to their narrative. Welch and Gonzalez (1999) refer to this as "the significance of the story, its meaning in the life of clients" (pp. 141–142).

How will you know when this communication has occurred? Clients often give you the answer through their responses. It isn't unusual for a client to react with some surprise or relief when you accurately understand both the content and meaning of the client's narrative. Expressions such as "Yes, that's exactly how I feel" or "Yes, that's it" indicate recognition of the level of your understanding.

Empathy has also been seen as a two-stage condition. Gladding (2007) identifies these stages as primary empathy, which involves communicating a basic understanding of what the client is feeling and the experiences and behaviors underlying these, and advanced empathy, which reflects not only what clients state overtly, but also what they imply or state incompletely. Egan (2010) refers to this second state as "basic" empathy. Being sensitive enough to catch what the client is implying or even stating incompletely suggests the challenge that accurate empathy carries.

One of the early researchers on empathy was Robert Carkhuff. To facilitate his study, he developed a 5-point empathy scale to assess how well the counselor was able to identify and communicate back to the client. The scale emphasizes movement to levels of feeling and experience deeper than those communicated by the client and that are additive in nature. Thus, level 1 reflects the lowest level of interpersonal functioning, and level 5 characterizes responses that go beyond what the client was able to express (advanced empathy). The Carkhuff scale was used primarily by researchers/observers as they rated counselor responses:

1. The counselor's responses either do not attend to or *detract significantly* from the expressions of the client.
2. The counselor responds to the expressed feelings of the client, but does so in such a way that it *subtracts noticeably* from the affective communication of the client.
3. The counselor's responses are essentially *interchangeable* with those of the client in that they express essentially the same affect and meaning (basically restating what the client had just said).
4. The counselor's responses *add noticeably* to the expressions of the client in such a way as to express feelings at a deeper level than the client was able to express.
5. The counselor's responses *add significantly* to the feelings and meanings of the client in such a way as to express accurately feelings some levels beyond what the client was able to express (Carkhuff & Berenson, 1967, pp. 9–10).

Carkhuff considered level 3 to be the beginning level for helpful, effective, empathic communication.

There is some question as to whether empathy is a learned counseling response, a personal quality, or some combination of the two (Hackney, 1978). Quite possibly, all human beings are born with a capacity to relate to others and their tribulations. If that is so, it is also possible that early life experiences either bring out that capacity or leave it dormant. Whether this is the explanation, it is a fact that not all would-be counselors are able to listen with the empathic ear, to project themselves into their clients' experiences in such a way as to experience, vicariously, each client's world. Curiously, actors tend to be highly empathic. They are able to project themselves into the role and bring it to life. Perhaps it is the creative imagination, paired with a sensitivity to feelings and nuances, that allows this to happen for the actor. Certainly, it is a product of experience, too. For these reasons, we believe that counseling students can develop strong and effective empathic skills through their preparation and experience.

Chung and Bemak (2002) observe that Western or traditional views of empathy fail to incorporate sufficient knowledge, awareness, or understanding of the complexities in negotiating cultural differences. To develop *cultural empathy* skills, they recommend that you help the client understand that (1) you have a genuine interest in learning more about his or her culture, (2) you have an awareness and sensitivity about some aspects of the client's culture but not necessarily all areas, (3) you have a genuine appreciation for cultural differences between yourself and the client, and (4) you make an effort to use culturally appropriate help-seeking behaviors and expectations in the counseling process. To this, it should be added that *cultural empathy* requires the same conditions as those laid out originally by Rogers (1957) already noted. Use the following exercise to see how well you can insert yourself into another person's world:

What does it mean to be a woman? What does it mean in the Muslim context to be a woman? What does it mean in the Detroit Arab American context to be a woman? What does it mean in the Irish context to be a woman? What does it mean in the Boston Irish context to be a woman? Does the Boston Irish woman see her world any differently than does the Detroit Arab American woman? Do their views of the role of women affect their views of themselves? Of their values? Of their world?

Strong empathic relationships are such that one person may begin a thought and the other person may complete it with accuracy, sensitivity, and emotion. Learning to understand is not an easy process if it does not come naturally. It involves the capacity to switch from your set of experiences to that of the other person as though you actually viewed the world through that person's eyes. It involves accurately sensing that person's feelings, as opposed to feelings you had or might have had in a similar situation. It involves skillful listening so you can hear not only the obvious, but also the subtle shadings of which perhaps even the client is not yet aware. Counselor empathy contributes to the establishment of rapport, the conveying of support and acceptance, and the demonstration of respect and civility. It helps the counselor and client clarify issues and contributes immensely to the collection of client information (Egan, 2010).

Genuineness

Genuineness refers to the counselor's state of mind. It means that the counselor can respond to the client "as a full human person and not just in terms of the role of therapist" (Holdstock & Rogers, 1977, p. 140). Egan (2010) describes genuine people as being comfortable with themselves. Genuineness includes being congruent, spontaneous, nondefensive, open to the experience, consistent, and comfortable with those behaviors that help clients (pp. 50–51). In short, it is being who you really are, without pretenses, fictions, roles, or veiled images. It suggests a large amount of comfort with yourself; thus, it is a quality that people acquire through life experiences.

If you are uncomfortable with who you are as a person, you will find it very challenging to be genuine with your clients. Your first task is to find ways to become more comfortable with yourself. Many aspiring counselors accomplish this by entering into a counseling relationship as clients.

This *quality* is often referred to as *congruence*, which means that your words, actions, and feelings are consistent—that what you say corresponds to how you feel, look, and act. Helpers who attempt to mask significant feelings or who send simultaneous and conflicting messages are behaving incongruently. For example, if I say that I am comfortable helping a client explore his or her sexual orientation issues but show signs of my discomfort with the topic, then I am in a state of incongruence. Such incongruence can contribute to client confusion or even mistrust. Ridley, Mendoza, and Kanitz (1994) add to this the notion of cultural self-awareness:

> The effectiveness of counselors in processing cultural information depends greatly on their ability to be self-analytical. They must distinguish their cultural assumptions from those of their clients. Then they must strive to overcome their prejudices, stereotypes and biases. In short, they must become culturally self-aware.

The word *spontaneous* is also used in reference to genuineness. This is the ability to express oneself easily and with tactful honesty without having to screen your response through some social filter. It does not mean that you will verbalize every passing thought to your client, nor does it give you license to blurt out whatever is on your mind. Spontaneity communicates your "realness" to the client and provides the client with a basis for understanding you and establishing a meaningful relationship with you.

Helpers who are genuine are often perceived by clients as more human. Clients are more likely to discuss private views of themselves when the counselor possesses a degree of nonthreatening self-comfort. Counselor genuineness also reduces unnecessary emotional distance between the counselor and the client. This is why it is referred to as a *facilitative condition*.

Positive Regard

Unconditional positive regard was one of the original conditions identified by Rogers as necessary and sufficient for positive personality change to occur. He defined it as prizing the client as a person with inherent worth and dignity, regardless of external factors such as the client's behavior, demeanor, and appearance. In a contemporary context, we think of it as a positive affirmation for the client as a human being. The counselor who experiences a positive regard for clients reflects not only his or her view of who that client is, but also embraces the client's worldview. This incorporates the client's ethnic and cultural sense of self, as well as other aspects of the client's life experiences that have shaped his or her worldview and his or her wish to change.

COMMUNICATING EMPATHY

It has already been noted that empathy is both experienced by the counselor and communicated to the client. The counselor's success in perceiving the client's world becomes important in the relationship only as it is communicated back to the client. Two sets of conditions are associated with the empathy experience: (1) conditions that allow the counselor to experience the client's world and (2) conditions that allow the client to understand that his or her world has been accurately experienced by another person.

Conditions That Affect the Experiencing of the Client's World

Focusing and relating are two necessary conditions if one is to experience another's world. By focusing, we refer to the suspension of all self-directed thinking and, instead, turning one's full attention to the other person. Only as you let go of your own concerns can you become free enough to experience another person's immediate concerns. And as you let go of your agendas, you can begin to relate to the other person's experience as though you were experiencing it yourself.

This is not an easy transition for most counselors. Kottler (1991) describes the challenge from the experienced therapist's perspective:

> There is not a single client I see with whom I do not, at periodic intervals, tune out what they are saying and go off into my own mental world. Most of the time, these are fleeting moments— flash images that are provoked by something the client said or did. Yet with some clients who I find especially difficult to be with, I leave the room more often than I would like to admit. I am, of course, uncomfortable about these self-indulgent lapses that, while excusably human, are nonetheless unprofessional. (p. 99)

Clearly, focusing is a self-disciplinary experience. It must be practiced as one might practice meditation.

Once you have achieved some self-control over your attention span so that the client's narrative can be followed closely, the second aspect of the empathic experience involves relating to the other person's experience in meaningful ways. This is much more than having an emotional experience. It involves searching one's own experience for similar situations and, beyond that, attempting to attach feelings from the full range of human emotion to the effect of such experience. It was noted earlier that advanced empathy involves recognizing even what the client may only be implying. In such cases, the empathic experience may require that the counselor interpret, or at least infer, what the client is trying to communicate. When the counselor must move beyond concrete communication to inferred communication, the risks of error multiply significantly.

Skills Associated With the Communication of Experienced Empathy

It is important to establish that we are really talking about a relationship in which two people are relating to one another at an intimate level of meaning. It is important not to think of this process as the mere implementation of skills. But there are also skills associated with such relating. How you sit as you listen to a narrative of pain unfolding, what you say in response, and how you feel as the client draws you into his or her very private world—all of these reactions are accompanied by outward, visible reactions, too. Just as you are asked to impose self-discipline on your attention span, you must also impose self-discipline on the outward manifestations of your experience in the moment. But beyond this, you must respond to your client, and help your client know that you are very present, sensitive, understanding, and accepting of the person your client is describing. The nonverbal and verbal attending responses discussed next will help build the relationship between you and your client by communicating your compassion and understanding.

RELATIONSHIP-BUILDING SKILLS

How does one create a positive relationship with a new client? Is it a matter of social competence? Self-comfort? Professional bearing? While all of these qualities are important, they do not address what you will be *doing* as you are talking to your client. The *what* that contributes to constructing a positive working relationship includes the following verbal skills:

Nonverbal attentiveness

Noting the client's gestures, body posture, nervousness, agitation, and physical reactions to you or to the topic

Verbal attentiveness

Using minimal verbal responses to let the client know that you are listening and following his or her story

Verbal reflections

Restating to the client what you are hearing him or her say

- *Affective reflections.* Reflecting the client's feeling statements
- *Cognitive reflections.* Reflecting the client's thoughts

Verbal paraphrases

Using your own (not the client's) words to communicate the depth of what you understand the client to be saying

Inferential responses

Making statements, usually framed as tentative hypotheses, that suggest you understand even beyond what the client is reporting

Enhancing responses

Making statements to the client that suggest confidence or hope that the client can handle the challenge

NONVERBAL ATTENTIVENESS.   As we noted in Chapter 2, clients often determine whether a counselor is attentive by observing the counselor's nonverbal behavior. In fact, even if a counselor states, "Go head and talk—I'm listening to you," the client may not believe this verbal message if the counselor is looking away, leaning back in the chair, or generally appearing disinterested. Whereas verbal communication is intermittent, nonverbal communication is continuous. When verbal and nonverbal messages contradict one another, the client will usually believe the nonverbal message (Gazda, Asbury, Balzer, Childers, & Walters, 1984). In part, this is because so much of the communication that occurs between people is expressed nonverbally rather than verbally. Effective nonverbal attentiveness includes the use of appropriate eye contact, head nods, facial animation, body posture, and distance between speaker and listener.

Ivey and colleagues (2007) have studied the differential effects of nonverbal behavior for different cultural groups. They found that the skills normally associated with "therapy" tend to include nonverbal gestures that are more typical of a Eurocentric orientation. That makes sense, of course, because most current theories of psychotherapy originated either in Europe or the United States. However, this does not reflect the realities of the 21st century in which multiculturalism is the norm rather than the exception. For example, the Eurocentric communication pattern includes things such as increased eye contact when listening and less frequent eye contact when talking, which is exactly the opposite of the pattern of eye contact in the African American culture. Similarly, a comfortable physical distance between two people having a personal conversation tends to be arm's length or greater among Eurocentric cultures, but it can be as close as 6 to 12 inches among Arab and Middle Eastern cultures.

The concept of time varies considerably among cultural groups as well. Northern European and western cultures tend toward a more linear view of time, with an emphasis on a more constant awareness of what time it is, what must be done at a certain time, and whether a time commitment must be honored literally. Mediterranean and South American cultural groups take a more casual view of time commitment and may not consider it as important to get to a 10:00 appointment no later than 9:59.

While these are generalizations about a cultural group, and certainly every cultural group has a range of behaviors, they tend to stand as norms. Thus, Hispanics have norms for body language that contain some uniqueness, and Asians have norms for facial expression that are different from those of African Americans. Can you identify some other examples of differences?

One of the problems many Americans have with discussions about multicultural difference is that they believe in the melting pot philosophy of U.S. culture. The melting pot philosophy means that, as immigrants to the United States become acculturated, they replace their culture of origin with a homogenized U.S. culture. It is true that over several generations, many Americans have modified their cultural expressions in the direction of a generic cultural norm. But if you scratch beneath the surface, you will find evidence of a person's culture of origin.

How might you know which behaviors would be understood and which might be misinterpreted by clients of different cultural origins from your own? The most obvious answer is to study cultures and become aware of their patterns of communication. But this could be a life's study in itself. The next best thing is to become highly sensitive to cultural variations among people; attempt to identify with their patterns of communication; and, in doing so, acknowledge or respect their uniqueness. Sometimes this effort becomes the subject of a respectful verbal discussion between you and your client.

VERBAL ATTENTIVENESS.   Nonverbal attentiveness is supported by verbal attentiveness—what is said to clients demonstrates an interest in them. There are different ways of expressing verbal attentiveness. One way is to allow clients to complete sentences. Cutting off a client's communication by interrupting discourages full expression, unless, of course, the client is rambling or telling stories in which case an interruption may be useful. Gordon (1969) observes that interruptions are not always verbal expressions; they include any behavior that distracts the client or interferes with the client's ability to continue with the interview at a particular pace.

The most common way to communicate verbal attentiveness is through the occasional use of short *verbal encouragers*, such as *mm-hmm*, *I see*, *go on*, and so forth. When used selectively, these short phrases can have a powerful effect in communicating your interest and encouraging expression. Overuse of these responses, on the other hand, can become a distraction and can impede client expression.

Another aspect of verbal attentiveness is verbal following, also referred to as *tracking* (Minuchin, 1974) or *attending* (Ivey et al., 2007). A person engages in tracking by following the content and actions expressed in the client's communication. The counselor is nonintrusive and leads by following, accepting, and encouraging the client's communication rather than initiating or changing topics.

Tracking can be used in a variety of ways. It is not restricted to just one type of response. It may be a statement or a question, and it may take the form of any number of different verbal responses, such as clarification, paraphrase, reflection of feeling, and open-ended question (see Chapter 2). The critical element in tracking is to support the direction your client's communication is taking.

The voice can also be a very powerful tool in communicating with clients. It is important to learn to use your voice effectively and to adapt the pitch, volume, rate of speech, and voice emphasis to the client and to the situation. An important concept to consider in using your voice is that of *verbal underlining*—the manipulation of volume and emphasis (Ivey, 1994). Verbal underlining is a way of using the voice to match the intensity of your nonverbal behaviors with those of the client. For example, if the client is speaking loudly about a situation that caused anger, you can also add intensity and emphasize key words in your response with your voice.

Finally, Ivey et al. (2007) introduce *focus* as an aspect of verbal attentiveness. Focus is better described as selective attending because the counselor is choosing which aspects of a communication to respond to. This is illustrated with a specific client statement, such as the following:

CLIENT: I really wonder what he might be thinking when I refuse to argue with him. He knows that my family never argues. We always discuss our issues and then find a compromise somehow.

To which the counselor might respond by focusing on the client, the client's spouse, the client's family background, the "problem," the counselor's reaction—a *we* focus that communicates communal effort on the part of the client and counselor, or a cultural/environmental context. Ivey et al. also believe that when the counselor is working from multicultural counseling theory, focus should reflect a balance among the individual, family, and multicultural issues.

REFLECTING CLIENT MESSAGES.   Sometimes the best way to communicate one's attentiveness is to give back to the client what you heard. This can be a brief restatement of the client's communication, or it may be a paraphrasing of the client's message. Generally speaking, your response will not be as complex as the client's message. Client messages may contain an objective or cognitive component and a subjective or affective component. The *cognitive* component includes thoughts and ideas about situations, events, people, or objects; it answers the question, What happened? The *affective* component refers to the client's emotions or feelings that accompany the cognitive component. Affective messages answer the question, How does the client feel about what happened? Notice the cognitive and affective portions of the following client message:

I really care for and respect my husband. He gives me just about all I need in the way of security, comforts, and so on. If only he could let himself give me affection, too. Sometimes even when I'm with him, I feel lonely.

The cognitive part of this message—what happened—is fairly obvious. The client thinks her husband is a good provider. The affective component—how she is feeling about the situation—refers to her emotional experience of loneliness.

Not all client messages contain easily recognized cognitive and affective components. Some messages have only a cognitive component, as when a client says, "I think my professors here are just average." Other messages may contain only the affective portion; for example, a client might state, "I feel lousy about this situation." In both of these examples, the other component was omitted from the message and must be discovered through indirect inquiry or inference.

PARAPHRASING CLIENT MESSAGES.   Another way to convey empathy is through the use of verbal responses that rephrase to clients the essential part of their communication. The response used to rephrase cognitive client messages is the *paraphrase*. (The response used to rephrase affective client messages is the *affective reflection*.)

Paraphrasing involves selective attending (focusing) on the cognitive part of a message—with the client's key words and ideas rephrased into other words in a shortened and clarified form. Thus, an effective paraphrase does more than simply restate or parrot what the client has said. Jessop (1979) points out that the goal is to rephrase the client's message so that it will lead to further discussion or to increased understanding of the message.

In the example that follows, the counselor has offered a tentative ("It sounds like") response, which softens the paraphrase. The counselor has also rephrased the client's "I can't seem to stop" to "You aren't able to control," which may invite the client to think more critically about his or her reaction. When a paraphrase is on target, the client is likely to say something to the effect of "Yes, that's exactly how it is." Well-targeted paraphrases often draw clients into exploring the topic in greater depth, in addition to feeling successful in communicating their message.

The Paraphrase

CLIENT: I know I shouldn't be so hard on myself. But I can't seem to stop second-guessing everything I do.

COUNSELOR: It sounds like you'd like to be easier on yourself, but you aren't able to control your reactions.

Formulating an effective paraphrase has four steps: recall, identification of content, rephrasing key words and constructs, and perception check. First, listen to and recall the entire client message. This process helps to ensure that you have heard the message in its entirety and that you do not omit any significant parts. Second, identify the content part of the message; that is, decide what event, situation, idea, or person the client is talking about. Third, rephrase the key word(s) and construct(s) the client has used to describe this concern in fresh or different words. Be as concise as possible in your paraphrase. Long paraphrases border on summarizations—a skill we describe in a later chapter. Finally, include a perception check that allows the client to agree or disagree with the accuracy of your paraphrase (e.g., "It sounds like . . ."). The perception check often takes the form of a brief question. However, counselors also check their perceptions of client messages by phrasing their statements in a tentative manner and by identifying client nonverbal reactions to their paraphrases.

Some counselors are hesitant to paraphrase for fear they might be wrong. Yet as Gilmore (1973) observed, "Within limits, it is better to risk giving an inaccurate paraphrase and stopping for clarification than to sit there with an all-knowing look, nodding your head as if you understand" just to avoid being wrong (p. 242). Clients are not likely to lose respect for you if you are occasionally wrong, particularly when they are given an opportunity to correct your misperceptions.

REFLECTING CLIENT FEELINGS.   The reflection of client feelings acknowledges the "other half" of a client's message: It acknowledges the affect that the client is communicating verbally or nonverbally. It can be affect that happened in the past, affect that is experienced in the present moment, or anticipated future affect.

The Affective Reflection

CLIENT: I have been working on this project for 6 months now. It seems like each time I get close to the solution, something comes up that takes me away from it. I can't tell you how sick I am getting with it.

COUNSELOR: It must be really frustrating to get right up to the solution and then have everything fall apart.

Learning to reflect client feelings involves three steps. The first is to recognize the client's feelings or affect tone. The second step involves choosing the words to describe those feelings. The third step is to give your perception back to the client in a manner that is reflective rather than prescriptive.

To identify the client's feelings accurately, you must become sensitive to certain verbal and nonverbal cues that are elements of the client's communication. Some of these cues are referred to as *leakage* because they communicate messages the client did not deliberately intend to communicate (Ekman, 1993; Ekman & Friesen, 1969). Other cues, primarily verbal, are more deliberately intended and are more easily recognized and identified.

In the case of affective leakage, it is important to account for the inferences you may draw. The statement "The client seems happy" is an inference. If you say instead, "The client is smiling and that may mean that he is happy," then you have accounted for your inference.

The total impact of a client's message includes verbal and nonverbal elements. The verbal element refers to certain nouns, adjectives, adverbs, and verbs that identify and modify the client's feeling state. In addition, there is the paralanguage element, in which emphasis is placed on certain words or phrases. For example, how many ways can the following sentence be stated?

"I'm really worried about finding the time to write."

1. I'm really *worried* about finding the time to write.
2. I'm really worried about *finding the time* to write.
3. *I'm* really worried about finding the time *to write*.

The affect word in this phrase is *worried*. However, the emphasis can change the meaning and thus the affect. Statement 3 does not communicate the same affect as statement 1 or 2.

Nonverbal cues can be seen from elements of the client's communication such as head and facial movement, position of the body, quick movements and gestures, and voice quality. Although no single nonverbal cue can be interpreted accurately alone, each does have meaning as part of a larger pattern. Thus, relationships exist between nonverbal and verbal aspects of speech. In addition to the relationship between nonverbal and verbal parts of the message, nonverbal cues may also communicate specific information about the relationship of the persons involved in the communicative process, in this case, the client and counselor. Nonverbal cues differentially convey information about the nature and intensity of emotions, sometimes more accurately than verbal cues (Ekman, 1993). For example, facial expressions do not appear to be culture-specific. Ekman (1993) reported that "no one to date has obtained strong evidence of cross-cultural disagreement about the interpretation of fear, anger, disgust, sadness, or enjoyment expressions" (p. 384).

After the counselor has identified the client's feelings from the kinds of verbal and nonverbal cues, the next step involves communicating those feelings back to the client using different words that convey the same or similar emotional tone. The choice of words used is critical to this skill because words can reflect either the same or different levels of intensity of feelings by the client. Ekman's (1993) research suggests that affect states may incorporate "emotion families." For example, "the anger family would include variations in intensity stretching from annoyance to rage" (p. 386). Because of this varying intensity of affect words and expressions, the reflection of client feelings can occur at two different levels. At the most obvious level, the counselor may reflect only the surface feeling of the client. At a deeper level, the counselor may reflect an implied client feeling with the same or greater intensity than that expressed by the client.

The more obvious level occurs when the counselor reflects an affect message that is overtly present in the client's message by using a different affect word that captures the same feeling and intensity expressed by the client. Here is an example:

> CLIENT: I don't like it when my wife tries to organize my life.

> COUNSELOR: You get angry with your wife. [reflection of overt message]

INFERRING CLIENT FEELINGS.   The more advanced level of empathy, when the counselor responds to what the client is implying or stating incompletely, may be communicated only by reading more into the client's statement than was actually said. In such cases, the counselor is inferring more into the message to provide added meaning. When used to facilitate advanced empathy, its purpose is to communicate the counselor's deep sensitivity to the client's feelings. Consequently, the *inferential response* is not evaluative or summative; rather, it is speculative or tentative.

For example, a client might be talking about the overload of her professional career and all of the pressures associated with it. The counselor could respond by inferring that all of this pressure probably spills over into the client's home life and personal relationships. The client hasn't said that. But the counselor speculates that, under typical conditions, such spillover is to be expected and, therefore, postulates that it is happening to this client.

This counselor response is tentative (this pressure *probably* spills over) rather than concrete. The counselor's acknowledgment, if accurate, says to the client that he or she understands even beyond what the client has revealed. Had the counselor asked, "How do you handle it when the pressure affects your family?" the effect is assumed, not presumed, and thus the counselor's response could be counterproductive. This is an important distinction because the tentative, or presumed, effect gives the client room to correct the counselor's presumption without losing the overall empathic objective.

The second kind of reflection is one that reflects an affect message that is implicitly expressed in the client's statement. Consider, for example, the implied affect message:

> CLIENT: I don't know why you just sit there and let me stew.

> COUNSELOR: It upsets you *when I don't take better care of you.* [reflection of implied message]

Notice that the reflection at a deeper level not only mirrors the implied feeling, but also reflects greater intensity of feelings. The most effective reflection is one that emphasizes what the client is concealing in his or her message.

The third step in reflecting client feelings involves a perception check. You can check out the accuracy of the reflection by asking the client a brief question or by recognizing client nonverbal reactions to the reflection. As with the paraphrase response, clients usually express confirmation and/or relief once their feelings have been identified accurately and understood. Occasionally, however, clients may respond by denying their feelings. In this case, you must decide whether the reflection was inaccurate or simply ill-timed.

Ivey, Ivey, and Zalaquett (2010) observe that, while it is important to note the client's feelings, it may not be appropriate to react or comment on your observations at a particular moment because timing can be critical to the process of helping a client acknowledge feelings.

The Inferential Response

CLIENT: I have been trying to find ways to cope with the pressure, but the job is unrelenting. As soon as I think I have gotten on top of my schedule, something new pops up.	COUNSELOR: With all that's going on at work, I would imagine that the pressure spills over to your home life and your family.

CONDITIONS THAT CONVEY GENUINENESS

Genuineness is also communicated through the counselor's verbal and nonverbal behaviors. Three classes of behavior, in particular, communicate genuineness or the lack there of:

1. Congruence
2. Openness and discreet self-disclosure
3. Immediacy

Congruence

Congruence means that your words, actions, and feelings all match or are consistent with one another. For example, when counselors become aware that they find a client's rambling to be directionless, they acknowledge this—at least to themselves—and do not try to feign interest when it does not really exist. Otherwise, they must conceal their reactions, producing the condition that leads to leakage of nonverbal deceptive behaviors referred to earlier.

The sensitive client will find counselor incongruence to be confusing or distracting and may view the incongruence as an indicator of the counselor's lack of competence or sincerity. Thus, counselor incongruence impedes development of the therapeutic relationship. In contrast, counselor congruence is related to both client and counselor perceptions of therapeutic helpfulness.

Counselors also need to be good observers of their own internal reactions and resulting behaviors; otherwise, they will send incongruent or mixed messages to clients. For example, if a counselor says disingenuously, "Sure, I want to hear what you have to say about this," his or her true reactions may be revealed through body language, attention span, or lack of attending behaviors. Most clients are sensitive to incongruent counselor behaviors although they may not know how to interpret them. If the incongruence persists, the client must attach some meaning to it, and the real danger is that it will be interpreted negatively.

Mindfulness—being aware of your words, feelings, and responses—will help you convey your own meanings more clearly and will lead to clearer interventions on your part. Moursund and Kenny (2002) note, "As you notice contradictions between the words you are saying and the way your body is responding, you can clarify your emotional reactions to the client and to the process that is unfolding between the two of you" (p. 17). You can become more congruent by sharpening your observation of your own experience and by noticing signals that may indicate that you are experiencing conflicting reactions to the client. Physical responses often prove to be more accurate guides to discrepancy and incongruence than do words.

Openness and Discreet Self-Disclosure

Openness is what Rogers originally referred to as *transparency* (Meador & Rogers, 1984). It is a willingness to let a client see through the counselor's intentions, motives, and agendas. Self-disclosure, on the other hand, is more intentional because it involves a decision to reveal information of a personal nature to the client. Many counselors believe that openness is a critical dimension of the therapeutic relationship because it communicates to the client a sense of equality and confidence in the client's power to change. Self-disclosure is a sharing of information that is not necessarily required by the client although it may be seen as helping the client understand how change occurs or how the client's expressed problem is one shared by others.

The nature and degree of self-disclosure have ethical and professional implications. Conflicting results have been reported among the numerous studies on the effect of self-disclosure. Donley, Horan, and DeShong (1990) concluded that "our data do not support the supposition that counselor self-disclosures have a favorable impact on either counseling process or outcome [and that] counselors ought to be quite circumspect about its use" (p. 412). More recently, Knox, Hess, Petersen, and Hill (1997) reported that "clients perceived self-disclosures to be important events in their therapies" (p. 280). Knox and colleagues do make a distinction between immediate and historical self-disclosure, noting that clients cite personal, nonimmediate self-disclosures as most meaningful. These authors conclude, however, that "even helpful therapist self-disclosures have the potential for some negative impact" (p. 281).

As a result of these and other research findings, it would seem wise to use self-disclosure discreetly emphasizing the counselor's historical rather than immediate events, and measuring carefully the apparent effect that such revelations have on each client.

Counselor openness is related to counselor genuineness. For example, clients sometimes ask counselors such questions as: Are you married? Why did you decide to become a counselor? Are you a student? Such direct questions are best handled with a direct, brief, and honest answer. You may then return to the discussion that preceded the questions. The point is that clients do have some need to know about their counselor. Not all of what they may wish to know is appropriate information for them to have. But some information is or may be necessary to help the therapeutic relationship grow.

If the request for personal information seems to be excessive, then there are some better ways to respond to the client's queries. For example, it may be more helpful for you to speak to the obvious by saying something like:

- "You seem anxious about talking about yourself today." [reflecting on the client's feelings of anxiety]
- "You've been asking a lot of questions about me." [reflecting on the process]
- "Does it feel good to get off the 'hot seat' for a moment?" [focusing on the reversal of roles]

The verbal skills associated with empathic understanding that were described earlier maintain a primary focus on the client. In contrast, self-disclosure shifts the focus to the helper. If the counselor uses self-disclosure as an intentional intervention, such as illustrating to the client that there are alternatives to how the client is reacting, then self-disclosure has a therapeutic purpose. But there are two hazards to using self-disclosure: (1) shifting focus from the client to the counselor alters the working alliance, and (2) it may suggest to the client that the counselor's reaction is the proper one or the "normal" response (Moursund & Kenny, 2002, p. 62).

The most effective self-disclosing responses are those that are similar in content and mood to the client's messages. This is referred to as verbal linking or *parallelism*, meaning that the helper's self-disclosure is closely linked to the client's preceding thematic response. Consider this example:

CLIENT: I just wish my father was more understanding and less critical of me. He always seems to want me to do better than I can or to be someone I'm not.

COUNSELOR: I do know what it's like to feel like you don't measure up to your parents' expectations. I can remember feeling that way sometimes when I was your age. [parallel response]

COUNSELOR: I don't like it either when people disapprove of me or my actions. Sometimes I wish people would try to be kinder. [nonparallel response]

Immediacy

Immediacy can be thought of as a special case of openness involving a particular kind of sharing with clients. It involves sharing a thought or feeling as it occurs in the counseling session. Cormier, Nurius, and Osborn (2009) identify three purposes that are served by counselor use of immediacy statements:

1. It brings out into the open something that you feel about yourself, the client, or the relationship that has not been expressed directly.
2. It may generate discussion or provide feedback about some aspects of the relationship or verbal interactions as they occur.
3. It is useful to facilitate client self-exploration and to keep the focus on the client or the relationship rather than on the counselor. (pp. 152–153)

Counselor immediacy brings covert, implicit feelings into the open and provides discussion of or feedback about aspects of the helping relationship. This kind of sharing not only aids in the development of the relationship but it can also be a highly effective kind of therapeutic intervention. Sometimes it's the counselor's own reactions to what the client is saying that can provide the client with insight into how he or she is being perceived. If the counselor waits until a later point in the process, the learning moment might be missed.

Cormier et al. (2009) have provided some guidelines for using counselor immediacy with clients: (1) The counselor should describe what she or he sees as it happens rather than waiting until later in the interview when the impact might be lost, (2) the immediacy statement should be in the present tense (e.g., "I'm starting to feel uncomfortable about this") to reflect the here-and-now nature of the response, (3) the counselor should be aware that using immediacy in an early session could be anxiety-producing for some clients, and (4) the counselor should be cautious to base an immediacy response on what is actually happening in the relationship and not to use immediacy responses to reflect countertransference issues.

Counselors may tend to avoid immediacy issues even when raised directly by clients. This may be especially true for beginning counselors, who are unaccustomed to talking about relationship qualities as they are occurring. Unfortunately, counselors who avoid using this response are likely to contribute to the development of a more cautious relationship.

CONDITIONS THAT CONVEY POSITIVE REGARD

Although unconditional positive regard involves an expression of caring and nurturance as well as acceptance, this condition can be conveyed to clients through the appropriate use of certain behaviors, including supporting nonverbal behaviors and enhancing verbal responses. Both of these may convey a sense of relationship warmth to clients.

Nonverbal Behaviors Associated With Positive Regard

When one person has a warm and caring regard for another, the clearest communication of that is through the person's nonverbals. Johnson (1993) describes some nonverbals that are associated with the expression of positive regard and warmth in a Eurocentric context:

> Tone of voice: soft, soothing
>
> Facial expression: smiling, interested
>
> Posture: relaxed, leaning toward the other person
>
> Eye contact: looking directly into the other person's eyes
>
> Touching: touching the other person softly and discreetly
>
> Gestures: open, welcoming
>
> Physical proximity: close (p. 163)

As we have already discussed, other cultures may communicate through quite different nonverbal patterns. For example, Native Americans "accept periods of silence, especially in unfamiliar circumstances such as counseling or psychotherapy. Speaking and silence should be allowed to come naturally and as part of a process" (Sage, 1991, p. 31). "Harmonious interpersonal relationships among Japanese Americans are maintained by avoiding direct confrontation. Therefore, much of the communication style . . . is indirect and is characterized by talking around the point" (Tomine, 1991, p. 93). And in the Vietnamese culture, "touching a young person on the head is offensive to them . . . [and] social touching of the opposite sex is usually not done . . . except [with] family members" (Tran, 1981, p. 7). Obviously, when a client is of a markedly different culture, the Eurocentric means for conveying a nonverbal message may lead to a misconstrued message or no communication at all. Under such conditions the counselor is unable to convey an affirming respect or other intended messages. Thus, it is important to recognize the unique qualities of the client's cultural patterns to enhance all communication and specifically to communicate an affirming respect for the client.

Enhancing Responses

There is one thing that all clients need from the counselor, particularly in the initial stages of helping: *acceptance*. Counselors convey acceptance by responding to client messages with nonjudgmental or noncritical verbal and nonverbal reactions. Thus, when a client states, "I know I'm pregnant again. It will be my fifth abortion. But I don't know who the father is, and I can't stand to use contraceptives," the typical reaction might be disapproval. But if you hope to establish a relationship with your client that allows you to be a positive influence through counseling, such a response would be self-defeating. You do not have to agree with or condone the client's behavior.

A verbal skill related to the communication of affirming respect and acceptance is the use of *enhancing statements*. Enhancing statements are those that comment on some positive aspect or attitude about the client and provide encouragement or support to the client in some fashion.

The Enhancing Response

The enhancing response provides positive feedback to the client, usually on process rather than on outcome criteria—for example:

"I can see you've really worked hard on this issue."

"You're allowing yourself to get close to your feelings now."

"You're able to take the risk now, even if it means finding out something uncomfortable or painful."

Enhancing responses can have a strong effect on the client and on the relationship. They are most effective when used selectively and sincerely. You know the feeling you have about someone who is always saying nice things about you—these statements lose their effect when used too often.

FUNCTIONS OF A THERAPEUTIC RELATIONSHIP

The core conditions and associated skills we describe in this chapter are derived from the person-centered approach to helping. Most other helping approaches or theoretical orientations also stress the importance of a sound therapeutic relationship in effective helping even though some approaches differ in the nature and degree of importance they attach to the role of relationships in counseling. Adlerian psychotherapy, for example, emphasizes the necessity of establishing a democratic and egalitarian relationship with the client. Behavioral approaches identify the importance of a good relationship as a potential reinforcing stimulus to the client.

One of the key ingredients of reality therapy—that of *involvement*—is based on the concept of the counselor's ability to relate to clients effectively. The family therapy approaches have placed less emphasis on relationship as a therapeutic condition but speak of joining with the client or family as a prerequisite to therapeutic work.

At least four primary functions are associated with a strong relationship bond between counselor and client. First, the therapeutic relationship creates an atmosphere of trust and safety for the client. This reduces client cautiousness, suspicion, or hesitancy to take risks, thus facilitating the client's disclosure of very personal and sensitive material without the fear of aversive or punitive consequences. Without such disclosure, counseling is likely to have little impact on clients because pertinent issues are not being explored.

Second, the relationship provides a medium or vehicle for intense affect. It permits and protects the client who needs to express strong feelings. Often, expression of such feelings is the initial step in diminishing their intensity and developing a greater sense of self-control.

Third, an effective therapeutic relationship allows the client to experience a healthy interpersonal relationship. Such an experience can assist clients in identifying and enhancing the quality of their relationships with others in their world. For example, clients may learn that it is all right to say how one feels, ask for what one needs, and share thoughts and feelings with others within the context of cultural restraints. They develop more effective forms of communication that are consistent with their worldview.

Fourth, it should be noted that relationships may be perceived differently, depending on one's gender. Males may define relationships in terms of similarities of interest, whereas females tend to define relationships in terms of shared feelings and experiences. In addition, relationships can be valued differently by males and females.

EFFECTS OF THERAPEUTIC RELATIONSHIPS ON CLIENTS

Clients' reactions to the counselor's level of involvement can range over several dimensions. Initially, some clients will feel pleased and satisfied with the quality of this interpersonal relationship. They may experience relief that someone finally seems to understand, giving them the opportunity to get burdensome or painful memories out in the open. They may also feel hopeful that someone seems to care enough to become involved in their lives.

Not all initial client reactions will be this positive, however. Some clients, unaccustomed to the informality or intimacy of the setting, may feel threatened, intimidated, or claustrophobic by the therapeutic relationship. They are uncomfortable with so much attention directed at them, with the counselor's expression of caring and concern, and with what they perceive as an insufficient amount of role distance.

Other clients may question the counselor's motives or sincerity and view the counselor and the relationship with a degree of skepticism. They may have trouble believing that the counselor's intentions are good. They may wonder how committed the counselor really is to them and to working on their behalf. These clients are often looking for assurance that counseling will not exploit in any way their vulnerability. Such clients often express their concerns with indirect or mixed messages designed to collect data about the counselor's trustworthiness. If counselors fail to respond to the underlying issue of trust and skepticism, the relationship may deteriorate or even terminate, with the counselor still unaware that the real issue was lack of trust.

Counselors may want to be careful about assuming that the conditions and quality of the therapeutic relationship always produce favorable client reactions. Current interpretations of empathy, for example, view it as a multistage process consisting of multiple elements (Egan, 2010). As such, empathy may be more useful for some clients and less effective with others. A leading authority on the person-centered approach has observed that, in the counseling process, empathy "will be helpful in certain stages, with certain clients, and for certain goals." At other times, however, it "can interfere with positive outcomes" (Gladstein, 1983, p. 478).

When clients respond to therapeutic involvement with apprehension or skepticism, it does not mean that the counselor stops reacting therapeutically or that the counselor denies involvement with the client or withdraws from the relationship. It does mean that the counselor makes a concerted effort to pay close attention to the client's feelings and attempts to relate to the client in a way that matches or tracks the client's feelings and frame of reference. Initially, this might mean moving a little more slowly, not pushing as much, or not conveying implicit or explicit demands for client progress and change. Your understanding of the skills and concepts of the therapeutic relationship may be enhanced by reading the following case. (Case illustrations will be provided throughout the book to illustrate the major stages and strategies of the helping process. The case examples should help you in the application of the material you read.)

CASE ILLUSTRATION OF RELATIONSHIP BUILDING

The Case of Amy

Amy is a 45-year-old woman referred to you by her physician after he failed to find any organic basis for her frequent headaches and depression. He thought her symptoms could potentially be complicated grief, a condition resulting from the untimely death of her husband 14 months earlier.

Her physician did prescribe an antidepressant and continues to monitor its effect.

Amy is an elementary school teacher and is highly regarded in her community. She is viewed as competent, very child-centered, and dutiful to all the tasks that relate to good teaching. At home, Amy is barely able to manage her schedule, which includes her children's activities, a large house, and daily family management. When he was alive, her husband assumed responsibility for most of these duties.

Amy has finally agreed to seek grief counseling, but she does not seem particularly receptive in the first interview. She sits in the most distant chair in your office, keeps her eyes down rather than making eye contact with you, and speaks in monosyllables during the first half-hour of the session. Finally, you ask her an important question: "Amy, would you tell me about your children?" She raises her head to make eye contact, and answers, "I have two children: Max, who is 17, and Jennifer, who is 12."

Because this is her first display of responsiveness in the session, you choose to stay with the topic. Your thought is that anything that will get Amy involved is an important first step in establishing a relationship, so you proceed to ask her questions about the children. It quickly becomes obvious that they are her prized reality at this point and she is able to talk about them. At the same time, you know that Amy was unable to talk earlier because the presenting problem, the loss of her husband, was simply too painful to talk about.

At the end of this session, you ask Amy if she is willing to meet again and if she is willing to bring pictures of her children. She is obviously reluctant to commit, but with some gentle urging, she agrees. As she is putting her coat on to leave, you remind her again to bring pictures to the next session and ask her if she would like an e-mail reminder. She says "No, but thank you."

Amy arrives at the second session 10 minutes late and apologizes, saying something came up at the end of the school day that delayed her. The two of you sit in the same chairs as earlier and discuss how her school assignment is going. She replies that parent conferences are starting soon and she is feeling pressure from that. In addition, the father of one of her students died in a car wreck and she has been quite involved with the child and her mother. You listen carefully to the story as Amy explains it, but you do not ask probing questions. Instead, you use your basic verbal and nonverbal counseling skills to help Amy describe the situation. You note that it is stressful for her to discuss this topic, but she seems to need to describe it. You avoid bringing up Amy's loss at this time, thinking that she will be able to get there as she discovers that it is a safe place to talk about such traumatic conditions. At the end of this session, as Amy prepares to leave, you ask for another session because you did not get to see her children's pictures or hear about their activities and school situations. Amy reluctantly agrees and a third session is planned.

At the third session, Amy arrives promptly but appears exhausted. You inquire about this and she says that she hasn't been sleeping the last couple of nights. You remember that she had said in the first session that parent conferences were coming up, so you take a chance and ask, "Have parent conferences started yet?" She says "Yes, this week." You look at her and ask, "Is that where the stress is coming from that is keeping you awake?"

At this point, Amy begins to weep softly and pulls herself back in her chair. Finally, she says in an almost inaudible voice, "I guess so." You do not respond, choosing instead to let her gather her thoughts and emotions. Finally, Amy looks up and says, "It's all so hard," and begins to sob. During this time, you respect her need to cry by offering Kleenex and support. "Go ahead and cry—don't rush this—take some time and let these feelings and tears come out." You attempt to respond with both warmth and spontaneity to her and to let her know that you are not uncomfortable with the intensity of her feelings even though she might be uncomfortable. "Sometimes feelings can be pretty overwhelming, especially if you have been holding them in for a long time. It may be helpful to try to express them any way that you can."

As the session winds down, Amy begins to talk about her own situation, her loss, and her feelings of inadequacy. Time and again, she indicates how incompetent she feels. You take this opportunity to direct her attention to her children, asking if she remembered the pictures. She nods and pulls them out of her briefcase. At this point, you move over to the chair beside her to look at them. Four or five pictures later, you remark about how much Jennifer looks like her. She smiles and adds, "Max looks just like his Dad, too." She agrees to schedule another session, this time without the same reluctance as before although she isn't exactly enthusiastic. As she leaves, she turns and says, "Thank you. I feel a little better."

Case Discussion

In this case, the counselor quickly recognizes that the client is very fragile and needs to be given as much emotional space as possible if a counseling relationship is to emerge. At the same time, the counselor knows that a relationship cannot emerge until some verbal interaction does occur. Finally, she is given an entry when the client mentions her children. This proves accurate when the client responds willingly to a question about the children. The counselor uses this information by asking the client to bring pictures of the children to the next session. At no time in the first session does the counselor bring up Amy's loss. She focuses instead on those concrete conditions of her present life: school, students, schedule. In the second session, Amy ventures into the world of feelings and talks a bit about her student who lost her father. The counselor does not try to use this as a bridge to get Amy to talk about her own situation, fearing that it is too soon and that Amy might retreat into her overwhelmed state. Instead, the counselor listens sympathetically and with understanding, hoping that this will help Amy realize that the counselor is a "safe" person to talk to. At the end of this session, the counselor reminds Amy that a goal of this session—viewing the pictures of her children—was unmet. This further reinforced the notion that the counselor was attentive to, cared about, and able to react to Amy in ways that Amy valued.

CHILDREN AND THE COUNSELING RELATIONSHIP

Thus far, we have discussed rapport and relationship in an adult context. Much of what we have observed may also apply to adolescents although the issue of trust is inherently more complex with adolescents, who are actively seeking to differentiate themselves from parents. For younger children, however, the matter of relationship is more variable. Children may be referred to counseling when they are exhibiting difficulty with peers, with responsibilities, or with adults. Sometimes parents will seek counseling for children when the family is undergoing stress, for example, the death of a family member, moving to a new community, and so on. With younger children, the trust issue is more likely to be whether to trust a stranger. Henderson and Thompson (2011) observe:

> Counseling seems to work better if children can control the distance between themselves and the counselor. Adults are often too aggressive in trying to initiate conversations with children. Children prefer to talk with adults at the same eye level, so some care needs to be given to seating arrangements that allow for eye-to-eye contact and feet on the floor. A thick carpet, comfortable chairs, floor pillows, puppets, dollhouses, and other toys to facilitate communication are also recommended for the counseling room. (p. 45)

Other developmental issues should be taken into account. The younger child has not learned many of the subtleties of adult communication. But at a less subtle level, younger children also lack the vocabulary of the adult world. It is important that you modify your adult behavior and vocabulary to match that of the child. A second concern is the physical domain. To young children, adults look like giants. Their appearance serves as a reminder of the child's powerlessness and vulnerability. Third, it is important to remember that the child's attention span, which is briefer than that of adults, has two implications: First, younger children will not be topic-bound for more than a couple of minutes at a time (they may return to a topic several times during a session). Second, the counseling session will not be as long as an adult or adolescent session. You may want to think in terms of 20-minute counseling sessions for younger children unless you are using play therapy. In play therapy, the session can be somewhat longer, but there will be more play than therapy. Beyond these immediate concerns, the establishment of rapport and a relationship with younger children also involves understanding, acceptance, a liking of children, and genuineness. Genuineness is especially critical. If young children sense that you are being disingenuous or not taking them seriously, their basis for trusting you will be destroyed and rapport will not occur.

Summary

Several conditions and ingredients contribute to the initial stage of building a therapeutic relationship with clients. Accurate empathy, counselor genuineness, and supportive respect are three counselor qualities that form the foundation of therapeutic relationships. These qualities are conveyed through the counselor's attitudes, and they are also expressed by certain helping skills, which include facilitative nonverbal behaviors and verbal skills such as paraphrasing, reflecting, self-disclosure, immediacy, sharing, and enhancing responses.

The greatest obstacle in this initial phase of helping is the counselor's tendency to move too quickly. This tendency may be precipitated by clients who want relief from pain and by helpers, particularly inexperienced counselors, who may need to prove something to clients and to themselves.

With all of this information as background, it is important to be sensitive and responsive to each client's worldview, which is composed of ethnic/racial, cultural, gender, lifestyle, physical, and age parameters. These unique qualities alter and shape the nature of helpful counseling relationships.

Exercises

I. Attentiveness and Empathy

This exercise involves you and a partner in two interactions. Each interaction will last about 5 minutes. After both have been completed, assess the impact of each interaction. Ask for your partner's reactions to each situation. In which one did he or she feel most comfortable? In which did he or she feel like stopping or leaving?

A. You are to listen carefully to what your partner is saying, but you will send your partner nonverbal signals that indicate boredom: look away, doodle, appear distracted, and so on. If your partner accuses you of being uninterested, insist that you are interested—you may even review what has been said—but continue to send nonverbal signs of boredom. Do not discuss or share these instructions at this time.

B. In the second exercise, listen carefully to what your partner is saying and send nonverbal signals that indicate your interest and attentiveness—eye contact, head nodding, facial animation, and so on. Make some attempt to ensure some synchrony between your partner's nonverbal behavior and your own.

II. Identifying Nonverbal and Verbal Affect Cues

To give you practice in identifying nonverbal and verbal affect cues, complete the following exercises:

A. Pick a partner. One of you will be the speaker; the other will be the respondent. After you complete the exercise, reverse roles and repeat the exercise. The speaker should select a feeling from the following:

contented, happy
puzzled, confused

angry, hostile
discouraged, depressed

Do not tell the respondent which feeling you have selected. Portray the feeling through non-verbal expressions only. The respondent must try to identify the feeling you are communicating as well as the behaviors you use to express the feeling. After he or she has done so, choose another feeling and repeat the process.

B. The speaker should select a feeling from the following list:

surprise
elation or thrill
anxiety or tension
sadness or discouragement
seriousness or intensity
irritation or annoyance

Do not inform the respondent which feeling you have selected. Verbally express the feeling in one or two sentences. Be certain to include the affect word itself. The respondent should try to identify the feeling in two ways:

1. Restate the feeling using the same affect word as the speaker.
2. Restate the feeling using a different affect word but one that reflects the same feeling, for example:

> SPEAKER: I feel good about being here.
> RESPONDENT: a. You feel good?
> b. You're glad to be here.

3. Choose another feeling from the list above and repeat the exercise.

III. Paraphrasing and Reflecting

Respond in writing to each of the following three client messages. (Feedback follows the chapter exercises.)

A. Client: "I'm tired of sitting at home alone, but I feel so uncomfortable going out by myself."

1. Cognitive part of message: _____

2. Affective part of message: _____

3. Paraphrase of cognitive part: _____

4. Affective reflection: _____

B. Client: "I don't know why we got married in the first place."

1. Cognitive part of message: _____

2. Affective part of message: _____

3. Paraphrase of cognitive part: _____

4. Affective reflection: _____

C. Client: "The pressure from my job is a lot to contend with, but I expected it" (said with strained voice, furrowed brow, twisting of hands).

1. Cognitive part of message: _____

2. Affective part of message: _____

3. Paraphrase of cognitive part: _____

4. Affective reflection: _____

IV. Self-Disclosure and Immediacy

Listed below are four client situations. For the first two, develop and write an example of a self-disclosure response you might make to this client. For the second two, develop and write an example of an immediacy response you could use with this client. Share your responses with other students, colleagues, your instructor, or your supervisor.

A. The client hints that he wants to tell you something but he is reluctant to do so because it is something he feels very ashamed of.

B. The client believes she is the only person who has ever felt guilty about a particular issue.

C. You experience a great deal of tension and caution between yourself and the client. You both seem to be treating each other with kid gloves. In your body you are aware of physical sensations of tension, which are also apparent in the client.

D. You and your client like each other a great deal and have a lot in common. Lately, you have been spending more time swapping life stories than focusing on or dealing with the client's presented concern of career indecision.

V. Positive Regard and Enhancing Responses

Take a few minutes to think of a person with whom you are currently in a relationship and toward whom you feel affirming respect.

A. What kinds of positive feelings do you have for this person? Jot them down.

B. What does this person do that you like and value? Jot these details down.

C. Based on your positive feelings for the person and on things he or she does that you like, develop some enhancing statements you could use to convey your feelings to this other person. List them.

D. How would you feel making these statements to the person? What might be the effect on the other person?

Feedback for Exercises

III. Paraphrasing and Reflecting

A. *Client Message 1*

1. The cognitive part of the message is "sitting at home alone." This is the event or situation.
2. The affective part of the message is "I feel so uncomfortable going out by myself."
3. Examples of paraphrase responses:
   a. "Sitting at home alone isn't a very good choice."
   b. "It's hard when neither choice is a good one."
4. Examples of affective reflection responses follow. Note that the first two are at the surface level; the second two reflect the implied meaning as well as the obvious message.

   a. "You feel uneasy about venturing out alone."
   b. "You're feeling apprehensive about going out on your own."
   c. "You're really feeling unsure about yourself. It would feel so good to have someone to go out with."
   d. "It's really difficult being alone."

B. *Client Message 2*

1. The cognitive part of the message is "we got married [but we're incompatible]."
2. The affective part of the message is "don't know why." *Don't know* reflects uncertainty; confusion; or, in this case, disbelief.
3. Examples of paraphrase responses:
   a. "It's hard to understand how two incompatible people ended up getting married."
   b. "Even with all of your differences, you still got married."

4. In the following examples of affective reflection responses, the first two are at the surface level; the second two reflect implied omission or what the client would like to have happen.
   a. "You're amazed that the two of you got married."
   b. "Given the basic differences that exist between the two of you, it's puzzling that you ended up together."
   c. "It sounds like you'd feel more comfortable if you weren't so different and shared more of the same interests."
   d. "And perhaps you are looking at yourself and questioning why you would make such a choice?"

C. *Client Message 3*

1. The cognitive part of the message is "pressure from my job."
2. The affective part of the message is implied from the client's nonverbal behavior—strained voice, furrowed brow, twisting of hands—all of which suggest tension.
3. Examples of paraphrase responses:
   a. "You're finding out just how much there is in your job that you have to cope with."
   b. "It's a very demanding job."
4. In the examples of affective reflection responses, the first two are at the surface level and the second two are at a deeper level.
   a. "You expected some pressure from your job, but this is starting to get very heavy."
   b. "The job is becoming a heavy burden."
   c. "From your nonverbals, you're really reacting to the job."
   d. "Even though you expected pressure, you're feeling pretty overwhelmed by the job's demands."

Discussion Questions

1. How do you approach a new relationship? What conditions do you require to be met before you open yourself to a closer relationship?

2. What are the unwritten rules in your family about interactions with nonfamily members? How do you think these unwritten rules will affect the way you relate to clients?

3. If you were a client, what kind of relationship would you expect and value? What conditions would you probably put on the relationship?

4. What do you think is the greatest problem faced by cross-cultural counseling relationships?

5. Is it always useful to be genuine with clients? Can you think of any instances in which an expression of genuineness might be inappropriate?

6. What do you suppose it would be like for two persons from different minority cultures to form a counseling relationship? What are the advantages? What are the disadvantages?

MyCounselingLab Assignment

Go to the Video Resource Library on the MyCounselingLab site for your text and search for the following clips:

• **Person-Centered: Individual Demonstrating Empathy**   What counselor behaviors did you observe that were discussed in the Empathy section?

• **Cognitive-Behavioral: Introduction**   What was the counselor doing to establish a *beginning* working relationship with the client?

• **Existential-Humanistic: The Power of Listening and Questioning**   What verbal responses did the counselor use to encourage the client to discuss her issues? Were all of the responses effective? Which seemed to work better?

Assessing Client Problems

PURPOSE OF THIS CHAPTER

In this chapter, we examine the process by which counselors can assess the client's presenting problems. That process involves the collection of information relevant to problem definition, conceptualization of that information into a cogent picture of the client in his or her world, and consideration of client resources. Cultural factors that affect client perceptions of their world and counselor perceptions of client problems are introduced.

Clinical assessment in counseling may occur at an in-take interview prior to assignment to a counselor. Or it may occur during the assigned counselor's sessions with the client. When it occurs prior to counselor assignment, it typically includes paper-and-pencil assessment instruments in addition to information gathering in the interview(s).

There are two approaches to clinical assessment: the psychodiagnostic method and the psychometric method (Drummond & Jones, 2010). In this chapter, we shall examine the psychodiagnostic approach, which has as its purpose the evaluation of client problems and contextual conditions in order to determine what type of counseling is needed, what types of interventions should be used, and how counseling is likely to progress.

Considerations as You Read This Chapter

▪ Defining a "problem" is a difficult process. People see problems differently. How does a professional counselor view problems?

▪ How does the professional counselor separate his or her worldview from that of the client to permit the objective definition of problems?

▪ What kinds of information are useful in understanding a stranger's problems?

▪ How do you determine the difference between seeking information that is significant in your client's life and merely going on a "fishing" expedition?

▪ How do the differences between crisis counseling and other forms of counseling reveal themselves?

These questions are at the root of the clinical assessment process. They affect the counselor and client alike. For this reason, it is useful to have some sort of guideline or outline to follow as one collects information and then assimilates that information into a definition of the client's presenting problem, the context in which that problem exists, and the alternatives available to the client in problem resolution.

In most instances, clients seek a counselor (or are encouraged to seek one) to help resolve concerns or problems that are interfering with their daily functioning or causing discouragement or despair. Consequently, clients come to counseling with a sense of vulnerability, yet hoping that counseling will lead to improvement in their lives.

Most beginning counselors enter new therapeutic relationships with similar feelings of hope and vulnerability. For the counselor, the vulnerability comes from self-expectations to do something to ease or improve the client's situation. This need can lead to thinking that, unless the counselor is always doing something—usually for or to rather than with the client—counseling will not be successful. Given such pressures, beginning counselors often have difficulty with the discipline of the assessment process. They may have a tendency to move as quickly as possible toward a solution. Or the counselor may feel a strong need to establish a nurturing relationship to ease the client's distress, thus neglecting to identify parameters of the problem.

Such inclinations can lead to inadequate or even unethical behavior. Seligman (2004) observes, "The assessment process should be a way of recognizing the importance and uniqueness of each person, a way of saying to the person, 'You are special and I want to get to know you and understand why you are the way you are'" (p. 85). Without such knowledge, the counselor might miss important conditions or characteristics of the client's problem(s) and thus might actually enter into a counterproductive therapeutic process.

PURPOSES OF ASSESSMENT

Assessment has many functions within the counseling process. It provides a systematic approach to soliciting and organizing relevant client information. It also aids in the identification of significant life conditions that contribute to a client's presenting problems. Seligman (2004) identifies 12 ways that the assessment process may actually enhance the counselor-client relationship:

1. Streamline the information-gathering process
2. Enable counselors to make an accurate diagnosis
3. Facilitate development of a treatment plan that is likely to be effective
4. Determine a person's suitability for a particular program or treatment
5. Simplify goal-setting and measurement of progress
6. Promote insight into a person's personality and clarify self-concept
7. Assess environment or context
8. Promote more relevant and focused counseling and discussion
9. Indicate the likelihood that certain events will happen, such as success in occupational or academic endeavors

   10. Promote the translation of interests, abilities, and personality dimensions into occupational terms
   11. Generate options and alternatives
   12. Facilitate planning and decision-making (pp. 86–87)

Assessment is not to be confused with acceptance or counselor judging. Instead, it is a means by which the counselor seeks to understand the client's world, both in terms of how the client perceives that world and how the client is able to report the factual world. This involves a process of exploring the conditions the client is experiencing; other persons, contexts, and time sequences that are part of that experience; as well as efforts to change those conditions or events the client would like to change.

It is also important to note that assessment can be reactive; that is, the process of obtaining specific information about problems may also cause some change in the problem. For example, a male client who reports that he is self-conscious around women may find that some of his self-consciousness dissipates as he begins to explore his behavior with the counselor and to monitor it more closely outside the counseling sessions. Thus, assessment can also contribute to desired client changes or outcomes.

DIMENSIONS OF ASSESSMENT

Assessment refers to anything counselors do to gather information and draw conclusions about client concerns. Although most of the major components of assessment occur early in the counseling process, some degree of assessment goes on continuously during counseling because counselors are always seeking missing parts of the puzzle and attempting to place them where they fit.

In-Take or History Interviews

The first identifiable component of assessment is usually referred to as the in-take or history interview. During this session, counselors are interested primarily in obtaining information about the range or scope of the client's problems and about aspects of the client's background and present situation that may relate to these problems.

An assumption behind the in-take interview is that the client is coming to counseling for more than one interview and intends to address problems or concerns that involve other people, other settings, and the future as well as the present. Most counselors try to limit in-take interviews to one hour. To do this, the counselor must assume responsibility and control over the interview. No attempt is made to make it a therapeutic session for the client. The second session can begin to meet those needs. In other words, the in-take interview is like an appendage that precedes the process of establishing a relationship with the client.

Because the in-take session is different from a regular counseling session, it is helpful if the counselor gives the client an explanation about the purpose and nature of the initial session. You might say something like "José, before counseling begins, I would like to get some preliminary background information about you. So today, I will spend the hour getting to know you and asking you some questions about your school, your work, your family, and so on. Then, next week, we will start focusing and working on the specific concerns that brought you to counseling. Do you have any questions about this?" If the client is in crisis during this first interview, the in-take is not conducted and the counselor addresses issues related to the crisis instead.

When writing the in-take interview, a few cautions should be observed. First, avoid psychological jargon. It is not as understandable as you might think. Avoid elaborate inferences.

Remember, an inference is a guess, sometimes an educated guess. An inference can also be wrong. Try to prevent your own biases from entering the report. Remember, assessments must be justified, both psychologically and legally. It is important to know what your agency or school guidelines are regarding client assessment and to stay within those constraints while giving an accurate picture of the client's world.

The information gained through in-take interviews takes on added significance at the worst times. Far too many counselors have confronted a client crisis lacking the information they needed to address the situation. Because beginning counselors are torn between relationship building and information gathering, they can neglect that vital bit of information that would be needed should the client became suicidal, severely depressed, or dangerous to someone else. In those moments, critical information about the client's medications, support network, and previous similar crises are vital to making decisions in the client's best interests.

I. Identifying Data

A. Client's name, address, and telephone number at which the client can be reached. This information is important in the event you need to contact the client between sessions. The client's address also gives some hint about the conditions under which the client lives (large apartment complex, student dormitory, private home, inner-city project, etc.).

B. Age, sex, marital status, occupation (or school class and year). Again, this is information that can be important. It lets you know if the client is still legally a minor, and provides a basis for understanding information that will come out in later sessions.

II. Presenting Problems, Both Primary and Secondary

It is best that these problems are presented in exactly the way the client reports them. If a problem has behavioral components, they should be recorded, too. Questions that help reveal this type of information include:

A. How much does the problem interfere with the client's everyday functioning?

B. How does the problem manifest itself? What are the thoughts, feelings, and so on, that are associated with it? What observable behavior is associated with it?

C. How often does the problem arise and how long has the problem existed? When did it first appear?

D. Can the client identify a pattern of events that surround the problem? When does it occur? With whom? What happens before and following its occurrence? Can the client anticipate the onset of the problem?

E. What caused the client to decide to enter counseling at this time?

III. Client's Current Life Setting

What is the background or context for the client's daily functioning?

A. How does the client spend a typical day or week?

B. What social, religious, and recreational activities does the client undertake?

C. What is the nature of the client's vocational and/or educational situation?

D. What special characteristics about the client—cultural, ethnic, religious, lifestyle, age, and physical or other challenges—must the client address on an ongoing basis?

IV. Family History

A. Father's and mother's ages, occupations, descriptions of their personalities, family roles, relationships of each to the other and each to the client and other siblings.

B. Names and ages of brothers and sisters, their present life situations, relationships between client and siblings.

C. Is there any history of mental illness in the family?

D. Descriptions of family stability, including number of jobs held, number of family moves (and reasons), and so on. This information provides insights during later sessions when issues related to client stability and/or relationships emerge.

V.   Personal History

A. Medical history: Include any unusual or relevant illness or injury from the prenatal period to the present.

B. Educational history: Include academic progress through high school and any post–high school preparation. This includes extracurricular interests and relationships with peers.

C. Military service history.

D. Vocational history: Where has the client worked? At what types of jobs? For how long? What were the relationships with fellow workers?

E. Sexual and marital history: Where did the client receive sexual information? What was the client's dating history? Any engagements and/or marriages? Other serious emotional involvements prior to the present? Reasons that previous relationships terminated? What was the courtship like with her or his present spouse? What were the reasons (spouse's characteristics, personal thoughts) that led to marriage? Are there any children?

F. What experience has the client had with counseling, and what were the client's reactions?

G. Alcohol and drug use: Does the client currently use alcohol or drugs? Has the client used alcohol or drugs in the past? To what extent?

H. What are the client's personal goals in life?

VI.   Description of the Client During the Interview

Here you might want to indicate the client's physical appearance, including dress, posture, gestures, facial expressions, voice quality, tensions; how the client seemed to relate to you in the session; the client's readiness of response, motivation, warmth, distance, passivity, and so on. Did you observe any perceptual or sensory functions that intruded on the interaction? What was the general level of information, vocabulary, judgment, and abstraction abilities displayed by the client? What was the stream of thought and rate of talking? Were the client's remarks logical? Were they connected to one another?

VII.   Summary and Recommendations

In this section, you want to acknowledge any connections that appear to exist between the client's statement of a problem and other information collected in this session. What type of counselor do you think would best fit this client (assuming that you are responsible only for the in-take)? How realistic are the client's goals for counseling? How long do you think counseling might require?

Problem Definition

The second dimension of clinical assessment involves a more extensive definition of the problem. This may begin as part of the in-take interview but will continue into the next one to two sessions. Problem definition differs from in-take information because specific details regarding the nature and context of the presenting problem(s) are explored. These details may include not only the one(s) presented initially by the client (referred to as the presenting problem) but may also include any others that might have been mentioned during the in-take or during subsequent sessions.

Frequently, clients will identify a presenting problem as their reason for seeking help and then, during the subsequent sessions, reveal something else that is the real object of their concern. In these instances, the client has been "testing" the counselor or the counseling process to determine whether this is a safe or appropriate environment in which to explore such issues. For this reason—and also because a sound therapeutic relationship is an important prerequisite to the proper identification of goals—it is usually a good idea to have one or more counseling sessions with the client before attempting to define the problem too specifically. The following are areas to explore in reaching a useful understanding of the client's problem(s):

I. Components of Problem (ways in which the problem manifests itself primarily and secondarily)
   A. Feelings associated with the problem (major feeling or affect categories to assess include confusion, depression, fear, anger)
   B. Cognitions associated with the problem (including thoughts, beliefs, perceptions, internal dialogue, ruminations, and self-talk).
   C. Behaviors associated with the problem (specific actions observable not only by the client but also by others, including the counselor).
   D. Physical or somatic complaints associated with the problem.
   E. Interpersonal aspects of the problem (effects on significant others and on the client's relationships with others, including family, friends, relatives, colleagues, peers; also the effects that significant others may have on the client or his or her problem).

II. Pattern of Contributing Events (Can the client identify a pattern or sequence of events that seems to lead up to the problem and also maintains it?)
   A. When does the problem occur? Where? With whom?
   B. What is happening at the onset of the problem?
   C. What is happening just prior to occurrence of the problem?
   D. What typically happens just after its occurrence?
   E. What makes the problem better? What makes it disappear?
   F. What makes the problem worse?

III. Duration of Problem (extent to which the concern disturbs the client and/or interferes with the client's everyday functioning)
   A. How long has the problem existed?
   B. How often does the problem occur?
   C. How long does the problem last when it does occur?
   D. What led the client to seek counseling at this time regarding the problem?
   E. In what ways does the problem interfere with the client's daily functioning?

IV. Client Coping Skills, Strengths, Resources
   A. How has the client coped with the problem? What has worked? What has not worked?
   B. How has the client coped successfully with other problems?
   C. What resources, strengths, and support systems does the client have to help with change efforts?
   D. What is the client's cultural worldview? Sociopolitical histories of the groups the client identifies with? Language(s) spoken? Impact of gender? Neighborhood the client grew up in? Religion the client practices?

In addition to this kind of information collected from problem-definition interviews, counselors can also obtain additional assessment information about clients and their problems by using adjunctive data, such as psychological tests, self-ratings, and so on.

Finally, problem definition can be approached in numerous ways, as determined by one's theoretical orientation, the use of the American Psychiatric Association's *Diagnostic and Statistical Manual*, 4th edition (DSM-IV-TR) (American Psychiatric Association, 2007), and/or by contextual realities. This latter context is an attempt to recognize that not all human problems originate within the individual; rather, they can be imposed by the environment in ways that impel the client's reactions. For example, the Americans with Disabilities Act recognizes the environment as the source, thus the target for change, of problems that persons who have disabilities experience related to their physical disabilities. Similarly, many minorities experience degrees of discrimination that, if remedied, would have a major impact on the client's "problem." Young children also experience problems imposed by environmental or contextual conditions. In these cases, the environment may be the source, thus the target for intervention, as well as the client.

CLINICAL ASSESSMENT WITH CHILDREN

Children pose a unique assessment challenge to the counselor. On the one hand, children are less inhibited than adults in talking about their concerns to a trusted counselor. On the other hand, children, especially young children, lack the cognitive development to describe problems with causal or contextual clarity. As a consequence, you must phrase questions so that you draw out the kinds of information that will allow you to conceptualize the child's world. Children's problems tend to fall into three areas: (1) environmental factors affecting healthy growth and development, (2) self-concept issues, and (3) relationship issues.

The obvious first step in child assessment is the establishment of a relationship bond with the child. Such relationships require a special sensitivity to the child's world, which can work both for and against forming a bond. For example, children who live in a threatening environment will be much more reluctant to engage in new relationships with strangers. On the other hand, once children have begun to accept you as a "safe" person, they will be more open and genuine than adults tend to be.

Once you have established a safe and trusting relationship with a child, you can begin the in-take/problem-definition process. This will differ from the adult in-take interview described earlier. Depending on the child's emotional state, in-take information may be drawn from other significant sources (e.g., parents, teachers, siblings, peers) as well as the child. Thus, the first contact with the child may find you already involved in problem-definition questions that draw out the child's emotional state, environmental factors contributing to the child's problem, self-views, and significant relationships with others. The highly verbal child will be able to respond to open-ended questions about self, family, friends, and environment. However, the less verbal child may need structured questions (Who? What? Where? How? When?) in order to respond to the counselor. Some child counselors prefer to avoid these types of questions because they also restrict the child's response and thus the range of information that is gained.

Given the special nature of communicating with children, it is important that the counselor have a plan before entering into the assessment process. This plan must take into account the child's developmental language level and ability to respond to concrete or abstract concepts. Younger children will not understand questions that are framed abstractly. It is also important to the process that you ask questions in a way that provides specific rather than general responses. All of this must be done in a time span that fits the child's attention span.

When working with young children, it is important to seek information that the child is likely to have and be able to share, to ask in such a way that the child can understand the questions, and to have some sense of the child's level of introspection and social skill. Finally, with older children, it is important to recognize the pressures the child is experiencing from family members, siblings, or peers. Such pressures only make it more difficult for the child to respond cooperatively to the counselor.

Issues Related to Child Clinical Assessment

A number of concerns have been raised by state legislatures, social service agencies, and the helping profession regarding the welfare of children. Many of these concerns are revealed in the child counseling process, including child abuse, the effect of divorce on children, the single-parent home, and poverty. The counselor will be faced with a fundamental question when he or she works with the young child: What is normal? What is normal physical, emotional, social, or moral development? What is normal child behavior? What is normal parent behavior? How wide a range of alternatives does the concept of "normal" include?

Defining normal or, more particularly, defining abnormal child behavior is the general domain of the DSM-IV-TR. This source is used by all service providers who conform to guidelines for repayment for psychological/psychiatric services by health insurance companies. It addresses wide-ranging behaviors, such as fighting, verbal and physical abusiveness, cruelty to peers or animals, destructiveness, temper tantrums, lying, disobedience and resistance, stealing, hyperactivity, inattentiveness, and failure to learn. It also includes behavioral descriptions for what must be observable by the counselor in order to classify a child as needing professional assistance for a specific problem.

For the child who falls outside the range of normal, the counselor's role will include involvement with others: physicians, psychologists, psychiatrists, social workers, marriage and family therapists, the court system, or the state child welfare system. The counselor will often be the person to initiate these other services. When this happens, it is rarely the end of the counselor's role. The more likely outcome is that the counselor will remain involved, either as a primary or secondary service provider to the child and family. As a primary provider, the counselor will continue the counseling relationship with the child, using the other resources as consultant or adjunct services. When the counselor becomes the secondary provider, his or her role is likely to be that of coordinating the school's participation in the larger therapeutic plan.

CLINICAL ASSESSMENT WITH COUPLES AND FAMILIES

Most professional literature on marital and family therapy emphasizes a systemic approach to working with couples and families (see Chapter 11). This approach represents a qualitative shift in the conceptual framework toward data about interactions among individual members rather than characteristics of each individual member. In other words, the question changes from what is the individual thinking, doing, or feeling to what is going on between the persons and how the interaction is shaping or supporting a particular outcome. Thus, the approach is referred to as systemic because it is concerned with how the system (persons) is interacting or functioning.

Given this systematic perspective, the types of questions that characterize the in-take and problem-definition interview address verbal and nonverbal interaction patterns between members of the identified system (family, couple, peer group, etc.). While it is still important to obtain demographic information and medical information about the couple or family, the counselor needs to refocus quickly on factors reflecting effects rather than intentions: the effects that one person's behaviors have on the behaviors of others and the way interpersonal sequences are organized. Questions that reflect this orientation include:

"Whenever Antonio does this, how are you likely to respond, Maria?"

"When Maria reacts, what is the next thing you are likely to say, Antonio?"

Note that the counselor does not ask, "Why do you respond this way?" because that would suggest to the clients that intention is more relevant than what the couple attempted to do about the problem.

THE FAMILY GENOGRAM.   One of the better ways to identify family structure and interaction data is the genogram. This type of diagram uses symbols to represent family members, typically

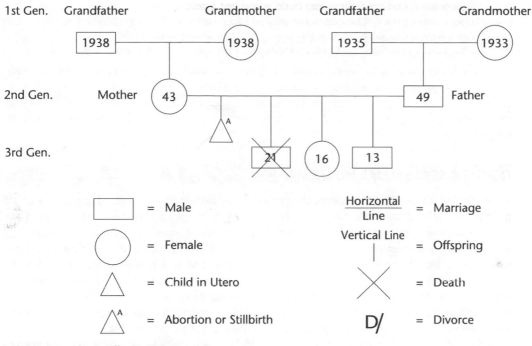

FIGURE 5.1 The Family Genogram

over three generations (see Figure 5.1). This exercise begins by explaining to family members how the genogram is drawn. Then the counselor begins to solicit information about various family members, beginning with the immediate family—for example, father and mother, each child, including those who might have died or were stillborn, and the birth dates of each. Children of the immediate family constitute the third (present) generation, whereas parents (mother and father) constitute the second generation. Added to this are the maternal and paternal grandparents (first generation) and any other family members who play active roles in the family's functioning.

Once the genogram has been drawn, it may be used to develop insights into family dynamics, including how family members perceive their relationships within the family, how they perceive their personal family role and the roles of other family members, how members are included or excluded verbally and nonverbally, who the protagonist is, who the peacemaker is, who hides, and so on. This discussion yields a family history as well as a pictorial format. Both may be used to help family members gain insight into the family's functioning, to repair relationships where a family member may have been cut off by other family members, and to make adjustments in organizational patterns. The genogram is probably most used by Bowen-oriented counselors, but it is a useful intervention exercise for all schools of family therapy.

Thomas (1998) describes a multicultural genogram that incorporates cultural origins as well as family history. It includes all of the traditional information found in the family genogram, but it adds "assessment of worldview and cultural factors that often influence behaviors of members [such as] differences in cultural values between family members" and spirituality/religion (pp. 25–26). Spirituality/ religion is assessed in the genogram through the following six questions:

1. What is the spiritual or religious history of the family?
2. What characteristics, values, and beliefs are influenced by spirituality or religion?

3. What is the relationship between spirituality and worldview?
4. If members differ in religious or spiritual beliefs, what are the similarities in values?
5. What are the differences in values and beliefs according to spirituality?
6. How are conflicts due to different religious values resolved? (Thomas, 1998, p. 30)

The importance of assessing cultural factors in families can be overlooked or under-appreciated. Kurilla (1998) emphasizes the importance of family cultural assessment for identifying factors such as strengths and natural resources that the family draws on through its cultural identity, and how sociocultural factors (e.g., poverty, racism, and sexism) affect these families.

USING ASSESSMENT INFORMATION

Counselors develop different approaches to using the information collected from in-take and problem-definition sessions. Some counselors look primarily for patterns of behavior. For example, one counselor noted that his client had a pattern of incompletions in life, including a general discharge from the Army prior to completing his enlistment, dropping out of college twice, and a long history of broken relationships. This observation provides food for thought. Are these events revealing a pattern of functioning? What happens to this person as he becomes involved in a commitment? What has this client come to think of himself as a result of his history? How does he anticipate future commitments? Another counselor uses the assessment information to look for signals that suggest how she might enter the counseling relationship. Is there anything current in the client's life that common sense would suggest is a potential area for counseling attention (e.g., Is the client in the midst of a divorce? Is the client at a critical developmental stage?).

The information that counselors collect during assessment is also invaluable in planning relevant counseling strategies and approaches to use with problems. For example, a client who reports depression describes the problem primarily in cognitive terms: "I'm a failure; I'm not good at anything. I can't stand it when people don't approve of me. When something goes wrong, it is all my fault." Has this client internalized a self-defeating set of beliefs and self-perceptions that are erroneous and not likely to be based on data or facts? The counselor would probably decide to use an approach or strategy with this client that deals directly with cognitions, beliefs, and internal dialogue.

In contrast, suppose another client is depressed because of a perceived inability to make friends, to form new relationships, and to maintain existing ones. In this instance, the counselor might look at the client's behavior in interpersonal relationships and use behavioral strategies that emphasize acquisition of social skills and interpersonal or systemic strategies that deal with relationships between people.

Counselors who fail to conduct assessment interviews are more likely to formulate erroneous conclusions about client problems and irrelevant or nonworkable counseling approaches and strategies. As a result, not only is more time spent on hit-or-miss counseling, but ultimately clients might leave with the same set of problems they brought to the first session.

To help you tie together the information revealed from assessment of a client with corresponding counseling strategies, we have organized the strategy chapters (Chapters 8 through 11) around the four components of a problem (feelings, behavior, cognitions, relationships). For example, strategies that deal primarily with feelings or have an affective focus are presented in Chapter 8. Cognitive-based strategies are described in Chapter 9, and Chapter 10 presents behavioral strategies. Strategies with an interpersonal or systemic focus are discussed in Chapter 11.

SKILLS ASSOCIATED WITH ASSESSMENT

Assessment is an intentional process. Each question, each intervention, each clarification, each line of discussion by the counselor has a purpose. The process of assessing client concerns is both current and contextual. Details surrounding the client's presenting issues are important to understand, but equally important are background details that shape how clients understand and define their world (Seligman, 2009).

In assessing client concerns, the counselor relies on all of the rapport and relationship skills described in Chapter 4 and data-gathering skills. Some of the skills most frequently used during in-take and problem-defining interviews include verbal and nonverbal attending, paraphrasing content, and using a variety of questions to facilitate the assessment process. Of these skills, questioning becomes the intentional instrument for introducing, leading, facilitating, and inferring what the client brings to the counseling event. Each of these types of questioning skills will be examined in greater detail to define how they differ and how they produce different types of information.

Assessment-Related Skills

Clarifying questions

Questions that ask the client for greater detail (e.g., Can you tell me more about how that happens?)

- "Could you try to describe that feeling in another way? I'm not sure I am following what you mean."
- "When you say 'fuzzy,' what's that feeling like?"
- "I think I got lost in that. Could you go through the sequence of events again for me?"
- "Is there another way you could describe that feeling?"

Open-ended questions

Questions that require more than a minimal response from the client, usually seeking for more detail (e.g., How?)

- "What is there in all of this that you have not seen?"
- "How do you react when she [he] says that sort of thing to you?"
- "What is keeping you from asking him [her]?"
- "What is the piece that would unlock the puzzle?"

Closed questions

Questions that ask for specific data (e.g., When? Where? Who? and so on)

- "How old were you when your parents died?"

- "Are you an only child, or do you have brothers and sisters?"
- "Are you taking any medications now?"
- "Have you ever received counseling or therapy?"

Linking statements

Statements that ask the client to make connections, explain relationships, and so on

- "So when you withdraw, he is more likely to overreact, right?"
- "You said earlier that your husband is 'high maintenance.' Is this an example of high maintenance?"
- "It sounds like she overreacts with anger whenever someone challenges her. Is that right?"

Confirmatory statements

Statements that seek to verify what the client has described to ensure accuracy of understanding

- "Let me be sure I understand. You say that...."
- "I assume you were serious when you described the relationship between your siblings as hostile?"
- "Let me be sure I'm on the right page with you. You definitely want to try to change some of the dynamics around the office, right?"

Clarifying Questions

Sometimes a client's responses sound cryptic or confused and the counselor is left wondering just what the client is trying to say. It is important to seek clarification in these moments rather than guess or assume that the communication is unimportant. The clarifying question asks the client to rephrase the communication and can be stated in several ways.

Clarifying questions are self-explanatory. The important point is that they can be over- or underused. When overused, they become distractors. Sometimes the counselor is reluctant to seek clarification lest it impede or distract the client from the topic. If you are simply unable to follow the client's train of thought, it is more important to seek clarification than it is to allow the client to proceed. Otherwise, you run the risk of drawing inaccurate conclusions.

Open-Ended Questions

Open-ended questions require more than a minimal one-word answer by the client. They are introduced with the words *what, where, when, who,* or *how. What* questions solicit facts and information; how questions are used to inquire about emotions or sequences of events; *where* and *when* elicit information about time and context; *who* yields information about people. It is important to vary the words used to start open-ended questions depending on the type of material you want to focus on and solicit from the client. The minimal reflection is a softer way of asking an open-ended question. It is a one- or two-word restatement of what the client just said:

> CLIENT: "I'm beginning to think I am burned out"
>
> COUNSELOR: "Burned out?"

A good open-ended question offers new energy to clients and helps to open them up in a different way. Three specific instances when open-ended questions are particularly useful during counseling sessions include:

1. *Beginning an interview*
   "What would you like to talk about?"
   "What brings you to counseling?"
   "How have things been this week?"
   "Where do you want to begin today?"

2. *Encouraging client elaboration*
   "What happens when you lose control?"
   "Who else is invested in this problem?"
   "When do you notice that reaction?"
   "How could things be better for you?"

3. *Eliciting specific examples*
   "What do you do when this happens?"
   "Exactly how do you feel about it?"
   "Where are you when you feel depressed?"

Closed Questions

As noted in Chapter 2, a closed question narrows the area or focus of discussion. Thus, when you need a specific piece of information (e.g., "Are you taking any medications now?"), it is best obtained by a closed or targeted question. Closed questions may be answered with yes or no or a specific piece of data. The closed question can also work against the counselor because it is the easiest to ask, and yet, it provides the most limited amount of discourse. For this reason, the closed question should be avoided except when specifics are needed.

The Linking Statement

Part of the counselor's task is to understand contexts or background factors that are operating in the client's life. Such contexts often play a significant role in how the client reacts or how the client interprets events. These connections can be subtle or even unrecognized. Consequently, an important aspect of counseling is to identify and examine the connectors that are operating in the client's life. Connections can be routinized or habitualized and thereby gain a power of their own in the client's life. Only by recognizing and consciously challenging these routinized connections can the client regain control over them. Not to be confused with interpretations, linking statements are exploratory and even hypothetical in nature. Their purpose is to invite the client to take an event, thought, feeling, or circumstance and look for connections between it and other events, thoughts, feelings, or circumstances.

Confirmatory Statements

Confirmatory statements are an important tool in the counselor's repertoire of responses. They establish the accuracy of understanding a particular piece of information. They also confirm to the client that the counselor is actively following the client's narrative. In addition, confirmatory statements often communicate a level of empathic understanding to the client. From the counselor's perspective, such statements may also lead the client into further or deeper exploration of a topic, feeling, or condition. When this happens, the client is open to greater self-examination and self-understanding. From an assessment perspective, confirmatory statements not only confirm what the client is saying, they may also confirm the counselor's hypotheses or speculations about the client's world.

EFFECTS OF ASSESSMENT ON CLIENTS

The assessment stage of counseling is likely to have a number of possible effects on clients. Although each client's reaction to an in-take or problem-definition interview is unique, it is also possible to describe some fairly predictable client patterns of reaction. Some of these patterns are positive; some are negative. On the positive side, assessing client concerns helps clients to experience various feelings, which they reveal in responses such as:

> *Understanding:* "I believe someone finally understands how terrible these last few months have been for me."
>
> *Relief:* "Well, it does feel good to get that off my chest."
>
> *Hopefulness:* "Now maybe something can be done to help me feel better or get a handle on things."
>
> *Motivation:* "Now that I have someone to talk to, I have some energy to do something about this."

On the negative side, assessment can result in client reactions and feelings such as the following:

> *Anxiety:* "Am I really that bad off? I guess so. This is a lot to deal with all at once."

Defensiveness: "Boy, do I feel on the spot. There are so many questions being thrown at me. Some of them are so personal, too."

Vulnerability: "How do I know if I can trust him with this? Can he handle it and not share it with anyone else?"

Evaluated: "I wonder if she thinks I'm really messed up? Crazy? Stupid? Maybe something really is wrong with me?"

Given these possible reactions, it is important to assess client concerns carefully and with much sensitivity. The ideal outcome is when the client's positive reactions to assessment outweigh the negative reactions. When this occurs, assessment has become a useful and productive part of counseling without jeopardizing the rapport and relationship the counselor and client have worked so hard to establish prior to this time. Client reactions to assessment are likely to be more positive when the counselor uses questions that are directly relevant to the client's concerns and are also used in proportion to other skills and responses.

Nothing can make a client feel defensive and interrogated more quickly than asking too many questions. Sometimes the same information can be gleaned by nonverbal attending behaviors, verbal following, or statements that paraphrase content or reflect affect. Inexperienced counselors seem to have a natural tendency to use questions more frequently than any other response, and they must be especially careful during assessment not to let this skill take over while their other newly learned skills go by the wayside.

CASE ILLUSTRATION OF THE IN-TAKE INTERVIEW

The Case of Angela

Angela is a middle-age female who works full-time as a teacher. She reports that she is divorced and has not remarried, although she maintains custody of two teenage children. Angela states that the reason she is seeking counseling at this time is to learn to have better control of her moods. She indicates that she often "flies off the handle" for no reason with her own children or with her students in the classroom. She also reports that she cries easily and "feels blue" much of the time.

The In-Take Interview

The in-take/history interview with Angela revealed the following information:

I. Identifying Data

Angela is 40 years old. She lives with her two children (ages 9 and 15) in a mobile home outside a small town. She has been divorced for 6 years. She teaches English to high school juniors.

II. Range of Problems

In addition to the problems first presented (feeling out of control and blue), Angela also feels that she is a failure as a wife and mother, primarily because of her divorce and her mood swings. Her self-description is predominantly negative.

III. Current Life Setting

Angela's typical day consists of getting up, going to work, coming home, doing something with her children, and then grading papers or watching TV. On weekends, she stays at home a great deal. She has few neighbors, only one or two close friends, and does not participate in any recreational, religious, or social activities on a regular basis. She reports a great deal of difficulty in carrying out her regular routine on days when she feels down. Occasionally, she calls in sick and stays home and sleeps all day.

IV. Family History

Angela is the youngest of three children. She was raised Roman Catholic in a second-generation, Italian American family. She describes her relationship to her two older brothers and to her mother as very close. She is not as close to her father although she reports that he was always very good to her. The family remains close and gathers whenever there is an occasion, a birthday, or a celebration. Angela also reports that, as the youngest child and the only girl, she was protected and pampered a great deal by her parents and her brothers while growing up. Currently, she lives a day's drive away from both her parents and her brothers and looks forward to seeing them on family occasions. To her knowledge, none of her immediate family members has had any significant mental health problems although she thinks that one of her aunts is chronically depressed.

V. Personal History

A. Medical: Angela reports that in the last year she has undergone major surgery twice—once for the removal of a benign lump in her breast and once for the repair of a disc. She also indicates that she has been diagnosed as having Addison's disease and is on medication for it, but she frequently forgets to take the medication as prescribed. The medication is prescribed by a general practitioner.

Angela reports some sleeping problems, primarily when she is distressed. At these times, she has difficulty falling asleep until 2:00 or 3:00 a.m. Her weight fluctuates by 5 or 6 pounds during a given month. When she is upset, she often eats little or nothing for a day or two.

B. Educational: Angela has a bachelor's degree in English and a master's degree in education. She appears to be of above-average intelligence and describes herself as a conscientious student to the point of worrying excessively about grades and performance. She occasionally takes graduate courses to renew her teacher certification.

C. Military: Angela has never served in the military.

D. Vocational: Angela has been a high school English teacher ever since graduating from college although she reports that she "dropped out" of her teaching after her first child was born 15 years ago. She resumed teaching again when she was divorced 6 years ago. Her children were then 3 and 9 years old. She describes her present job as marginally adequate although not very challenging and not very financially rewarding. She stays with it primarily because of job security and because of the hours (summers off). She reports satisfactory relationships with other teachers although she has no good friends at work.

E. Sexual and marital: Angela's first sexual experiences were with her former husband, although she reports she received a good bit of sex education from her parents and her older brothers. She asserts that this is a difficult subject for her to discuss. She states that although she felt her sexual relationship with her husband was adequate, he became sexually involved with another woman prior to their divorce. Angela indicates that before her marriage, she had only two other love relationships with men, both of which were terminated mutually because of differences in values. She describes her marital relationship as good until the time she discovered through a friend about her husband's affair. She has very little contact with her ex-husband although her two children see him every other weekend. She reports that the children have a good relationship with their father and that he has been helpful to her by taking the children for periods of time when she is feeling depressed and overwhelmed by her life situation. Angela repeatedly indicates that she blames herself for the failure of the marriage.

F. Counseling: Angela reports that she saw a counselor for depression during her divorce (about 12 sessions). She terminated the counseling sessions because she thought she had things under control. Now she is concerned about her ability to manage her feelings and wants help to learn how to deal better with her moods, especially with feeling upset, irritable, and blue.

VI. **Counselor's Observations of Angela**
During the in-take interview, you observe that Angela generally seems to have little energy and is rather passive, as evidenced by her slouched body position, soft voice tone, and lack of animation in facial expressions and body movements. Angela appears to be in control of her feelings although she cried much of the time while describing her marital and sexual history.

Integration of Material from In-Take

Following an initial interview, it is important to tie together the information obtained from the client in some meaningful fashion. In Angela's case, you know that she is a 40-year-old female who although she has been divorced for 6 years, has not ever really resolved the divorce issue in her mind. Her concern with mood fluctuations and feeling so blue appears to be substantiated not only by her nonverbal demeanor, but also by her verbal reports of symptoms and behaviors typically associated with mild depression:

- She perceives herself as a failure, particularly in her role as a wife and mother.
- She blames herself for the divorce.
- She describes herself negatively.
- She experiences a reduced level of energy and rate of activity when distressed.
- She has very few close relationships with others.
- She experiences some sleeping difficulties and loss of appetite when distressed.
- She does not appear to have any concrete goals or plans for the future apart from her role as mother.

This picture is complicated by Angela's health. She has undergone two operations in the last year and suffers from a fairly complex endocrinological problem that because of her lack of compliance in taking prescribed medication, probably makes her mood fluctuations and depression more intense and more frequent.

Angela's family is a strength. She is on good terms with her family and enjoys the occasions when they get together. Knowing that strong family ties are characteristic of the Italian American family, this is likely to be a source of significant support. On the other hand, the distance between her home and that of her family poses a problem.

Continuing beyond the in-take interview, it is important for the counselor to continue developing an understanding of the presenting problem. This involves assessment of the components of the problem, intensity, and possible controlling variables associated with Angela's feelings of dysphoria. Some of the information she gave during the in-take session will serve as suggestions on which to build during the process of problem definition.

Problem-Definition Analysis

COMPONENTS OF THE PROBLEM

Feelings. Angela describes her predominant feelings as irritable, upset, and "down" or "blue." Primary somatic reactions during times of stress include loss of appetite and insomnia.

Cognitions. When you ask Angela to describe specific things she thinks about or focuses on during the times she feels depressed, she responds with statements such as "I just think about what a failure I am," "I wish I were a better wife (or mother)," and "I should have been able to keep my marriage together and because I didn't, I'm a failure." Her cognitions represent two areas or trouble spots often associated with feelings of depression—shouldism and perfectionism. She does not report any thoughts or ideas about suicide.

Behaviors. Angela has some trouble specifying things she does or does not do while depressed. She finally says that she often withdraws and retreats to her room or that she becomes irritable, usually to her students or children. She also cries easily at these times.

Interpersonal Relationships. Angela notes that once she feels down, no one around her can pull her out of it. But she also says that she does not have close friends to share her feelings or problems with. She believes her depressed feelings interfere with her relationship with her children because they tend to avoid her when she gets into a period of depression. However, she also acknowledges that she can use her feelings to get her children to do things "her way."

PATTERN OF CONTRIBUTING EVENTS. When Angela describes what seems to lead up to these feelings, she notes the following:

- Seems to be the worst a week before her menstrual period
- Failure to take her medication
- Being reminded or reminding herself about her divorce
- Hassles with her children and/or ex-husband

In describing what seems to stop the feelings or make them better or worse, she observes:

- Having her period end
- Taking her medication
- Doing something with her children
- Having to go to work
- Having telephone or other contact initiated by her brothers or parents

INTENSITY OF THE PROBLEM. With depression, it is important to assess whether it is a long-term, chronic condition or a short-term response to a situation or event. Angela reports that she has felt more depressed for the last 6 years since the divorce. However, she acknowledges that as a child and even during her marriage, she was frequently able to use tears to get her way. Thus, her crying at least had value for her in the past, and even currently she can use it to manipulate her children. She states that, on average, she gets quite depressed for one week out of every month. She rates the intensity of her feelings at about 8 on a 1 (low) to 10 (high) scale. When she feels down, she usually does so for several days. This is the time when she is most apt to call in sick or to become irritable with her students and her children.

CLIENT COPING SKILLS, STRENGTHS, RESOURCES.   Angela is not readily aware of anything she does to cope effectively with her depressed feelings. She seems to believe that the onset and termination of these feelings are mostly out of her control. She does describe herself as a good student and a good teacher. Her strengths are her reliability and dependability. She does indicate that she has a lot of perseverance and tenacity when she decides she wants something to work out. Angela's family of origin is a resource to be explored.

CRISIS ASSESSMENT

Crisis has become a very common condition in our world. For the individual, crisis is much like a life-threatening medical diagnosis, a divorce, a death, or a job loss. Under such stresses, clients can experience the event as an intolerable difficulty that exceeds their current resources (James & Gilliland, 2005). When clients come to counseling in crisis, there is an urgency that presents unique challenges.

Crisis assessment requires that the counselor do three tasks: (1) seek to understand the nature of the client's crisis event, (2) determine the needs and strengths of the individual in crisis, and (3) determine the strengths and deficits of the client's recovery environment (Collins & Collins, 2005, p. 10). Making this assessment involves most of the stages described in Chapter 3. If the client is in crisis, however, relationship building is less of a priority than stabilizing the client. More important is assessing whether the client is in emotional or physical jeopardy. In addition, issues such as goal setting, assessment, and intervention planning take on a much shorter-term focus. Crises can include personal loss, physical or sexual abuse, emotional instability, natural disaster, or any combination of these.

Consider Angela's case. Is she in crisis? More specifically, is she in danger of self-harm or emotional collapse? What is the intensity of her presenting problem(s)? What coping skills, strengths, and resources can she potentially mobilize?

INTEGRATION OF PROBLEM-DEFINITION INFORMATION WITH TREATMENT PLANNING

The information obtained from this problem-definition session and initial session is of direct value in selecting and planning relevant counseling strategies to help Angela. In Angela's case, the depression seems partially maintained by two potential physiological sources—Addison's disease and premenstrual syndrome (PMS). Therefore, part of your planning would involve having her health assessed and monitored by a physician. It is evident that the cognitive and interpersonal spheres are major components and contributing causes of these feelings. Thus, it would be important to select counseling strategies that focus on the cognitive and interpersonal modalities. Strategies such as cognitive restructuring, reframing, irrational thought analysis, systemic analysis, social skills training, and family counseling are all useful possibilities. (These strategies are described in Chapters 9 and 11.) It is also possible that some of Angela's difficulties stem from dissonance she feels with the cultural values of her childhood and family.

Summary

Assessment is invaluable for seeking pertinent information about clients and their presenting problems. In addition to the value of information garnered, assessment can also be reactive; that is, it can initiate the process of change for clients. Assessment is usually started by in-take sessions that gather information about the client's background and history. Assessment is very important in the early stages of counseling to help counselors formulate hypotheses, but it is also an ongoing process during counseling because presenting problems and accompanying conceptualizations of issues often change. Specific assessment interviews obtain information about components of the problem, pattern of contributing events, intensity of the problem, and client coping skills. Skills used to obtain such information frequently include paraphrasing content, reflecting affect, summarizing, and asking a variety of questions.

Exercises

I. In-Take and History Interviews

A. Identify a current or existing problem in the life of a member of your family. It might be a family or relationship conflict, a love or sex issue, a financial problem, or a work- or school-related concern. Select someone with whom you feel comfortable discussing this problem. Your task is to discuss how your relative's background and history have affected the development and maintenance of this concern. You may want to refer to the in-take and history outline in this chapter to guide your discussion.

B. Using triads, identify one person as the client, another as the counselor, and one as an observer. The assigned tasks are as follows:

Client. Describe a present or ongoing concern or issue in your life.

Counselor. Conduct an in-take or history session with this client following the outline given in the chapter. If possible, record the session.

Observer. Be prepared to give feedback to the counselor following the role-play and/or to intervene and cue the counselor during the role-play if he or she has difficulty and gets stuck. Rotate the initial roles two more times so that each person has an opportunity to be in each role once. Time requirement: 1 hour.

II. Problem Definition

A. Using the same problem you identified for Exercise I.A, identify:

1. Various components of the problem
2. Contributing conditions
3. Intensity of the problem
4. Client's resources, strengths, and coping skills

You may wish to do this alone or in conjunction with a partner, colleague, instructor, or supervisor. It may be helpful to refer to the outline in this chapter to jot down some key words as you go through this process.

B. Read Chapter 16, "Italian Families" (Joe Giordano, Monica McGoldrick, and Joanne Giordano Klages. (2008). In M. McGoldrick, J. Giordano, and Nydia Garcia-Preto [Eds.], *Ethnicity and Family Therapy*, 3rd ed. [pp. 616–628]. New York: Guilford). Then do an analysis of Angela's in-take interview within the context of her family of origin. What insights about Angela may be gained through an understanding of her cultural background? How might her background and her family be utilized as part of her counseling?

III. Questions

A. In this activity, identify whether each of the questions listed is a clarifying, open-ended, or closed question. Use the key below to record your answers in the blanks provided. Feedback follows the exercises.

C = Clarifying
O-E = Open-ended
Cl = Closed

_____ 1. "What is it like for you when you get depressed?"
_____ 2. "Have you had a physical exam in the last two years?"
_____ 3. "Are you saying you don't give up easily?"
_____ 4. "How does this job affect your moods?"
_____ 5. "Do you mean to say that you have difficulty letting go?"
_____ 6. "Do you have many children?"

B. In this activity, you are given five client statements. Practice formulating a question for each client statement. Share your questions in your class or with your instructor or a colleague.

1. *Client (a teenager):* "I've got to graduate with my class. If I don't, everyone will think I'm a real screw-up."

2. *Client (an elderly man):* "It's just so hard to make a living on a fixed income like I do. If I had it to do over, I'd do it a lot different."

3. *Client (a young girl):* "I hate my dad. He's always picking on me."

4. *Clients (a couple married for 4 years):* "It's just not turning out the way we thought. We

wanted our marriage to really work. But it's not."

5. *Client (a middle-age person):* "There are just so many pressures on me right now from all sides—family, work, friends, you name it."

Feedback for Exercises

III. Questions

1. O-E
2. Cl
3. C
4. O-E
5. C
6. Cl

Discussion Questions

1. In-take interviews and the problem-definition process are time-consuming and may seem to delay the counseling process. Assume you are the clinical director for a private mental health agency. How would you justify the use of these assessment interviews to the administrative director or to the agency's board of directors?

2. Suppose you are seeing a client who presents a crisis situation (e.g., recent rape, decision over abortion, spouse/child abuse). You probably will not have the luxury of devoting a session or more to conduct a complete in-take/problem-definition process. What information about the problem and about the client's background and history would be most important to obtain

in a 15-minute time period? Discuss with other class members.

3. Assessment with young children (ages 6 to 10) calls for a different type of interaction. How would you modify your approach for this age group? What kinds of information would you solicit? What do you know about yourself that would either facilitate the assessment process or provide obstacles to your success with this age group?

4. How do you think the assessment process may be viewed differently by women and by men? Can you also think of instances in which the impact of assessment may vary with the cultural/ethnic background of the client?

MyCounselingLab Assignment

Go to the Video Resource Library on the MyCounselingLab site for your text and search for the following clips:

- **Gina: Individual Diagnostic Assessment**   How does the counselor gain the client's assistance in the assessment? What did you learn in this video clip that you would use in your counseling?

- **Child: Tracking Questions**   What is the counselor doing to obtain information from this child? What do you think the counselor is hoping to learn about

the child? Wht are the unique challenges in child assessment?

- **Collaborative Interviewing: Exploring Beliefs About the Problem**   What kinds of counseling responses does the counselor use as he explores the client's views of the problem? What do you think the counselor was looking for in this interview segment? What is your reaction to the client's perception of his problem?

Developing Counseling Goals

PURPOSE OF THIS CHAPTER

When the counselor and client first meet, there are two stories to be told. The client's story is whatever he or she is bringing to counseling: a troubled relationship, a failing career, a personal crisis, a sense of impossibility. The counselor's story is about what happens in counseling, what success or failure in life is all about, who is responsible for client change and improvement, what the counselor is actually *doing* as the client engages and explores, the role of counseling in the bigger picture of life itself, and, of course, achieving a desirable outcome. This chapter examines the process by which the counselor and client can work collaboratively to define what that desirable outcome might or will be. We first engaged the issue of the client's worldview and how that directs the counselor's effort in Chapter 4. Now, in choosing the goals of counseling, those values, beliefs, and practices that compose the client's worldview really come into play. This chapter identifies some of those factors.

Considerations as You Read This Chapter

■ There is a great divide between needs and wants. In the context of counseling, how can we differentiate between our needs and our wants?

■ Who is best able to judge what are wise wants or goals? The counselor? The client?

■ How does one make these decisions?

■ What is the impact of one's choice of goals on the counseling process?

Often, counselors (or sometimes clients) will complain, "The session didn't go anywhere" or "I felt like we were talking in circles." As part of the assessment process, it is important to translate general client concerns into specific desired goals. Goals give direction to the therapeutic process and help both the counselor and the client to move in a focused direction with a specific route in mind. They represent the results or outcomes the client wants to achieve at the end of counseling. Without goals, it is all too easy to get sidetracked or lost. Goals help both the counselor and client to specify exactly what can and cannot be accomplished through counseling. In this respect, goal setting is an important extension of the assessment process in counseling. Recall that during assessment, clients focus on specific concerns and issues that are difficult, problematic, or not going very well for them. In goal setting, clients identify, with the counselor's help, specific ways in which they want to resolve these issues and specific courses of action they can take for problem resolution.

FUNCTIONS OF COUNSELING GOALS

Goals serve four important functions in the counseling process. First, goals can have a motivational effect. When clients are encouraged to specify desirable changes in their lives, they are more likely to work toward accomplishing those outcomes. This is particularly true when clients actively participate in the goal-setting process.

Goals also have an educational function in counseling. Over and over again, helpers realize that clients have not been successful in managing their lives because they do not know how to set positive, achievable goals. Such goals can help clients acquire new life responses. By going through a goal-setting process, clients learn not only how to structure their lives but also what changes in behavior or thinking may be involved in the new vista. Dixon and Glover (1984) explain the benefits in this way:

> Once a goal is formulated and selected by a problem solver, it is likely to be rehearsed in the working memory and stored in long-term memory. A goal encoded in this way, then, becomes a major heuristic for the problem solver as he or she interacts with the environment. (pp. 128–129)

This is quite evident in the performance of highly successful performers and athletes who set goals for themselves and then use the goals to rehearse their performance over and over again in their heads. Concert pianists, for example, cognitively rehearse the way they want a particular passage to sound; champion divers visualize themselves performing a particular dive in a desired fashion both before the competition and on the platform.

Goals provide an evaluative function in counseling. The type of outcomes or change represented by the client's goals helps the counselor to select and evaluate various counseling interventions that are likely to be successful for a particular client pursuing a specific goal or set of outcomes. Goals also contribute to the evaluative function in counseling because a goal represents a desired outcome, a point at which counseling would be deemed successful. Thus, when outcome goals are established, both the counselor and the client can evaluate client progress toward the goals in order to determine when they are being attained and when the goals or the counseling intervention may need revision. But goals need to be defined so that clients can measure their progress. This means that goals must be observable and measurable rather than global and nonmeasurable. When goals are observable and measurable, clients can recognize when efforts are succeeding or when efforts need to be revised because they are not succeeding.

Finally, goals serve a treatment assessment function in counseling. As the impact of managed care on counseling practice continues to grow, peer review of the effectiveness of treatment becomes increasingly important. In this context, goal setting by the counselor becomes part of the formal treatment plan. (See Chapter 7 for a more extensive discussion of treatment plans.) Typically, these goals are derived from the goals that have been identified in the counselor-client discussion. Others will be developed by the counselor after reviewing and interpreting data from the assessment phase of counseling.

PARAMETERS OF GOAL SETTING: PROCESS AND OUTCOME GOALS

The counseling process involves two types of goals: process goals and outcome goals. Process goals are related to the establishment of therapeutic conditions necessary for client change. These are general goals, such as establishing rapport, providing a nonthreatening setting, and possessing and communicating accurate empathy and positive regard. They can be generalized to all client relationships and can be considered universal goals. Process goals are the counselor's primary responsibility; you cannot expect your clients to share the responsibility for these goals. Most of what was discussed in Chapters 4 and 5 are process goals.

Unlike process goals, outcome goals are different for each client. They are the goals directly related to the life changes your clients hope to accomplish through counseling. As you help each client understand his or her concerns, you will want to help each client understand how counseling can be useful in responding to those concerns. The two of you will begin to formulate tentative outcome goals together. As counseling continues, the original goals may be modified through better understanding of the problems and through the development of new attitudes and behaviors that will eliminate or reduce problems. Goal setting should be viewed as a flexible process, always subject to modification and refinement. Most important, outcome goals are shared goals—goals that both you and your client agree to work toward achieving.

Outcome goals that are visible or observable are more useful because it is easier to determine when they have been achieved. But not all outcome goals are stated as visible goals. For example, consider these two outcome goals:

1. To help your client develop his or her self-esteem
2. To increase the number of positive self-statements at home and at work by 50% over the next six weeks

Both of these could be considered outcome goals. They might even be so closely related as to be the same goal in terms of outcomes. (That is, the person who is saying more positive things about him- or herself may be well on the way to developing positive self-esteem.) Your client may be more attracted to less explicit goals (e.g., better self-esteem) because most people are inexperienced in making specific, measurable goals.

You may want to view the development of self-esteem as a composite of many smaller and more specific changes. To state it a little differently, self-esteem is a quality that is reflected in many behaviors. It is inferred through those observed behaviors. Using enhanced self-esteem as your goal, you have no way of knowing the types of activity that your client will enter into while proceeding toward the goal. As a result, you and your client may spend a lot of time talking about self-esteem and how much he or she has or doesn't have, but things that can be done to enhance self-esteem are not addressed. Consequently, the first goal (number 1 in the list above) does not provide as much information about how counseling should proceed as does the second goal.

When outcome goals are stated precisely, both you and your client have a better understanding of what is to be accomplished. This better understanding permits you to target your client's problems or concerns more directly and reduces tangential efforts. Equally important are the benefits you are able to realize in working toward specific behavioral goals. You are able to enlist the client's cooperation more directly because your client is more likely to understand what is to be done. In addition, you are in a better position to select appropriate interventions and strategies when your client has specific objectives. Finally, both you and your client is in a better position to recognize progress when it happens—a rewarding experience in its own right.

THREE ELEMENTS OF GOOD OUTCOME GOALS

Perhaps you have noticed from our previous examples that outcome goals are different from process goals in several respects. A well-stated outcome goal includes the behavior to be changed, the conditions under which the changed behavior will occur, and the level or amount of change. One client may want to modify eating patterns; another may wish to reduce negative self-appraisals; a third may wish to increase assertive requests or refusals.

The second element of an outcome goal indicates the conditions under which the desired behavior(s)—clients might say desired outcomes—will occur. It is important to weigh carefully the situations or settings in which a client will attempt a new behavior. You wouldn't want to set your client up to fail by identifying settings in which there is little hope for success. The client might agree to modify eating habits at home during the evening but not to attempt to modify those eating habits at the company picnic on Saturday.

The third element of outcome goals involves the choice of a suitable and realistic level or amount of change. That is, how much of the new behavior will a client attempt? Some clients begin diets with the expectation that they will reduce their consumption from 3,000 calories per day to 900 calories per day. A more realistic and attainable goal might be 1,800 to 2,000 calories. This brings up another thought about goals. As you modify goals, you come closer to the ultimate goals of the client. Each time you set a goal, it is a closer approximation of the client's ultimate objective. Successive approximations are very important. They allow a client to set more attainable goals, experience success more frequently, and make what might be dramatic changes in his or her lifestyle.

OBSTACLES IN DEVELOPING SPECIFIC GOALS

As noted earlier, most clients are unaccustomed to thinking in terms of specific, concrete goals. Instead of saying, "I want to be able to talk to teachers without getting nervous," the client is likely to say, "I am shy." In other words, a personal characteristic has been described rather than the ways in which the characteristic is expressed. It then becomes the counselor's job to help the client describe the ways in which the characteristic is expressed and, consequently, could be expressed differently. Taking nonspecific concerns and translating them into specific goal statements is no easy task for the counselor, who must understand the nature of the client's problem and the conditions under which it occurs before the translation can begin.

What can you expect of yourself and your clients in terms of setting specific goals? First, the goals that are set can never be more specific than your understanding, and a client's understanding, of the problem. This means that, at the outset of counseling, goals are likely to be nonspecific and nonbehavioral. But nonspecific goals are better than no goals at all.

Clients tend to move from nonspecific to intermediate goal setting and then from intermediate to specific goal setting as they move through the process. In other words, a client will not jump from "I want to be happy" (nonspecific) to "I want to have more friends" (specific). Rather, the client will probably move to the intermediate level of goal setting, as in "I want to have a social life."

As you and your client explore the nature of a particular problem, the type of goal(s) appropriate to the problem should become increasingly apparent. This clarification will permit both of you to move in the direction of identifying specific behaviors that, if changed, would alter the problem in a positive way. These specific behaviors can then be formulated into goal statements; as you discuss the client's problems in more detail, you can gradually add the circumstances in which the client will perform the behaviors and how much or how often the target behaviors might be altered.

SKILLS ASSOCIATED WITH GOAL SETTING

Two kinds of skills are associated with goal-setting activities in counseling: the *verbal skills* the counselor uses to open and guide discussions about client goals, and the *structuring skills* that the counselor uses to help the client formulate or conceptualize life goals. The counselor should be informed during the assessment stage about the client's ability or insight into the process of goal setting. Some clients will be able to take verbal guidance in the process. Others, especially those who are more visually based, will require visual aids to help them conceptualize goals.

Goal-Setting Skills

Verbal skills

Counselor responses that allow clients to examine and assess their short- and longer-term objectives

- Visualizing activities help clients define changes they would like to introduce into their lives.
  1. "Imagine how it would be different if you and Bob could agree on how to raise the children."
  2. "Can you describe how you would like your life to be different 5 years from now?"
  3. "You've mentioned three or four things you would like to see change. Which of these would make the greatest improvement in your life?"
- Verbal confrontations challenge clients to face issues they may not recognize or may be avoiding.
  1. "You say school isn't very satisfying, but your grades are excellent." [discrepancy between stated conditions and behavior]
  2. "You indicated that you have resolved that conflict, but are you aware of the emotion

in your voice when you talk about it?" [discrepancy between stated feeling and communicated affect]
  3. "A while ago you said you never want to see Bob again, and now you say he's your best friend." [discrepancy between two verbal messages]
- Affirming responses communicate the counselor's confidence or a client's potential for accomplishing a particular objective.

  1. CLIENT: I'd like to be able to tell him what I really feel, but if I do, I believe he'll get upset.

     COUNSELOR: Perhaps you could find some positive ways to tell him if you think about it.

  2. CLIENT: I can't imagine how I could ever feel positive about myself.

     COUNSELOR: I think if you had a plan or a structure for facing this problem, you could make some real headway toward liking yourself.

Structuring skills

Aids that help clients to plan and organize their thinking, activities, and self-assessments

- The goal-setting map provides a visual hierarchy of achievable, interconnected goals and how they lead from one level of attainment to another.
- Time lines help clients organize activities in reasonable and achievable order.

- Behavioral assessment allows clients to reconceptualize their feelings and consequences within the context of precipitating behaviors, interchanges, and progression of achievements.
- Successive approximation helps clients order their goals in the most achievable sequence of objectives.
- Reaching logical conclusions is a means of conceptualizing problem formation and solution planning.

Verbal Goal-Setting Skills

Counselors utilize all the verbal skills presented in preceding chapters when working with clients in the goal-setting process, including verbal attentiveness, reflections, paraphrases, enhancing statements, and various types of questions. In addition to these core responses, counselors also use *visualizing, confrontations*, and *encouraging responses* to facilitate goal setting.

VISUALIZING. Visualizing invites clients to consider how their world might be different or how they would wish to make their world different. It is usually introduced as a targeted question, such as, "When you finish school next year, what would be the ideal job to move into?" Asking about "ideal jobs" is akin to asking about dreams, so the counselor is really asking the client to dream a bit about the future, or his or her relationships, or self-perceptions. Visualizing can be used with almost any topic and often yields information that clients might be shy about stating at first. And indeed, some clients find it almost impossible to visualize a different world, perhaps because their reality is so bleak that hope seems like a dangerous activity.

CONFRONTATION. One of the most useful counselor responses is the confrontation. The word *confrontation* has acquired some excess emotional meanings. It is sometimes misconstrued to mean "lecturing," "judging," or "punishing." It is more accurate to view the confrontation as a response that enables the client to face that which is being avoided, be it a thought, a feeling, or a behavior. Avoidance is usually expressed as one part of a discrepancy present in the client's message. Thus, the confrontation helps the client to identify a contradiction, a rationalization or excuse, or a misinterpretation. The discrepancy or contradiction is usually one of the following:

1. A discrepancy between what the client is saying and how the client behaves (e.g., the client says that he is a quiet type, but in the interview he talks freely)
2. A contradiction between emotions and behaviors that the client presents (e.g., the client says that she is comfortable, but she continues to fidget)
3. A discrepancy between two verbal messages (e.g., the client says that he wants to change his behavior, but in the next breath he places all blame for his behavior on his parents and others)

Operationally, the confrontation is a compound sentence. The statement establishes a "you said–but look" condition. In other words, the first part of the statement is the "you said" (a paraphrase or affective reflection). It repeats a message given by the client. The second part of the statement presents the contradiction or discrepancy—the "but look" of the client message.

Sometimes the "you said" part can be implied rather than said, particularly if the discrepant message has just occurred. For example:

CLIENT: I just can't talk to people I don't know.

COUNSELOR: [implied] But you don't know me all that well.

The confrontation describes client messages, observes client behavior, and presents evidence. However, the confrontation is not meant to accuse, evaluate, or solve problems. Use of the confrontation serves four important purposes:

1. It assists in the client's effort to become more congruent by helping the client recognize when discrepancies exist.
2. It establishes the counselor as a role model for direct and open communication; if the counselor is comfortable acknowledging contradictions, perhaps the client can become more comfortable challenging them, too.
3. It is an action-oriented response. Unlike the reflection that mirrors the client's feelings, the confrontation mirrors the client's behavior. It is useful in initiating action plans and behavior change.
4. It is useful for exploring conflict associated with change and goal setting.

THE ENCOURAGING RESPONSE.   The encouraging response is intended to say to the client, "I know you have within you the capability to do this" or "to be this." It is often introduced with such phrases as "You could," "You might," and so on. It is an important statement from the counselor and should be used discreetly; that is, it should not be used if the counselor has any doubts about the client's potential to carry out an activity. Although the encouraging response can sound like advice, it can be used effectively as a way to identify alternatives available to the client. It is misused when, in oversimplification, the counselor attempts to suggest or prescribe a solution; the effect is to negate or ignore the client's concerns.

Structuring Goal-Setting Skills

Structuring skills are particularly useful tools when clients need help in understanding the goal-setting process. It was mentioned earlier that clients often don't know how to set goals or, more precisely, how to set appropriate goals. They may literally need to be taught how to select goals that are achievable. Structuring skills often involve visual aids, such as a goal-setting map, a time line, or successive approximation.

GOAL-SETTING MAP.   A goal-setting map is a useful tool to help clients learn how to set goals (see Figure 6.1). The map provides a visual representation of the goal-setting process and requires the client to focus on the steps that lead to change. The first step is to help your client establish a desired outcome (main goal). Then encourage your client to identify three (or more) changes that have to happen for this goal to be realized (subgoals). Finally, the client must identify two or three behaviors that he or she must do for each of the subgoals to happen (immediate tasks).

When several subgoals are identified, they are usually arranged in a sequence or hierarchy, from easiest to attain to most difficult. Similarly, the immediate tasks related to each subgoal are arranged in a logical sequence and are accomplished in that order. The client completes one subgoal before moving on to another. By gradually completing the activities represented

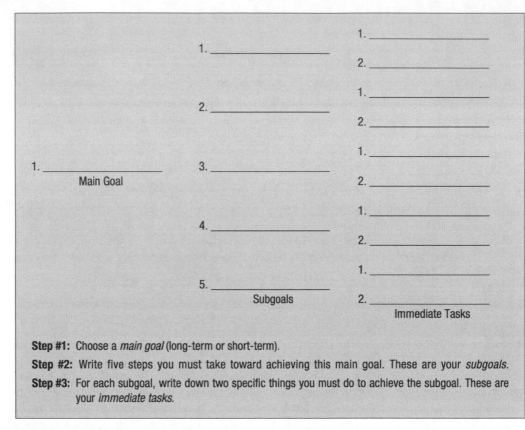

Step #1: Choose a *main goal* (long-term or short-term).

Step #2: Write five steps you must take toward achieving this main goal. These are your *subgoals*.

Step #3: For each subgoal, write down two specific things you must do to achieve the subgoal. These are your *immediate tasks*.

FIGURE 6.1 The Goal-Setting Map

by the subgoals and immediate tasks in a successful manner, the client's motivation and energy to change are reinforced and maintained. Successful completion of subgoals always represents actions that move clients in the direction of the desired goal. There are several ways to ensure that counseling subgoals are effective:

- Build subgoals on existing client resources and assets.
- Base subgoals on client selection and commitment.
- Make subgoals congruent with the counselor's and client's values.
- Identify subgoals with immediate tasks the client can reasonably be expected to accomplish.

TIME LINE. The time line is another visual aid that helps clients gain a time perspective for their goals. Clients often can't visualize potential progress and have unrealistic expectations for what they can accomplish. The time line involves a discussion between the counselor and the client that introduces reality checks for how quickly something might happen (see Figure 6.2).

SUCCESSIVE APPROXIMATION STAIRS. Successive approximation is a way to define change by breaking down the process into a logical sequence of easily achievable steps. It is how humans

Subgoal #1:

Immediate Task #1:	Immediate Task #2:	Immediate Task #3:

By date: _____   By date: _____   By date: _____

FIGURE 6.2   The Time Line

first learned to walk, talk, read, play, socialize, work, and so on. Even though everyone has had these experiences, many adults cannot analyze goal attainment in terms of steps or stages. They may need to be taught the concept and may need help in defining the steps that are inherent in a particular goal. O ne way this lesson may be presented is with a visual drawing of the process (see Figure 6.3). Using a visual like the one in Figure 6.3 often helps the client visualize the process more easily. By asking the client to help you fill in the blanks for each step in the process, the client becomes involved in the goal-setting procedure.

EFFECTS OF GOAL SETTING ON CLIENTS

The process of setting goals can have important effects on clients. Most are positive or helpful although an occasional client may resist the goal-setting process. The advantages of establishing concrete goals are several. Clients feel clearer about themselves and their wants and needs. Goal setting helps clients sort out the important from the unimportant, the relevant from the trivial of their lives. Goal setting encourages clients to make decisions and choices that represent their most significant values and priorities. As a consequence, clients often feel more enlightened and clearer about what they really want for themselves.

Goal setting is often the first time during counseling that clients begin to take specific action in response to a problem or issue. Sometimes the problem has existed for a long time. Through goal setting, clients can feel better about themselves by overcoming a sense of inertia, by mobilizing their forces, and by starting to set in place a chain of events and behaviors that will

My ultimate goal!
_____

Where I will be in three weeks.
_____

Where I will be in two weeks.
_____

Where I will be next week.
_____

Where I am now.
_____

FIGURE 6.3   Successive Approximation Stairs

lead to problem resolution. As a result, clients often feel a great sense of accomplishment during and after the goal-setting process.

Goal setting affords clients a different view of their problems and concerns. The process of establishing specific goals can be reactive; that is, the act of selecting and defining results can contribute to desired changes in itself. This is particularly true when clients are heavily invested in the goal-setting process.

It is generally agreed among professional counselors that clients progress more rapidly when they have been involved in the goal-setting process and have a clear understanding of how achievement of those goals would enhance their lives. When clients understand and commit to outcomes in counseling, they become co-participants in that process of growth and change.

Research into client perceptions of various aspects of the counseling relationship supports the importance of goal setting (Halstead, Brooks, Goldberg, & Fish, 1990). In the results of their research, Halstead et al. observe

> that clients perceived the goal portion of the alliance as being stronger than their counselors did. A possible explanation for this finding, again, may be associated with the nature of the client's personal investment. One would expect the counselor and client to have a common understanding of the explicit goals that help to guide the counseling process. These goals, from the counselor's frame of reference, serve as a beacon by which to set a course to help the client. To the client, however, the goals of counseling, especially in early sessions, may be associated directly with a way to relieve emotional pain. The goals in counseling may represent a real sense of hope for the client. Therefore, it is likely that clients form stronger personal attachments to their goals in that goals can serve to create solutions to what may look like overwhelming situations. (p. 216)

GOAL SETTING WITH CHILDREN

As we have noted earlier, counseling children imposes certain special conditions that alter the goal-setting process. Foremost among these is the need to recognize the child's developmental level. This includes cognitive development (Is the child able to think abstractly because many goals have an abstract future dimension?); affective development (Is the child able to identify and discuss advanced levels of feelings?); moral development (Is the child able to discriminate between socially appropriate and inappropriate goals?); and spiritual development (Is the child able to explore the abstractions of self, power, and destiny?). Assessment of developmental stage is a critical precursor to goal setting for these reasons. When appropriate assessment has been made, however, the counselor still must accommodate and adapt to the child's developmental level of functioning.

Children can be amazingly good about goal setting. Perhaps this is because they do not play mental games with their world. Instead, they go straight to the heart of the matter and are very concrete about what they would like to be different.

CRISES AND GOAL SETTING

When clients are in crisis, the notion of goal setting might seem to be the least likely of all activities. However, crisis dictates that certain goals must be achieved. Even if the contact is to be a single session (which is often the case in crisis counseling), three process goals are necessary:

1. The counselor must establish that the client is safe and lethality is reduced.
2. The client is psychologically stable and has attained short-term stability of self and situation.

3. The client has been connected to appropriate formal and informal supports/resources. (Collins & Collins, 2005, p. 47)

To accomplish these three goals, the counselor must solicit appropriate information about the client's cognitive, affective, behavioral, and environmental conditions during the in-take portion of the contact.

GOAL SETTING AND MULTICULTURAL ISSUES

Within the multicultural counseling context, the effect of goal setting is less well understood by counselors. Although there has been only limited research in this area, Taussig (1987) proposes that clients with varying racial/ethnic backgrounds respond positively to the goal-setting process. However, a note of caution is necessary. We have already observed how important it is that the counselor has a realistic and accurate understanding of the client's worldview and the client's world.

Sue and Sue (2008) state that, as a counseling goal, insight is not highly valued by many culturally diverse clients. People from lower socioeconomic classes frequently do not perceive insight as appropriate to their life situation and circumstances. Likewise, many cultural groups do not value insight (pp. 109–110).

Helping clients to identify goals that address conditions in their environment might be as important as goals that involve a change in their perceptions of their environment. Steenbarger (1993) illustrates this point:

> Multicultural approaches . . . are derived from contextualist models of development that posit problems as a function of poor person-environment fit. Thus, client problems are not intra-psychic in this view, but instead are derived from a fundamental tension between the demands and resources of the environment and the needs of the individual. (p. 10)

Another multicultural issue that affects goal setting is racial/cultural identity development. Numerous authorities have described the personal adjustment issues that are related to identity development (Atkinson, Morten, & Sue, 1989; Cross, 1971; Hall, Cross, & Freedle, 1972; Helms, 1990; Jackson, 1975; Sue & Sue, 1990). This work originally focused on black identity development but has been adapted to other minority groups and to white majority identity development as well. The developmental stages begin with Conformity (Stage I) and continue with Dissonance (Stage II), Resistance and Immersion (Stage III), Introspection (Stage IV), and conclude with Integrative Awareness (Stage V) (Atkinson et al., 1989). Each of these stages manifests developmental issues that are related to one's attitude toward self, attitude toward others of the same minority, attitude toward others of different minorities, and attitude toward the dominant group. Although the literature has not applied this developmental model to other groups (e.g., lesbian/gay clients or persons with disabilities), there would appear to be some appropriateness of fit to other multicultural groups, too.

This range of issues related to multicultural development and personal adjustment have obvious goal-setting implications when you are working with a minority client. Your client is experiencing not only those problems that he or she is able to report to you, but also racial/cultural identity developmental issues of which the client is not even aware. Sue and Sue (1990) note that "therapists may often respond to the culturally different client in a very stereotypic manner and fail to recognize within-group or individual differences" that could be explained by racial/cultural identity development (p. 93). Consequently, it is important that counselors be aware not only of skills related to working with minority clients but also of those identity issues that might make these clients different from clients of the majority culture.

EXISTENTIAL AND SPIRITUAL GOAL SETTING

Occasionally a counseling student will ask, "Why are all goals stated as behaviors? Aren't some client goals meant to change how one thinks, or to change how one feels?" The answer to this question is a complicated yes. It is complicated because many conditions that bring clients to counseling are maintained by their behavior. Feelings may or may not be caused by behavior, but they certainly can be maintained by unconstructive behaviors. Similarly, spiritual issues may not be caused by behavior, but they, too, can be maintained by unconstructive behavior. So goals are frequently behavioral in their formation. Nevertheless, we do wish to address the issue of existential or spiritual crisis as a special form of goal setting.

Existential and/or spiritual crises arise from a number of sources:

- A loss of personal identity or meaning of life
- A need to explore one's conception of divinity and what it means
- A loss of connectedness to life, to the universe, and to others and its implications for daily living
- A need to experience a relationship to the mystery of life; that is, how to live with doubt in a world that demands fact or reason
- A need to find quality leisure time without succumbing to the pressures to perform, achieve, or progress
- A need to experience life more fully and meaningfully
- A need to integrate personal meaning, relationship to a supreme being, connectedness to life, relationship to uncertainty in life, sense of worthiness in leisure, and fully experiencing life into one's being

Notice how these goals are nonspecific, nonbehavioral, and even noncognitive. Nevertheless, they can be very meaningful goals for some clients. Their resolution is far more in the power of the client than the counselor. That is, the counselor can facilitate the exploration of such goals, but the quest is dictated by the client's own sense of purpose and direction.

CLIENT PARTICIPATION IN GOAL SETTING

Some counselors may construe goal setting to mean that they listen to the client, make a mental assessment of the problem, and then prescribe a solution or goal. In fact, such a procedure is likely to be unsuccessful. The nature of counseling is such that the client must be involved in the establishment of goals. Otherwise, the client's participation is directionless or, even worse, counterproductive. An example will illustrate this point.

A beginning counselor was seeing a client who was overweight, self-conscious about her appearance, reluctant to enter into social relationships with others because of this self-consciousness, and very lonely. Realizing that the problem of being overweight was an important factor, the counselor informed the client that one goal would be for her (the client) to lose 1 to 3 pounds per week, under a doctor's supervision, of course. With this, the client became highly defensive and rejected the counselor's goal, saying, "You sound just like my mother."

Goal setting is highly personal. It requires a great deal of effort and commitment on the client's part. Therefore, the client must select goals that are important enough to make sacrifices to achieve. In the preceding example, the client's resistance could have been prevented if the counselor had moved more slowly, permitting the client to identify for herself the significance of her being overweight and the importance of potential weight loss. At this point, both the counselor and the client could then work together to determine the specific goals and subgoals that, when achieved, might alleviate the client's concerns. As with other aspects of the counseling relationship, goal setting should be an interactive process for which both counselor and client assume responsibility.

RESISTANCE TO GOAL SETTING

Occasionally, a client may be reluctant to participate in goal setting or make a commitment to change. Although it doesn't happen frequently, sometimes clients simply can't or won't participate. When this happens, the counselor must deal with the questions of why the client is not participating and if it is a lack of skill or it is resistance.

On the other hand, it may be that the client's reluctance to participate in goal setting is related to resistance issues. In dealing with client resistance to goals, it is helpful to realize that such behavior is purposeful; that is, what the client does or avoids doing achieves some perceived desirable result for the client (whether or not the client realizes it). You might find that the client who resists setting goals could be protecting the very behavior that is in need of modification because that behavior is also serving some desirable purpose. An example is the chronic smoker. Although an individual may recognize the negative consequences of smoking, including its addictive properties, he or she also clings to the habit, believing that it helps him or her relax during stressful moments, or that it increases the enjoyment of a good meal.

It becomes your task to get clients to identify what they gain from their current behavior. In so doing, you may help clients determine whether that gain or outcome can be achieved in more desirable ways. For example, a young student may reject the teacher's authority in order to gain attention from peers. Gaining attention may be a desirable outcome; it is the method that is the problem. Therefore, finding more appropriate ways of gaining increased attention would be a functional goal for counseling.

Sometimes clients resist attempts to establish goals because they feel that the counselor (either overtly or subtly) is pushing them in a certain direction. Unless clients can determine some personal goals for counseling, the probability of any change is minimal. You can avoid creating client resistance to goals by encouraging active participation by clients in the goal-setting process.

Finally, some clients resist goal setting because they are genuinely confused about their desired priorities, needs, and wants. They know what is wrong in their lives, but they cannot visualize a better life. These clients may resist goal setting because it puts them in touch with their confusion, and also because there is an implicit demand for them to sort things out and look beyond their reality. With such clients, it is often very helpful to acknowledge their confusion directly.

> COUNSELOR: Lawanda, I can see you trying and I do know that it's really difficult to imagine a different or an improved situation.

If you give clients permission to move at their own pace, the pressure to set goals does not compound their already building sense of frustration and powerlessness. Indeed, the process of identifying desired priorities, needs, and wants is a goal in itself.

Three other possible strategies to help clients set goals include:

1. Language work. Ask the client to complete open-ended sentences such as "I want. . .," "I do not want. . .," "I need. . .," "I do not need. . .," "I choose to. . .," and so on.

2. Imagery and visualization. Ask the client to imagine him- or herself in an ideal situation and describe it—or to visualize someone else who embodies the qualities and behaviors the client desires. What are those qualities?

3. Role-play and enactment. Ask the client to attempt to reenact the problem through a role-play.

Some clients may be very conflicted about competing priorities and needs. They may identify several possible directions or options, but they may still be in conflict and thus unable to choose which course of action is the best one to pursue. These clients resist goal setting because it exposes the conflict, which often feels uncomfortable or painful. It looks easier to mask or avoid than to deal with the issue head-on. With such clients, it is often helpful to use confrontation (described earlier in this chapter) to point out the apparent conflict:

> COUNSELOR: Lucy, on the one hand, you're saying that you want to have some stability in your life. At the same time, you're saying you are considering a job offer in which you will be required to move every 2 years.

Confrontation is particularly useful for identifying and describing the conflict. For actual working through the conflict, additional counseling strategies—such as gestalt dialoguing (see Chapter 8), transactional analysis redecision work (Chapter 9), and reframing (Chapter 11)—are helpful. It would be important to use such strategies with these clients at this point in counseling because very little progress is likely to be made until this initial conflict is resolved.

Assessing Counseling Goals

The obvious reasons for setting goals are to determine the direction counseling should go *and* to determine when counseling has been successful. An unmet goal can mean numerous things. It may indicate that counseling was unsuccessful, that the client was not committed to change, or that the goal was somehow inappropriate (either immeasurable or unrelated to the problem).

People tend to think of goals in broad, grandiose terms rather than concrete, measurable terms. Grandiose goals are almost impossible to achieve. Concrete goals are *observable* and *countable*, thus *measurable*. The following case of Angela illustrates how concrete goals may be conceptualized using the goal-setting map in Figure 6.1.

CASE ILLUSTRATION OF GOAL SETTING

In this example, we illustrate how the counselor can help Angela (from Chapter 5) identify desired outcome goals for counseling. Recall that Angela described her problem as a depressed state in which she perceives herself as a failure; engages in few meaningful activities or relationships; and, in general, lacks a purpose in life apart from her role as parent. Also, recall that part of Angela's depressed moods seems to be precipitated and/or maintained by a physiological condition—Addison's disease.

After you and Angela probe the facets of her concerns, you can consider the specific changes Angela would like to make. Gradually, these changes can be translated into an outline of desired goals (see Figure 6.1). Angela and the counselor discussed goals and identified the following:

Continuation of the Case of Angela

I. *Outcome Goal Number 1* Angela wishes to become significantly more positive about herself over the next 3 months. (not measurable)

   A. Angela must learn to recognize when she is involved in negative and self-defeating thoughts or self-talk about herself each day.

     1. Angela will start noting the number of times each day that she says or thinks something negative about herself. (observable and measurable)

     2. Angela will begin to keep a list of general topics she tends to use in putting herself down. (observable and measurable)

     3. Angela will start noting what time of day she finds herself involved in negative and/or self-defeating behavior to determine if she is more vulnerable at certain parts of the day or night. (observable and measurable)

   B. Angela must develop a list of positive or self-enhancing statements about herself.

     1. Angela will begin focusing on her positive qualities with the counselor's help. (measurable)

     2. Angela will write each positive quality statement she identifies on 3 × 5 cards and keep these cards handy during those parts of the day that seem to be her most vulnerable times. (measurable)

     3. When Angela gets negative, she will faithfully read a positive quality card and focus on it until she has overcome the negative surge. (measurable)

   C. Angela will examine the setting(s) in which she is most likely to become self-defeating or negative to determine the effect of setting on her moods.

     1. With the counselor's help, Angela will look for a time-of-day pattern to her tendency to become negative or self-defeating. (observable and measurable)

     2. With the counselor's help, Angela will look for other conditions that might be associated with her moods (e.g., being alone, having a lot of tasks, etc.). (measurable)

     3. With the counselor's help, Angela will identify settings to avoid and develop a list of alternative activities when she finds herself in a self-defeating setting. (measurable)

II. *Outcome Goal Number 2* Angela wishes to control any negative effects from the Addison's disease that might contribute to her moods. (not measurable)

   A. Angela will make an appointment with her physician (which she has been avoiding) for an examination and consultation on the possible progression of her Addison's disease.

     1. She will call within 3 days and will make the appointment within 2 weeks. (measurable)

     2. Between now and the appointment, Angela will keep a record of her bouts with the blues, including day, time, situation, and duration of the feelings. She will take this record when she goes for the appointment. (measurable)

   B. With the physician's help, Angela must determine what changes of behavior, use of medication, and so on, would counteract any effects of Addison's on her moods.

     1. With the counselor's help, Angela will use this information to identify how her daily habits must change. (measurable)

     2. Angela will begin a preventive program, based on the plan she and her counselor develop. (measurable)

     3. Angela will keep a daily record of her new activities until they become part of her normal routine. (measurable)

     4. Angela will monitor the intensity of her moods on a 1 to 10 scale in at least three different time periods on a daily basis over the next 3 months. (measurable)

III. *Outcome Goal Number 3* Angela wishes to be more aware of her daily activities and relationships and their meaningfulness or value to her. (not measurable)

   A. Angela will determine the relative importance of her work and leisure activities and relationships. (not measurable)

   1. Angela will monitor and log all daily work and leisure activities for a week and, with the counselor's help, will categorize these activities into "pleasant" or "unpleasant" categories. (measurable)

   2. Angela will determine which of the unpleasant activities are within her control to change or reschedule. (measurable)

   3. With the counselor's help, Angela will attempt to reframe the meaning of those unpleasant activities so they become at least neutral, perhaps pleasant. (measurable)

   4. Angela will do the same analysis with her relationships. (measurable)

   B. Angela will establish a more positive balance between negative and positive work/leisure activities and relationships. (not measurable)

   1. With the counselor's help, Angela will analyze her typical weekly schedule to determine whether it is overbalanced by negative activities and relationships. (measurable)

   2. With the counselor's help, Angela will identify new sources of positive activities and relationships associated with her work and leisure time. (measurable)

   3. With the counselor's help, Angela will seek to establish and maintain a positive balance in her weekly work/leisure activities and relationships. (measurable)

IV. *Outcome Goal Number 4* Angela would like to have a sense of meaning for her life and some sort of "plan" for the next 5 to 15 years, and she would like to feel like she is working toward fulfilling that plan. (measurable or not measurable?)

   A. Angela knows that she must have a better understanding of her values and must determine what kinds of goals and accomplishments are really important to her.

   1. With the counselor's help, Angela will do some values clarification activities to get a better sense of her life priorities. (measurable or not measurable?)

   2. Angela will begin to look at her present activities and priorities to see if they match her life priorities. (measurable or not measurable?)

   3. With the counselor's help, Angela will consider how her family background relates to her situation (how well or poorly would her family function if they were in her present circumstances). (measurable or not measurable?)

   4. With the counselor's help, Angela will consider what "family solutions" would be prescribed for her present circumstances. (measurable or not measurable?)

   5. With the counselor's help, Angela will look for any value conflicts between her present worldview and the worldview she was taught as a child by her family. (measurable or not measurable?)

   6. With the counselor's help, Angela will attempt to resolve any value conflicts she discovers. (measurable or not measurable?)

   B. Angela would like to feel more independent of her ex-husband.

   1. Angela will attempt to be more resourceful about taking responsibility for the children during times when she is feeling blue. (measurable or not measurable?)

   2. Angela will try to view the children's relationship with their father as a positive factor in her life rather than as a potentially threatening factor. (measurable or not measurable?)

Notice the process by which these outcome goals are established. First, they begin as overall goals (Roman numerals) that are directly related to the client's specific or general complaints. Then specific and observable changes (subgoals) (capital-letter items) are identified, which must occur if Angela is to succeed in accomplishing each overall goal. Finally, specific tasks (numbered items) are identified that will allow Angela to accomplish each of the subgoals. In this way, goal setting moves from general goals (related to the presenting problem) to specific subgoals and then to specific tasks.

Summary

Goal setting is such a central part of the change process that people often take it for granted. Yet many people (including many counselors) are not very skilled at setting their own goals or helping others to identify and set goals. In this chapter, we have differentiated two types of goals that are part of the counseling process: process goals and outcome goals. Process goals affect the therapeutic relationship. Outcome goals affect the results of counseling and determine the specific counselor interventions that will be used in counseling. Goals can help motivate clients to make desired changes and can also prove useful as the counselor attempts to evaluate therapeutic progress. Parameters of effective goal setting include identification of what broad changes the client wishes to accomplish, specific situations that would have to change if this broad goal is to be achieved, and specific tasks the client would have to undertake if the intermediate objectives are to be realized. Goals are also affected by the circumstances surrounding the client's functioning. Clients from different cultural backgrounds than those of the counselor pose a challenge to be understood and aided in ways that might be different from the counselor's solutions. A keen sensitivity to multicultural forces is essential when helping clients of different backgrounds set counseling goals.

Exercises

I. Identification of Client Goals

Martin is a college freshman. In his first semester, he concentrated on his studies and tended to avoid social scenes. As a result, several students in his residence hall "singled him out" as weird and teased him. Late in the semester, they began accusing him of being gay, a turn that deeply distressed him because, since childhood, he had felt different from other boys. He went home for semester break and his parents immediately noticed his emotional changes. They convinced him to go to the counseling center when he returned after the break. He did agree and made contact with the counseling center late in January. His counselor was female, experienced, and sympathetic to gay issues, and he developed a genuine liking for her. After the third session, she asked him what he would like to explore or change in his world. He didn't know how to respond to this question, so she asked him to give it some thought before their next session.

A. Put yourself in Martin's position. Identify a few goals that you think might be appropriate, using the suggested goal outline in Figure 6.1. After each goal, indicate whether the goal is safe or risky.

B. Are the goals in your list specific or vague? How would Martin know when he had achieved these goals? How would achieving them affect Martin's concerns?

C. As Martin's counselor, what process goals would you set for yourself? How would these process goals relate to Martin's presenting problems?

II. Multicultural Issues and Goal Setting

Jimmy Huang is a young (late twenties) Asian American who lives in a large urban environment. He was referred to you by a friend who knows you as an acquaintance. His friend thought you could help Jimmy because he has had difficulty both in seeking and obtaining employment that pays enough to support his family (wife and child), support he feels a strong obligation to provide. In the first session, Jimmy is somewhat reluctant to talk about his situation. He appears to be reserved and polite, but not trusting. He is willing to talk about the mutual acquaintance who referred him and, to some extent, he is willing to talk about his employment history and skills.

   A. As Jimmy's counselor, what process goals would you set for yourself? How would these process goals be affected by Jimmy's cultural background?

   B. Put yourself in Jimmy's position. Using the suggested goal outline in Figure 6.1, identify a goal that Jimmy might think is appropriate in the counseling process, and include subgoals and immediate tasks.

   C. Is your goal statement specific or vague? How would Jimmy know when he had achieved this goal? How would achieving this goal help Jimmy?

Feedback for Exercises

I. Identification of Client Goals

There are two ways to approach Jimmy's situation. You could key in on the problems as he verbalized them (his sense of responsibility for his family and the associated shame if he fails his family). Or you could look at possible factors that might be producing the problem (his approach to job searching, and his reluctance to seeking better-paying jobs). If Martin agreed to the second set of factors, it would be easier to develop a set of goals, subgoals, and tasks than if he pursued the first set of factors.

II. Multicultural Issues and Goal Setting

Clearly, the first step in working with Jimmy Huang is to get to know him and the cultural heritage that drives his behavior, values, family obligations, and so on. Without an accurate sense of his worldview, you could not participate in a goal-setting process with Jimmy Huang that he would find meaningful. In fact, there might be aspects of your worldview that would be in direct conflict with Jimmy Huang's values and beliefs. Therefore, the first process goal would be to attempt to relate to Jimmy Huang within the context of his cultural background. This could mean that you are in the role of learner and Jimmy Huang is the teacher. Although this is a reversal of power structure from the traditional counselor-client relationship, it is more likely to be perceived by Jimmy Huang as a sign that he is being shown respect.

Discussion Questions

1. In this chapter, we discussed possible reasons for client resistance to goal setting. Identify some reasons why counselors might also resist developing outcome goals with clients.

2. In what ways do outcome goals help the counselor assess client progress? Describe what you think it would be like to assess counseling progress when no goals have been formulated.

3. Identify a recent problematic situation that you or a close friend experienced. What kinds of solutions came to mind for the person? Was goal setting part of the process? What are the pros and cons if goal setting had been part of the process?

4. Based on your multicultural counseling knowledge, what precautions or advice would you give a counselor who is helping a client of a different culture to identify goals, subgoals, and immediate tasks?

5. Consider the differences between a "typical" counseling session and a session in which the client is in crisis. How would you handle goal setting with the client in crisis?

MyCounselingLab Assignment

Go to the Video Resource Library on the MyCounselingLab site for your text and search for the following clips:

• **Goals, Expectations, and the Meaning of Life**   Identify what verbal skills the counselor is using to get the client to start talking about goals. What was the effect on the client? Respond to the questions on the notes page at the end of the clip. How would you translate the client's goals into observable outcomes?

• **Goal Setting**   How is the counselor's approach to goal setting different from that shown in the Existential/Humanistic clip? How are they similar?

Defining Strategies and Selecting Interventions

PURPOSE OF THIS CHAPTER

Once you and your client have collaboratively established goals for counseling, the next step is to develop a therapeutic plan for counseling that is tailored to the client's goals. This process involves identification of a case strategy (with an accompanying rationale for the choice) and identification of counseling interventions that would serve the strategy and address the therapeutic issues present in the case. This therapeutic or working alliance between counselor and client involves more than the two persons. It also includes the environmental contexts of both individuals. How those contexts affect each person is critical information to be incorporated into the strategic plan if the counseling process is to be effective.

Considerations as You Read This Chapter

- Planning is a major part of every complex activity. What are you like as a planner?
- When you become involved in a complex activity without a plan, what do you do?
- When you form new relationships with friends and colleagues, what do you find yourself mainly focusing on? What they talk about? How they think? What activities they are involved in? Or who they seem to be when they are in their social environment?
- Are the people you get to know best more like you or very different from you?
- How might these questions relate to you as a counselor?

Thus far, we have described a process in which the counselor and client meet, a therapeutic relationship begins to take form, and an assessment of the parameters of the problem occurs; from this, goals to be accomplished in the counseling relationship begin to emerge. In this chapter, we shall examine the case conceptualization process that supports the counseling plan.

Most models of case conceptualization involve three components: (1) the plan organizes a broad range of client information into a small number of categories, (2) the product is a concise understanding of the client, and (3) the plan facilitates the processes of diagnosis and treatment planning (Seligman, 2004, p. 280). Each of these components is, in itself, a thoughtful process involving the counselor's theoretical orientation, the worldviews of both client and counselor, mutually agreed upon therapeutic goals, the diagnosis of the presenting problem, the time orientation, the identification of appropriate treatment strategies or interventions, and client characteristics that will either contribute to or impede therapeutic progress. Thus, case conceptualization is a thought process the counselor utilizes in preparing to work with the client.

CASE CONCEPTUALIZATION SKILLS

Theoretical Bases

Counselors work from theoretical orientations that can be broadly classified as affective, behavioral, cognitive, or systemic in nature. Based on existing research, it is increasingly common for counselors to use a hybrid model that incorporates more than one orientation (e.g., cognitive-behavioral).

Worldview

How we view and interpret life experiences plays a major role in how we understand and define our problems. It is as true for the counselor as it is for the client that worldview shapes how counseling will proceed and be experienced.

Diagnostic Acuity

Case conceptualization must include the identification or ruling out of psychopathology.

Therapeutic Goals

Solutions are an obvious component in the definition of counseling. Solutions, or objectives, should be realistic, appropriate to the level of the problem, and acceptable to both the client and the counselor.

Time Orientation

The counselor must be able to assess the time dimension of the problem, how long it has persisted, how long it might require to change, and whether the client is in a crisis state.

Treatment Strategies

The interventions that are selected by the counselor should have some demonstrated effectiveness with problems similar to those the client presents. And the counselor should be able to assess the effectiveness of a selected strategy and alter the treatment plan when necessary.

Client Characteristics

The client's background and interpersonal history may work against as well as facilitate the counseling process. The counselor must be able to assess the client's potential for cooperative participation in counseling.

THEORY AND CASE CONCEPTUALIZATION

Counseling theory attempts to provide explanations about (1) why people live their lives in productive and sometimes unproductive ways and (2) how people can change their lives when change is needed. Theory can be used by the counselor as either foreground or background in the counseling process. Used as foreground, the counselor embraces a specific theory, uses its guidelines to understand and explain client behavior patterns, and projects ways in which those patterns could change. When theory is used as background, counselors are more likely to emphasize cognitive consistency as their guide in working with cases. Either way, the counselor is using theory as one of the components for conceptualizing each client's world. In Chapter 1, we discussed the range of theories that represent the counseling profession. These theories, although numerous, reflect a finite number of philosophical viewpoints, personality development patterns, change processes, and relationship alternatives.

One could argue that all human beings embrace five forces—feelings, thoughts, behaviors, interpersonal activity, and spirituality—and that would be accurate for the most part. However, each person also tends to be more pronounced in one of the five areas, relying on the other areas when human understanding calls for it. Thus, one person views feelings as the core of being. Another person believes that it is not what one says but what one does that matters. Yet another person believes that it is the meaning one makes of experiences that matters most, a fourth person views interaction with others and with nature as most important, and a fifth person views the soul and a higher being as the source of meaning. Finding one's theory is partly determined by finding oneself in the context of theory choices. It is also determined by the nature of one's professional training and the orientation of one's coaches.

WORLDVIEW AND CASE CONCEPTUALIZATION

The counselor's theoretical orientation will be influenced by his or her worldview. In an earlier chapter, we described worldview as the total perception one has of self, others, environment, and relationships. One's view of others includes a very wide range of culturally based differences. Many multicultural specialists would argue that all counseling is multicultural in nature. This would seem obvious if one considers the many impacts that race, ethnicity, religion, gender, sexual orientation, and physical limitation have on the human condition.

This multicultural perspective can be approached from culture-specific orientations, in which the counselor is aware of and responding to the unique cultural qualities of the client, or it can be approached from a culture-general perspective that emphasizes similarities across cultures. Which is the better direction to take remains an issue of discussion in the counseling profession. Some fear that the culture-specific approach might lead to overlooking the personal characteristics and humanness of the client. Others have argued that only a culture-specific approach can fully reflect the nature and qualities of a person's ethnicity although it is not clear how any one counselor can master the vast variety of cultures reflected in the diversity of race and ethnicity.

One way to negotiate this issue is to examine how client orientations vary across cultures. The Afrocentric or African worldview is holistic, emotionally vital, interdependent, and oriented toward collective survival. The Afrocentric view also emphasizes an oral tradition, uses a "being" time orientation, focuses on harmonious blending and cooperation, and is highly respectful of the role of the elderly. Cheatham and colleagues (2002) contrast this perspective with those of Euro descent:

> The North American Eurocentric worldview tends to divide the world into discrete, "knowable" parts; handles emotion somewhat carefully, even to the point of emotional repression; focuses on self-actualization and independence as a goal of life; emphasizes the clarity and precision of the written word; is oriented toward a linear "doing" view of time; stresses individuation and difference rather than collaboration; and is more oriented toward youth than toward the elderly. (Cheatham et al., 2002)

Sue and Sue (2008) add to this perspective with a discussion of how traditional Asian societies focus on the family for identity, whereas in the Eurocentric view, one develops an individual identity. The authors illustrate this in a discussion of guilt (Eurocentric) versus shame (traditional Asian), noting that guilt is an individual response to a situation, whereas shame is viewed as a family response.

These contrasts lead to our first guideline for working with clients of differing cultures.

When working with clients of different cultures, it is important to determine where the client's identity	emphasis lies: within the individual or within the family/community.

The western (United States and Eurocentric) orientation to counseling involves heavy dependence on verbal expressiveness, emotional disclosure, and examination of behavior patterns. Other cultures may differ on one or more of these conditions. Sue and Sue (2008) point out that in traditional Japanese culture, "children have been taught not to speak until spoken to," a value that will also have been transmitted in many Japanese American families. They also observe that traditional Hispanic and Asian cultures emphasize that maturity and wisdom are associated with one's ability to control emotions and feelings, [which] include public expressions of anger and frustration [as well as] expressions of love and affection. This offers us a second guideline for multicultural counseling:

When working with clients of different cultures, it is important to determine the client's orientation	toward verbal expressiveness and cultural values regarding emotional expression and disclosure.

Finally, it has been noted that many psychotherapies rely heavily on client insight as one of the goals of counseling. Sue and Sue (2008) again note that the traditional Asian advice for handling such feelings as anger, frustration, or depression is "to keep busy and don't think about it," an orientation that goes in the opposite direction from insight.

This leads to a third guideline for multicultural counseling:

When working with clients of different cultures, it is important to determine the client's orientation	toward introspection and insight as opposed to taking action on the external problem.

CONCEPTUALIZING PRESENTING PROBLEMS

Successful interventions are related to the nature or character of the client's presenting problem. Best results are achieved when selected interventions match the components of the problem. Thus, if the client's presenting problem appears to be predominantly affective or emotional in nature, interventions would be targeted to the affective complaints. Similarly, if a client seems to be using his thought processes to sabotage himself, then the counselor would want to select interventions that addressed the cognitive sources. On the other hand, it is important to realize that most client problems are multidimensional. A problem with negative self-talk ("I'm constantly telling myself I'm no good") is not just cognitive; it also reflects an affective dimension ("I feel lousy about myself"), a behavioral dimension ("I choose to stay home and watch a lot of TV"), and a systemic or interactional dimension ("When I do go out, I avoid contact with others because they find me strange, or I behave strangely and others react to me accordingly").

Although problems tend to have multidimensional aspects, the counselor does not have to address all aspects. Frequently, a behavioral aspect, if altered, will lead to different social consequences that will, in turn, alter the client's interactional aspect, too ("If I am able to think more kindly about myself or my problem, I may find that I worry less and behave less self-consciously"). Thus, if the counselor chooses to intervene at the affective door to the problem, changes in the client's affective state will have concomitant effects on the cognitive, behavioral, and interactional aspects of the client's world. This ecological interconnectedness suggests that positive change can occur, regardless of how the problem is experienced by the client. However, it may prove less efficient and less effective if the helper chooses to intervene behaviorally when the client is experiencing the problem affectively (or if the client is culturally disposed toward one aspect and the counselor uses an intervention reflecting a different aspect). Figure 7.1 illustrates how a problem can be explored from different perspectives. Even though these several perspectives will yield different information about the problem, the larger context of the problem is the same.

How does one plan a strategy for counseling intervention if multiple choices exist and "all roads lead to Rome"? A general guideline for selecting counseling strategies is that clients are more receptive when the choice of strategy matches their cultural history and how they experience the problem. If the client experiences the problem as an emotional trauma, then an

1. How does the problem make your client feel? How do her feelings affect her effort to change the problem? How might her feelings maintain the problem? What different feelings might change the problem? What is your client's cultural perspective toward feelings associated with the problem?	2. What kinds of things does your client do when the problem is "in charge"? How do these behaviors support or maintain the problem? What behaviors could she change and thereby reduce the effects of the problem? What are her cultural predispositions toward *doing* as opposed to *feeling*?
CLIENT'S PRESENTING PROBLEM Your client has been experiencing repeated failures in her college courses. She is starting to feel hopeless and is thinking about dropping out of college. She doesn't know what she might do, but wonders if she might try to revive an old high school love and perhaps marry.	
3. What kinds of things is your client saying to herself? How might her messages be part of her problem? What cultural messages are part of her self-talk? What roles do her cultural values play in the self-statements that she makes, and what alternative self-statements are available?	4. What are your client's relationships with other students like? With men? How do her professors fit into the picture? How have her parents functioned in her absence? In what ways do relationships support the problem? What are the cultural expectations on her to marry?

FIGURE 7.1 The Various Ways to Approach a Client's Problems

affective intervention strategy might seem more plausible to the client. Inconsistency between the client's experience of the problem and the helper's counseling strategy can lead a client to conclude that the counselor has failed to understand. This is not to suggest that the counselor's interventions would be exclusively affective in this case. As counseling proceeds, and as the multiple dimensions of the problem become apparent to the client, counseling can begin to address these other dimensions. For example, affective reactions are often reinforced by the client's self-talk. An affective strategy would focus on the client's affective reactions but might include cognitive interventions that addressed the negative self-talk. In this example, the base for this working alliance would be the affective domain. In a different counseling case, the client's experiencing of the problem might be behavioral (for example, excessive drinking), thus suggesting that the counseling plan should be behaviorally based. This would involve behavioral interventions, with cognitive, affective, and systemic/interactional excursions from the behavioral component as appropriate.

Sometimes the client's experience of a problem fails to produce the best understanding of how that problem should be confronted, and so the counselor chooses a strategy that yields only qualified success. When this occurs, you should reexamine your rationale for selecting a particular strategy. For example, if a woman presents a problem of poor self-concept, the counseling strategy may be to address her cognitive self. As she begins to feel and become more competent, however, her new self may lead to a crisis in her marriage, causing her to back off her recent gains. It may be that her husband's expectations are for her to remain less competent, thus maintaining a relationship in which he is superior. In this situation, the problem may have been experienced as a cognitive and/or affective issue, yet the underlying issues really represent a systemic/interactional problem.

DIAGNOSIS AND CASE CONCEPTUALIZATION

It cannot be assumed that your clients will always be free of pathology. This reality emerges with increasing frequency as stress and violence grow in the school, the community, and the family. Consequently, it is important that you be able to identify or rule out client psychopathology early in the counseling relationship (Nelson, 2002). We do not assume that you are preparing to treat psychopathology, but even if you are not, you must be able to recognize psychopathology when it exists in order to make appropriate referrals to other clinicians. The standard source for diagnostic direction is the Diagnostic and Statistical Manual of Mental Disorders (DSM-IV-TR) (American Psychiatric Association, 2007).

Professional counselors who work in schools, community agencies, pastoral settings, or private practice will encounter psychopathology on a fairly regular basis. Depression is occurring with increasing frequency among school-age children and youth. It can be as mild as the "blues" or as serious as clinical depression. If you work in schools, you are also likely to encounter attention deficit hyperactivity disorder (ADHD), but this condition is increasingly recognized in adult clients, too. Other pathologies that you may encounter include phobias, adjustment disorders, and bipolar disorders. Nelson (2002, p. 419) advises that clients who show signs of clinical depression, ADHD, or other mental disorders should be referred for consultation with a physician—a psychiatrist or a general practitioner trained to diagnose and treat mental illness. Today, most state licensure laws require professional counselors and clinical mental health counselors to have formal coursework in diagnostic procedures as part of their graduate training.

TIME ORIENTATION AND CASE CONCEPTUALIZATION

Time is an extremely important part of the working alliance. It includes the amount of time de-voted to each session, the amount of time devoted to the process, how long the problem has been experienced by the client, and the amount of time required to address the problem fully. If the client comes to counseling in crisis, time may be seen as a critical aspect of the problem. Time also has its cultural dimensions. In some cultures, time is a friend; in others, time is a factor to be controlled.

Time also enters into the equation when goals of counseling are considered. Some goals are short-term, whereas others may have lifetime implications. Client tolerance for ambiguity and process is a direct reflection of the client's view of time. Generally speaking, clients choose goals that represent either choice or change, or a combination of the two. Clients who commit themselves to choices usually have the prerequisite skills and opportunities to take a particular course of action but have not yet committed themselves to do so. Clients who commit them-selves to changes may very well lack the necessary skills, opportunities, or behaviors needed to achieve those changes. Thus, the fundamental alternative between choice goals and change goals will have time ramifications because change will likely require more time than choice.

Questions about how long counseling should take are probably on the mind of most clients as they enter the process: What is a reasonable amount of time for me to solve my problems? Will a "good" counselor speed up that process for me? How patient must I be in waiting for the good feelings to return? How long should I wait before deciding that counseling isn't the right solution to my pain? Such questions are rarely verbalized but are often thought by clients.

Counselors think of time issues, too: How much time should I devote to building rapport? To assessment? To the process of goal setting? How long will the client commit to counseling? What is a reasonable amount of time to wait before seeing some evidence of progress? How long should most counseling take? These are important questions. They reflect the counselor's theoretical underpinnings, tolerance for ambiguity, belief in the process, and understanding of client differences.

GOALS AND TREATMENT PLANNING

Goals are directly related to the counselor's choice of strategy and intervention. Goals may be classified as immediate, intermediate, or long term (Cormier & Hackney, 2012). Generally, a combination of these goals will be reflected in the treatment plan. There are exceptions, of course. When working with clients in crisis, most goals must be short term and crisis-mediating in character. Once goals have been identified through counselor-client discussion, the treatment plan is developed.

Treatment planning has long been part of the counseling process, but in recent years, as third-party reimbursement has been tied to managed-care systems, the treatment plan has be-come an essential step in case conceptualization. Although this may not be necessary for coun-selors who do not rely on insurance reimbursement, the practice of preparing treatment plans is nonetheless good counseling practice.

Treatment plans include four types of information: the goals that have been established; the kinds of interventions that will help clients realize their goals; the anticipated length of time (or number of sessions) it would reasonably take to achieve success; and the format or milieu that will be used to deliver interventions, usually referred to as the mode of treatment. Because client characteristics may also affect the outcome of a strategy and thus affect goal attainment, they become part of the planning process that leads to the treatment plan. In fact, some scholars would argue that client characteristics are the most powerful sources of influence affecting the outcome of treatment.

Cormier, Nurius, and Osborn (2009, Chapter 10) provide six guiding principles in the preparation of treatment plans that reflect client characteristics:

1. Make sure your treatment plan is culturally as well as clinically literate and relevant; that is, the plan should reflect the values and worldviews of the client's cultural identity, not your own.
2. Make sure your treatment plan addresses the needs and impact of the client's social system as well as the individual client, including (but not limited to) oppressive conditions within the client's system.
3. Make sure your treatment plan considers the role of important subsystems and resources in the client's life, such as the family structure and external support systems.
4. Make sure your treatment plan addresses the client's view of health and recovery and ways of solving problems. The client's spirituality may play an important role in this regard.
5. Consider the client's level of acculturation and language dominance and preference in planning treatment.
6. Make sure the length of your proposed treatment matches the needs and time perspective held by the client.

Although the treatment plan is primarily a tool to guide you and to provide a means for assessment of progress, information contained in the plan may also be most valuable to the client. Given the change in recent years toward client-as-consumer and client rights, it is appropriate to provide clients with accurate information about intervention strategies that make up the treatment plan (see Appendix B for a sample treatment plan). This information (Cormier, Nurius, and Osborn, 2009, Chapter 10) includes:

1. A description of all relevant and potentially useful treatment approaches
2. A rationale for each procedure that will be used
3. A description of the counselor's role in each intervention
4. A description of the client's role in each intervention
5. Possible discomforts or risks that may occur as a result of the intervention
6. Expected benefits that will occur as a result of the intervention
7. The estimated time and cost of each intervention

STRATEGY SELECTION

In addition to choosing strategies that reflect client expectations and preferences, counselors also must consider available client resources and characteristics. For example, does the client have sufficient internal ego strength or self-discipline to carry out a particular intervention? Does the client live and work in a context in which support from others is fully given or withheld? Is the client likely to apply a particular procedure outside the counseling session? Does an intervention require the client to do something (such as engage in imagination), and is the client capable of doing this? Are certain types of interventions outside the clients' experience or worldview? Is the intervention developmentally or age appropriate?

Proposed strategies also need to take into account previous client attempts to solve their problems. When dealing with problems, clients often arrive at solutions that are both inadequate and irrelevant. When this happens, an all-too-common situation arises: The solution becomes the problem. This can be illustrated by the person whose world contains so many pressures that relaxation is very difficult. Seeing the need to escape from the pressures and routines, the client embarks on a course of action that includes hobbies, travel, and reading. Soon, the client realizes that these diversions have taken on the same character as the original problem. Hobbies have become compulsive activities, travel necessitates extraordinary planning, and reading has become a quest to absorb more books than last month's record. In other words, the solutions only added more pressure; consequently, the problem is exacerbated by the solutions.

It is vitally important for the counselor to understand, as much as possible, the client's world. It is also important to understand the frustrated needs the client is experiencing in that world. Finally, it is critical to understand what the client has been doing or thinking as part of the solution. We often find that clients have a very limited repertoire of solutions, and they apply these limited solutions indiscriminately. The result is a more complicated, less successful world than even before the "solution" was applied.

CATEGORIES OF COUNSELING INTERVENTIONS

Counseling interventions may be described within the major categories through which problems are enacted: affectively experienced problems, cognitively experienced problems, behaviorally experienced problems, and problems that are interactional/systemic in nature.

Affective interventions (see Chapter 8) elicit and respond primarily to feelings and emotions. They may also involve body awareness activities that focus on somatic components of a problem because emotional states often involve the musculature and the expenditure of physical energy.

Cognitive interventions (see Chapter 9) deal with thoughts, beliefs, and attitudes one has toward self and others. Such interventions are intended to help the client think differently about a situation, person, fear, enemy, boss, spouse, and so on.

Behavioral interventions (see Chapter 10) are used to help the client develop new behaviors or skills and/or control or eliminate existing behaviors that are counterproductive. They may be used to modify habits, routines, or interaction patterns with others.

Interactional/systemic interventions (see Chapter 11) address relationship patterns with other persons, tasks, or situations. The source may be one's family, work setting, neighborhood, church, or any social setting in which interactional patterns have been established.

Table 7.1 describes therapeutic interventions used by counselors to accomplish these tasks. They are classified under the four categories mentioned here and include typical client presentations that might call for their use. This categorization system is based on previous classification systems, particularly Hutchins's thought-feeling-action (T-F-A) model and L'Abate's emotionality-rationality-activity (E-R-A) model.

As you will recall from Chapter 5, client problems typically are multidimensional (including any combination of feeling, thinking, behaving, and interacting with others). In categorizing counseling interventions along these dimensions, the intent is to illustrate how selected interventions may be suitable for specific expressions of client problems. The intent is not to oversimplify the therapeutic process but rather to lay out the range of options that counselors have when working with specific client problems. And, of course, affective interventions may be functional with more than affectively expressed problems, and so, too, with the other three categories. In fact, if one views human beings as total persons rather than parts to be added together, then interventions in any of these four dimensions will produce effects in all of the other dimensions of the problem. Let us revisit Angela, our fictional client from Chapter 5, to illustrate how the working alliance and intervention selection might be implemented.

TABLE 7.1 Counseling Strategies and Corresponding Manifestations of Client Problems

Affective	Cognitive	Behavioral	Systemic
Person-centered therapy; Gestalt therapy; Body awareness therapies; Psychodynamic therapies; Experiential therapies:	**Rational-emotive therapy; Beck's cognitive therapy; Transactional analysis; Reality therapy:**	**Skinner's operant conditioning; Wolpe's counter-conditioning; Bandura's social learning; Lazarus's multimodal therapy:**	**Structural therapy; Strategic family therapy; Intergenerational systems:**
Active listening; empathy; positive regard; genuineness; awareness techniques; empty chair; fantasy; dreamwork; bioenergetics; biofeedback; core energetics; radix therapy; free association; transference analysis; dream analysis; focusing techniques	A-B-C-D-E analysis; homework assignments; counterconditioning; bibliotherapy; media tapes; brainstorming; identifying alternatives; reframing; egograms; script analysis; problem definition; clarifying interactional sequences; coaching; defining boundaries; shifting triangulation patterns; prescribing the problem (paradox)	Guided imagery; role playing; self-monitoring; physiological recording; behavioral contracting; assertiveness training; social skills training; systematic desensitization; contigency contracting; action planning; counterconditioning	Instructing about subsystems; enmeshment and differentiation; addressing triangulation, alliances, and coalitions; role restructuring; clarifying interactional systems; reframing prescribing the problem (paradox); altering interactional sequences; genogram analysis; coaching; defining boundaries; shifting triangulation patterns
Manifestations	*Manifestations*	*Manifestations*	*Manifestations*
Emotional expressiveness and impulsivity; instability of emotions in problem solving and decision making; sensitivity to self and others; receptive to feelings of others	Intellectualizing; logical rational, systematic behavior; reasoned computerlike approach to problem solving and decision making; receptive to logic, ideas, theories, concepts, analysis, and synthesis	Involvement in activities; strong goal orientation; constant need to be doing something; receptive to activity, action, getting something done perhaps at expense of others	Enmeshed or disengaged relationships; rigid relationship boundaries and rules; dysfunctional interaction patterns
Client Issues	*Client Issues*	*Client Issues*	*Client Issues*
Stress; anger; fear of failure; defensiveness; anxiety; moody; insecure; conflicted; parenting issues; spiritual issues	Anger; anxiety; panic; depression; insomnia; parent training; self-esteem; addictions; marital problems; spiritual issues	Anxiety; phobias; classroom behavior; health problems; behavior disorders; stress; substance abuse	Family dysfunction; parenting issues; marital problems; job issues; divorce and remarriage

Case Illustration of Strategy and Interventions Selection: Angela

Based on information derived from an in-take interview with Angela, the counselor summarized Angela's complaints using the four-dimensional analysis (see Figure 7.2). Next, the counselor examined the six factors for establishing a counseling strategy for this case:

1. **The counselor's theory.** The counselor prefers an affective approach, with elements of person-centered theory and existentialism. The counselor also subscribes to systemic explanations of human problems.
2. **Counseling experience.** The counselor has practiced for about 4 years and has taken several training workshops since completing her formal counselor preparation program. She has worked with several depressed clients.
3. **Character of the problem.** Angela's problem may have a medical dimension in addition to affective, cognitive, behavioral, and systemic dimensions. Her presenting concern is how to have better control over her moods.
4. **Typical responses to her problem.** Based on her training and experience, the counselor

knows that clients who feel inadequate will need to examine their support system, identify what outcome their moods may be serving, and develop alternative and more facilitative behavior patterns.

5. **Character of the goal.** Angela identified three main goals (see Chapter 6) that she would like to achieve in counseling: (1) to become significantly more positive about herself over the next 3 months, (2) to control any negative effect that the Addison's disease and PMS may be contributing to her moods, and (3) to become more aware of the meaningfulness of her daily activities and relationships.
6. **Client's characteristics.** Angela appears to be functioning at a minimal level, personally and socially. She was raised in a family in which she was not expected to be responsible for attending to her needs. She does not seem to be able to create social support. And she quickly feels overwhelmed when life's demands begin to accumulate. In her former marriage, her husband took responsibility for "cheering her up."

DEFINING A COUNSELING STRATEGY

The first step in developing a counseling strategy is to synthesize what is known about the case and define a plan of action that is consistent with those factors. This synthesis would take into account both the four-dimensional analysis and the six factors for establishing a counseling strategy. We note that (1) Angela presented her problem as affective (mood swings, feelings of inadequacy) and the counselor is predisposed toward an affective approach; (2) the presence of possible medical concerns should be addressed by a physician; (3) Angela set as a goal to become more positive about herself, which corresponds to her cognitive negativity; (4) Angela tends to retreat from others (behavioral and systemic) as well as from her problem (cognitive) and hides in her affective self when stress builds up; and (5) Angela's problem has spilled over to interpersonal relationships (children, students, social life), which relates to the counselor's systemic interests. In addition, she continues to lean on her ex-husband for help when she is in emotional distress and this tends to undermine her self-confidence even more.

Possible Strategies

The counselor has several viable choices of direction to take. She might choose to work from an affective context because she suspects that Angela is carrying several unresolved issues from her

Affective	Behavioral
Angela often feels irritable, upset, or depressed; feels sorry for herself when things go wrong; feels inadequate; feels abandoned by her ex-husband.	Angela retreats into her room when she feels blue; takes out her feelings on her children and students; occasionally has sleep problems; avoids social contact; has no regular recreational activities.

ANGELA'S PRESENTING PROBLEMS

Angela (see Chapter 5) is seeking counseling to learn how to have better control over her moods. She indicates that she often "flies off the handle" for no reason with her children or with her students in the classroom. She suffers from PMS and occasional difficulties sleeping. She feels like a failure as a wife and mother, primarily because of her divorce and her mood swings. Her self-description is primarily negative.

Cognitive	Systemic
Angela has a lot of negative self-talk; thinks her divorce was primarily her fault; blames herself for her inability to control her moods; thinks she is not giving her children the atmosphere they need.	Angela doesn't date; she seems to have no support network; has little contact with her family of origin; "uses" her children to avoid others; asks ex-husband to take children when she is overwhelmed.

FIGURE 7.2 Four-Dimensional Analysis of Angela's Case

former marriage (failure feelings) and her mood swings, the effect of which produce increased stress, interpersonal issues, and possible exacerbation of her PMS difficulties and Addison's disease. This would seem to be a promising approach, particularly because the counselor does have an affective predisposition and Angela's initial complaints were affective in nature.

Angela's problem could support a different strategy. Rather than address her emotional baggage from her former marriage, the counselor might choose to examine how Angela presently places herself into situations that remind her of her former marriage. In other words, she might address the systemic and cognitive links that connect Angela's present to her past and, in so doing, seek to establish more facilitative cognitive responses. In addition, with the counselor's aid, Angela might challenge her self-defeating thinking about her past, her potential, and her interpersonal relationships. This approach might allow Angela to reassess her priorities, view her unchangeable life factors in a more positive light, and identify new goals and activities that would support a more desirable lifestyle. Because the counselor has not shown a strong inclination toward cognitive counseling approaches, this strategy could be more difficult to implement.

A third way that the counselor could conceptualize the case is to focus on Angela's behavior patterns, both in terms of how she responds to herself and to her children, students, and adults. The fact that Angela withdraws when she feels depressed probably exacerbates her affective response and becomes self-defeating. It was noted that Angela appears to be functioning at a low level, personally and socially. It may be appropriate to help Angela identify and strengthen certain behavior patterns that she could turn to when she begins to feel overwhelmed, depressed, or self-negative. The rationale would be that if she could intervene in this downward spiraling pattern, then she would be spared the undesirable consequences.

Finally, there seem to be clear links between Angela's present functioning and her role in her family of origin and her relationship with her ex-husband. The counselor may wish to explore this linkage with Angela by seeking to clarify how her interaction patterns reflect her family's views of interdependency and family unity, how she manifests these patterns with her children and her students, and how her social linkage with her family is similar to her social linkage to other adults. She might encourage Angela to examine how this pattern has repeated itself with her reliance on her ex-husband, and she could help Angela address issues of differentiation versus unity. In other words, is Angela in conflict with her ethnic (family) values? The counselor may wish to include the children in the counseling process as a means of revealing patterns of interaction; assumptions; and family rules, roles, and structure. This might logically lead to a cognitive reassessment of Angela's approach to family and social groups through the use of a strategic family therapy approach. Because the counselor does subscribe to systemic explanations, this is an attractive approach, except that the counselor does not feel adequately prepared to conduct this type of counseling.

Selecting Interventions

Each of the four strategies embraces a repertoire of counseling interventions that are theoretically consistent with the assumptions of each strategy. For example, the affective approach emphasizes exploration of feelings in a safe and understanding environment, the development of insight into and mindfulness of one's feelings, and ultimately the acceptance of oneself. Counselor activities such as empathic understanding of the client's situation, active listening, and acceptance are endemic to this strategy. Similarly, the cognitive, behavioral, and systemic approaches also identify counselor interventions that support the objectives of these respective strategies. Chapters 8 through 11 examine these interventions and illustrate how they complement the strategy in question.

Choosing the Preferred Strategy

The character of the problem may be addressed through any one of a variety of counseling strategies, including behavioral, cognitive, affective, systemic, or any combination of these (e.g., cognitive-behavioral, cognitive-systemic). Your choice of strategy probably will reflect your personal explanation of human problems and how they can best be resolved (your personal theory). On the other hand, multiple or sequential strategies may be needed to work with the entire character of the defined client problem. For example, anxiety may be experienced somatically (behaviorally), cognitively (anticipatory), affectively (depression), and systemically (emotional distancing from others). When more than one component is involved, usually more than one intervention is also necessary. You may still approach the case from your preferred vantage point for conceptualization, but you may find that your interventions should address all aspects of the problem.

STRATEGIES FOR WORKING WITH CHILDREN

Children pose special issues in the counseling relationship because they have little power or control over their environment. How children view themselves (self-esteem) is bound to have environmental linkages. Similarly, how children behave is interconnected to the behaviors of others in the world. A child's potential to change that environment—be it the home, the neighborhood, or the school—is highly problematic without the involvement of significant others. Consequently, any effort to intervene in a child's problems will necessarily involve relationships with siblings, parents, friends, teachers, and other adults. For this reason, a systemic view of the problem, if not a systemic strategy, will prove appropriate. The systemic view involves relationship patterns and their concomitant behavioral and cognitive components. The counselor can work with the child on an individual basis and seek to produce systemic change through the child, or the counselor can involve other participants in the child's system and seek to invoke direct change in the interactional patterns of the system.

The school counselor may include in this systemic counseling process three other systems: other children; the teacher and the child; or the parents, teacher(s), and the child. If the problem, and thus the goal, is primarily learning-related, then the process may be contained totally within the school setting. But if the problem is familial, then the counselor's goal may be to generate parental awareness and responsibility for the problem, at which time a referral to a family counselor would be appropriate. Counselors working with children in community settings probably will seek to include the family in the counseling process. Given the more diffuse nature of community counseling clientele, child problems that come to the counselor probably require family participation if successful resolution of the presenting problem is to be achieved.

Summary

Counseling strategies constitute the plan within which most therapeutic work and change take place. The strategic plan of action must reflect a number of divergent factors, including those related to the counselor's theory, experience, and expertise, as well as the client's presenting problem, goals, and environmental contingencies. In the case of children, the other significant players in the child's world assume a particularly significant role. Culturally different clients also reflect needs that are both personal and environmental. Counselors must work with clients to identify interventions that will address both the character of the problem and the goals that have been identified. Client expectations, preferences, capabilities, and resources are other important criteria to consider in choosing workable strategies. In the following four chapters, we shall examine different counseling interventions, how they are implemented, what they are intended to achieve, and how clients typically react to their introduction in the counseling process.

Exercises

I. Choice or Change Issues and Related Counseling Strategies

A. By yourself or with a partner, list four to six issues or problems you are currently experiencing in your own life. Identify whether each is a choice issue or a change issue. Remember, choice issues are ones in which you have the skills and opportunities to follow a course of action but feel conflicted about which direction to follow. Change issues are ones in which you need to develop new options and behaviors or modify existing ones. Finally, note whether the choice or change for each issue is under your control and can be initiated by you. If it is not, identify the other people in your life who are also part of this choice or change.

B. With a partner, or in a small group, brainstorm possible strategies that might be suitable interventions for one of the issues or problems from your list in Part A. Next, evaluate the probable usefulness of each strategy. In your evaluation, consider the six guidelines for selection of counseling strategies described in this chapter.

1. Is the strategy consistent with your theoretical orientation?
2. Do you have any expertise and experience in working with this strategy?
3. Are you knowledgeable about typical responses to and effects of this strategy?
4. Does the strategy fit the character or nature of the problem?

5. Does the strategy fit the character or nature of your desired goal?

6. Does the strategy meet your expectations and preferences and does it avoid repeating or building on prior unsuccessful solutions?

(*Note:* You do not have to select complex or sophisticated counseling strategies. If you have not yet been exposed to counseling theories and techniques, rely on common-sense approaches and interventions because the emphasis in this activity is on the process of strategy selection rather than on the actual strategies you select.)

C. Continue this activity with your partner or group. For the strategy your group selected in Part B as the best or most effective one, generate the following information about the strategy:

1. A rationale—how it seems to work
2. A description of the counselor's role in the strategy
3. A description of the client's role in the strategy
4. Possible discomfort, negative effects, or spinoffs from the selected strategy
5. Expected benefits of the strategy
6. Estimated time involved in using this strategy

D. Role-play the strategy information in Part C. One person will assume the client's role and present the issue. The other person will assume the counselor's role, suggest the recommended strategy, and provide the client with enough information about the strategy to help the client make an informed choice about accepting or rejecting the suggestion. Additional members of the group will function as observers and will take notes and provide feedback to the counselor after the role-play. Follow up with a group discussion of the exercise.

II. Relationship of Problem Components to Strategy Selection

In this exercise, we present three client cases. For each case, determine the primary component(s) of the problem that would need to be addressed during the intervention strategy phase of counseling. There may be more than one significant component. (Feedback for the exercise can be found in the next section.)

A. Angel is a 16-year-old eighth-grader who has been in and out of trouble for the past 5 years. He belongs to a street gang that is known to be involved with drugs, and he has been to county jail twice for "aiding/abetting in drug activity." In the past year, he has been considering leaving the gang and as he puts it, "starting all over again." Leaving the gang is not so easy, however, because the gang does not allow members to leave and enforces this rule heavily. Angel is caught between the desire to start over and the probable consequences if he tries.

Primary Components

Affective: _____
Cognitive: _____
Behavioral: _____
Systemic: _____
Cultural: _____

Preferred strategy: _____

B. Marguerite is a 28-year-old single woman who has been diagnosed with multiple sclerosis, a progressive disease. Her mobility has become increasingly constricted in the past 6 months, such that she has encountered increasing situations in which she has limited access. This has both frustrated her and angered her. At the same time, she knows that the disease will only get worse and that she should be using her energies to try and accept and adapt. She lives at home with her parents, who give her too much sympathy (she thinks) or turn their frustrations on the society that is so "insensitive" to such situations.

Primary Components

Affective: _____
Cognitive: _____
Behavioral: _____
Systemic: _____
Cultural: _____

Preferred strategy: _____

C. Mary and Bob have come for marriage counseling. During the first session, Bob dominates and Mary sits passively while he describes their "problem." When he refers to their problem, he stares at her and she looks down at her hands in her lap. Finally, Mary explodes and shouts that the problem is that Bob is having an affair with her best friend. At this point, Bob becomes enraged and leaves the therapy room. Mary begins to cry and says that she is at her wits end. She doesn't want a divorce but she doesn't think the marriage can be saved. You ask Mary if they ever discuss their problems at home and she shakes her head no. You ask if Bob is ever physically abusive and she says quietly, "Sometimes he pushes me." When you ask if she has ever shared this with her family members, she says that they just wouldn't understand because they are traditional Catholics and believe that she should stick it out.

Primary Components

Affective: _____

Cognitive: _____

Behavioral: _____

Systemic: _____

Cultural: _____

Preferred strategy: _____

Feedback for Exercises

II. Relationship of Problem Components to Strategy Selection

A. There are three components to Angel's problem that would need to be addressed by counseling interventions.

Affective. How Angel experiences relationships in the gang. How he feels about himself as a member; as an ex-member; his fear of retaliation.

Behavioral. Angel's continued involvement in the gang; his need to find a way to separate from the gang; his need to assess the level of danger.

Systemic. The gang's rules for involvement; whether anyone has ever left the gang.

B. There are three areas of concern regarding Marguerite: an affective factor, a behavioral factor, and a systemic (family) factor.

Affective. Marguerite's emotional adjustment to her condition; her parents' emotional adjustment.

Cognitive. The need to examine what she is saying to herself regarding her increasing

dependence on others; her need to identify alternative strategies.

Behavioral. Marguerite's need to develop strategies for adapting to her limitations and strategies for dealing with social justice issues.

Systemic. The need to address relationship with her parents regarding her disability, and how they might relate more productively to her disability.

C. Mary and Bob have multiple components to their presenting problem(s).

Affective. Mary's attempts to hold her emotions in and then exploding; Bob's escape from affect by leaving the session.

Cognitive. Mary's thoughts about the marriage; Bob's thoughts about the marriage.

Behavioral. Bob's escape behavior; Mary's avoidance behavior.

Systemic. Mary's relationship with her parents.

Cultural. Mary's parents' religious expectations for her.

Discussion Questions

1. Identify and discuss the attributes of a good counseling strategy and of a poor counseling strategy. From your perspective, what factors make a strategy good or effective?

2. How much influence do you believe a person's cultural values have? How aware do you think people are of their cultural values?

3. What has been your exposure to people of different cultures? What knowledge have you gained from this

exposure? What cultural knowledge deficits do you possess? How will that affect your counseling?

4. Identify a problem situation that you have experienced (or have observed in a close relationship) in which the attempted solution became the new problem or made the existing problem worse. To what extent was the person in question aware of this complication? How was the problem finally resolved?

MyCounselingLab Assignment

Go to the Video Resource Library on the MyCounselingLab site for your text and search for the following clips:

- **Gina: Individual Diagnostic Assessment**   How does the counselor gain the client's assistance in the assessment? What did you learn in this video clip that you would use in your counseling?
- **Child: Tracking Questions**   What is the counselor doing to obtain information from this child? What do you think the counselor is hoping to learn about

the child? Wht are the unique challenges in child assessment?

- **Collaborative Interviewing: Exploring Beliefs About the Problem**   What kinds of counseling responses does the counselor use as he explores the client's views of the problem? What do you think the counselor was looking for in this interview segment? What is your reaction to the client's perception of his problem?

8

Affective Interventions

PURPOSE OF THIS CHAPTER

Ask someone why people seek counseling and you are likely to get an answer that identifies emotion as the cause. We hear terms like *emotional imbalance*, *emotionally disturbed*, or *emotionally upset* as conditions that get people into psychological difficulty. Although feelings certainly are not the source of all human difficulties, it is nonetheless true that many, if not most, people come to counseling for help in dealing with overwhelming emotions. This chapter discusses the role that emotions play in the process of counseling and describes counseling interventions that are specifically used to help clients identify emotions; modify troublesome feelings; and, when appropriate, accept feelings that are present.

Considerations as You Read This Chapter

- Feelings have been described as basic to all human experience. Yet many people do not seem to understand their feelings. Some will disavow having certain feelings. Others will treat their feelings as an embarrassment or a sign of weakness. Some cultures treat feelings as private events.

- What are your views? Would you be described as "wearing your heart on your sleeve" or as the stoic type? On a continuum from high emotions to low emotions, where would you place yourself?

- What role does emotion play in people's problems? Is it the source? The result?

- How do people change the way they feel about something? If a feeling changes, for example, from indifference to liking, will that be reflected in the person's perceptions of his or her world?

People feel happy when things are going well, sad when they experience loss, angry or frustrated when their desires are blocked, and lonely when they are deprived of contact with others. Many times, feelings can be accessed only indirectly through a person's verbal expression or behavior. A client may feel depressed, but only through verbal and nonverbal communication, physical cues, or acting out can the counselor make contact with that feeling state. But feelings cannot be manipulated in the same fashion as thoughts or behaviors. Counselors must work with client feelings by generating client awareness and subsequent client valuing and integration of those feelings.

The role that feelings play in counseling and psychotherapy is an unsettled issue. Feelings can be viewed as peripheral phenomena that accompany but do not affect therapeutic change, or they can be viewed as essential to or evidence of change. Whichever is the case, most, if not all, of human thought and behavior have a feeling dimension. Perhaps because this is so, feelings can be the source, or a significant part, of the problems one experiences. We noted above how the counselor accesses the client's affective state, but the client may also lack access to feelings. This bottling up of feelings may be due to one's early training or to the intensity of an emotion that threatens and overpowers the person. Generally, boys are often taught to deny those feelings that are associated with weakness, failure, or powerlessness. Similarly, girls are often taught to deny feelings associated with characteristics such as dominance, control, power, or even intellect. Consider the child who is raised in a perfectionist environment. If that child internalizes the environmental demands, then the need to be perfect without the skills to do so will lead to excessive threat and emotional difficulties throughout childhood and into adulthood. When these unacknowledged or even undetected feelings begin to build up, some people are ill-equipped to find release, and counseling or psychotherapy becomes an appropriate recourse.

Helping the individual to develop the capacity to find release of emotional difficulties and to cope better with life demands are central goals of many therapeutic approaches. The affect-oriented theories have made major contributions to the counselor's repertoire of interventions. Generally speaking, those theories with an affective orientation rely heavily on the development of affect awareness, exploration, and integration of feelings. They do not discount thought processes or behavior patterns. Rather, they emphasize the emotional context in which thought patterns, beliefs, and behaviors occur.

THEORIES THAT STRESS THE IMPORTANCE OF FEELINGS

Most affective or emotion interventions derive from the phenomenological therapies. Phenomenologists make a distinction between what is (objective reality) and one's perceptions of what is. This inner world of perceptions becomes one's personal reality. By far the most dominant of these therapies is Carl Rogers's person-centered therapy. Probably next in its impact would be the contributions of gestalt therapy, followed by the existential approaches of Binswanger, Boss, Frankl, and May. Other therapeutic approaches that are sometimes identified as affective therapies include Kelly's psychology of personal constructs; Gendlin's experiential counseling; psychoanalytic therapy; and the body work therapies, such as bioenergetics and core energetics.

Wittmer and Sweeney (1995) have proposed an Adlerian-based wellness approach to human problems. As a concept, wellness may constitute the ultimate goal or objective of counseling because it encompasses a number of dimensions, including intellectual, emotional, physical, social, occupational and spiritual wellness (Chandler, Holden, & Kolander, 1995). This approach has been labeled holistic, meaning that the entirety of the individual is considered and utilized in the process of counseling. Wellness also emphasizes prevention as a tool toward healthy living. Within the psyche, three conditions of wellness are operating: intellectual (cognitive), emotional, and spiritual. For our purposes, we shall consider emotional and spiritual wellness as conditions residing within the affective or feeling dimension of counseling. Intellectual wellness will be considered in Chapter 9. Finally, constructivist theory considers feelings (as well as thoughts) as highly significant to the process of client perception and exploration.

AFFECTIVE INTERVENTIONS

In one respect, referring to affective interventions is a philosophical contradiction. The affect-focused counselor is more likely to emphasize the personhood of the client and the interpersonal relationship between counselor and client, rather than the techniques that would be used. Nevertheless, the affective counselor is doing something in this process, and these counselor behaviors are the focus of this chapter. Affective interventions that the counselor uses include both basic and advanced communication skills that help the client identify a feeling. As we explore these interventions, which are listed below, keep in mind that the interventions become gimmicky and ineffective if the therapeutic relationship between the counselor and the client has been given a lesser priority.

Affective Intervention Skills

Basic Skills

Restating Feelings

Using the client's words to describe a feeling the client has presented

Paraphrasing Feelings

Using your own words to describe a feeling the client has presented

Summarizing Feelings

Using your own words to gather or to connect more than one feeling presented by the client

Affective Intervention Skills

Identifying Feelings

Helping the client recognize or categorize a presented or implicit feeling

- Using nonverbal cues. The client's physical qualities (e.g., posture, gestures) may be the first indicators that affect is present.
- Using verbal cues. The client's language is a second indicator that affect is present.

Sorting Out Feelings

Helping the client identify the type of feeling to be explored

- Emotions inventory. This is a checklist of feelings that the client can use (even during in-take) to identify feelings that are present.
- Emotions balloons. This is an exercise that children are able to use.

Focusing Technique

Helping the client achieve a receptive state of mind in which feelings are able to emerge into consciousness

Role Reversal

Allowing the client to view interactions from another person's perspective

Alter-Ego Exercise

Helping the client recognize alternative or competing emotions within him- or herself

Empty-Chair Exercise

Using a dialoging exercise in which the client is able to carry on a conversation or even an argument with him- or herself or with another person

Using Dream Work

Using the client's recurring dreams to explore ways in which they are meaningful to the client

Emotive Imaging

Helping the client explore the affective dimension of an experience

The Goals of Affective Interventions

The primary goals of affective interventions are to (1) help the client express feelings or feeling states; (2) identify or discriminate between feelings or feeling states; (3) alter or accept feelings or feeling states; or, (4) in some cases, to contain feelings or feeling states.

Some clients come to counseling with awareness that something is wrong in their lives but are unable to articulate or discuss that condition. Talking about problems or feelings may be a new experience for them. This is often the case for the person who grew up in a family or culture in which problems were never discussed openly or the expression of feelings was discouraged or forbidden through injunctions such as "Don't be angry," "Don't cry," "Don't feel." Child clients may not have reached the developmental stage at which skills and affect sensitivity are acquired; consequently, they may lack both the skills of expression and the awareness that expression of feelings can be helpful.

At a somewhat more complicated level, the client may come to counseling flooded with emotional reactions. When this happens, it is experienced as an emotional overload, and the protective response often is to tune out the emotions, to become emotionless. Or the response may be confusion or disorientation. When this happens, the client must be helped to recognize and to sort out or contain the variety of affect responses that are being experienced. This condition is frequently found when a person has experienced a long period of emotional turmoil, such as occurs in a divorce, death of a family member, poor physical health, or other life tragedy, or it may be a more serious psychopathologic blocking of affect.

At the most complex level of affect intervention, the counselor and client are involved in the integration or alteration of feeling states. This may include value clarification, acceptance of hitherto unacceptable feelings, reconsideration of old feelings, or even redefinition of self-perceptions. This process is common when the client is beginning to differentiate self from family, self from spouse and children, self from job or career, or self from culture, or is otherwise laboring with the question, Who am I?

In this chapter, we describe and illustrate the more common affective interventions that facilitate the expression and examination of feelings. These interventions include feeling inventories, counselor modeling, scripting and role rehearsal, dialoguing and alter-ego exercises, identifying affect blocks, differentiation among competing feelings, role reversal, the empty chair, affect focusing, and dream work.

HELPING CLIENTS EXPRESS AFFECT

Experiencing a feeling, even knowing that somehow feelings are related to one's problems, does not lead naturally to the expression and examination of the feeling. Part of the counselor's role is to help clients find ways to express feelings, both in ways that capture the meaning of the feeling and convey that meaning to others. The counselor's task may be a matter of setting the stage, creating the proper conditions for a reticent client to open up.

Many authors have described the conditions that are necessary for such an involvement. These conditions—an accurate understanding of the client's situation and an unconditional valuing of the client—were discussed in Chapter 4. Beyond the conditions that create the atmosphere of helping, the counselor becomes involved in the client's process of emotional exploration through selective attention and reflective listening, also described in Chapter 4.

The exploration of emotions is a process more than a set of verbal responses and involves the counselor's conceptualization of what the client is trying to understand and the acknowledgment of that effort. Sometimes the process also serves to focus the client's awareness on what he or she seems to be saying. And the process usually involves sharing the satisfaction of having accomplished the task. Given that it is a process rather than a series of behavioral events, the counselor must rely nonetheless on verbal interaction with the client and close observation of nonverbal communication. This metacommunication interaction incorporates many stylistic responses of the counselor and counseling.

Cultural Variables and Affect Expression

The expression of affect runs counter to the values of some cultures. Research indicates that the English and Italians endorse the display of distress and anger across relationships more than do the Japanese (Argyle, Henderson, Bond, Iizuka, & Contarelo, 1986). This is also borne out in research by Noesjirwan, who "found that Indonesians agreed with the rule of keeping quiet and hiding feelings when one is angry at one's boss, while Australians endorsed expressing anger in the same situation" (Gudykunst & Ting-Toomey, 1988, p. 181). Sue and Sue (2008) observe that Asian Americans value the restraint of strong feelings and that self-disclosure is particularly difficult for black clients working with white counselors. Similarly, the expression of inner thoughts and feelings by Native Americans cannot be expected to occur until trust is well established. It is not that affect is less accessible in some cultures than others; rather, in collectivistic cultures (as opposed to individualistic cultures) affect expression is more likely to be withheld (Gudykunst & Ting-Toomey, 1988, p. 179). To summarize, when cultural variables come into play, the role of affect is not as predictable as it is within a culturally homogeneous group.

NONVERBAL AFFECT CUES

A major way in which clients show feelings is through nonverbal cues or body language. Early work by Ekman and Friesen (1967) indicated that nonverbal information can be inferred from elements of the client's communication such as head and facial movement, body position, movements and gestures, and voice qualities. Although no single nonverbal cue can be interpreted accurately in isolation, each does have meaning as part of a larger pattern or gestalt. Thus, there are relationships between nonverbal and verbal characteristics of client messages. In addition to these relationships, nonverbal cues may also communicate specific information about the relationship between individuals involved in the communicative process, in this case, the counselor and client. Some nonverbal cues convey information about the nature and intensity of emotions more accurately than verbal cues. The nature of the emotion is communicated nonverbally primarily by head cues—for example, setting of the jaw, facial grimaces, narrowing of the eyes. The intensity of an emotion is communicated both by head cues and body cues such as muscular rigidity.

The counselor may or may not choose to acknowledge these nonverbal cues. In some cases, acknowledging them ("You've been looking very tight since you started talking about this matter") can invite the client to share the intensity of the emotion. At other times, the counselor's observation may be rejected outright or may bring out a defensive response. Thus, timing as well as accuracy of perception is a factor in what the counselor chooses to say. As you get to know your client, you will be able to determine how to respond to nonverbal cues.

Nonverbal Cues and Cultural Differences

In Chapter 2, we discussed how different cultures use nonverbal cues. Sue and Sue (2008) observe that many nonverbal cues have distinct cultural meanings. The messages communicated through facial expressions, degree of eye contact, or head movements can be quite different across the range of cultures, from Eurocentric to Japanese, African American to Mexican, Puerto Rican to Malaysian. To make accurate inferences about nonverbal messages, we need to know about factors such as cultural deference to age or authority, and emotional expression. Sue and Sue (2008) note that there are complex rules regarding when to speak or when to yield to another person that vary across cultures.

Edward T. Hall's early research differentiated between high-context cultures and low-context cultures. High-context cultures are those in which communication relies heavily on non-verbal cues, whereas low-context cultures rely much less on nonverbal cues for communication purposes. Hall also proposes that U.S. culture (presumably the majority white culture) is a low-context culture, although not as low as the cultures of Germany, Switzerland, or Scandinavia. On the other hand, Asian Americans, African Americans, Hispanic Americans, Native Americans, and other minority groups in the United States emphasize high-context cues (Sue and Sue, 2008). This would suggest that certain ethnic groups in the United States are much more attuned to and adept at reading nonverbal messages. However, Ekman (1993) emphasizes that "no one to date has obtained strong evidence of cross-cultural disagreement about the interpretation of fear, anger, disgust, sadness, or enjoyment expressions" (p. 384).

VERBAL AFFECT CUES

Although there are many different kinds of feelings, most feelings that are identified by words or moods fit into one of four mental states: positive/affirming feelings, aggressive/defensive feelings, fear/anxiety feelings, and spiritual/existential feelings. Many of these feelings can be identified by certain affect word usage. In addition, there are subcategories of affect for each of the major affect categories. In using words or moods to identify affect, it is important to remember that words may occasionally mask more intense feelings or even different feelings. It should also be noted that the language of emotions can vary across cultures. In fact, some cultures may not have a word for a particular emotion although Ekman (1993) adds that if the language of a culture does not have a word for a specific emotion, it does not mean that the emotion is not present in that culture but simply connotes the lack of specific terms to represent certain feelings.

Verbal Cues for Positive Mental States

Positive expressions or moods reflect good or accepting feelings about oneself and others and indicate positive aspects of interpersonal relationships. Verbal mood cues in a client's communication are revealed by the presence of words that connote certain feelings. For example, if a client uses the word *wonderful* in describing an event, a location, or a person, that descriptor suggests an accepting, preferred, or desirable mental set toward the referent. Sometimes, the client will be more nonspecific about such reactions but will nonetheless communicate a mood reaction. Some examples of word or mood cues that connote this positive affect are shown in Table 8.1. Often, nonverbal cues occur simultaneously with these positive affect cues. The most frequent nonverbal mood correlates are facial ones. The corners of the mouth may turn up to produce the hint of a smile, the eyes may widen slightly, worry wrinkles may disappear. There may be a noticeable absence of body tension. The arms and hands may move in an open-palm gesture of acceptance, or the communicator may reach out as though to touch the object of the affect message. When clients are describing feelings about an object or event, there may be increased animation of the face and hands.

TABLE 8.1 Positive Mental State Cues

EMPOWERED	HAPPY	ENJOY	LOVING/LOVED	TRUSTING
able	blissful	beautiful	adored	assure(d)
appreciated	cheerful	delight	appreciated	believe
authorized	creative	enjoy	beloved	certain
capable	delighted	good	care	confident
confident	elated	happy	cherished	depend
confirmed	excited	indulge	choose	expect
enabled	extravagant	nice	close	faith
important	fascinating	pleasing	desired	hope
intelligent	glad	relish	esteemed	rely (reliance)
proud	happy	satisfy	friendly	secure
respected	joyful	terrific	idolized	trust
satisfied	merry	tremendous	like	
smart	playful	zestful	love	
supported	sexy		needed	
valuable	stimulating		treasured	
worthwhile	thrilled		want	
			worthy	

Verbal Cues of Aggressive/Defensive Mental States

Feelings serve functions. Although aggressive or defensive responses sometimes represent an obstruction to be removed, they can also be a signal to protect oneself or to fight for one's rights or even survival. These are not pleasant feelings to experience, and many clients seek counseling or are referred with the idea of having them relieved or eliminated. However, attempting to make them go away without looking to see what function they may serve might not be in the client's best interest therapeutically. Often, these feelings mask a more vulnerable reaction, such as hurt, shame, or inadequacy. Clients may need help in learning how to understand the origins of such mental states, or they may need to learn how to express their feelings in an assertive way rather than in an aggressive/defensive manner. Most people are well acquainted with the words or moods that represent aggression and defensiveness (see Table 8.2).

TABLE 8.2 Aggressive/Defensive Mental State Cues

AGGRESSIVE	GRIM	QUARRELSOME	DEFENSIVE
angry	austere	argumentative	against
annihilate	cruel	belligerent	cagey
argue	foreboding	cantankerous	careful
attack	frightful	combative	cautious
criticize	grave	contentious	guarded
destroy	grumpy	disagree	opposition
fight	harsh	hotheaded	prepared
hit	merciless	irritable	protective
hurt	ruthless	litigious	resent
offend	severe	scrappy	resistive
overcome	solemn	tempestuous	withholding

Certain vocal qualities are associated with aggression and defensiveness. Many times, the voice will become louder, deeper, or more controlled. The pacing of the communication may become more rapid or more deliberate. Usually, communicators make distinct departures from their normal communication when these mental states are present.

It is possible that a client can experience aggressiveness or defensiveness without immediate awareness of it. Old anger, deep insecurity, or alienation can become so normative that a person accommodates a responsive mental state as though it, too, were normal behavior. Thus, the counselor may find that the client is unaware, at a surface level, of a departure from "wellness." In this case, the counselor's acknowledgment of the condition may be perceived as confrontation by the client. A simple, tentative observation, such as "You sound as though you may be angry," can bring a defensive reaction. This serves as a signal that deeper, gentle exploration of the client's reactions may be appropriate.

Verbal Cues of Fear/Anxiety Mental States

Fear is a reaction to some kind of danger to be avoided. Anxiety is a more latent or generalized response to the same perceived dangers. Either may signal a need to withdraw from a threatening situation, from oneself, or from other people and relationships. The person experiencing fear or anxiety may also feel isolated. The implicit presence of danger that is signaled by these responses is the likely focal point for counseling. Cultural characteristics may also be linked to the expression of these mental states. Verbal cues that suggest fear or anxiety in a client's communication may be classified into five categories (see Table 8.3).

As was the case with aggressive/defensive responses, some physical cues are associated with fear and anxiety. The face may express surprise or suspicion, the body may recoil or appear ready to spring into action. The breathing rate may become more rapid and shallow. As anxiety and tension increase, the number of speech disturbances—such as errors, repetitions, stuttering, and omissions—may also increase. The person may speak at a faster than normal rate, or the voice may take on a more guarded quality.

When the client appears fearful, the counselor may wish to explore the ramifications of that fear. How realistic is the fear? How physically threatening is the feared situation? Is the situation more threatening to one's identity or spiritual self than to one's physical self? How accurate are the client's perceptions of the feared situation?

Verbal Cues of Spiritual/Existential Mental States

Thus far, we have discussed emotional conditions that have direct or concrete connections to a client's physical world (e.g., a fear of speaking to strangers, or anger associated with a particular

TABLE 8.3 Fear/Anxiety Mental State Cues

FEARFUL	DOUBTING	PAINED	MISTRUSTING	AVOIDING
anguished	confused	angst	aversive	copping out
anxious	failure	dismayed	dislike	denying
concerned	insecure	fearful	doubt	escaping
nervous	stuck	hurt	questionable	fleeing
scared	stupid	struggling	shady	neglecting
worried	unsure	suffering	suspicious	running

TABLE 8.4 Spiritual/Existential Mental State Cues				
PEACEFUL	**HOPEFUL**	**EMPTY**	**DISILLUSIONED**	**DESPAIRING**
calm	anticipate	abandoned	cheated	depressed
composed	assurance	adrift	cynical	desperate
content	believe	dejected	disappointed	despondent
loving	confident	directionless	discouraged	disconsolate
mellow	expect	disconnected	disheartened	empty
pensive	faith(ful)	distraught	dissatisfied	forlorn
placid	insipring	downhearted	failed	gloomy
relaxed	optimistic	heartsick	let down	hopeless
satisfied	providential	hopeless	lost	lost
serene	rely	meaningless	punished	morose
thankful	trust(ing)	purposeless	unattainable	powerless
thoughtful	uplifting	sad	unfair	sullen
untroubled	wish(ful)	sorrowful	unworkable	weary

event). But as you know, some feelings do not seem to be anchored in day-to-day events or people. They may have more to do with self-doubt, purpose, or connection to life. And the client's response may be equally vague: a general sense of unwellness or unease, restlessness, or doom. The feelings themselves can be most unsettling because they don't seem to be associated with causative events.

Spiritual/existential mental states actually form a continuum from wellness to distress (see Table 8.4). When a person feels congruent with his or her spiritual self, a sense of peace and hopefulness is experienced. When a person is out-of-sync with her- or himself, feelings of disillusionment or despair are experienced. Somewhere in between lies a psychic space of neither hope nor despair. It is a feeling of emptiness, which can range from vague discomfort to outright craving for relief. Bishop (1995) observes that "issues such as locus of control, acceptance of responsibility, belief in God, and guilt and shame [often] play a role in problems presented by clients" (p. 64).

Spirituality, as presented here, is distinguished from religion or religiosity. Religion may be identified as the institutional response to matters of the self and God. Spirituality is the noninstitutional response to these same matters. As such, spirituality does not seek to replace the role of religion in one's life but in fact may tide one over in periods of religious alienation. Similarly, religion may be the appropriate approach to addressing a client's spiritual issues, particularly when the client is aware of a personal religious base to life. Richards and Bergin (1997) define spiritual interventions as

> those that are more experiential, transcendent, ecumenical, cross-cultural, internal, affective, spontaneous, and personal. Examples include private prayer, spiritual meditation, spiritual imagery with images that are personally meaningful to the client, encouraging forgiveness, and keeping a spiritual journal. (p. 237)

Morgan (2000) addressed these issues as they apply to counseling:

> For counselors today, the task is to understand the particular experiences, communal contexts, and historical-cultural elements that shape a client's spiritual perspective and practice. How does this person experience transcendence, or a higher power, or ultimacy in his or her life? What attitudes and values are important for him or her to live by, in order to feel connected with the spiritual realm? What practices keep the client "on track" in his or her search for meaning? (p. 174)

Powell (1996) described a case in which a 16-year-old depressed female, whom he diagnosed as experiencing a Major Depressive Disorder, Single Episode (DSM-IV-TR) and who was the daughter of missionary parents, received treatment over a period of 18 months. The focus of treatment was on spiritual values clarification, addressing losses that the client had not acknowledged or grieved, and understanding the stresses and pressures her parents were undergoing.

This association of depression with spiritual upheaval is not uncommon. When you become aware that your client is experiencing feelings of emptiness, disillusionment, or despair, it is appropriate to ask some questions that would reveal the extent of the mental state in order to identify any self-destructive inclinations and to determine whether your client also needs referral to a physician for medication. Following are some questions that would help determine the extent and nature of your client's emotional pain.

Exploring Dimensions of Depression

How well do you sleep at night?

Do you have difficulty going to sleep?

Do you wake up in the middle of the night and find it difficult to go back to sleep?

Are you sleeping less (more) than is your typical pattern?

What are your eating patterns?

Are you disinterested in eating?

Are you eating obsessively?

Do you feel guilty about your eating?

What is the state of your physical well-being?

Do you feel normal?

If not, what seems unusual about your physical well-being?

Is this a recent change?

Do you experience lengthy bouts with fatigue?

Do you have a high, medium, or low energy level?

Do you consider your sexual feelings to be normal?

What kinds of social contact do you have?

Has your social pattern changed recently?

Do you prefer to be alone or with people?

Do you have friends or relatives that you are comfortable calling at inconvenient times?

What are your self-views like?

What do you think about yourself?

When do you tend to think about yourself?

How much time do you spend thinking about yourself?

What kinds of things distract you from thinking about yourself?

Do you ever think about suicide?

If so, have you thought about how you might commit suicide?

Do you have a current suicide plan?

Have you ever attempted suicide? When?

Has any member of your immediate family ever attempted or committed suicide?

Questions such as these provide cumulative information about the client's inner well-being. If the client appears to be withdrawing from social contact, sleeping poorly, eating poorly or erratically, and focusing extensively on self, then the counselor should seek consultation or refer the client to a physician or psychologist. If the client is contemplating suicide or has attempted suicide before, referral may be made to a physician or psychiatrist because medication may be a necessary part of treatment.

HELPING CLIENTS SORT OUT FEELINGS

Some clients enter counseling aware of their emotions but they are overwhelmed by either the complexity or quantity of their unresolved feelings. Such a condition is often triggered by a traumatic life event, such as the death of a parent, spouse, or child; a divorce; or the loss of a career. These traumatic events stimulate feelings associated with the event and, perhaps more significantly, feelings associated with the person's self-worth. Typically, the person is attempting to resolve unanswerable questions, such as: Why did it happen? Why did it have to happen to me? Could I have prevented it from happening?

The counselor's role in this situation is that of facilitator, guide, and supporter. Counseling interventions include being a sounding board as the client attempts to uncover a complex series of feelings, helping the client recognize the source of various emotional reactions, and helping the client develop a sense of emotional control. Sometimes, the counselor will begin this process with a simple paper-and-pencil exercise if the client is unable to address feelings. At other times, the counseling scene takes on the qualities of a play rehearsal. Often, the scene is one of intensely experienced emotions, tears, fears, relived hurts, and anger. Ultimately, it leads to hope, clearer understandings, and new decisions.

A second condition can occur in which the client enters counseling with an overload of emotions. When this happens, a common survival mechanism is to deny or screen out the intensity of the emotions while still acknowledging the emotions.

Whether the crux of the client's problem is the quantity or complexity of emotional experience, the process aims to help clients develop some structure or system for managing those feelings. This process is not as simple as it might sound. The tendency, particularly for the inexperienced counselor, is to offer a structure, a way of viewing the client's concerns. External structures may make cognitive sense, but they usually miss the point. The point is, of course, that most emotional overloads are illogically structured by clients. Therefore, when the counselor provides a logical structure, it does not address the client's illogic. Instead, the counselor must encourage the client to reprocess situations, personal explanations, and conclusions so that an alternative and more logical structure may emerge. This process allows clients to conceptualize their life situations in new ways that are personally meaningful.

Several interventions, exercises, and discussions can help clients sort out feelings. No one intervention is effective with all clients. Thus, you must explore and experiment with each new client to find the activities that are acceptable and meaningful for that individual. The interventions range from very simple paper-and-pencil exercises to rather complicated and dramatic reenactments of emotional experiences.

Early in counseling, the most appropriate strategy is to use activities that generate expression and classification of feelings. These activities include counselor recognition and reflection of client's expression of feelings, verbal statements, and counselor empathy for the client's emotional description. Chapter 4 contains a full discussion of empathy, affective reflections, and restatements. Other activities include an emotional percentages chart and emotions checklist (which is very effective for the client who says, "I can't describe my feelings") and the emotions balloons chart (which is a helpful aid for young children).

It is important to note that not all counselors are comfortable with strong feelings, either the client's or their own. Teyber and McClure (2011) believe that this can be explained by several possible factors: the counselor's need to be liked, a misperception of the counselor's responsibility, rules learned from the counselor's family of origin, or situational conflicts in the counselor's own life. Under such circumstances, the counselor is likely to respond ineffectively.

Teyber and McClure describe a number of ways in which counselors respond ineffectively when these circumstances prevail, including:

- Interpreting what the feelings mean and intellectually distancing themselves
- Becoming directive and telling the client what to do
- Reassuring the client that everything is okay or will work out all right
- Becoming anxious and changing the topic
- Falling silent or emotionally withdrawing
- Self-disclosing and moving into their own feelings
- Diminishing the client by trying to rescue him or her
- Over-identifying with the client and becoming controlling—pressuring the client to make some decision or take a particular action in order to truncate the therapist's own unwanted feelings (p. 224)

Emotions Inventory

An effective way to introduce adolescents and adults to a discussion of emotions is the emotions inventory (see Figure 8.1). This inventory is a checklist of a wide range of emotions that clients frequently report in their counseling sessions. It can be given to the client to fill out prior to or during the first counseling session. The client is asked to identify those feelings that describe his or her life experience in the past 3 months or in the present moment. In the session(s) following, the client's responses may be used as a basis for early discussion and exploration of counseling concerns. As an exercise, look at the emotions inventory in Figure 8.1 and check the feelings that describe your world right now.

Emotional Percentages Chart

Some adults have difficulty focusing on feelings. This doesn't mean that they lack feelings; rather, they are probably unaccustomed to talking or thinking about their feelings. Often a visual aid helps them begin to think or focus on their feelings. The emotional percentages chart

_____ abandoned	_____ disoriented	_____ mad
_____ adrift	_____ doubtful	_____ nervous
_____ afraid	_____ empty	_____ offended
_____ angry	_____ fearful	_____ outraged
_____ annoyed	_____ frustrated	_____ panicked
_____ anxious	_____ furious	_____ pessimistic
_____ bewildered	_____ grumpy	_____ resentful
_____ confused	_____ hassled	_____ sad
_____ defensive	_____ heartsick	_____ scared
_____ depressed	_____ hopeless	_____ skeptical
_____ desperate	_____ hurt	_____ sorrowful
_____ despondent	_____ insecure	_____ tense
_____ directionless	_____ irritable	_____ tired
_____ discouraged	_____ irritated	_____ uneasy
_____ disillusioned	_____ lonely	_____ unsure

FIGURE 8.1 Emotions Inventory

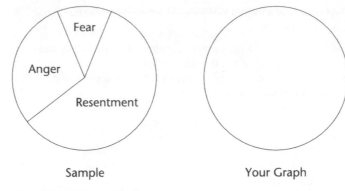

FIGURE 8.2 Emotional Percentages Chart

(see Figure 8.2) is an exercise that can be quite effective early in counseling. On a sheet of paper, two circles are drawn. One is a pie graph that illustrates a number of different feeling states and how much of the total pie each emotion occupies. The other circle is empty, and the client is asked to draw in his or her emotional percentages. You may want to refer your clients to the emotions inventory if they are having difficulty labeling personal emotions to use in the chart. The emotional percentages chart allows clients to identify the intensity or preoccupation with a particular set of emotions. It also allows the counselor to invite clients to discuss the interrelationships of those identified emotions in the chart.

Emotions Balloons Chart

Young children pose a special problem for the counselor. Emotional awareness is a process that develops as the child develops. Very young children may know only happy, sad, mad, and bad. As children grow and as their vocabularies increase, they are able to recognize the subtleties that exist within these emotions. Even so, the counselor must relate to the child at the child's level of experience. In part, this means that you will use the toys and tools of the child's world to relate to the child's emotions. One example of this is the emotions balloons chart (see Figure 8.3).

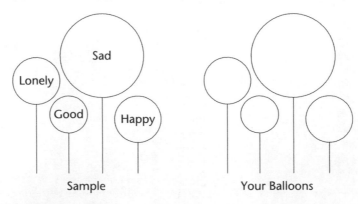

FIGURE 8.3 Emotions Balloons Chart

The child is given the following instructions about this activity:

Sometimes people have several different feelings at the same time. Some of those feelings are strong and are very hard to forget, while others are important but are sometimes forgotten. Using the chart I am going to give you, write into the large balloons which of your feelings are biggest and hardest to forget. Then write into the small balloons the feelings you do sometimes forget. You can use feelings like mad, happy, lonely, scared, upset, proud, or excited to label your balloons.

Another good aid is the happy/sad/angry faces chart, which allows the child to point to the face(s) that best describe his or her feelings.

FOCUSING TECHNIQUES

Focusing techniques are used to encourage and facilitate introspection so that problems can be clarified and conceptualized by the client. Focusing emphasizes present feelings toward either present or past circumstances. Iberg (1981) described this process as

holding one's attention quietly at a very low level of abstraction, to the felt sense. Felt sense is the bodily sense of the whole problem. In focusing, one doesn't think about the problem or analyze it, but one senses it immediately. One senses all of it, in all its complexity, as the whole thing hits one bodily. (p. 344)

After suggesting that the client find a comfortable sitting position, the counselor invites the client to become quiet and to allow feelings to enter into consciousness. The client is then asked to associate words with this undifferentiated mass of feelings and to allow awareness to generate naturally. The instructions for using this intervention that follow have been adapted from Gendlin (1969) (see Iberg, 1981, p. 506).

Affect-Focusing Instructions

I am going to explain how you can focus on a general or overall feeling you have about some concern or problem. Be silent for a moment and relax. . . . [Pause: Have the client close his or her eyes and relax] Now let the tension drain from your body. . . . [Longer pause] See what comes to you when you ask yourself, "How am I now?" "How do I feel?" Let any thoughts emerge. Try not to screen your response. . . . [Longer pause] Think about what is a major problem or concern for you. Choose whatever seems most meaningful to you. . . . [Shorter pause]

Focusing Process

Try to pay attention to [focus on] what all of the problem [concern] feels like. Allow [let] yourself to feel the entire mass of the feeling. . . . [Longer pause]
    As you pay attention to [or receive] the entire feeling of your problem, you may find that one special concern comes up. Let yourself pay attention to that one aspect or feeling. Don't explain it or talk to yourself about it. Just feel it. . . . [Extended pause] Keep following one feeling. Don't let it be just words or pictures. Wait and let words or pictures emerge from the feelings. . . . [Extended pause] If this one feeling changes, or moves, let it do so. Whatever it does, follow the feeling and pay attention to it. Feel it all. Don't decide what is important about it. Just experience it. . . . [Extended pause] Now take your fresh and new feeling about your problem and give it space. Try to find some new words or images or pictures that capture what this feeling tries to say. Find words or images to say what you are feeling now . . . [Extended pause]

Following the focusing instructions, the counselor should ask the client to describe the words or pictures that entered awareness during the exercise. This description can be continued for the remainder of the session.

CASE ILLUSTRATION OF FOCUSING

The Case of Constance

Constance is a 26-year-old divorced woman who requested counseling to help her deal with her divorce. In the first session, she reported feeling overwhelmed by emotions and the demands of her 2-year-old daughter. She vacillated among the feelings of anger, resentment, guilt, and back to anger (usually directed at her ex-spouse). When this circular process really gained control of her, she would begin to feel stuck, caught, or lost (her words). She showed strong evidence of being rational, realistic, and in control, except for these emotional bouts. There was no past history of depression or life-threatening acts by either Constance or any other family member. She did have her good days as well as her bad days and could say that she believed this terrible time would pass eventually.

Based on this information, the counselor decided that Constance did not show suicidal tendencies but did ask her to make an appointment with her family physician for a complete physical examination. The counselor also decided that paper-and-pencil exercises were not needed because the client seemed quite able to verbalize her feelings and did not seem confused or unable to differentiate between anger and guilt. On the other hand, it did seem desirable to help Constance examine these various feelings and to find the meaning or relevance of the pattern in which they seemed to occur (anger . . . resentment . . . guilt . . . anger . . .).

By providing facilitative conditions (understanding, accurate empathy, respect), the counselor gradually produced an atmosphere in which Constance began to relax and do some self-confrontation. She was able to talk about her misgivings regarding the causes of the divorce. She began to talk about the heavy burden of single parenthood. Invariably, however, she would reach a dead end (which she referred to as an "insurmountable wall") in talking about these feelings.

After three such sessions, Constance began to feel frustrated, and the counselor suggested that they try a focusing exercise. Following an explanation of the process and its purpose, they decided together to use the next session as a focusing experiment. Constance arrived at the next session showing some nervousness, but this soon dissipated. The counselor began the focusing exercise and Constance quickly became a cooperative participant. At its completion, Constance reported that when she tried to let the anger, resentment, and guilt merge into one larger feeling, the word *responsibility* kept entering her awareness. The counselor wisely suggested that they repeat the exercise, but that Constance should focus on the responsible response this time. At the end of the second round, Constance talked with a sense of discovery about the experience.

"I think I have been running away from my responsibilities, my responsibility for the end of the marriage, my responsibility for my daughter, and most of all my responsibility for myself. In the exercise, I reached the point of 'giving these responsibilities away,' but there is no one I would want to give them to. They are too valuable to give away."

"What do you mean, they are too valuable?" the counselor asked.

"If I give them away, I must also give away my independence, my freedom to be who I am. And that is very valuable to me. I must learn to accept some of these fears about causing the divorce or not liking some parts of being a mother if I'm going to be independent. Otherwise, I'd be right back in the same place I was as a child."

Hinterkopf (1998) suggested that the focusing method "may be used for the remediation of religious and spiritual problems, the enhancement of already existing spiritual experiences, and the facilitation of new, life-giving connections to spirituality, [all of which] are essential for spiritual wellness" (pp. 2–3). She describes a six-step process by which the focusing method is introduced to clients (pp. 52–55):

1. Clearing a space. Helping the client identify problems or issues, then mentally "setting them aside" as though they were no longer present, and observing the effect of their removal
2. Getting a felt sense. Asking the client to attend to the whole complexity of the problem(s) and issues and reporting the result
3. Finding a handle. Identifying words to describe the "felt sense" of Step 2. Such words "help the client hold on to or stay in touch with the vague felt sense or 'pull it back' if awareness of it is lost"
4. Resonating. Examining the words identified in Step 3 and seeking better words to identify the felt sense, if appropriate
5. Asking. Having the client ask him- or herself, What is it about this issue (problem) that leaves me feeling this way? (Hinterkopf refers to this as "giving the felt sense a 'friendly hearing.'")
6. Receiving. Helping the client integrate the "felt shift" that occurs as a result of the focusing process, including those bodily felt changes that the client experiences

HELPING CLIENTS INTEGRATE OR CHANGE FEELING STATES

It was noted in the preceding section that people sometimes cope with emotions by creating a psychological distance from their feelings. This can happen when a person is bombarded by multiple affect reactions stemming from traumatic life situations. It can also happen when a person is confronted by a strong but unacceptable emotional situation. The result of this affect distancing is to postpone the immediate demand to respond to the affect. A normal example of this condition is the grieving process. But to postpone an adaptive demand is not a long-term solution. Thus, even the grieving individual must ultimately come to grips with the loss and alter perceptions in whatever way the loss demands.

Replacement of dysfunctional feelings or establishment of functional feelings is a complicated process. Some theorists hold that it requires a cathartic moment in which the client experiences a sudden release of bad feelings followed by a flood of emotional relief. Other theorists believe it occurs only when dysfunctional feelings are replaced by more functional feelings through conscious and rigorous efforts to identify and replace. Still other theorists believe dysfunctional feelings are present but unrecognized by the client, and only when the client becomes fully aware of these hidden feelings can they be addressed and dealt with by the client. Through this process, the counselor is an active participant, either in leading the client or responding empathically to the client so that the dysfunctional feelings can be recognized and addressed. A case illustration might illustrate this integration of new feelings.

CASE ILLUSTRATION OF INTEGRATING NEW FEELINGS

The Case of Janice

Janice is a 36-year-old attorney for a major New York bank. She graduated from law school at 26 and married Ralph when she was 32. Both she and Ralph were having such success in their careers that they were not tempted to start a family. A year ago, Janice began feeling restless and showing irritability at work and at home. When those feelings occurred, she would chastise herself and remind herself that working had been a choice based on her ambition. Finally, she had a serious conversation with Ralph and admitted that she was feeling the need to start a family. Ralph was completely supportive and proposed that she go off birth control, which she agreed to do. Several times in the past few months, however, she has intended to stop the pill and each time, she didn't.

Finally, Janice realized that she was fearful of getting pregnant and having to give up her career.

She decided to seek counseling to help resolve this conflict. A skilled professional counselor helped her realize that her career needs were related to some unmet personal needs for achievement and recognition. The issue for Janice was twofold: Should she allow these recurring feelings to be admitted into her perceptions of self and family? And if she did acknowledge these feelings, what would be the implications for her, her career, and her marriage?

Janice's situation illustrates how emotional undercurrents can intrude into a person's consciousness and disrupt emotional commitments and daily routines. It also illustrates the interrelatedness of feeling, thought, and behavior, as well as the need to come to some resolution of value conflict and incompatible emotional states.

At issue here is the nature of Janice's presenting concern. Are her issues (irritability at home and work; restlessness) associated with her career decision (cognitive), her feelings about the decision to start a family (affect), maintaining her career status (behavioral), or her relationship with Ralph (systemic)? The counselor concluded that Janice was not acknowledging feelings that were associated with giving up career ambition and replacing it with less exciting responsibilities. The counselor also surmised that Janice's decision was complicated by family values conflicts (short-term family commitment to seek employment versus long-term family commitment to have children). The counselor developed a treatment plan that would address affective issues first, with the reasoning that these conflicts are probably driving her behavior as well as her cognitive assessment of how to resolve her needs to be a mother (see Figure 8.4).

A number of counseling interventions are derived from person-centered, gestalt, and existential counseling to aid the client with such problems. In this section we shall examine role reversal, the alter-ego exercise, and the empty-chair (or two-chair) exercise, all of which may be used with Janice's problem.

Role Reversal

Role reversal is a useful exercise when a client is experiencing a conflict of values or feelings or a conflict with his or her self-image but is unable to isolate and understand the nature of the conflict. The purpose of role reversal is to project the client into a paradoxical examination of views, attitudes, or beliefs. This exercise may meet initial resistance because it asks the client to challenge safe (albeit dysfunctional) roles or attitudes. However, if the client is encouraged to try playing devil's advocate, to demonstrate that he or she is, in fact, able to discuss both sides of an issue, the exercise can be quite effective.

The counselor becomes an active participant in the role-reversal enactment. He or she must be able to identify the splits or different roles that the client is experiencing. In the following case, Vincent had come to counseling because of a problem he was having at work. The counselor soon realized that the conflict was between Vincent and his boss, and so decided to set up a role reversal to help Vincent explore all aspects of his conflict. The counselor reversed Vincent's role by having him enact an encounter as his boss. The counselor also participated in the enactment in the role of Vincent. Thus, Vincent's role was reversed.

Outpatient Treatment Plan (see Appendix B-4)

Type of Treatment: Insight/Affective, Supported by Cognitive-Behavioral

Goal #1: To help Paolo examine feelings associated with his new family status
Time frame: Two to three months
Success indicator: Paolo will be able to evaluate family and career values separately

Subgoal A: Paolo will be able to identify values associated with being a new father
Intervention strategy: Affect focusing; values clarification
Time frame: Three to six weeks
Alternate intervention/strategy: Visualization with and without new baby

Subgoal B: Paolo will be able to identify and contrast career values/family values
Intervention strategy: Role reversal (Paolo dialoguing as parent and as employee)
Time frame: Two to three weeks
Alternate intervention/strategy: Visualization as father and as successful employee

Subgoal C: Paolo's assessment of experience of values clarification and roles
Intervention strategy: Cognitive-behavioral assessment
Time frame: Two to three weeks
Alternate intervention/strategy: Homework assignment: To write a report of his life five years from now, using pretherapy motives and posttherapy goals

---

FIGURE 8.4 Counselor's Initial Treatment Plan Strategies (Paulo)

CASE ILLUSTRATION OF ROLE REVERSAL

The Case of Vincent

Vincent entered counseling for the purpose of solving "career problems." As counseling progressed, the problem became more clearly defined as an interpersonal conflict between Vincent and his boss. Vincent found it easy to explore his feelings toward his boss even though he liked his job. However, these explorations always seemed to lead up blind alleys when the counselor raised the question of solutions. Vincent would become flustered and would jump to the conclusion that the only solution was to change jobs. After this pattern repeated itself for four sessions, the counselor suggested that they try the role-reversal exercise. Vincent responded somewhat suspiciously, but after some discussion of what the exercise involved, he agreed to participate. The next session began as follows:

VINCENT: I don't know what this exercise is going to prove. Every time we discuss my problem, I end up at the same place. My boss is insensitive and completely unconcerned about my situation. He'll never change, and I'm not going to change, so the only solution is for me to look for another job.

COUNSELOR: Before we reach that conclusion, let's try the role-reversal exercise we discussed last week. It may not change anything, but at least we can say we looked at the problem every way we could imagine. Are you still game?

VINCENT: Well, I can't imagine what you have in mind, but I'll go along with whatever it is.

COUNSELOR: Good. I'd like you to play devil's advocate with your problem for a few minutes. I'd like you to imagine that you are your boss, and I'll be you, and we'll talk about the problem. Try to be as accurate as possible in your boss's role. That way, I'll have a much better idea what your boss is like. And I will try to be as accurate as possible in my role as you. If I tend to respond inaccurately, stop the exercise and give me coaching on how I should respond. Are you ready?

VINCENT: I suppose so. I know I can imitate him. I know him like the back of my hand. But I don't see how it can do any good.

COUNSELOR: Maybe you're right. Let's give it a try and see what you think. You begin as your boss.

VINCENT: Vincent, I see you have missed another deadline for the pro-duction report. What the hell's going on?

COUNSELOR: I couldn't get the information I needed, and I didn't want to bother you because you were busy yesterday.

VINCENT: What the hell do you mean, "You didn't want to bother me"? If you have to bother me to get the report done, then bother me. But don't miss another deadline. Do you understand?

COUNSELOR: Okay, okay, I hear you. But I knew you would have lost it if I interrupted you yesterday. too.

VINCENT: Look Vincent, you can't have it both ways. If you don't ask for help when you need it and that leads to missing deadlines, then you have to expect some consequence. And if anger is the consequence, then you had better understand that it is due to your avoiding me. You've got to stop avoiding me.

COUNSELOR: Well, Vincent, what do you think of that scene?

VINCENT: I guess it took an unexpected turn. His anger does upset me, but I haven't been thinking about bringing it on myself.

COUNSELOR: Do you think it might help to work on how you react to his anger?

As you can see in this illustration, Vincent acknowledges his avoidance in a safe confrontation with his boss. This acknowledgment does not mean that Vincent will return to his job with new methods for coping. It may be that counseling will move on to an exploration of how Vincent can develop new approaches to working with his boss. Or maybe he will end up changing jobs. For the moment, however, Vincent has broken through a resistance that would otherwise block the resolution of his job difficulties.

Alter Ego

This exercise is similar to role reversal, but with a novel twist. Webster's defines *alter ego* as "another side of oneself, another self." The notion is that each individual has another dimension of his or her personality that is more aware, more honest, more perceptive of personal motives, values, and hidden agendas. People's alter egos nag them when they neglect their duties or avoid their responsibilities. Thus, the alter ego knows and is a more honest report of one's inner motivations.

In this exercise, the client is asked to become his or her alter ego, and the counselor assumes the client's public self. Because the counselor must produce an accurate portrayal of the client's public self, and because the client must feel safe enough with the counselor to allow the alter ego to emerge, this exercise should not be used early in the counseling relationship. When the alter-ego exercise is effective, it allows clients to confront themselves more honestly. This kind of self-confrontation can be far more effective than confrontations by the counselor. The result is that the client can introduce issues, refute self-rationalizations, or question self-motives in a therapeutic encounter with the self. The following illustrates the use of the alter-ego exercise in a counseling setting.

CASE ILLUSTRATION OF THE ALTER EGO

The Case of Wanda

Wanda is a 35-year-old homemaker married to a 50-year-old auto mechanic. She has an 11-year-old son, Tim, by a previous marriage. Wanda entered counseling because she was concerned about Tim's emotional and academic development. Tim had been identified as a gifted child by the school he attended. However, his grades have deteriorated in the past 6 months, and this had become a source of family concern. As Wanda discussed her concerns for Tim, she would shift from her personal issues to how she felt that her husband did not recognize Tim's needs. When this occurred, she would become angry toward her spouse, and then Tim's issues would become lost.

The counselor had asked Wanda to involve the stepfather and Tim in counseling, but Wanda said her spouse refused and that Tim's school schedule would not permit his participation. The counselor wondered about these explanations, but she accepted Wanda's judgment. Because Wanda was a bright and introspective client, the counselor decided that she was a good candidate for the alter-ego exercise, which, she believed, would help Wanda better understand her own emotional reac-

tions. Wanda, who liked counseling, readily agreed to the counselor's suggestion.

COUNSELOR: In this exercise, I am going to be you, as I have come to know you. I'll try to represent you honestly and accurately. I want you to be the private Wanda, the person I don't really know yet. In this exercise, we are going to talk to each other, the public you (my role) and the private you (your role). We might even have an argument, but that's okay. Do you understand?

WANDA: I think so. I'll try.

COUNSELOR: Good, I'll go first. [as Wanda] I just don't know what to do with Tim. He is so bright, but he is wasting his ability.

WANDA: [as alter ego] You always think you ought to know what to do and you don't.

COUNSELOR: Yeah, and that's why I think Bob [husband] ought to be helping. He disappears when I need him most.

WANDA: You think Bob knows more about Tim than you do? You just don't want to be responsible for Tim.

COUNSELOR: It's not that I don't want to do it alone. I don't think I can do it alone. And besides, I want Bob and Tim to have a parent–child relationship, and that isn't happening.

WANDA: It's not happening because you won't let Bob do the important parenting jobs, like discipline.

COUNSELOR: What do you mean, "I won't let Bob be a parent"?

WANDA: I think you're afraid to let Bob be a real parent because Tim might decide he likes Bob better than he likes you. So you keep Bob away.

COUNSELOR: That's not true. Bob really doesn't love Tim enough to worry about him.

WANDA: That's not true, Wanda, and you know it. Bob loves Tim a lot. He worries about Tim. But he worries more about you and your relationship to Tim, and that's why he doesn't get involved.

COUNSELOR: I hate it when you say these things.

WANDA: I know it hurts, but you better wake up, Wanda, or you're going to lose both of them someday.

The counselor and Wanda ended the exercise at this point. Wanda had said some very self-revealing things and was beginning to show some discomfort with her revelations. The counselor sensed that Wanda was beginning to reach a saturation level, so she decided to allow her some time to integrate the ideas and feelings that had been brought up. After stopping the exercise, they took time to discuss the confrontation. During this discussion, Wanda began to relax and look more comfortable with herself. It was a very significant session and proved to be a turning point in Wanda's counseling, when she acknowledged to herself for the first time that her husband was conflicted between his love for Tim and his concern for her relationship with Tim.

The Empty Chair

The *empty chair* is a dialoguing exercise made popular by gestalt therapists but used increasingly by counselors from a wide range of orientations. It is used to help clients explore and develop awareness of subtle feelings that are not surfacing but are affecting client functioning. The exercise may be used with interpersonal issues (in which case, the enactment will be between the client and the other relevant person) or with intrapersonal issues (in which case, the enactment will be between the client and the client's other self).

The counselor begins by explaining that this is a dialogue or imaginary conversation either with oneself or with a specific person who is also involved in the client's problem. The counselor explains that his or her role will be to observe, choreograph the conversation, and at times interrupt to ask questions or share observations. If the client agrees, the next step is to define who the two principals in the conversation will be—that is, with whom the client will converse. This might be the "embarrassed self" or the "intimidated self," or it might be the client's parent, spouse, or significant other.

The counselor must be able to recognize the splits in awareness or the potential conflicts in order to define the elements of the dialogue. The next step is to explain to the client how the process works.

> In this exercise you will be both the "caring you" and the "angry you." And the two "yous" will talk it over and explore both points of view, both sides. Let's start by having the caring you explain why you don't want to talk to your parents about their decision. Then I'd like the angry you to react to the caring you. Is it clear what you will do? Remember, I'll be right here, coaching when you need help.

Greenberg (1979) refers to this arrangement as the *experiencing chair* and the *other chair*. The experiencing chair is similar to what happens in most therapeutic settings. The other chair represents the internal objects—opposing will, conflicting values, or motivations—of which the client is possibly unaware but which have a significant effect on the client's emotions, actions, and choices. The case of Paula illustrates how the counselor helps the client begin this exercise.

CASE ILLUSTRATION OF THE EMPTY CHAIR

Paula and the Empty Chair

Paula, a young woman in her mid-twenties, has just landed the job of her life. In addition to this, she is currently involved in a most fulfilling intimate relationship with another woman, Sue, who is in medical school and will be starting her residency next year. Sue has an opportunity to stay at the local hospital, but she is also exploring several opportunities to do specified residencies in other states. Paula has mixed feelings about this. On the one hand, being in love with Sue, she wants what is best for her even if that means Sue has to leave town to get the best training. On the other hand, Paula has her own interests to look out for and she doesn't want Sue to leave because the relationship is so good.

Paula wanted to explore these conflicting feelings, and so the counselor suggested the empty-chair intervention as a way to do this. When Paula agreed, the counselor described the exercise and then asked Paula which of her conflicted feelings seemed the strongest. She identified the feelings associated with Sue's leaving. Then the counselor asked Paula to begin in one chair by explaining to the empty chair across from her those feelings associated with Sue's possible departure.

PAULA 1 [WHO WANTS SUE TO STAY] TO
       PAULA 2:   I just don't want

her to go. We have such a good thing going. I don't understand why she has to leave when she could do her residency here.
[Counselor directs Paula to move to the other chair and be the other Paula]

PAULA 2 [PART WHO WANTS SUE TO DO WHAT IS BEST FOR SUE]: Well, you know the answer to that. Staying here probably isn't the best thing for her—she'll get better training somewhere else. She's so talented she needs to get the best training she can.
[Counselor moves Paula back to Chair 1]

PAULA 1: But if she really loved me, she'd stay...
[Moving to Chair 2]

PAULA 2: And if you really loved her, you'd feel freer to let her go....
[Paula starts to cry]

COUNSELOR: Let's stop a minute. What are you aware of right now, Paula?

PAULA: I feel sad, really sad.

COUNSELOR: Okay, stay with that feeling and see where it takes you.

PAULA: You mean from this chair?

COUNSELOR: Yes.

PAULA 2 [STILL WEEPING]: The sadness feels deep. It feels like I really do want to let her go—I wouldn't want her to stay just because of me—but letting go is hard for me and I do feel sad [weeps now more easily].

COUNSELOR: Try to accept how you are feeling and allow it to exist for a little while. [silence]

After a few minutes, Paula began to talk again. Although she didn't feel wonderful, she felt much clearer about her feelings and her position on this issue.

Note that the counselor directed Paula's awareness to her feelings and then encouraged her to be accepting of the feelings that were aroused.

There are two distinct advantages to be derived from the empty-chair technique: (1) Paula's defenses that characterize the conflicting elements tend to diminish as she enacts the dialogue, thus permitting her to see elements of the relationship that she could not easily let herself see, and (2) Paula is able to accept two seemingly incompatible feelings and say to herself, Both of these feelings are me.

Dream Work

A number of counseling approaches, including psychoanalysis, gestalt therapy, individual (Adlerian) therapy, and analytical (Jungian) therapy, use dreams in the therapeutic process. In some cases, the dream content is taken as relevant insight into the client's psyche. In other cases, the dream is a metaphor to be used in the session to explore alternative realities. This can be illustrated through the gestalt treatment of dreams in which the client is asked to explore the different elements of a dream to search for or allow awareness to emerge. The meaning of the various elements of the dream is always provided by the client.

There are several guidelines to follow while working with dreams:

1. As a first step, have the client describe the dream from beginning to end without interruption.
2. Describe the procedure for role-playing the dream (dialoguing).
3. If the client appears uncertain about the process, give an example.
4. Be the director of the role-play. Ask the client to be each of the several parts of the dream.
5. Proceed with different parts of the dream in the order of their occurrence in the dream.
6. Do not allow yourself to make interpretations of the elements of the dream. Only the client can do that. Ask the client if he or she can find any relationships. If not, proceed to the next part of the dream.

The use of dream work is an advanced technique that is probably best used only by the more experienced counselor.

CLIENT REACTIONS TO AFFECTIVE INTERVENTIONS

The point was made at the beginning of this chapter that many clients lack the introspective and interpersonal skills to express their feelings accurately and adequately. This does not mean that they do not experience feelings, nor does it mean that they do not need to express their feelings.

The inability to express what one is feeling is often experienced as a pressure-cooker effect in which bottled-up emotions accumulate and add to a person's tensions and anxiety. Eventually, the emotions find an outlet, either through psychosomatic illness, substance abuse, physical violence, temper tantrums, or some other socially destructive expression.

Given this kind of condition and its very limited alternatives, most clients experience relief at the expression of feeling states. Some also feel a kind of embarrassment, as though they have broken some unwritten rule about their behavior. The counselor can soften this effect by normalizing the feeling. To normalize is to point out that this reaction is a normal reaction and will pass. Occasionally, a client will continue, almost without limits, to talk about current or old feelings. It is as though an emotional dam has finally been broken. With white middle-class clients, the most common client response is a sense of relief, catharsis, and renewal that can lead to further change. Clients of some minority cultures in which the expression of feelings is not part of the culture's values will not find a sense of relief and may, in fact, experience intense personal embarrassment.

Culture will be a major consideration in determining client reactions to affective interventions. Clients of nonwestern cultural backgrounds may be less inclined to express or even work on feelings. Indeed, it may go against a client's cultural values to express feelings openly or even to view feelings alteration as the solution to personal problems. In such cases, it would be far better for the counselor to use interventions described in following chapters with these clients.

Summary

In this chapter, we have examined the very complex subject of human emotions and their expression. You may think of affective interventions as efforts to aid clients in the expression of their innermost fears, hopes, hurts, resentments, and frustrations. Such expression often involves teaching clients how to express their feelings, and helping them to give themselves permission to express emotions. At another level, you may work with clients who are able to express emotions but who are unable to sort out or conceptualize what they feel. Finally, at the most complex level, you may become involved in helping clients either to accept or integrate affect states or to change affect states.

Whatever your involvement might be, it is vitally important to recognize that human emotions are central to human functioning. Consequently, when therapists work with emotions, they are working near the core of most human beings' reality. Thus, therapists are creating and walking through what amounts to a highly vulnerable passage for clients. Respect for this condition, and appreciation that clients invite professional helpers into their inner world, is both appropriate and essential.

Exercises

I. Understanding Feelings

Choose a partner. One of you will be the speaker; the other will be the listener. The speaker should select one of the four emotions identified (positive affect, anger, fear, and emotional pain) and communicate that feeling state to the other person. The listener should record on paper all verbal and nonverbal cues observed but should not respond to the speaker. After 3 to 5 minutes, the exercise should be concluded, and the listener should identify the speaker's feeling state and the cues that support that choice. Check with the speaker to verify your choice.

II. Identifying Feelings

The following is an exercise in verbal affect identification. Identify the feeling state(s) in each of the four client communications, which have been taken from actual counseling interviews. If more than one feeling state is present in the client response, place an asterisk (*) next to the one that you believe has the greatest bearing on the client's concern. After identifying the feeling states, discuss your choices with other class members.

    A. "Well, uh, I'm happy just being in with people and having them know me."

    B. "And, and, uh, you know, they always say that, you know, some people don't like to be called by a number; well, I don't either."

    C. "In speech, I'm, uh, well, in speech, I'm not doing good because I'm afraid to talk in front of a bunch of people."

    D. "It seems to me like working in that lab is really harmful; I mean, I enjoy my work, and the people, but that lab, that worries me."

III. Practicing the Process

This exercise is to be done in triads. One of you is the first respondent, another one is the listener, and the third is the observer/recorder. Rotate all roles twice so each person is in each of the three roles.

Listed below are some incomplete sentences. The observer's role is to feed each sentence to the respondent and to record the respondent's response. The respondent's task is to respond as quickly as possible without thinking. If, as the respondent, you can't come up with a response, just say, "Blah, blah, blah." The listener's job is simply to face the respondent directly—watch, listen, and receive. After you have completed each round, give the respondent time to observe and process his or her affective states.

Incomplete sentences:

_____ 1. Something I want you to know about me is….

_____ 2. Something I don't want you to know about me is….

_____ 3. Being angry for me is….

_____ 4. When I'm angry, I just want to….

_____ 5. Being sad for me is….

_____ 6. When I'm sad, I just want to….

_____ 7. Right now I'm feeling….

Discussion Questions

1. Does any part of working with clients' affective states worry you? How?

2. Two goals of affective interventions are (1) to help the client express feeling states and (2) to help the client identify and discriminate between feeling states. This implies that clients may be able to express feelings but still not be able to identify or sort out those feelings. Do you think this is possible? Isn't it likely that the expression of a feeling carries with it the awareness of what it is? Discuss this with other classmates or colleagues.

3. Which nonverbal cues communicate anger? Do these same cues communicate some other emotion? If yes, what emotion? How would you know which emotion is being communicated?

4. What are the potential therapeutic gains when using role reversal with a client? What kinds of clients might not be able to participate effectively in a role-reversal exercise?

MyCounselingLab Assignment

Go to the Video Resource Library on the MyCounselingLab site for your text and search for the following clips:

- **Family Systems Connecting Feelings and Behaviors** What is the client's difficulty in espressing feelings? How does the counselor help the client identify the block to his expression of feelings? Do you know anyone who also has this difficulty expressing her or his feelings?

- **Gestalt Child: Role-Play** How does the counselor engage this child to talk about his feelings? What is the "role" she asks him to use? What is the child's reaction to the counselor's efforts?

9

Cognitive Interventions

PURPOSE OF THIS CHAPTER

How many times have you gotten yourself in trouble by thinking too much? Or by talking to yourself? Or because you had a bad attitude? This chapter examines the ways that clients think themselves into problems and describes interventions that the counselor can use to reverse this situation. These interventions address mistaken beliefs, attitudes, or patterns of thinking and give the client the tools to change to more productive and accurate thoughts. Some cognitive interventions are quite simple. Others (e.g., the paradox) can be quite sophisticated. In this chapter, we describe a variety of interventions and the manner in which they are applied in counseling.

Considerations as You Read This Chapter

■ Many people apparently find it difficult to differentiate between their thoughts and their feelings. It is fairly common to hear a person say, "I feel like you're right," when the more accurate statement is, "I think you are right." A lot of thinking people have mislabeled their thoughts as feelings. Is this also the case with you?

■ Thinking is a very special capability that human beings possess. But it also can be misused. When this happens, people can become depressed, physically ill, even suicidal. How does one get out of such difficulties? How does one get into these difficulties in the first place?

■ What skills does a skilled counselor need to be able to help people who have thought themselves into trouble?

C ognitions include people's thoughts, beliefs, and attitudes toward themselves and others, and their perceptions of the world around them. Many people would say that cognitions determine who they are, what they do, and how they feel. This view holds that errors in thinking, sometimes called faulty thinking, are especially likely to produce distressing emotions and/or problematic behavior. For example, the person who expects to fail prepares herself for failure, and the result is that she approaches life events from a failure orientation. With this much going against her, the probability is great that this person will fail. She could be described as having low self-esteem or lack of confidence, but, in fact, she is approaching life with a self-defeating mentality, an "I don't think I can do it" life view. This type of person may benefit from strategies that focus primarily on changing beliefs, attitudes, and perceptions about self and others.

The application of cognitive therapeutic interventions is extensive. They have been applied as the primary intervention for problems such as anxiety reduction, stress management, anger control, habit control, obesity, depression, phobic disorders, and sexual dysfunction. Characteristics of clients who seem to have the most success with cognitive interventions include:

- Persons of average to above-average intelligence
- Persons with moderate to high levels of functional distress
- Persons with the ability to identify feelings and thoughts
- Persons who are not in a state of crisis, psychotic, or severely debilitated by the problem
- Persons possessing an adequate repertoire of skills or behavioral responses
- Persons who can process information visually or aurally
- Persons whose cultural orientation is toward analytical activity

THEORIES THAT STRESS THE IMPORTANCE OF COGNITIVE PROCESSES

Most of the cognitive approaches to counseling and psychotherapy address rational processes and derive from the philosophical school known as essentialism. They include theories such as rational emotive behavior therapy (REBT) (Dryden & Ellis, 2001; Ellis & Wilde, 2002), cognitive therapy (Beck, 1995), and transactional analysis (Berne, 1964; Harris, 1967). In addition, some include the constructivist approach in this group of theories, noting that the constructivist perspective views individuals as complex beings who continually adapt their thoughts as a way to create meaning out of the world (Neukrug, 2007).

Whether traditional or constructivist, the emphasis on thoughts and thought processes is the common thread of cognitive therapy. Thus, interventions that are designed to alter thought processes are defined as cognitive interventions.

In recent years, the strong linkage between thoughts and behaviors has been translated into an approach called cognitive-behavioral therapy. This is because change in thinking is only observed when behavior changes. On the other hand, a change in behavior does not necessarily require a change in thought. For the purpose of learning how to counsel, we believe it makes better sense to separate cognitive from behavioral practices.

GOALS OF COGNITIVE INTERVENTION

The overall aim of any cognitive intervention is to reduce emotional distress and corresponding maladaptive behavior patterns by altering or correcting errors in thought, perceptions, and beliefs. Changes in behavior or feelings occur once the client's distorted thinking begins to change and is replaced by alternative, more realistic ways of thinking about self, other persons, or life experiences. Thus, a cognitive intervention is intended to alter a client's manner of thinking about a particular event; person; self; or, in the larger context, life. Clients are viewed as direct agents of their own changes rather than as helpless victims of external events and forces over which they have little control although there are some cognitive interventions that help clients by nudging them out of habitual ways of thinking. Isn't this a little bit like mind control or brainwashing? No. With cognitive interventions, the issue of responsibility always remains with the client. That can happen only when the client chooses to think a particular way or to change the way he or she is thinking about something. This even includes choosing to participate in a cognitive intervention as part of the counseling strategy.

CULTURE AND COGNITIVE PROCESSES

Culture embraces how people think about themselves and how they view (think about) the world. Culture and cognition are very closely related. People's thought processes, especially when considered within a cultural context, are powerful and pervasive. They affect how one feels about oneself, one's behavior, and one's relationships with others. Cognitive processes reflect one's cultural determinants more than feelings, behavior, or even interaction with other persons. When a counselor works with clients of differing cultures, the differentiations that must be made involve understanding the difference between those cognitions that are culturally determined (thus shared by others in that culture) and the cognitions that are unique to a specific client. In addition, the counselor must strive to understand how the client's cultural cognitions affect his or her feelings, behavior, and interactions with others. Cognitive patterns can change, but when they are as fundamental as one's cultural values and beliefs, they are more resistant to change. Indeed, it is ethically questionable whether the counselor should embark on such change.

ASSESSMENT OF COGNITIVE PROBLEMS

Cognitive strategies rely heavily on a particular manner of problem assessment. We shall begin with the assumption that people construct their reality based on their childhood experiences, their beliefs, and their resultant attitudes. Some of that construction is distorted if a person's perceptions of self or others are distorted. Why would anyone distort perceptions? People learn these distortions from their parents, their peer groups, their teachers, and/or their cultural groups. They then apply these distortions, along with their more accurate perceptions, to their view of reality. Cognitive distortion assessment requires that the counselor and client, together, analyze these perceptions, looking for the flaws, errors, or inaccuracies that underlie one's conclusions. Only at that point can cognitive interventions be applied to change errors in thinking, repair cognitive flaws, or correct inaccuracies.

In a format similar to an in-take assessment, Judith Beck (1995) has developed a series of questions for the counselor to use in defining the nature of the client's presenting cognitive distortion(s).

- What is the client's "core belief"?
- What experiences contributed to the development/maintenance of this core belief?
- What is the client's most central belief about self?
- What positive belief/assumption helps the client cope with the core belief?
- What negative belief(s) counter this assumption?
- What behaviors help the client cope with the core belief?

- What is the immediate problematic situation that reveals the cognitive distortion?
- What goes through the client's mind in this problematic situation?
- What is the client's meaning of the automatic thought(s) under these circumstances?
- What emotion does the client associate with the automatic thought(s)?
- What is the client's (behavioral) reaction to these thoughts? (p. 126)

Cognitive Skills

The cognitive approaches to counseling involve a set of counselor skills and strategies that are designed to recognize and help clients recognize thought patterns, to assess the relationships between client thinking and client problems, to help clients confront unproductive thinking and replace it with productive or positive thoughts, and to provide clients with strategies for maintaining and strengthening productive thinking. The basic assumption that the counselor begins with is that clients acquire faulty thinking habits or patterns without recognizing the effects of those thought patterns. As a result, they are unable to correct life problems without changing the thought patterns that support those problems.

The counselor's challenge lies in recognizing faulty thinking as the client presents it and helping the client recognize the patterns as faulty, too. But awareness of faulty thinking doesn't lead to change; rather, the counselor then must help the client implement strategies that will effect change. This is done through various assignments and exercises that are designed to stop faulty thinking and replace it with productive thoughts.

Cognitive Intervention Skills

Cognitive Skills

Eliciting Thoughts

Helping the client to differentiate between thoughts and feelings and to express opinions, beliefs, self-rules, and so on

Modifying Thoughts

Helping the client to change thought patterns when it is deemed appropriate

Problem Solving

Helping the client to identify how he or she solves problems, evaluating those processes, and developing more effective problem-solving strategies

Information Giving

Determining what information the client requires to make sound decisions and helping the client obtain that information

Decision Making

Helping the client to develop sound decision-making practices

Cognitive Interventions

A-B-C-D Analysis

A (activating event), B (belief system), C (consequence), D (disruption). Helping the client to analyze his or her thought patterns

Disputation

Challenging the client's thought and behavior processes by confronting assumptions and practices

Decibels and Countering Interventions

Identifying and replacing or disputing thoughts that are linked to disturbing feelings

Redecision Work

Examining injunctions the client received as a child (e.g., "Don't be a child") and making a conscious decision whether to continue following those injunctions as an adult

Cognitive Restructuring

Helping the client to identify and replace negative self-statements

Thought Stopping Helping the client to develop ways of halting destructive or unproductive thoughts about self and others	***Reframing*** Helping the client to recognize more constructive or realistic interpretations to events that he or she formerly interpreted negatively
Positive Self-Talk Showing the client ways to replace his or her negative self-talk with positive (confidence-building) self-talk	***Symptom Prescription*** Confronting the client's apparent lack of control over problems by having the client initiate the problem
Anchoring Helping the client to replace unsupportive reactions to situations with positive or supportive responses to those situations	***Resisting Therapeutic Change*** Suggesting to the client that change may not happen readily or may not be lasting

ELICITING THOUGHTS. One of the counselor's tasks is to understand how clients determine meaning in their lives. From a constructivist perspective, this includes how one interprets life events, circumstances, and interactions. The age-old question of whether the glass is half full or half empty captures this idea of meaning. It is human nature to try to make sense of life, but the sense that is made may be close to reality or it may have little relationship to reality, depending on the individual's logic and faithfulness to detail and observation.

Consequently, it is important to draw out the client's thoughts, interpretations, and conclusions about life events in order to examine their relationship to "reality." Eliciting client thoughts is really no different from eliciting client feelings. The basic skills described in Chapter 2—reflecting, paraphrasing, and summarizing—are used to understand the client's cognitive processes. Similarly, the affective intervention skills of Chapter 8 are adaptable to cognitive exploration, that is, identifying thought patterns, sorting out thoughts, and helping the client focus on logical conclusions.

MODIFYING THOUGHTS. Thought modification involves changing stabilized thought patterns. Everyone has natural or habitual responses to recurring situations. And, for most people, some of those patterns do not follow logically from event to reaction. When this happens, it can lead to undesired consequences, whether turning on oneself, assuming defeat, or feeling unloved.

PROBLEM SOLVING. Humans learn how to solve problems. Some acquire excellent problem-solving skills, others use hit-or-miss strategies, and some simply "fold" when faced with a problem to be solved. Yet problem solving is a critical skill in life. The counselor often encounters clients who have developed either poor or inadequate problem-solving skills. Counseling, then, involves helping the client to learn effective problem-solving skills.

INFORMATION GIVING. Although counselors are frequently cautioned not to become advice givers, they are sometimes called on to become information givers. It is important to be able to make the distinction between advice and information. It is also important to help the client find needed information. But there are occasions when counseling involves the giving of information, career counseling being a case in point.

DECISION MAKING. Decision making is an assessment process that leads to a commitment. Alternatives are weighed, consequences are considered, personal investment is examined, and willingness to commit is evaluated. Even at this point, there is the final move from one course of action to another course of action. Many clients find the several points along this process to be troublesome and even blocking in nature. The counselor will frequently encounter clients who are struggling with or blocked in some way from making decisions that even they acknowledge are the right course of action.

COGNITIVE INTERVENTION STRATEGIES

Several different strategies for change have come from cognitive and clinical psychology. Most of them are exercises that help the client modify existing thought patterns, remind the client to avoid undesirable thoughts, or even help the client assess events more constructively. These strategies derive primarily from the work of Albert Ellis and Aaron Beck, pioneers in the cognitive therapy movement.

A-B-C-D Analysis

The A-B-C-D analysis is a cognitive strategy associated with rational-emotive therapy. This approach was created in the 1950s by Albert Ellis, who developed a formula for counselors to follow as they analyze the client's patterns of thought. A represents the activating event that begins the faulty thinking pattern; B is the client's belief system through which all life experiences are filtered; C represents the consequence, emotional or cognitive, that is produced by the interaction of A and B. These three steps represent the analysis portion of the formula. Once the cognitive errors have been detected, the counselor moves on to the therapeutic intervention, which involves disputation (D) of the irrational beliefs or thought patterns.

Differentiating between rational and irrational beliefs is the responsibility of the counselor. Rational beliefs are those that are truly consistent with reality—in the sense that they can be supported with data, facts, and/or evidence and would be substantiated by a group of objective observers. Rational beliefs may result in moderate levels of consequence (Cs), or emotional consequences, and are useful in helping people attain their goals. Irrational beliefs, on the other hand, are those that are not supported by reality through data, facts, and/or evidence and would not be substantiated by a group of objective observers.

Most irrational beliefs are reflected in one or more of Ellis's 11 irrational beliefs (see Figure 9.1). According to Ellis, people both create and maintain unnecessary emotional distress by continually reindoctrinating themselves with their irrational beliefs. Self-indoctrination is analogous to playing a recording in one's head again and again until the recording's contents are the only reality the person knows. In the A-B-C-D analysis, the client learns to recognize activating events (A), corresponding beliefs about the event (B) that are in one's head, and the emotional-behavioral consequences (C) of interpreting the activating event by using the irrational belief(s). The counselor then teaches the client a variety of ways to dispute (D) the emotional beliefs that are leading to the consequence and to replace these irrational beliefs with more accurate and rational beliefs. An example of the irrational thinking is illustrated in the following description of the case of Alan.

1. I believe I must be loved or approved of by virtually everyone with whom I come in contact.
2. I believe I should be perfectly competent, adequate, and achieving to be considered worthwhile.
3. Some people are bad, wicked, or villainous, and therefore should be blamed and punished.
4. It is a terrible catastrophe when things are not as I would want them to be.
5. Unhappiness is caused by circumstances that are out of my control.
6. Dangerous or fearsome things are sources of great concern and their possibility for harm should be a constant concern for me.
7. It is easier to avoid certain difficulties and responsibilities than it is to face them.
8. I should be dependent to some extent on other persons and should have some person on whom I can rely to take care of me.
9. Past experiences and events are what determine my present behavior; the influence of the past cannot ever be erased.
10. I should be quite upset over other people's problems and disturbances.
11. There is always a right or perfect solution to every problem, and it must be found or the results will be catastrophic.

FIGURE 9.1   Ellis's 11 Irrational Beliefs About Life

The Case of Alan

Alan entered counseling with the complaint that he feared that he would never get a job. He has a bachelor's degree in business administration and was hired out of college by a major sports equipment company as a sales representative. For 6 years, Alan was successful and received an annual salary bonus. Fourteen months ago he was let go from his job when the company downsized, with the explanation that the economy forced the company to tighten its operations. Alan received unemployment insurance benefits for 6 months while he searched for an equivalent position with other sports companies. He had no successful contacts and was running out of money to pay for his rent and monthly expenses. Finally, he took a job as a part-time salesman in a local liquor store. This cost him his unemployment benefits, and he moved in with his parents. During this time, Alan's efforts to find a new job have decreased and he has become increasingly discouraged that he will be able to find full-time employment.

In the first session, the counselor encouraged Alan to describe his employment dreams as well as his fears. Each time he was directed to identify a dream, Alan froze and shrugged his shoulders in defeat. Finally, the counselor asked Alan to describe his job with the sporting goods company and his job with the liquor store and identify the similarities and differences. Alan was able to go into detail with this exercise, and gradually the picture began to emerge that what Alan valued was a degree of autonomy, challenge, potential for growth, and a chance to set goals for himself. The counselor then asked Alan if he no longer felt able to set personal goals and he said yes.

The second session was spent discussing how Alan could use his skills of personal goal setting to help him emerge from this job discouragement he found himself in. Throughout the session, Alan seemed unable to extract himself from the countless failures he had experienced during the past 12 months. Finally, he said, "I just don't think I'm good enough or competitive enough to land a job in this environment."

Getting to the A

The activating event is usually some obnoxious or unfortunate situation or person in the client's life, and often the presence of this situation or person is part of what prompts the client to come for counseling. A client may say, "I've lost my competitive edge in the marketing world," or

"Potential employers do not see me as competitive with younger applicants." In helping clients identify the A, it is important for them to understand that this external situation or event does not cause their feelings (which are their reactions to how the external situation makes them feel).

It is also important to discriminate between activating events that can be changed and those that cannot. For those that can be changed, clients can use good problem-solving skills to bring about change. For those situations that are outside the client's control, it is important to focus on reactions to the event rather than the event itself.

Getting to the C

The emotional consequences of the activating event are often what propel the client into counseling. People cannot tolerate bad or uncomfortable feelings too long, and if such feelings persist, they may be motivated to seek outside assistance. Examples of emotional consequences that lead clients into counseling include guilt, long-term anger, fear, depression, and anxiety.

To identify the C accurately, the counselor must be alert to the presence of affect words that the client uses and the supporting body language or nonverbal cues indicative of emotion. The counselor then proceeds to ask the client what he or she is saying to him- or herself about the activating event. Often, this question must be asked several times before the client begins to realize what the message is. In particular, clients often fail to realize the self-evaluative component of the message (i.e., "My failure to find a job with the same status of the one I lost is a huge discouragement to me, and, therefore, I will be unhappy as long as I work in a place with lesser status").

Getting to the B

Identifying the B, or the client's belief system, is a major focus of this particular therapeutic intervention. The client's beliefs about a specific activating event may be exhibited in one of two forms—rational beliefs (RBs) or irrational beliefs (IBs). Both RBs and IBs represent a client's evaluations of reality and self.

Rational beliefs are truly consistent with a person's reality in the sense that they can be supported with data, facts, and/or other evidence and would be substantiated by a group of objective observers. Rational beliefs result in moderate levels of consequences and tend not to be destructive. It is irrational beliefs that cause people problems. As a person accumulates more IBs, that person becomes more troubled, not realizing that it is his or her belief system that is the source of the problem.

Disputing (D) Irrational Beliefs

Generally, clients have to be convinced that their belief systems are at the root of their problems. This is done by questioning and challenging the conclusions they have drawn regarding a particular event. Even when challenged, deeply committed irrational thinking must be addressed again and again until it transforms from "I feel defeated by my job status" to "I choose to feel defeated by my job status." At the point of recognizing choice, the client gains control of the situation and is free to choose a different reaction. The goal of disputation is twofold:

1. To eliminate the irrational beliefs
2. To acquire and internalize a new, more rational belief system

To achieve these goals, disputation occurs in two stages: First, a sentence-by-sentence examination and challenge of any irrational beliefs must take place; second, the irrational belief system must be replaced by a more rational and self-constructive belief system. Disputation can take any of three forms. It can be cognitive, or based on one's thoughts; imaginal, or drawing on one's fantasies of how life is; or behavioral, based on events that happen to the client.

The following case about James illustrates how A-B-C-D analysis can be used with a case that extends over a period of time. The client was seen weekly for approximately 20 sessions.

CASE ILLUSTRATION OF A-B-C-D ANALYSIS

The Case of James

James is a 30-year-old Ph.D. student who hopes to complete his degree in the next year and find a position as a college professor, preferably in a southern state. He came to the United States with his Vietnamese family when he was 8 years old. James has a younger brother and two younger sisters. As the oldest male in the family, James always had a privileged position in the family and with that felt a heavy responsibility to be, in his words, "the perfect son."

James was an excellent student during his early school years, and his parents sent him to private school for high school, an expense that strained the family budget. He received a full scholarship to attend a highly regarded eastern college, but he performed poorly and lost the scholarship his junior year. After that time, James was riddled with shame and felt he could never face his parents again. That was when the headaches began, and through the remainder of James's college education, they intensified and were ultimately diagnosed as migraine.

When James finally sought counseling on the advice of his neurologist, he found it to be an oppressive experience and almost terminated after two sessions. His counselor finally convinced him to continue, indicating that the migraines would never get better with medication alone. At that point, James committed to a serious effort with counseling. He reported that, in addition to the headaches, he experienced frequent bouts of depres-

sion. At this point, the counselor suspected James's issues were caused by what he was doing cognitively and proposed that they use a tool called the A-B-C-D analysis to track James' thought patterns.

The counselor began with an assignment that had James identify any situations that he believed might be contributing to his emotional distress. James immediately said, "If I hadn't screwed up in undergraduate school, I'd still have my parents' respect." At this point, the counselor helped James explore that statement and determine whether he had the power to change. He said that was why he continued with his doctoral studies, but when he returned home for holidays, he felt that his parents were still waiting for him to fall on his face again. This would always lead to intense migraines that lasted the whole visit. Thus, it was out of his power to change if his parents didn't change first. The counselor confronted James at this point: "But you're doing well in a very challenging doctoral program, aren't you?" to which he had to agree. The counselor pointed out to James that he was carrying two contradictory visions, James the failure, and James the scholar. Using the A-B-C-D method, the counselor began to help James recognize when his thoughts would sabotage him and how his mind would take on a pattern that inevitably led to his expectation of failure, depression, and migraine attack.

At this point, the counselor and James are ready to spend some time working with his beliefs, thoughts, or internal self-talk. The counselor reiterates that some beliefs can cause unnecessary levels of emotional distress, particularly those beliefs that are self-defeating or that cannot be supported by external evidence. The counselor gives some examples of James's irrational beliefs and then contrasts them with more rational or self-enhancing beliefs. When faced with a new academic challenge, James immediately returned to his sophomoric failure (the *Activating Event*). Thoughts such as "I'm a failure" and "It's my fault my parents no longer have faith in me" (his *Belief System*) are presented to James as self-defeating and inaccurate. They lead James to stress levels that bring on his migraines (*Consequence*). Thoughts such as "I screwed up in college, but that doesn't mean the future has failed" and "I lost a full scholarship but I am still intact" would be more consistent with external evidence and thus more rational (*Disputation*). The counselor also has James practice saying to himself, Just because I almost flunked out does not mean I have to feel terribly upset and depressed.

As James grew increasingly able to dispute his irrational beliefs without the counselor's interventions and to make a shift to different feelings and responses in his imagination, the counselor introduced systematic homework assignments designed to help James think and behave in new ways in his real-life environment. Through these homework assignments and his continued discussions with the counselor, James became increasingly skilled at recognizing the vulnerable trouble spots in his belief system and was able to replace them with more rational self-statements. As this process unfolded, he also realized that he was more comfortable and in greater self-control when he was in his cognitive context as opposed to his affective context. Counseling was terminated when James decided he was able to advance his progress on his own.

Cognitive Disputation

Cognitive disputation makes use of persuasion, direct questions, and logical reasoning to help clients dispute their irrational beliefs. This is one of the few times in counseling where why questions are useful. Cognitive disputation is driven by specific types of questioning, such as:

Is that good logic?

Is that true? Why not?

Can you prove it?

Why is that so?

Could you be overgeneralizing?

What do you mean by that term?

If a friend held that (self-defeating) idea, would you accept it?

In what way?

Is that very good proof?

Explain to me why. . . (e.g., you're so stupid; you don't belong in college).

What behaviors can you marshal as proof?

Why does it have to be so?

Where is that written?

Can you see the inconsistency in your beliefs?

What would that mean about you as a person?

Does that follow logically?

What's wrong with the notion that you're special?

How would you be destroyed if you don't. . .?

Why must you?

Let's assume the worst. You're doing very bad things. Why must you not do them?

Where's the evidence?

What would happen if. . .?

Can you stand it?

As long as you believe that, how will you feel?

Let's be scientists. What do the data show?

Counselors who use cognitive disputation need to recognize that this method can lead to client defensiveness. Counselors who rely on this disputation method need to be sensitive to resulting client responses, particularly to their nonverbal cues. It is important to realize that clients may have difficulty with the disputation process because they are unable to discriminate between irrational and rational beliefs. When this occurs, persistence is called for, often supplemented by counselor modeling of the difference between an irrational and a rational belief.

Imaginal Disputation

Imaginal disputation relies on client imagery, and particularly on a technique known as rational-emotive imagery (REI). This intervention is based on the assumption that the emotional consequences of *imagery* stimuli are similar to those produced by real stimuli. There are two ways this intervention can be applied. First, clients imagine themselves in the problem situation (the A) and then try to experience their usual emotional turmoil (the C). Clients are instructed to signal to the counselor (usually with a raised index finger) when this occurs. As soon as they signal, the counselor asks them to focus on the internal sentences they are saying to themselves (usually irrational). Next, the counselor instructs them to change their feelings from extreme to moderate. The counselor points out that, in doing this, they are making the cognitive shift they need to make in real life.

In the second application of REI, clients are asked to imagine themselves in the problematic situation, and then to imagine themselves feeling or behaving differently in this situation. As soon as they get an image of different feelings and behavior, they are instructed to signal to the counselor. The counselor then asks them to notice what they were saying or thinking to themselves in order to produce different feelings and responses. The counselor points out that these are the kinds of sentences or beliefs they need to use in real-life situations to produce different effects.

REI is an excellent therapeutic technique for taking rational ideas and mental pictures that initially "feel wrong" and making them quickly start feeling right. Specialists recommend that, for maximum results, clients use REI several times daily for at least a week or two.

Counselors who use REI may do well to forewarn clients not to expect instant success and to remember to be patient with themselves, even to the point of expecting the new feelings and responses generated during the imagery to feel a little strange at first. Some clients may report that distracting thoughts intrude during REI. In these instances, it is usually helpful to encourage clients to let these thoughts pass and ignore them, but not force the distracting thoughts out of their awareness. Other clients may report difficulty doing REI work because they cannot generate clear and vivid images during the imagery process. The production of strong images is not crucial to the success of the technique, as long as clients continue to focus on rational self-talk and on expected new feelings and behaviors as intensely as possible during their daily practice sessions. Also, clients who cannot picture rational self-talk and new feelings and behaviors can be instructed to think about these aspects of the process instead.

Behavioral Disputation

In *behavioral disputation*, the client issues a challenge to irrational beliefs by behaving in different ways, often in the opposite manner from previous ways of responding. Ultimately, behavioral disputation is almost crucial if the client's adoption of a more rational philosophy is to result in behavior change. Behavioral disputation usually takes the form of bibliotherapy (reading books and self-help manuals) and systematic homework assignments that involve both written and in vivo practice. Two specific disputation interventions are desibels and countering.

Desibels Intervention

The desibels intervention (*desibels* stands for "DESensitizing Irrational BELiefS") is used to help clients become aware of disturbances in thinking, which simultaneously eliminates consequent distressing feelings. The intervention is usually introduced during the counseling session and then assigned as daily homework. Clients are asked to spend 10 minutes each day asking themselves the following five questions and to either write their responses on paper or record them:

1. What irrational belief do I want to desensitize and reduce?

2. What evidence exists for the falseness of this belief?
3. What evidence exists for the truth of this belief?
4. What are the worst things that could actually happen to me if I don't get what I think I must (or if I do get what I think I must not)?
5. What good things could I make happen if I don't get what I think I must (or if I get what I think I must not)?

The desibels intervention may be more effective if daily compliance is followed by some form of client self-reinforcement, such as engaging in an enjoyable activity.

Countering Intervention

Countering involves activities such as having the client identify and state thoughts that argue against any self-defeating ideas, even aggressively, if necessary.

Countering Intervention

The *countering intervention* involves a process similar to desibels. Clients are asked to identify, both orally and in writing, counterarguments for each of their significant irrational or problematic beliefs, using the following six "rules."

1. Counters must directly contradict the false belief. For example, if the irrational belief is, "I'm a failure if my wife leaves me," a contradicting counter would be, "My wife's behavior is independent of my own success and accomplishments."

2. Counters are believable statements of reality. For example, a reasonable or believable statement of reality is, "I don't have to get straight *As* in high school in order to get a reasonably good job," whereas "I don't have to go to high school to get a reasonably good job" is not.

3. Develop as many counters as possible in order to counteract the effects that the irrational beliefs have produced over time.

4. Counters are created and owned by the client. The counselor's role in developing counters is limited to coaching. This rule is important because clients are likely to be more invested in counters that they themselves generate. Also, effective counters are often highly idiosyncratic to specific clients.

5. Counters must be concise. Lengthy, long-winded counters are easily forgotten. The most effective counters can be summarized in a few words.

6. Counters must be stated with assertive and emotional intensity. It has been suggested that if the client attempts a counter but is unconvincing, the counselor should have the client first repeat the counter nasally; then mechanically (without feeling); and then with vigor, filling her or his lungs with air and vehemently stating the new belief. This helps make an indelible memory for the client.

After counters are developed, clients practice them in counseling and at home until they convince themselves of the wisdom of the counter. When this has occurred, their thinking pattern has changed from an irrational and dysfunctional thought to a rational and highly functional thought.

INJUNCTIONS AND REDECISION WORK

Transactional analysis (TA) offers another type of cognitive intervention called the *injunction*. An injunction is defined as a parental-like message (verbal and/or behavioral) that tells children what they have to do and be in order to survive and to get recognition and approval. According to TA, children make early decisions based on the kinds of injunctions they have been taught about life. Although many of these early learned injunctions were appropriate for the situations in which children were taught, they are often inappropriate when carried into adulthood and applied to dissimilar situations. This cognitive TA intervention is meant to help clients become aware of the specific injunctions they accepted as children, to reexamine the effect of the intervention(s) for an adult, and then to decide whether they want to continue living according to the injunction(s) or to make a new decision. In the application of this technique, specific attention is given to thoughts or beliefs that accompany the long-ago learned injunction that may no longer be true or valid. These are then replaced (with the client's help) by new or different beliefs and thoughts that are needed to support a new decision.

Transactional Analysis Injunction

The injunction intervention uses the following counselor monologue with clients:

1. When you were growing up—say, between the ages of 4 and 8—what things did Mom say to you that sounded negative or bad to do?

2. Now recall anything that Dad said to you that sounded negative or bad to do.

3. From the following list of injunctions, recall two or three that were used most frequently in your home when you were growing up:

Don't

Don't be

Don't be close

Don't be important

Don't be a child

Don't grow

Don't succeed

Don't be you

Don't be sane

Don't be well

Don't belong

Don't feel

4. Select one of these injunctions. Write or talk about the decision you made about yourself or your life based on that injunction.

5. What thoughts occur to you about this decision? Are they true? Should they affect how you feel and behave?

6. Determine whether this decision is appropriate for you now. If not, rewrite the decision in a way that makes it appropriate for the present. In your new decision, specify what you can realistically do to change your behavior. How will this new decision make you feel?

7. Develop a plan to put the new decision into effect. What could interfere with this new decision? What thoughts could undermine this? What thoughts do you need to support your plan?

Redecision work may be particularly useful with clients whose current behavior is inappropriate in many situations and appears to be based on one or two parental-type messages they still hear or "play" as tapes in their heads.

CASE ILLUSTRATION OF INJUNCTIONS AND REDECISION WORK

The Case of Marie

Marie is a 40-year-old woman who is married; has two teenage children; works outside the home as an attorney; and cannot understand why she is so fatigued, overworked, and generally burned out. In the past year, she has developed chronic tension headaches and a stomach ulcer. Marie discloses that she has attempted "to do it all and do it all perfectly" and has never really considered asking for help from family or friends, nor has she expressed her growing irritation and resentment over their lack of help and support.

In the second session, the counselor asked Marie to close her eyes and recall what it was like as a child growing up in her house. Next, the counselor asked Marie to recall anything she remembered Mom telling or showing her not to do when Marie was a child, or anything Mom said that sounded negative. Marie revealed that her mother always told her to do things as well as possible, preferably without any help. Marie recalled that her mother was a perfectionist, an independent woman who never seemed to have any needs of her own and was always doing things for others.

When the counselor asked Marie to recall what she remembered Dad saying or doing, she stated that Dad always said, "Hold your tongue. Don't get upset or angry with other people even if they really make you mad." Marie described her father as a very calm person outwardly, who never showed much feeling. He died of heart disease at the age of 50.

The counselor helped Marie identify the typical injunctions she heard as a child that she still hears or follows in her present life. Marie identified three:

Don't ask for help or show needs or weaknesses.

Do everything as perfectly as possible.

Don't get angry.

Marie also revealed that she had decided to "work as hard and as independently as possible," and "keep all negative feelings to myself."

The counselor helped Marie explore how these decisions may have been useful as a child. For example, Marie learned to please her Mom and get approval from her by doing things without error and by not "bugging" her for help. Similarly, she learned to please her Dad and obtain recognition from him by being "just like Dad—a chip off the old block—able to handle anything without getting upset."

From a feminist perspective, the counselor has a responsibility to help Marie develop awareness of how growing up in a patriarchal culture produces and reinforces these sorts of injunctions, especially for women. So part of Marie's redecision work would be to develop consciousness about ideas she learned from her family and culture as a way to "keep her in her place" or to be a "nice girl." Part of becoming a woman is reevaluating those societal injunctions that prevent Marie from reaching her full potential as a person.

The counselor and Marie considered whether these two decisions were useful or were interfering in her present life. Marie concluded that her decisions to work independently and contain her feelings had resulted not only in severe stress for her but had also kept her family and friends at a distance. When she expressed a desire to change these decisions, the counselor helped her to identify what new decisions would be helpful and realistic.

Over the next few sessions, Marie decided she would like to continue to be a hard worker but to ask for help and to express negative feelings whenever her stress approached a certain level. The counselor helped her develop a plan to supplement the new decisions with specific attention to the thoughts or cognitions that could impede or support the plan. Marie identified the following thoughts that could interfere with the plan:

I don't have the right to ask for help.

I should be able to do it all by myself.

I shouldn't burden anyone else with my feelings or needs.

Together, Marie and the counselor developed some alternative thoughts to support the plan:

I am a person who is worthy of asking for and getting help from others.

It is unrealistic for me to do everything alone.

I want my family and friends to be more involved in my life.

During the remaining sessions, the counselor continued to encourage Marie while she tried to implement her plan based on the new decisions she had made for herself. Gradually, Marie realized that she, rather than other people, presented the main obstacles to making the plan a success. She continued to work on ways in which she would support and carry out her new decisions.

COGNITIVE RESTRUCTURING

Cognitive restructuring (CR), also called *cognitive replacement*, involves identifying and altering irrational or negative self-statements of clients (usually considered to be automatic thoughts, such as fear of falling) and helping the client replace them with neutral or positive self-statements. This intervention has been used to help athletes modify high-performance anxiety, change unrealistic expectations of couples in marital therapy, and alter cognitions around food for bulimic clients. Cognitive restructuring has also been used successfully in treating depression in children, adolescents, and older adults; influencing career indecision; treating phobias and panic disorders; and enhancing self-esteem.

Cognitive restructuring begins with an exploration of the client's typical thoughts when in a troublesome situation. These thoughts may include both self-enhancing (rational) thoughts and self-defeating (irrational) thoughts. The counselor uses closed questions to help the client identify specific thoughts that occur before, during, and after the problematic situation. If the client has trouble recalling specific thoughts, the counselor may want to ask the client to start by monitoring what goes through his or her head when problems arise and keep a written record of those thoughts.

Another way to help clients identify their thoughts in problematic situations is to visualize a situation in which the client typically has difficulties and then have the client describe the inner dialogue that takes place. For example, "Imagine yourself boarding a commercial airplane. Listen to your internal dialogue as you look for your seat, find it, sit down, and strap yourself in. What kinds of statements are you making to yourself during this sequence of events?"

Clients need some preparation or structure to use cognitive restructuring. Without structure, the client cannot be a productive contributor and the process will be ineffective. By way of introduction, the counselor should explain what automatic thoughts are and give examples, then explain the process by which those thoughts are replaced with more productive or rational thoughts. Following is a sample of how the counselor can introduce the technique of cognitive restructuring.

Introducing Cognitive Restructuring

One of the things we all do involves "automatic thoughts." When I have automatic thoughts, I am repeating a habitual thought rather than a rational thought. For example, if I trip while walking across the room, I might say, subconsciously, "You are such a klutz!" A more rational thought might be, "Slow down. When you get in a hurry, you often get clumsy." The first thing you must do is to become aware of these silent forces. We will start by making a list of negative self-statements. Then we will identify rational (more accurate) statements to counter them. Eventually, we want to replace the negative statements with neutral or positive statements. Once the replacement statements have become typical, we will have achieved our objective and you won't be attacking yourself, and your real strengths will emerge.

Cognitive restructuring can be a potent tool with a client whose self-talk is destructive or erodes confidence. The range of client conditions that can be addressed include fear, anxiety, eating habits, compulsive behaviors, communication problems, memory recall, parenting, perfectionism, self-esteem issues, addiction issues, and excessive worry. Negative self-talk does not cause these problems; rather, it is the negative self-talk that maintains the issues, keeping them from receding or dissipating.

Introduction and Use of Coping Thoughts

After the client has identified typical, negative self-statements or thoughts surrounding problem situations, the learning process begins for substituting a variety of coping self-statements or thoughts. These are similar in both content and function to the assertive thoughts used in the thought-stopping procedure. The use of coping thoughts is crucial to the overall success of the CR intervention. Awareness of negative or irrational self-statements is necessary but not usually sufficient to result in enduring change unless the client learns to produce incompatible self-instructions and behaviors.

When introducing coping thoughts, the counselor emphasizes their importance and their role in affecting the client's resulting feelings and behaviors. To help the client understand the difference between coping and noncoping thoughts, the counselor may give examples of each. Often, it is helpful to teach clients a variety of coping thoughts when the need to cope or intensity of a feeling may vary with the situation. For example, the client may find it helpful to use a particular type of coping before a problematic situation occurs. Or during the situation, the client may need to utilize coping thoughts that help to confront a challenge or to cope with a difficult moment. After the situation, clients can learn coping thoughts to encourage themselves or to reflect on what they learned before, during, and after the problem situation occurred.

Example of a Coping Thought

Self-defeating statement: I am afraid of this airplane.	**Coping statement:** This airplane has just been inspected by a specialist in aviation safety.

Shifting from Self-Defeating to Coping Thoughts

After identifying coping thoughts, the client must still learn how to shift from well-practiced self-defeating thoughts to the new coping thoughts. This is not an easy or natural process. It must be practiced once the client has learned to recognize the intrusion of the self-defeating thought. Sometimes it helps for the counselor to model this process for the client first. For example, a counselor could model the shift for a client who is waiting for an important job interview:

> *Okay, I'm sitting here waiting for them to call my name for this interview. Wish I didn't have to wait so darn long. I'm getting really nervous. What if I blow it [self-defeating thought]? Now, wait a minute. That doesn't help [cue to cope]. It will probably be only a short wait. Besides, it gives me a chance to sit down, relax, pull myself together, take some deep breaths, and review not only what I want to emphasize but also what I want to find out about this employer. I'm going to be sizing up this person, too. It's not a one-way street [coping thought established before the situation in the form of planning].*
> *Okay, now they're calling my name. I guess it's really my turn now. Wow, my knees are really shaking. What if I don't make a good impression [self-defeating thought and cue to cope]? Hey, I'm just going to do my best and see what I can learn from this, too [coping thought].*

Thought Stopping

Thought stopping is perhaps the first line of response when working with clients who tend toward negative self-talk or self-defeating thinking. Thought stopping is the process of interrupting a particular thought or line of thinking by commanding oneself to stop that thought. It is as though the client creates in his or her imagination a "little commander" who orders the thought to cease.

Positive Self-Talk

Self-talk is a common human activity. It can be subverbal or it can be whispered, and it is as though we are having a conversation with ourselves. Typically when we self-talk, however, we are not consciously focused on that inner monologue. When the monologue drifts toward negative descriptions of oneself and one's motives and actions, it becomes a drag on the psyche. Often, clients simply do not know how to break out of these negative self-talk patterns.

Positive self-talk involves the client's recognition of the existing negative patterns, paired with some type of internal alarm that negativity is in control of his or her mental processes. Only then can the client attempt to replace this negativity with positive (and true) self-talk. Thus, this intervention involves an assessment process and a replacement process. Perhaps the best example of negative self-talk comes from the person one would describe as having a weak self-image. When faced with a challenge, the self-talk may sound like "I could never do this." Such an internal judgment can be far from accurate. In fact, the person may have responded effectively in similar past situations. With the counselor's assistance, this realization needs to be brought to the surface and acknowledged by the client.

Once this acknowledgment has happened, the counselor suggests (strongly, if need be) that the "I could never do this" response is in error and must be replaced with the more accurate "I have succeeded in similar situations." Because internal self-talk is strongly entrenched, this reminder by the counselor may need to be repeated numerous times before the client can start taking over the process.

Anchoring

One of the problems in helping clients change entrenched behavior patterns is that the patterns have become like autonomic responses. They are not consciously driven. This makes the recognition or even the anticipation of such responses difficult for clients to manage. Anchors are signals that the counselor and client have agreed on that alert the client to an impending undesirable response, such as a negative self-thought. The anchor that alerts can be external (e.g., visual, behavioral, auditory) or internal (e.g., a feeling). When the anchor is recognized, the client is alerted and can respond with the new learned response. For example, the person with a weak self-image experiences much anxiety or impending doom. This feeling can become the anchor alert. So the counselor coaches the client, "When you first become anxious, quickly ask yourself, 'What am I saying, what am I thinking right now?' Then, instead of following your typical thought pattern, replace it with the phrase we have agreed on." This anchor-based replacement needs to be rehearsed in the counseling session. The drill might involve the counselor making the client's negative self-statement and the client responding with the replacement (e.g., "No, I am able to do this").

PARADOXICAL INTERVENTIONS

Another form of cognitive restructuring is often referred to as *paradoxical thinking*. The paradox often is just the opposite of what would seem rational to the client although it may be rational from a different perspective.

It perhaps comes as no surprise that not everything that you or I think is rational. But unless questioned or challenged, I choose to think of my cognitive processes as rational. The meanings that I attach to objects, persons, or situations may not all pass the test of rationality. In fact, many may not. How does one challenge a client's irrationality? The most commonly used paradoxical interventions include reframing, symptom or problem prescription, restraining, and positioning.

Reframing

Reframing is the gentle art of viewing or thinking about a situation differently. Within a counseling context, it is much more than a Pollyanna view of life. In fact, reframing (also called reformulation) is the counselor's attempt to take the definition of the problem and redefine it so that it opens the door to viable solutions. It has been favored by an interesting variety of theories, ranging from existentialists to strategic family therapists. Sometimes, reframing amounts to redefining an unsolvable problem as solvable or viewing the problem as not a problem at all. Other times, the reframe cuts through unfounded assumptions about either the person or the problem and provides a fresh and uncomplicated approach to the issue at hand. Madanes (1981) even includes bizarre behavior as reframable, suggesting that it be relabeled "as discourteous communication, in that others cannot understand it or in that it upsets others" (p. 130). In its simplest form, reframing takes a relatively simple thought or opinion that is subject to interpretation and offers a differing interpretation to that which is held.

Therapeutic reframing is most effective when it redefines an offensive motive or behavior as inept but well intended, thus making the behavior more personally or socially acceptable. It may be used equally well with the individual client who is dealing with intrapersonal issues or with the person who is reacting to interpersonal issues. The critical test for an effective reframe is that the alternative meaning is totally credible and believable. Thus, a mother's overbearing behavior may also be viewed as her inability to communicate her love, or a student's compulsive behavior may be viewed as her attempt to lighten her mother's parenting responsibilities. Only when this credibility criterion has been met is the client likely to accept the new meaning and discard the dysfunctional older meaning.

Symptom Prescription

Symptom (or problem) prescription involves having the client intentionally display the undesired behavior or even to exaggerate the behavior in order to imprint the ineffectiveness or uselessness of the behavior. In this way, the client recognizes the undesired behavior more quickly and also recognizes that the behavior is unnecessary or inappropriate.

When the symptom prescription is in the form of a paradoxical intervention, it produces a therapeutic double bind. For example, if the client follows an instruction to deliberately become more anxious, the client's compliance with the instruction actually brings the anxiety under the control of the client. Discovering that the anxiety is controllable is a first and necessary step toward symptom control.

Types of problems that lend themselves to symptom prescription are those in which the client feels no sense of control, such as compulsive worrying. For example, let's say you have a client who suffers from insomnia and reports a long list of solutions that have been tried but found lacking. Insomnia tends to be accompanied by excessive or even compulsive rumination. The typical complaint is, I just can't seem to turn my mind off when I go to bed.

Given this complaint, you might wish to prescribe the symptom, which would be for the client not to try to go to sleep even if it requires doing some other task. The point of this intervention is that one can be trapped into fighting oneself when trying to control a spontaneous process (falling asleep). Trying to control its opposite (staying awake) somehow manipulates the person's internal processes such that he or she can then let go. Yet another example, one that is used frequently and with considerable success, is to warn the client not to expect to get over a crisis too quickly. By prescribing the symptom—in this case, the client's fear that the crisis will not recede—the counselor may actually help the client recover more quickly. Such is the paradoxical nature of the psyche.

Resisting Therapeutic Change

This paradoxical intervention can come in the form of cautioning clients against change or warning them that they are improving too quickly. When used in this manner, the paradox is called *restraining*. It offers a preventive prescription to client resistance to change and can be used alone or as part of a more complex intervention. There are many cases in which the counselor can outline what needs to be done to improve a situation but can then add a caution to the considered change. Clients can be warned that they are improving too rapidly and should slow down the process of change. For example, a client in divorce counseling might be cautioned if he or she is feeling "single" too soon (sooner than the statistics indicate is normal). If the person suffers a relapse, the counselor has buffered the setback by saying it is normal; if the person continues to change in a therapeutic direction, then the implication is that the client is making a better than normal recovery.

CASE ILLUSTRATION OF PARADOXICAL RESTRAINT

The Case of Sue

Sue is a 29-year-old who has been divorced for 3 months. She has made a dramatic adjustment to the divorce, a fact she attributes to her long and emotionally draining predivorce separation. Nevertheless, she sometimes wonders if she is moving too quickly.

The counselor picks up on this concern and decides to introduce a paradoxical restraint. Suggesting that Sue might be deceived by the rapid progress she has made, the counselor cautions that Sue might encounter a temporary relapse during the course of her adjustment. She accepts this caution and thanks the counselor for the warning. The caution achieved two important results: (1) it was indeed possible that Sue would have a temporary relapse and, should it happen, she would be less likely to fear that all her gains were imagined, and (2) the notion that Sue remained somewhat vulnerable led her to exercise some caution as she made new growth decisions. (As a postscript, the relapse never happened.)

Positioning

Everyone has encountered persons who elicit positive statements from others by being overly negative about themselves. Examples include the office worker who volunteers that she is poorly organized so that she draws praise from others regarding her good organization, or the student who complains about not understanding when clearly the student is in full command of the subject. When this occurs in the counseling session, and if the counselor agrees with a client's negative self-assessment, it sabotages the power game implicit in the client's communication patterns. Some authors have even suggested that the counselor can enhance the power of the strategy by exaggerating the negative statement, often eliciting a response such as "I'm not that bad!" from the client (Dowd & Milne, 1986). The positioning response can be effective with clients who use negative self-assessments as a manipulative tool. It should not be used with clients who have truly negative self-images, however, because it could exacerbate their problem.

Example of a Positioning Response

CLIENT: I'm not any good with the computer. As soon as I try to do something, it does something weird and I just can't figure out what to do next.	COUNSELOR'S POSITIONING RESPONSE: So it sounds like the computer will always be beyond your intelligence or your capability, so why try to do anything using the computer?

COGNITIVE INTERVENTIONS WITH SPIRITUAL ISSUES

In their classic review of spirituality and counseling, Richards and Bergin (1997, p. 240) define *cognitive spiritual interventions* as interventions designed to help clients by changing their religious and spiritual beliefs and understandings. They describe "treatment packages" that use cognitive interventions with spiritual or religious issues, including Probst's religious cognitive therapy approach, the 12-step program of Alcoholics Anonymous (AA), and Ornish's *Program for Reversing Heart Disease*. Such programs use a variety of interventions, ranging from disputation to metaphor (pp. 242–249). Disputation has been used with religious clients who suffer from perfectionist tendencies and involves both theological and religious imagery. Both the AA 12-step program and Ornish's *Program for Reversing Heart Disease* utilize imagery involving acknowledgment of one's problem and one's inability to conquer the problem without divine intervention (see Richards & Bergin, 1997).

Metaphors and Spirituality

The use of metaphor is particularly compatible with spiritual interventions, in part because it is commonly used in the writings of many world religions. The use of metaphor is also compatible with the philosophical position that believes that all change comes from within rather than outside the individual. Whether inspired by the sacred or the secular, the metaphor presents a contextually different scenario from the problem, but the scenario is close enough to allow the client to draw conclusions and gain insights about the problem. Pearce (1996) observes that "metaphor functions in the affective realm despite the fact that it is delivered and apprehended by the cognitive, intellectual realm" (p. 3). He explains the therapeutic value of metaphor:

> Precisely because metaphor straddles the worlds of cognition and affect, it expedites thought process in the world of feeling. Metaphor can, from its position in the unconscious realm, initiate behavior change. [It] enables clients to transform a painful or unresolved experience by enabling them to transfer the meaning of such events beyond the critical junctures, resulting in an improved destiny or frame of reference. (p. 3)

Metaphors are usually delivered as stories. Examples from the Judeo-Christian heritage include Jacob's wrestling with God (Genesis 32:22–32), David's victory over Goliath (1 Samuel 17), and the parables of Jesus.

Most uses of metaphor present an opportunity for the client to gain insight and meaning or to view a situation or condition in a different and more spiritually meaningful way. For example, the counselor who is trying to help a quarrelling couple get beyond their combative positions might offer the Buddhist story of two monks arguing:

> Two Monks were arguing about a flag. "The flag is flapping," said one. "No," said the other, "the wind is flapping." The argument went back and forth. The Master happened to be passing by. He told them: "Not the wind, not the flag; your minds are flapping." (Reps, 1981, p. 114)

This story would be delivered without explanation. Instead, the counselor would allow the couple to find their own meaning in the story—for example, "Are we each distracted by our need to be right?"

Metaphors also come from folk and fairy tales. Pearce (1996) reminds us that Freud turned to folklore, fairy tales, and other forms of imaginative literature to label and categorize symptoms. Bettelheim (1976) extended this use of fairy tales in his book *The Uses of Enchantment: The Meaning and Importance of Fairy Tales*. In this book, he proposes that fairy tales allow children to work through life's great mysteries in socially acceptable ways. But adults can also gain insight into their beliefs, values, and blind spots through the revisiting of fairy tales. The meaning that is gained must be provided by the client, however. If a client can see no meaning or relevance in a metaphor or story, then the only thing for the counselor to do is to move on to something else.

CLIENT REACTIONS TO COGNITIVE STRATEGIES

Clients are likely to either respond beautifully to cognitive interventions or find them totally meaningless. When clients respond positively to these approaches, they are likely to be people who are intelligent, are witty, present neurotic symptoms, generate pictures or internal dialogue easily, and value the art of logical thinking. Clients who are turned off to cognitive approaches may be in crisis or have more severe problems, want or need a great deal of emotional support and warmth from the counseling relationship, process information kinesthetically, and react to issues and make decisions emotionally. It is difficult to use cognitive strategies successfully with clients who are resistant to them. Other types of interventions may be more useful with these individuals.

In addition to these various reactions, other typical reactions are likely to occur soon after introducing cognitive interventions. By anticipating these reactions, you will be better able to handle them when and if they occur. One reaction has to do with the language or labels employed by some counselors when using cognitive interventions. When the counselor describes the client's thoughts or beliefs as irrational, mistaken, or illogical, clients sometimes perceive that they themselves, as well as their ideas, are being attacked. This may be especially true for some types of clients (rebellious teenagers or rigid adults, for example). Clients are also likely to have negative reactions if the counselor's labels are given in the context of a highly directive, active, and confrontational therapeutic style, particularly if the counselor has not established a strong rapport with the client from the outset.

You can circumvent this reaction from clients in several ways. One is to avoid the use of emotionally charged terms. For example, one study (Baker, Thomas, & Munson, 1983) found that teenagers were much more amenable to a cognitive approach when the phrase *clean up your thinking* was used in place of *you need to change your irrational thoughts*. Another way to avoid this potential pitfall is to remove yourself from the position of determining which of the client's beliefs are rational or irrational. Instead, this procedure can be performed by the client (if he or she is capable), thus eliminating the possibility of a power struggle or misunderstandings between you and the client.

A second fairly typical client reaction is initial disbelief at the counselor's proclamation that the client's thoughts, rather than external events or other persons, cause distressing feelings. A client may say, "I told you I wouldn't feel this way if it weren't for her" (or "for it," meaning "for an outside event"). In fact, in initial interviews with clients, many of them believe that everything except their thinking is causing the problem. In their eyes, the problem is a parent or a spouse, their family of origin, how they were raised as children, unconscious material, and so on.

How can a counselor deal with a client's disbelief in a sensitive and yet informative manner? One way is to spend an adequate amount of time describing the rationale on which cognitive interventions are based, thus providing an adequate conceptualization of these strategies to the client. Often, this may mean that the counselor devotes at least one session to instructional purposes regarding the nature of human problems and possible corresponding treatment approaches. It is important for counselors to do this with clinical sensitivity in a way that avoids blaming or repudiating the client's ideas. Meichenbaum (1977) observes:

> The purpose of providing a framework is not to convince the client—perhaps against his will—that any particular explanation of his problem is valid but rather to encourage him to view his problem from a particular perspective and thus accept and collaborate in the therapy that will follow. (pp. 150–151)

For cognitive interventions to work, it is important in your rationale to refute the "situation/people cause problems/feelings" theory and to subsequently explain how thoughts create undesired feelings and behaviors. This explanation usually is more helpful if realistic examples and analogies are used. For example, McMullin and Giles (1981) use the following sorts of examples with clients:

> When my daughter was three, she used to watch monster shows on TV and get scared. When she was five, she watched the same shows and laughed like crazy. The situations were the same, but the consequences were different. Why do you think this was so?
> A New Yorker went to Texas to visit his friend. As they were driving in the desert, the New Yorker spotted what he thought was a boulder in the road, and frantically tried to grab the wheel. The Texan, however, said, "Relax. It's just a mesquite bush." Do you see that it was what the New Yorker thought about the bush that caused his panic?
> Two men over-ate one night and woke up the next morning feeling sick. One went to the doctor in a panic, and the other simply took it easy until he felt better. The first man was saying something pretty scary to himself. What do you think that might have been? (p. 34)

Clients can also be asked to describe examples from their life in which beliefs affect feelings or to provide examples of how a belief affects the behavior or feeling of a friend or relative. Another technique involves asking clients to describe a myth, fairy tale, or superstition they believed as a young child but no longer believe as an older child, teenager, or adult (McMullin & Giles, 1981).

Clients can be helped to realize that their thoughts can affect feelings and behaviors by using the distancing technique (Beck, 1976; McMullin & Giles, 1981). The client is given a list of either irrational beliefs or beliefs that often contribute to emotional distress and asked to pick one belief from each list (e.g., "Other people should do what I want them to do") and to imagine that this belief is "injected" into the head of a passerby. The client is then asked to state how this person's behavior and feelings would be affected by having this new belief in his head.

Finally, there is always the possibility that cognitive interventions do not produce desired changes in particular clients' feelings and behaviors. If, after repeated use of a cognitive procedure, the client's level of distress does not diminish, the counselor's original assessment of the client's problem may have to be reexamined.

When Clients Resist Change

Perhaps one of the more frustrating conditions that counselors face is when a client appears unable or unwilling to change. This condition, first recognized by Freud, has is known as client resistance. Cognitive therapists have modified Freud's conception of resistance somewhat, choosing to think of it as "serving a natural and often healthy function in protecting core organizing processes from rapid or sweeping reconstructive assaults" (Mahoney, 1988, p. 300). In other words, each person constructs his or her view of the world so that it makes internal sense, at least to the individual. And he or she does not release that internal logic easily.

Cowan and Presbury (2000) believe that resistance "expresses a protective wisdom that can never be fully verbalized by the client" (p. 412). Whether the resistance is based in wisdom or not, the reality is that, to move beyond dysfunctional thought processes to more freeing thoughts, resistance must be confronted. Cowan and Presbury argue for a gentle approach, using counselor empathy to help the client break through the resistance. Cognitive therapists have generally proposed a more challenging approach by confronting the irrational thought process and encouraging the client to move toward more rational assessments and conclusions. This is a matter of personal choice for the counselor. If your approach is more comfortable in the gentle approach, the implications are that you will need to be more gently persistent with the client's thought patterns but not less determined to help the client through the barriers that resistance presents.

Summary

This chapter describes those empirically supported counseling interventions that help clients recognize how they think themselves into difficulties and how those thoughts can be challenged and altered in a more constructive direction.

Critical to this type of counseling is the assessment process. Identifying illogical thinking patterns involves the counselor's communication skills, while altering those illogical patterns requires specific counseling interventions. The important point is that most illogical thinking patterns are so habitual that clients rarely recognize them as self-defeating. Thus, finding ways to help clients recognize these dysfunctional patterns is a major part of the counselor's role.

Strategies that have demonstrated effectiveness include real and imaginal disputation and behavioral disputation. These strategies draw heavily upon rational emotive behavior therapy (REBT) for their rationale and application. Changing dysfunctional thought patterns requires that the counselor actively use cognitive restructuring interventions, such as introduction of coping thoughts, thought-stopping, positive self-talk exercises, and anchoring.

Finally, altering dysfunctional thought patterns often requires more subtle interventions, such as the use of paradox, reframing, symptom substitution, and the introduction of metaphors. Such interventions are not used in a mind-control manner. Rather, they are introduced with the client's awareness and as an aid to help the client understand alternatives to those patterns that prove resistant to change.

Exercises

I. Conduct A-B-C-D Analysis for a Problem You Experience Personally

A. Identify an external event (person or problem situation) that consistently evokes strong and unpleasant feelings for you. Identify and list in writing typical thoughts you have about this situation. Examine them. Do your usual thoughts indicate that you believe this situation is what causes your distressed feelings? If so, try to write examples of different or new thoughts about the situation in which you take responsibility for your feelings. For example, you might try using an "I message": "I feel _____" rather than "This situation or person makes me feel _____."

B. Identify the specific emotions or feelings that are distressing or uncomfortable. List them. Next, rate the usual intensity of such feelings on a scale of 1 to 10 (1 = not intense; 10 = very intense).

C. For each emotion or feeling you listed in Step B, identify any thoughts or self-talk that goes on before and during the occurrence of these feelings. If this is difficult for you, ask yourself questions such as "What goes through my mind when I feel this way?" "What am I thinking about before and during these feelings?"

List these thoughts in writing for each emotion. Examine your list and categorize your thoughts as either rational, true beliefs or irrational, false beliefs. Remember that if the belief can be supported by data, facts, or evidence and can be substantiated by an objective observer, it is an RB. If it cannot be supported, it is an IB.

You may need to continue Step C during actual situations. As these distressing feelings actually present themselves, become aware of your thoughts surrounding these feelings.

D. Examine and challenge each IB you listed in Step C on a sentence-by-sentence basis. Use questions such as the following to challenge each of these beliefs: What makes it so? Where is the proof? Let's be scientists—find the supporting data. Where is the evidence for that?

Next, for each IB on your list, develop at least two "counters" for that belief. Recall that a counter is a statement that is directly opposite to the false belief yet is a believable statement of reality. Make each counter as concise as possible. After developing these counters, repeat them aloud—first, mechanically, next with as much vigor and emotional intensity as possible. Finally, practice countering your IBs by whispering or thinking the counter to yourself. During the next 2 weeks, use the counters with actual situations. Each time you become aware that you are starting to think an IB, whisper or think to yourself the counters you have developed to challenge that IB.

E. Become aware of any new effects of using this process over the next few weeks. Identify and list any behavioral effects—new or altered responses—as well as any emotional effects—new or altered feelings. Discover what has happened to the frequency and intensity of the feelings you listed earlier in Step B.

II. TA Redecision Work

Use the list of injunctions and the outline of the process of redecision work described on pages 000–000 to identify any injunctions you used as the basis of an early decision. Determine whether this decision is still appropriate for you. If not, rewrite the decision in a way that makes it appropriate for the present. Develop a plan to put the new decision into effect, with particular consideration to any thoughts and beliefs that could undermine your plan and any thoughts and beliefs necessary to support your plan. Although you can complete this activity on your own, it might help to stimulate your thinking by sharing this process in a group setting.

III. Cognitive Restructuring

This activity can be done either for yourself or for another person.

A. Identify a situation in which your performance or behavior is altered or inhibited because of unproductive thought patterns. It may be something such as making a presentation in front of a group, a job interview, encountering a difficult person, taking a test, and so on.

B. During the next two weeks, keep a log of the kinds of thoughts that occur before, during, and after this situation, whenever the situation (or thoughts and anticipation of it) occurs. Identify which of these thoughts are negative or self-defeating.

C. For each negative or self-defeating thought from your list in Step B, develop an incompatible thought or a coping thought. Try to develop coping thoughts that will help you before, during, and after the problematic situation. Make sure the coping thoughts are suitable for you. Try them out and see how they sound. Practice saying them aloud, in the sequence in which you would actually use them. Use an appropriate level of emotion and intensity as you engage in such practice.

D. Practice making a deliberate shift from the negative or self-defeating thoughts to the coping thoughts. Learn to recognize and utilize the self-defeating thoughts as a signal to use the coping thoughts. First, talk yourself through the situation. Later, practice making this shift subvocally. Use role-play, if necessary, to help you accomplish this. Start to engage in this process whenever the trouble situation occurs in vivo.

IV. Application of Cognitive Intervention Strategies

In this exercise, you are given six client descriptions. Based on the information we give you, decide whether cognitive strategies would be appropriate or inappropriate treatments for each client. Explain your decision. An example is given. (Feedback follows the exercise.)
Example: The client is a third-grade boy who is acting out in school and, because of limited ability, is having difficulty working up to grade level.

Cognitive interventions are not suitable for this client. Because of his developmental age and possible ability limitation, it would be too difficult for him to systematically apply logical reasoning to faulty thinking.

A. The client is a young Asian American male adult who is a college senior. He feels depressed over the recent deterioration of his grades and its effect on his graduate school plans for next year.

B. The client is a 6-year-old boy who is an only child. According to his teachers, he is having trouble interacting with the other children in his class and spends much of the time alone. His parents confirm that previous opportunities for interactions with other children have been very limited and have occurred on a sporadic basis.

C. The client is a middle-age man who is referred to you by his family. From talking with him, you observe flat affect coupled with "loose" or incoherent talk. Occasionally, the client refers to acting on instructions he has been given by a saint.

D. The client is a middle-age woman who is employed as an elementary school teacher. She was recently elected to a community taskforce and reports feeling terrified by the prospect of having to get up and speak in front of a potentially unfriendly audience. She explains that she is constantly worried about making a mistake, forgetting her speech, or in some way embarrassing herself.

E. The client is a 12-year-old seventh-grader who comes in to talk to the school counselor because she doesn't think she's as pretty or as smart as the other girls in her class and, as a result, feels sad.

F. The client is a 72-year-old retired woman who complains about her retired husband's chronic dependency on her. According to the client, her husband seems unable to get tasks accomplished without her help. The client is well-defended; seems unable to identify any feelings she is having about this issue in her life; and appears to have strongly held beliefs, which are expressed in a rather dogmatic and rigid fashion.

Feedback for Exercises

IV. Application of Cognitive Intervention Strategies

A. This client is possibly suitable for cognitive approaches and strategies. He is likely to be sufficiently intelligent to apply logical reasoning and to understand the concepts of cognitive interventions. It is probable that his distress over the recent grades is maintained by self-defeating thoughts or self-talk. However, another significant factor in this case is that the counselor needs to recognize and respect that this client's cultural background might also suggest that he experiences a sense of shame over his recent performance.

B. This client is not likely to benefit from cognitive approaches and strategies. First, he is probably too young to have mastered the kind of cognitive developmental tasks necessary to use a cognitive intervention effectively. Second, it appears that his presenting problem is more related to skill deficits and lack of opportunities to develop social skills than to inappropriate cognitions or beliefs.

C. Cognitive strategies are inappropriate for this client because of his flat affect, loose associations or stream of thinking, and the presence of auditory hallucinations, all of which suggest severe pathology.

D. Cognitive interventions are likely to be quite helpful for this client. Her stress and anxiety appear to be directly related to troublesome cognitions ("If I should fail, it will be awful"). She is likely to have the intellectual capacity to understand the principles and rationale of cognitive strategies.

E. Cognitive strategies will probably be helpful to this client. She is just about at the age where she has probably mastered enough cognitive developmental tasks to understand the concepts of these strategies and to apply logical reasoning to problem situations. Her sad feelings seem to be directly related to errors in thinking.

F. Cognitive strategies are probably not going to be too helpful for this client. Although she can probably understand the principles of these strategies, her strong defenses, lack of self-awareness, dogmatism, and need to disavow responsibility for any part of the relationship problem do not make her a very suitable candidate for cognitive strategies.

Discussion Questions

1. A basic assumption of any cognitive intervention is that thoughts cause feelings. What is your reaction to this assumption? What effect might your reaction have on your application of cognitive interventions with clients?
2. Discuss the characteristics of people you think would be very suitable for cognitive strategies. For what kinds of clients or problems might cognitive interventions not be appropriate?
3. In what ways might some clients resist working with a cognitive strategy? What might this resistant behavior mean? How could you handle it?

MyCounselingLab Assignment

Go to the Video Resource Library on the MyCounselingLab site for your text and search for the following clips:

- **Identifying Specific Beliefs About the Problem**   How does the counselor explain cognitive interventions so the client will understand? What counseling interventions is the counselor using to help the client grasp cognitive thoughts?

- **Cognitive Intervention**   In this video clip, the counselor is giving a homework assignment for the client to follow. How does the assignment help the client identify thoughts that are helpful and thoughts that are unhelpful?

10

Behavioral Interventions

PURPOSE OF THIS CHAPTER

Most of our behavior is not *new* behavior. In fact most of our behavior patterns, whether they be how we put on our shoes, eat our meals, walk the dog, or pay our bills, have such a history that we probably can't remember why we started doing them the way we do. These behavior patterns have power in our lives—power to make our lives less complicated, and a competing power to make our lives more resistant to change. In this chapter, we examine how persons change patterns of behavior that have become dysfunctional, less effective, or even unnecessary. Some patterns relate to behaviors that interfere with a client's goals, hopes, or needs. Others are behaviors that might be missing from a client's patterns of interaction, leading to a failure to achieve desired goals, hopes, or needs. Perhaps the most important aspect of this chapter is the emphasis on a client's responsibility in this process of change, and how the client and counselor work together to accomplish the client's objectives. A variety of symptoms can be treated using the behavioral interventions described in this chapter, including affective symptoms such as phobic responses, cognitive symptoms such as compulsive thought patterns, and behavioral/systemic patterns.

Considerations as You Read This Chapter

- Behavior is the part of human existence that communicates to others how a person feels, what a person thinks, and who a person is. Because it is available to others through their observations, behavior becomes the communication channel that connects an individual to other people.

- Behavior is the tool or means by which people accomplish, perform, or in other ways achieve the goals that they set.

- Behavior can be the cause of a person's failures, mistakes, or disappointments.

■ Because behavior is the outward manifestation of a person's inner self, it may sometimes seem to be unconnected to him or her. Many client problems involve some manifestation of behavior. And often the best approach to working with client problems is by addressing behavioral changes.

Thus far, we have examined how feelings and thinking can lead to human problems, and how affective and cognitive interventions can alleviate those same problems. In this chapter, we address problems that are established in behavior patterns—the things people do, or fail to do. Behavioral interventions are intended to help clients change their habits when they interfere with achievement of their goals, ambitions, or values, or when they contribute to negative outcomes. Behavioral strategies on which specific interventions are based utilize theories and processes of learning. As such, these theories have a philosophical connection to Lockean thinking and to logical positivism. That is, they are based on the assumption that human behavior (as well as all things in the universe) is governed by lawful relationships within one's environment.

Although a large number of strategies can be classified as behavioral in nature and focus, perhaps the most common ones are based on imitation learning, skills training, relaxation training, successive approximation, systematic desensitization, and self-management exercises.

THE IMPORTANCE OF BEHAVIOR

Most behavioral interventions can be traced back to three originating schools of behavioral thought: Pavlov's original conceptualizations, called classical conditioning; B. F. Skinner's later modifications of Pavlov's work, known as operant conditioning; and Albert Bandura's additions to these approaches, referred to as social modeling.

The classical conditioning model was based on Pavlov's animal experiments in which he sought to understand how learning occurs. It assumed that existing behavior changes when new environmental patterns emerge. When his dogs learned to associate the ringing of the bell at the gate to their kennels with feeding, they began to anticipate the feeding time whenever the bell rang. In other words, when the smell of pie in the oven typically means eating something delicious, just the aroma can change one's mood. This model for learning tended to address very basic human physiological responses.

B. F. Skinner used the research laboratory to explain more complicated learning patterns, which also seemed to be more typical of human behavior. Again, by using animals to study patterns of learning, he looked at how a behavior or skill is acquired. He found that newly acquired skills could be refined, polished, and shaped by the manner in which rewards were given. This approach, called shaping, is based on the axiom:

The likelihood of occurrence of any future event is directly related to the consequences of past similar events.

Stated in the vernacular, the chance that Billy will obey when told by his teacher to sit down is directly related to what happened to Billy yesterday and the day before when his teacher told him to sit down. In fact, perhaps one of the better examples of how shaping happens in the real world occurs in the kindergarten classroom at the beginning of the year. The successful teacher knows that children will gradually learn what is expected of them and will conform to the social rules of the classroom if the teacher structures the environment in such a way as to gradually and consistently encourage their behavior to move toward a specific social norm.

Skinner called this the operant conditioning method, meaning that the subsequent rewards that are given operate on the focus behavior so that it gradually changes in the desired direction. Basic to this approach is a planned structure for the change, known as successive approximation. Again, the kindergarten teacher serves as a good example. Based on the folk wisdom that "you must crawl before you walk," the lesson is laid out in successive logical steps that are to be taken, each one building on the previous one, until the ultimate goal is achieved.

Bandura (1969) viewed both Skinner's model and Pavlov's model as basic but not complete explanations for how most human learning occurs. He reasoned that most people learn in a "safe" way, by observing other people learning and then imitating their behavior. As early as third grade, most children have learned that this really works, especially if the teacher is at all intimidating. Bandura called this approach social learning. It has also been referred to as observational learning, vicarious learning, and imitation learning. It is based on the use of a model, someone or something to observe carefully and then imitate. The more influential the model, the more quickly learning occurs. It helps explain why professional golfer Tiger Woods is frequently seen in advertisements for golf equipment.

All three of these models are based on experimental study of human learning. People use all three of these patterns when they learn something new. So it makes some sense that these learning models might also be viable when desirable behavior change is called for. This is the rationale for introducing behavioral interventions into the counseling process.

Behavioral interventions share certain common beliefs and elements:

- Maladaptive behavior (behavior that produces undesirable personal or social consequences) is the result of learning, not illness, disease, or intrapsychic conflict.
- Maladaptive behavior can be weakened or eliminated, and adaptive behavior can be strengthened or increased through the use of psychological principles, especially principles of learning that enjoy some degree of empirical support.
- Behavior (adaptive or maladaptive) occurs in specific situations and is functionally related to specific events that both precede and follow these situations. For example, a client may be aggressive in some situations without being aggressive in most situations. Thus, behavioral practitioners attempt to avoid labeling clients using such arbitrary descriptors as aggressive. Instead, emphasis is placed on what a client does or does not do that is "aggressive" and what situational events cue or precipitate the aggressive response, as well as events that strengthen or weaken the aggressive response. A thorough assessment phase (or behavior analysis) similar to the process described in Chapter 6 is the basis for choosing behavioral interventions.
- Clearly defined outline or treatment goals are important for the overall efficiency of these interventions and are defined individually for each client. Thus, counselors attempt to avoid projecting their desires for change onto clients. Instead, they help clients specify precise outcomes they want to make as a result of counseling.
- Behavioral interventions focus on the present rather than the past or future and are selected and tailored to each client's set of problems and concerns. Behavioral approaches reject the "all-purpose counseling" notion that assumes that one method or approach is generally appropriate for most clients.

Characteristics of clients who seem to have the most success with behavioral interventions include:

- A strong goal orientation—people who are motivated by achieving goals or getting results
- An action orientation—people who need to be active, goal focused, participating in the helping process (this includes several cultural groups, including Asian Americans and African Americans)
- An interest in changing a discrete and limited (two to three) number of behaviors

Behavioral interventions have also been used extensively and found to be very suitable in schools, agencies, or situations with time-limited counseling. They tend to derive primarily from Bandura's social learning or imitative learning model.

In recent years, the behavioral theories and the cognitive theories reflected in Chapter 9 have been merged into what are called cognitive-behavioral approaches. These tend to be more cognitive in method but emphasize behavioral outcomes.

GOALS OF BEHAVIORAL INTERVENTION

The overall goal of behavioral interventions is to help clients develop adaptive and supportive behaviors to recurring situations. The definition of the term *behavior* has expanded in recent years to include covert or private events such as thoughts, beliefs, and feelings (when they can be clearly specified), as well as overt events or behaviors that are observable by others. Developing adaptive behavior often involves weakening or eliminating behaviors that work against the desired outcome (e.g., eating snacks when you wish to lose weight), acquiring or strengthening desirable behaviors (e.g., asking for things that you want or need), or both. Nonadaptive or maladaptive behaviors can be harmful to a person's health, lifestyle, or welfare. Adaptive behaviors help a person meet biological and social needs and avoid pain and discomfort (Wolpe, 1990).

Behavioral interventions have been used in many different settings (such as schools, agencies, business and industry, and correctional institutions), with a great variety of human problems (including learning and academic problems, motivational and performance problems, marital and sexual dysfunction, skills deficits, and anxiety), and with maladaptive habits (such as overeating, smoking, and procrastination). In this chapter, we focus primarily on the behavioral interventions that seem to be most useful for working with people in the general population (as opposed to those in institutional settings). These include social modeling, behavioral rehearsal and skills-training approaches, relaxation training, systematic desensitization, and self-management interventions. Cognitive behavioral strategies are not discussed because of their inclusion in the previous chapter.

Behavioral Intervention Skills

Behavioral Skills
Defining Behaviors
Helping the client understand the complexity of behavioral tasks; breaking tasks down into sequential behaviors

Modifying Behaviors
Helping the client change behavior patterns when it is deemed appropriate

Goal Setting

Helping the client assess goal difficulty and plan goal sequences for change

Visualization

Helping the client imagine an event, behavior, or process and how it would unfold in the desired fashion

Contracting

Helping the client establish commitments, time lines, and record keeping for change

Supporting and Reinforcing

Helping the client assess and recognize levels of progress toward goals

Behavioral Interventions

Social Modeling

Using examples from other sources to teach the client how to change and what to change

In Vivo (Live) Modeling

Using live (physically present) models of the targeted behavior(s) to teach the client what to emulate

Symbolic Modeling

Using video- or audio-recorded examples of the targeted behavior(s) to teach the client what to emulate

Covert Modeling

Using visualization to help the client create an image of the process of change

Role-Play and Rehearsal

Using simulations to examine and rehearse new behaviors, verbal interactions, and so on

Hierarchy Contruction

Arranging behavioral subgoals in order of difficulty or complexity, to be used as a plan for change

Relaxation Training

Helping the client assume control over muscular or mental processes

Systematic Desensitization

Using competing relaxation responses to reduce anxieties and phobias

Self-Monitoring

Helping the client learn how to observe and manage behavior patterns over time

Self-Reward

Helping the client learn how to allocate self-praise or other type of desired consequences when behavioral goals are achieved or maintained

Self-Contracting

Similar to contracting (above) but helping the client manage the process for the accomplishment of goals outside the counseling process

BASIC BEHAVIORAL SKILLS

Counselors working on behavioral change use a number of basic skills in their work. These skills involve ways of conceptualizing behavior and behavior change. The starting point is to think of behavior as *physical movement*, or *verbal production*. This involves a description of microbehaviors.

Describing Behaviors

Describing one's behavior is not as easy as it might appear. Athletes and coaches have become most adept at behavior description because they must break behavioral processes down (e.g., a golf swing) into the many subbehaviors that are part of the behavior. Thus, their description for a golf swing includes how the body is positioned over the ball, how the weight shifts from the backswing through to addressing the ball, and so on. In short, the process becomes so complicated that many people have never mastered this beginning element of golf.

But if you take a golf lesson, one of the first things the instructor will do is analyze your present actions and then reconstruct them toward the "model" golf-swing behavior. Counselors helping clients make behavioral changes do much the same thing. Consequently, counselors need to understand how to do behavioral analysis and how to restructure behavior patterns so they can "coach" their clients in this change process.

Modifying Behaviors

As we have noted, many people simply do not think behaviorally. Before the counselor can gain a commitment from clients to enter into behavioral change processes, the client must recognize the relationship between certain target behaviors and their consequences. Thus, you might find yourself saying, "It seems like every time you do this, then that happens. Do you agree? Because you don't like that when it happens, perhaps we could start thinking about ways of breaking the pattern." Saying this will not resolve the issue, however. The point is that you will find it necessary to help clients understand the process of behavior change as well as giving them strategies to implement change.

Goal Setting

Goal setting was discussed extensively in Chapter 6. Those same skills are used when planning for behavior change. Planning the subgoals and immediate tasks (see Figure 6.1) will involve specific behaviors and patterns. It will also be useful to help the client understand the goal process by using the successive approximation concept (see Figure 6.3). Planning the process by using goal setting is important to achieving client investment in change.

Visualization

If you have ever watched an Olympic diver standing on the high platform for what seems like minutes, you might assume that he or she is working up the courage to lift off. Not so. What the diver is doing is visualizing the perfect dive, from balancing on toes to entering the water without a splash. In this way, the diver establishes a mind-set for the task, and always the criterion is perfection. This same process is used by counselors to give clients a way to visualize, or imagine, what they would do with a newly sought behavior. Walking the client through this visualization process to learn how to do it when the counselor is not present is an important behavioral skill.

Contracting

Several times we have mentioned the importance of gaining client commitment with counseling goals. One demonstrated way to do this is the counseling contract. It seems to be a human quality to feel more committed to a task if a contract is involved. Sometimes the contract is developed between the counselor and client. Another approach is to ask the client to develop a self-contract, not unlike what people sometimes do when they decide to start a weight reduction program. The interesting part about contracting is that a contract tends to be more effective when the client actually signs his or her name to it. There is nothing legal about this act, but psychologically it does seem to make a difference for clients. Whether or not the client signs the contract, writing down the conditions of the contract *together* is quite important. We will discuss this in more detail later in this chapter.

Supporting and Reinforcing

As clients begin risking to change behaviors that have long been part of their repertoire, and thus are familiar, they often need support and reinforcement. This can be as simple as telling the client, "You can do it" or "That was a good effort." Not to give the client this kind of feedback will be interpreted by some that they are not doing it right or that they are failing. It is also possible to overdo these supporting words. If that happens, the comments begin to lose their effect, or you will be viewed as having lower standards than the client has.

USING BEHAVIORAL INTERVENTIONS

Social Modeling

Much of the work associated with social modeling has been initiated or stimulated by Bandura (1977). Three approaches or models have emerged: the overt model, the symbolic model, and the covert model. Each of these approaches can be used in working with clients.

The *overt social modeling* approach uses one or more persons as a model to illustrate the behavior to be learned or refined. The overt model may be live (also called in vivo) or recorded for video or audio playback. It is overt because it is apparent that this model is something to be observed and imitated.

The *symbolic social modeling* approach might include animated cartoon or fantasy characters, schematics, narratives, or slides. A good example would be the training videos that are produced to help a person learn how to use new computer software. The process takes the learner through a step-by-step process, with the ultimate goal that the learner can repeat the process later without the help of the training video.

The covert *modeling approach* uses imagination in the learning process. The tutor— whether a person, beast, cartoon character, or schematic diagram—is imagined rather than shown. Covert models may be the client (called self-modeling) or someone else enacting the behavior with increasing deftness. Various cues (e.g., specifying sensory images or inner reactions) can be supplied to support the imagined scenario. This approach is particularly applicable with the intervention called *role visualization*, an extension of cognitive restructuring described in Chapter 9. A significant number of counseling interventions, such as self-as-model, in vivo modeling, bibliotherapy, role visualization, role-play and behavior reversal, assertiveness training, and dialoguing, have originated in the social modeling approach.

LIVE (IN VIVO) MODELING.   With live modeling, the desired behavioral response is performed in the presence of the client. Live models can include the counselor, the teacher in a developmental guidance class, or the client's peers. Usually, the counselor will provide a modeled demonstration via a role-play activity in which he or she takes the part of the client and demonstrates a different way that the client might respond or behave. We have found live modeling to be quite effective when working in counseling groups.

Live modeling can be a most versatile tool for the school counselor, the correctional counselor, or the family counselor, to name only a few. Scenarios can vary from helping youth understand how to begin thinking about careers (by observing a videotape of other youth talking about career study), to helping high school students deal with peer pressures (through group counseling in which students talk about their successes in resisting pressures), to helping family members see a new way to communicate. The counselor's role can vary from being an actor in the scenario to being the choreographer or being the narrator of the scenario. Following is a modeling session in which the counselor served as narrator. The scene is a group guidance session involving 12 seventh-graders. The counselor has been working with 6 of the students on a project, "Using the Library to Learn about Careers." The second 6 students are new to the group and are just beginning the project.

Using Live Modeling With Middle School Students

COUNSELOR: Today, we have some new faces in our group. I think all of you already know each other. For convenience, I'm going to call you the "old-timers" and you the "new bunch." The old-timers have been working on a project to learn about jobs. I'm going to ask them to demonstrate some of the things they have been doing. We will use something called a fishbowl. What that means is that the old-timers will sit in a small circle. The rest of us will sit outside the circle and observe the old-timers as they talk about their project. We will do this for about 15 minutes and then we will trade places. The "new bunch" will come into the inner circle and the old-timers will sit around the outside. Any questions? [Nervous noises, chairs moving, people getting settled. The old-timers are familiar with this exercise. They were introduced to it when they were in the role of the new bunch a few weeks earlier.] Now, if everyone is ready, old-timers, I would like for you to talk to each other about the topic: "Fifty ways to choose a career—all in the library."

OLD-TIMERS: [A discussion begins, slowly at first, about how to use the library to find out about careers. Different members of the group talk about how they got started, who in the library helped them find the right books, which books were most helpful, how they preferred the computer career software for some of the research, funny things they discovered about some careers, and so on. There is a lot of joking. It doesn't look like a great learning experience, but the point is made that learning about jobs can be fun and that the library is a neat place to get career information. They also learned the process of approaching the right librarian and knowing what to ask for. After about 15 minutes, the counselor interrupts, summarizes what was said, and asks the two groups to trade places. Many groans, teasing, playful putdowns follow as students change seats.]

COUNSELOR: Now, new bunch, it's your turn. I'd like for you to show the old-timers what you can do. This time the topic will be "Things I am going to do in the library to learn about jobs."

NEW BUNCH: [More groans, jokes, moving of chairs. Talk begins slowly. Someone makes a joke. All laugh. Finally, someone gets into the spirit and says she would like to find out about becoming an astronaut. Everyone laughs. Counselor intervenes, commends student for her question, challenges group to come up with a plan for using the library to help her find out about becoming an astronaut. The group begins, more or less in earnest, and the information that characterized the first group's discussion comes out again, this time focusing on the topic of finding out about becoming an astronaut.]

Live modeling is particularly useful in instances in which the client does not have appropriate response alternatives available. The modeled demonstration provides cues that the client can use to acquire those new responses. For example, a client who wishes to be more assertive may benefit from seeing the counselor or a peer demonstrate such behaviors in role-played situations. The following exchange between the counselor (model) and the client (wishing to be more assertive) illustrates how such a session might go.

Modeling Assertive Responses

COUNSELOR: Today, Nancy, I thought we might do a role-play—that's where you and I enact someone other than ourselves, and our "play" will be a scenario in which you are returning some unusable merchandise to a local store.

NANCY: That sounds awful. I don't like to have to return things to the store.

COUNSELOR: I know. But you said you wished you could do that sort of thing without getting so upset. Don't worry. I'm going to play you and you are going to play the part of the store employee. Okay?

NANCY: [smiling] Well, that's a little better. Okay.

COUNSELOR: You will begin first, by asking me if I need some help.

NANCY: Hello, can I help you?
[AS EMPLOYEE]

COUNSELOR: Yes. I purchased this baptismal
[AS NANCY] gown for my daughter's baby but after the baby was born, my daughter realized it was too small. I'd like to exchange it if I may.

NANCY: How long ago did you purchase it?
[AS EMPLOYEE]

COUNSELOR: Two months ago, I'm afraid. I
[AS NANCY] know your return policy is 30 days but I hope you will accept it in exchange.

NANCY: Well, since you only want to
[AS EMPLOYEE] exchange it, I think we can do that.

Following the role-play, the counselor and Nancy discussed the interaction and then they conducted a second role-play, this time with Nancy as herself and the counselor as the store employee. Then they evaluated Nancy's performance and identified some ways she could improve. This was followed by a third role-play in which Nancy again was herself. Her performance in the third role-play was much improved and she felt successful. Live modeling in which the client is a participant is limited by the client's willingness to participate in an imagined situation as an actor, unless you and the client can take an impending real situation that both of you can rehearse. If your client is particularly withdrawn, you may wish to use other persons as the modeling participants.

SYMBOLIC MODELING. Although live models have much impact on the client, they are sometimes difficult to use because the counselor cannot control the accuracy of the demonstration of the behavior being modeled. To correct for this, many counselors use symbolic models through video recordings, audio recordings, or films in which a desired behavior is introduced and presented. For example, symbolic models could be used with clients who want to improve their study habits. Reading about effective study habits of successful people and their scholastic efforts is a first step to help clients identify desired behaviors. Next, clients can listen to a recording or watch a video illustrating persons who are studying appropriately (such a recording can be produced by the counselor with the help of the school librarian). Once effective symbolic models are developed, they can be stored easily and retrieved for future use by the same or different clients.

COVERT MODELING. Covert modeling, also called imaging, is a process in which the client imagines a scene in which the desired behavior is displayed. The imagined model can be either the client or someone else. This approach is used frequently and with much success by professional and amateur athletes. The first step is to work out a script that depicts the situation(s) and desired responses. For example, if an avoidant client desires to learn to communicate more successfully with a partner, scenes would be developed in which the client is having a successful discussion. One scene might be:

It is Friday night. You would like to go to a movie but your partner is very tired. You acknowledge your partner's tiredness but suggest that a movie might prove relaxing as well as entertaining. Your partner thinks about it for a moment and then agrees.

Imaging serves two purposes: It brings the appropriate behaviors into focus, and it serves to construct a success image into the person's self-concept. Both are desired outcomes. Perhaps the best example of this is the Olympic diver who, while standing on the high platform, imagines him- or herself balancing, then springing, then turning, and finally entering the water, all perfectly. The behavior then follows the pattern established by the image. This procedure is also referred to as covert self-modeling and has the potential for augmenting the client's personal involvement in the process and subsequently effecting greater facilitation of desired behavior (Rimm & Masters, 1979, p. 130).

CHARACTERISTICS OF THE MODELED PRESENTATION. The way in which a presentation is modeled can affect the client's ability to pay attention to and remember the demonstration. It is important that the model be presented in a way that engages the client. The first part of the modeled presentation should include instructions and cues about the features of the modeled behavior of activity. Prior instructions can minimize competition for the client's attention. A rationale for the use of modeling should also be given to the client prior to the demonstration.

Scenarios or responses to be modeled should minimize the amount of stress that the client might experience in the presentation. Distressing and anxiety-provoking modeled stimuli may interfere with the client's observation powers, processing, or remembering.

Complex patterns of behavior should be broken down and presented in smaller, more easily understood sequences. If too many behaviors or an overly complex model is presented to the client at one time, the likelihood of learning is greatly diminished. You can seek the client's input about the presentation of modeled responses to ensure that the ingredients and pace of the modeled demonstration are presented in a facilitative manner.

Perry and Furukawa (1980) advise the counselor to have either the model or a narrator comment on the important features of the modeled behavior as well as on the general principle or rule that governs the model's performance when a modeling scenario is particularly complicated. They provide an example of how this might be done:

> Suppose a model were demonstrating assertive behavior to a withdrawn, socially inept observer. The scene involves ordering dinner in a restaurant and discovering that the steak is too tough to eat. The model exhibits an assertive response in this situation by requesting the waitress to bring him another steak. The model can comment at this point: "That was an example of an assertive response. I was entitled to a good steak and was willing to pay for it. I explained the difficulty in an open and friendly manner to the waitress and asked her to bring me another steak. Afterwards, I felt good about myself and enjoyed my meal." By listening to the model highlight the essential characteristics of an assertive response, the observer is more likely to remember the behavior and is in a better position to apply this form of response in a variety of different situations. As an additional aid to retention, the observer can be asked by the therapist to summarize the main features and general rules associated with the model's behavior. Several studies (for example, Bandura, Grusec, and Menlove, 1966) have found that observers who actively summarize the model's behavior are better able to learn and retain this information. (p. 139)

Practicing the goal behavior or activity also increases the effectiveness of the modeling procedure. In addition to practice in the counseling session, the counselor might assign homework to the client for practice outside the session. Self-directed practice can enhance the generalization of the modeling treatment from within the session to real-life situations. If a client experiences difficulty in performing a particular activity or behavior, instructional aids, props, or counselor coaching can facilitate successful performance.

MODELING AND SELF-EFFICACY.   Self-efficacy refers to the perception a client has about his or her ability and confidence to handle a situation or to engage in a task successfully. It has been found to be a major variable that affects the usefulness of modeling interventions (Bandura, 1988). It is not sufficient to assume that clients will simply observe a model—either live, symbolic, or covert—and acquire the skills to achieve desirable results. Clients "must also gain enough self-efficacy [confidence] that they can perform the needed acts despite stress, changes, moments of doubt, and can persevere in the face of setbacks" (Rosenthal & Steffek, 1991, p. 75). Thus, modeling interventions must be designed that emphasize not only outcomes but also attitudes and beliefs about oneself. As an example, Ozer and Bandura (1990) developed a modeling program to teach women self-defense skills. The program not only included modeling various self-defense skills, but also modeled ways in which the women could acquire trust in their self-defense skills, particularly in the face of adverse situations. So self-efficacy is not a global concept—that is, it does not reflect self-confidence in general—but rather it refers to the confidence in oneself to deal with particular goals. Modeling interventions will be more successful when they also teach clients how to develop confidence for the tasks being modeled.

DESIRABLE CHARACTERISTICS OF MODELS.   Clients are more likely to learn from someone whom they perceive as similar to themselves. Characteristics such as age, gender, prestige, ethnic background, and attitudes should be considered when selecting potential models. In the case of cross-cultural counseling, however, cultural sensitivity may be sufficient to account for perceived competence and modeling effectiveness. Atkinson, Casas, and Abreu (1992) studied the differential effects of cultural similarity and cultural sensitivity and found that "counselors who acknowledge the importance of culture in client problems are perceived as more culturally competent by ethnic minorities than are counselors who ignore cultural variables" (p. 518). On the other hand, gender sensitivity may not be sufficient to enhance modeling effects. Citing Carli (1989), Nelson (1993, p. 203) suggests that gender plays a significant role in the social influence (modeling) process in that same-sex dyads tend to interact differently than do different-sex dyads.

Similarity between model and client assures clients that the behaviors shown are appropriate as well as achievable. With some clients, there is no better model than the client. Hosford and deVisser (1974) write that arranging conditions so clients see themselves performing the desired response can be a very powerful learning tool. In their procedure, called self-as-model, the client is captured on a video or audio recording actually performing the desired response. For example, a client who wishes to stop stuttering listens to and practices with a recording in which all stuttering has been edited out. Having a client observe both inappropriate and appropriate behaviors may actually weaken acquisition of the desired responses and promote the undesired behavior. Presumably this is explained by the eroding effect on the client's confidence when he or she hears the problem behavior.

Meichenbaum (1971) suggests that a coping model might be more helpful to clients than a mastery model. A client may be able to identify more strongly with a model who shows some fear or some struggle in performing than the model who comes across perfectly. Clients can also learn more from modeling when exposed to more than one model. Multiple models may have more impact on a client because the client can draw on the strengths and styles of several different persons (Kasdin, 1973). Warmth and nurturance by the model also facilitates modeling effects.

When modeling fails to contribute to desired client changes, the counselor should reassess the characteristics of the selected model(s) and the mode and format of the modeled presentation. In many cases, modeling can provide sufficient cues for the client to learn new responses or to extinguish fears. In other instances, modeling may have more impact when accompanied by practice of the target response. This practice can occur through role-play and rehearsal in the counseling session or as assigned homework.

Role-Play and Behavior Rehearsal

Role-play and *behavior rehearsal* interventions promote behavior change through simulated or in vivo enactment of desired responses. Role-play and behavior rehearsal originated from Salter's conditioned reflex therapy, Moreno's psychodrama technique, and Kelly's fixed-role therapy. Common elements in the application of role-play and rehearsal interventions include the following:

1. A reenactment of oneself, another person, an event, or a set of responses by the client
2. The use of the present, or the here and now, to carry out the reenactment
3. A gradual shaping process in which less difficult scenes are enacted first and more difficult scenes are reserved for later
4. Feedback to the client by the counselor and/or other adjunct persons

Depending on the therapeutic goal, role-playing procedures are often used by dynamic therapies as a method to achieve catharsis, by insight therapies as a means to bring about attitudinal changes, by gestalt therapy as a tool to promote conflict resolution and increased self-awareness, and by behavior therapy as a way to facilitate behavior changes. In this chapter, we discuss role-play as a way to achieve the latter objective. Gestalt dialogue work and role-play to promote attitudinal change were discussed in Chapter 8.

Role-Play as a Method of Behavior Change

Behavior rehearsal uses role-play and practice attempts to help people acquire new skills and to help them perform more effectively under threatening or anxiety-producing circumstances. Behavior rehearsal is used primarily in three situations:

1. The client does not have but needs to learn the necessary skills to handle a situation (response acquisition).
2. The client needs to learn to discriminate between inappropriate and appropriate times and places to use the skills (response facilitation).
3. The client's anxiety about the situation needs to be reduced sufficiently to allow the client to use skills already learned even though the skills are currently inhibited by anxiety (response disinhibition).

Suppose you have a client who wants to be more self-disclosing with others but doesn't know where to start learning how. In this case, the client might have a deficit repertoire (lack of skills and knowledge) in self-disclosure and needs to learn some new communication skills. Or the client may have the necessary communication skills but needs clarification or discrimination training to learn when and how to use those skills to self-disclose. Many clients have the skills but use them inappropriately. A person may self-disclose too much to disinterested persons and then withhold with persons who are interested in them. In another case, the client's anxiety can inhibit the use of these skills. Role-play and behavior rehearsal can then be used to help the client gain control over the anxiety reaction.

In addition to the practice effects gained from behavior rehearsal, the intervention can often provide important clues about how the client actually behaves in real-life situations. For example, it isn't unusual for clients to describe a behavior or interaction one way and then portray the interaction in a different way. Such contradictions need to be resolved in the session. Experts believe that the role-played behavior is far more likely to be accurate than the interaction as described by the client. In other words, we are likely to portray a scenario more accurately than when we describe the interaction. This makes role-laying an important part of the assessment process, too.

The nuts and bolts of behavior rehearsal consist of a series of graduated practice attempts in which the client rehearses the desired behaviors, starting with a situation that is manageable and is not likely to backfire. Psychologists call this process *successive approximation*. The rehearsal attempts may be arranged in a hierarchy according to level of difficulty or gradations of stress. Adequate practice of one situation is required before moving on to a scene with more advanced skills. The practice of each scene should be very similar to the situations that occur in the client's environment. To simulate these situations realistically, you may wish to use props and portray the other person involved with the client as accurately as possible. This portrayal should include acting out the probable response of this person to the client's new or different behavior.

Behavior rehearsal can be either overt or covert (imaged). Both seem to be quite effective. Probably a client could benefit from engaging in both of these approaches. Initially, the client might practice by imaging and then move on to acting out the scenario with the counselor. Covert rehearsal can also be assigned as a homework intervention. Lazarus (1966) provided guidelines for knowing when to move from one scenario to the next level:

1. The client is able to enact the scene without feeling anxious.
2. The client's general demeanor supports the client's words.
3. The client's words and actions would seem fair and reasonable to an objective onlooker.

Feedback is an important part of role-play and behavioral rehearsal interventions. It is a way for the client to recognize both the problems and successes encountered in the practice attempts. To be effective, evaluative feedback should be measured by the client's willingness to change and by the potential for helping clients identify other effective alternatives. Feedback also should be nonpunitive, constructive, and directed toward behaviors the client can potentially change. Feedback may be supplied by video- and audio-recorded playback of the client's practices. These taped playbacks are often more useful objective assessments of the client's behavior than verbal descriptions alone. You may find that your evaluations are more important early in the feedback process, but eventually, it is desirable for the client to begin using accurate self-assessments in the feedback process.

MODELING, REHEARSAL, AND FEEDBACK: COMPONENTS OF SKILL TRAINING

Skill training is an intervention composed of several other interventions that we have already discussed: successive approximation, modeling, behavioral rehearsal, and feedback. Skill training may take a variety of forms, including problem- solving skills, decision-making skills, communication skills, social skills, and assertion skills. To develop a skill training program, you must first identify the components of the skill to be learned. Then you arrange components in a learning sequence that reflects a continuum from less difficult to more difficult. Training then proceeds by modeling each skill component, having the client imitate the modeled behaviors, providing evaluative feedback, and repeating the sequence if appropriate. Skill training protocols exist for most skills that might be taught in the counseling setting and may be found in the professional counseling literature. To illustrate how a training package might be developed, we will describe an assertion training protocol.

Assertion training is a tool for overcoming social anxiety that inhibits a person's interactions with others. Typical assertion skills involve the ability to make requests; to refuse requests; to express opinions; to express positive and negative feelings; and to initiate, continue, and terminate social conversations. In assertion training, you begin by having the client identify one situation in which he or she wants to be more assertive. Then identify what assertive behaviors are involved and what the client would like to say or do. The situation is modeled and role-played consistently in the interview until the client can be assertive without experiencing any anxiety. Then the learned skill is transferred to situations outside the counseling setting through homework assignments. Once the client is able to exhibit the desired skills independently of counseling, the process is deemed successful. Success at assertiveness will generalize to other situations, too; that is, it will be become easier for clients to be assertive on their own without assistance and feedback.

As an illustration, suppose you are working with a student who reports a lack of assertive classroom behaviors. You and your client would first specify the desired classroom skills. You may need to observe the student in the classroom setting to identify these target behaviors. In counting the number of times the student engages in assertive classroom behavior (asking questions, voicing opinions, engaging in group discussion, giving reports, volunteering for chalkboard work, initiating conversations with the teacher, etc.), you can obtain a fairly accurate idea of the kind of assertive behaviors that are most prevalent in the client's repertoire and the ones the client needs most to strengthen. After identifying the desired behaviors to strengthen, you must choose the type of modeling to use to teach the target behaviors: live, symbolic, or covert modeling, or some combination of these. After the client has seen, listened to, read about, or imagined these modeled behaviors, he or she can demonstrate and practice brief scenarios in which the behaviors are demonstrated. Following practice and successful demonstration in which the client becomes comfortable with the new behaviors, the client is asked to begin to transfer the skill to classroom settings.

Many persons who need assertiveness training describe an early history in which they have been taught that the rights of others supersede their own rights. This is not to imply that in assertiveness training, one learns to be aggressive but rather to treat oneself and others with a reasonable amount of respect. In some cases, assertiveness training involves helping clients learn the legitimate expression of anger so that their rights are not consistently violated. Researchers have observed that the expression of anger and consequent inhibited assertive expression are often particularly hard for some female clients who have been socialized to put others first and themselves last (Laidlaw et al., 1990). Assertiveness training may be useful for women as long as it doesn't encourage women to develop skills simply to meet the prevailing patriarchal social standards. Assertiveness training also may be useful in assisting gay, lesbian, and bisexual clients who are in the coming-out process (the process of asserting their sexual identity to friends, family, coworkers, etc.). It must also be recognized, however, that the meaning of assertiveness varies among culturally diverse groups. Meichenbaum (1985) cautions, "In some cultures, people tend to cope with stressors passively, by trying to endure them rather than viewing them as challenges and problems to be solved. Stress management training must reflect these cultural preferences" (p. 17). Cheek (1976) illustrates some of the problems of meaning in assertiveness training with African American clients:

> You see the authors on assertiveness have not sufficiently considered the social conditions in which Blacks live—and have lived. That blind spot in many ways alters or changes the manner that assertiveness is applied. . . . Current assertive authors have a great approach—it's an approach which can really aid Black folks, in fact they need it—but at the time these authors are unable to translate assertiveness training into the examples, language and caution that fit the realities of a Black lifestyle. (pp. 10–11)

CASE ILLUSTRATION OF SKILL TRAINING

The Case of Jack

Jack is a 27-year-old Caucasian male who initially sought counseling because he wanted to improve his social relationships. Assessment revealed that Jack has had a series of interpersonal encounters in which the relationship ended when Jack began to feel dominated by the woman involved. As this pattern repeated itself, Jack reported that his confidence sagged to new depths, and lately he has avoided social relationships as a result. He describes himself as weak and powerless in relationships. At this point, the counselor determined that Jack might need some skill training related to interpersonal skills in addition to the exploration of his feelings and thoughts about himself.

First, the counselor explained the process of assertiveness training, noting that it involves a good bit of role-playing. The counselor also drew on paper a continuum of possible behaviors—ranging from passive to assertive, to aggressive—to illustrate the differences among being passive, assertive, and aggressive. This distinction is very important because formerly passive people often attempt to overcompensate initially in their interactions with others by behaving aggressively rather than assertively. In Jack's case, this could have a very negative effect on future relationships.

Then Jack and the counselor discussed Jack's past relationships and identified a series of situations in which Jack has trouble being assertive with women. Most of these centered on his social relationships but several also involved his mother. Each social skill was discussed thoroughly so that both Jack and the counselor had a good idea of what actually happened in the social encounters. Then Jack and the counselor arranged the identified skills in a hierarchy— starting with ones that were the least difficult for Jack and presented the least difficulties for him when he wished to be assertive. Jack and the counselor identified six situations on which Jack wanted to work:

1. When shopping with a companion, identifying a shopping plan he would like to include and not following her shopping plan only
2. Choosing what to wear on a date without asking his companion's opinion first
3. Identifying some places to go to before asking a companion out to dinner
4. Telling his mother he can't come over to see her
5. Telling his mother he can't fix something for her
6. Telling his date that he really doesn't want to see a particular movie

At this point, Jack was ready to start working with the first situation on the list. The counselor had him participate in an imaginary shopping trip to the local mall, beginning with the drive to the mall. She took on the role of the companion and described what she wanted to do when they got there. Jack had to describe what he wanted to do. They imagined themselves getting out of the car and walking to the entrance. She said to him, "Do you have something you want to get or do you want to come with me?"

Jack's role was to describe to her what he wanted to do and then to negotiate when and where they would meet. Over the next few counseling sessions, they rehearsed this scenario until Jack was quite comfortable with his role. At that point, the counselor gave Jack a homework assignment to invite a date to go shopping. He announced that he had already done so the past weekend and that the experience had worked out very much to his liking. The remaining items on Jack's list went much faster as he gained self-confidence and skill.

There is a tendency during skill training for counselors to terminate role-playing with too few trials, possibly because the counselor has a higher skill level than the client and becomes bored or assumes clients are more comfortable with the new skills than they really are. The counselor may also want to discuss how the client can handle unexpected or varied responses from the other party who is involved in the scenario. For example, in Jack's situation, Jack and the counselor discussed ways that he could respond if his date insisted he accompany her into the store she selected.

Operant Conditioning Interventions

Skinner's operant conditioning learning model has contributed significantly to the counselor's repertoire of behavioral interventions. The operant model makes an important assumption.

Once a behavioral goal has been established, it is assumed that some rudimentary form of that behavior already exists in the client's behavioral repertoire.

For example, Mary has been plagued over the years with what she calls her "shyness." It emerges as social withdrawal with anyone except her closest friends. Her goal in counseling is to develop some new social skills and build her confidence in them. One of her goals is to walk up to someone she doesn't know and introduce herself. Mary and her counselor determine what behaviors are involved in this act of introduction. Then they identify behaviors that are already part of Mary's normal repertoire that resemble this action. These existing behaviors become the starting point for behavioral skill development. This same process would be followed for each of Mary's counseling goals that uses an operant conditioning intervention.

A large number of counselor interventions are derived from the operant conditioning approach. Mentioned earlier, in the successive approximation approach, a goal behavior is broken down into smaller, logical behavior steps, each of which becomes a subgoal. Successive approximation can be applied to a wide variety of counseling goals, not just behavioral goals. Systematic desensitization, used to reduce dysfunctional anxieties, is built on the successive approximation model. It relies on *muscle relaxation training*, also called progressive relaxation. The concept of successive approximation has also become an important approach to development of counseling goals. These and a number of other interventions with operant conditioning roots will be described in this chapter.

Anxiety Reduction Methods

Many clients who seek help do so because of strong negative emotions labeled as fear or anxiety. Researchers have identified several types of anxiety, including *somatic anxiety*, which may manifest itself in body sensations such as stomach butterflies, sweaty palms, and rapid pulse rate; *cognitive anxiety*, which may be apparent in an inability to concentrate or in intrusive, repetitive, panicky, or catastrophic thoughts; and *performance* or *behavioral anxiety*, typically manifested by avoidance of the anxiety-arousing situation.

Some anxiety is believed to be helpful and can actually lead to successful performance; however, when it reaches an intolerable or uncomfortable level, a person should seek help for it. Various strategies are used for anxiety reduction. In this chapter, we describe two of the more common behavioral interventions: relaxation training and systematic desensitization.

Relaxation Training

The most common form of relaxation training used by behavioral counselors is called progressive relaxation or muscle relaxation (Jacobson, 1939). Muscle relaxation has long been used to treat a wide variety of problems, including generalized anxiety and stress, headaches and psychosomatic pain, insomnia, and chronic illnesses such as hypertension and diabetes. Relaxation training is often used as an adjunct to short-term counseling. Relaxation can be an effective way of establishing rapport and a sense of trust in the counselor's competence. Muscle relaxation is also a major component of systematic desensitization, which we discuss in the next section.

The basic premise of using muscle relaxation to treat anxiety is that muscle tension exacerbates or adds to anxiety and stress. At the same time, relaxation and anxiety are not compatible states. Consequently, an individual can experience a reduction in felt anxiety by causing relaxation to occur in muscle groups on cue or by using self-instructions. The procedure involves training clients to contract and then relax various muscle groups, to recognize differences between sensations of muscle contraction and relaxation, and to induce greater relaxation through the release of muscle tension and suggestion. Suggestion is enhanced by counselor comments throughout the procedure, directing the client's attention to pleasant (relaxed) sensations, heavy or warm sensations, and so on. These suggestions are not unlike hypnotic inductions; however, muscle relaxation is not hypnosis, and some clients may need to know that they are not going to be hypnotized. After going through the procedure several times with the counselor's assistance, clients are encouraged to practice it on their own, daily if possible, and often with the use of recorded instructions as a guide. (Commercially prepared relaxation CDs and DVDs are available, or you can record the session in which you are teaching the client how to relax muscle groups and send that CD or DVD home with the client to practice.)

Relaxation training should occur in a quiet environment free of distracting light, noise, and interruptions. The client should lie on a couch, reclining chair, or a pad on the floor. (This latter option is most practical when working with a relaxation training group.) The counselor uses a quiet, modulated tone of voice when delivering the relaxation instructions. Each step in the process (tensing and relaxing a specific muscle) takes about 10 to 15 seconds, with a 10- to 15-second pause between each step. The entire procedure takes 20 to 30 minutes, and it is important not to rush. The process is illustrated in the following instructions.

Tension Release Through Muscle Relaxation

First, let your body relax. Close your eyes and visualize your body letting go. [Pause] Now we are going to the muscles of your face. First, smile as broadly as you can. Tighter. Relax. [Pause] Good. Now again, smile. Smile. [Pause] Relax. Now your eyes and forehead. Scrunch them as tightly as you can. Like a prune. Tighter. [Pause] Relax. Good. Note the difference between the tension and relaxation. Feel the warmth flow into the muscles as you relax. Now, again, make a prune face. Tighter. [Pause] Relax. Relax.

Let all of the muscles in your face relax. Around your eyes, your brow, around your mouth. Feel your face becoming smoother as you let go. [Pause] Feel your face become more and more relaxed.

Now, focus on your hands. Clench them into fists and make the fists tight . . . tighter. Study the tension in your hands as you tighten them. [Pause] Now release them. Relax your hands and let them rest. [Pause] Note the difference between the tension and the relaxation. [Pause] Now, tighten your hands into fists again. Tighter . . . tighter. Relax. Let them go. Feel the tension drain out of your hands as they release. [Pause]

Now bend both hands back at the wrists so the muscles in your lower arms tighten. Tighter . . . Relax. Again feel the tension flow out of your arms and hands. As the tension releases, a warmth enters your muscles to replace the tension. Try to recognize the warmth flowing in. [Pause] Bend both hands back and tense your lower arms again. Tighter. Relax. Feel the warmth replacing the tension. Relax further. Deeper. Good.

Now we will move to your upper arms. Tighten your biceps by pulling your bended arms to your chest. Tighter. Tighter. [Pause] Relax. Let your arms drop. Let the tension flow out. Let the warmth flow in. Relax. Deeper. Try to reach an even deeper level of relaxation of your arms.

And now your shoulders. Shrug your shoulders and try to touch them to your ears. Feel and hold the tension. Tighter. [Pause] Now relax. Relax. Let go. Feel the tension leave. Deeper. Good. Tighten your shoulders again. [Pause] Relax. [Pause] Relax. Feel all of the muscles in your hands, arms, shoulders, face. Feel them letting go. Deeper into relaxation. Deeper.

As these muscles relax, direct your attention to your chest muscles. Tense them. Tighter. [Pause] Relax. Again. Pull your chest muscles tighter and tighter. Tighter. [Pause] Relax, relax. [Pause] Now your stomach muscles. Tighten your stomach. Harder. Tighter. [Pause] Relax. Feel the tension flow out of those muscles. Feel them grow softer. Relax. Feel the warmth. Relax. [Pause] Now tense the stomach muscles again. Good. Tighter. Relax, relax. Feel the difference. Good.

Focus now on your buttocks. Tense your buttocks by holding them in or contracting them. Feel the tension. Tighter. Relax. [Pause]

Now tighten them again. Tighter. [Pause] Relax. Let your whole body go. Feel the tension flow out of your body. Feel the warmth flow into your body. Feel the warmth pushing the tension out. Let go. Relax. [Pause]

Now locate your legs. Tighten your calf muscles now by pointing your toes toward your head. Tighten them. Relax. Let your feet drop. Feel the muscles letting go. Again now. Tighten your calf muscles. Point your toes toward your head. Tighter. [Pause] Relax. Good. Feel the muscles go soft, smooth, warm.

Stretch both legs out from you. Reach as far as you can with your legs. Extend them. Extend them. [Pause] Relax. Let them drop. Feel the difference in your muscles. Feel the leg muscles relax. Concentrate on the feeling. Now stretch your legs again. Point your toes. Extend, extend. [Pause] Relax. Drop your feet. Relax. Deeper. Feel the warmth rush in. Let the tension go. Let your legs relax even deeper. Let them relax deeper still. Feel your whole body letting go. Feel it. Remember the feeling. Relax.

Now I am going to go over all of the muscle groups again. As I name each group, try to notice whether there is any tension left in the muscle. If there is, let it go. Let the muscle go completely soft. Think of draining all of the tension out. Focus on your face. Explore your face for tension. If you feel any, drain it out. Let the face soften, become smooth. Your hands. Let the tension drip from your fingertips. Visualize it dripping out, draining from your hands, your arms. [Pause] Your shoulders. Is there any tightness, tension there? If so, let it loose. Open the gates and let it flow outward, filling the space with warmth. Now your chest. Let your mind explore for any tension. Your stomach. Let the tightness go. Softer. Your buttocks. [Pause] If you find any tension in your buttocks, let it flow out. Down through your legs, your calfs, your feet to your toes. Let all of the tension go. Sit quietly for a moment. Experience the relaxation, the tension is gone. Your body feels heavy, soft, relaxed. [Pause] With your eyes still closed, record this memory in your mind. What it feels like to be so relaxed. [Pause]

Now, before you open your eyes, think about how relaxed you are. Think of a scale from 0 to 5 where 0 is complete relaxation, no tension. A 5 is extreme tension, no relaxation. Tell me where you place yourself on that scale right now.

Systematic Desensitization

Systematic desensitization is an anxiety-reduction intervention developed by Wolpe (1958, 1990) and based on the learning principles of classical conditioning. This type of learning involves the pairing (occurring close together) of a neutral event or stimulus with a stimulus that already elicits or causes a reflexive response such as fear. Desensitization employs *counterconditioning*— the use of learning to substitute one type of response for another—to desensitize clients to higher levels of fear or anxiety. In desensitization, a counteracting stimulus such as relaxation is used to replace anxiety on a step-by-step basis. Wolpe (1982) explains this process:

> After a physiological state inhibiting anxiety has been induced in the [client] by means of muscle relaxation, [the client] is exposed to a weak anxiety-arousing stimulus for a few seconds. If the exposure is repeated, the stimulus progressively loses its ability to evoke anxiety. Successively stronger stimuli are then similarly treated. (p. 150)

Desensitization is often the treatment of choice for *phobias* (experienced fear in a situation in which there is no obvious external danger) or any other disorders arising from specific external events. It is particularly useful in instances in which the client has sufficient skills to cope with the situation or perform a desired response but avoids doing so or performs below par because of interfering anxiety and accompanying arousal.

On the other hand, desensitization is inappropriate when the target situation is inherently dangerous (such as sky diving) or when the person lacks appropriate skills to handle the target situation. In the latter case, modeling, rehearsal, and skill training approaches are more desirable. Counselors can determine whether a particular client's anxiety is irrational or is the result of a truly dangerous situation or a skills deficit by engaging in a careful assessment of the presenting problem. Effective desensitization usually also requires that a client be able to relax and to engage in imagery although occasionally responses other than relaxation or imagery are used in the intervention.

The intervention involves three basic steps and takes about 10 to 30 sessions, on average, to complete, depending on the client, the problem, and the intensity of the anxiety. Those steps are:

1. Training in deep muscle relaxation
2. Construction of a hierarchy representing emotion-provoking situations
3. Graduated pairing through imagery of the items on the hierarchy with the relaxed state of the client

Training in deep muscle relaxation follows the procedure we discussed earlier. If the client is unable to engage in muscle relaxation, some other form of relaxation training, such as that associated with yoga or meditation, may be used.

Hierarchy Construction

Hierarchy construction involves identification of various situations that evoke the conditioned emotion to be desensitized, such as anxiety. It may involve situations the client has already experienced or anticipates in the future. It may also involve something extrinsic to the client, such as snakes or airplanes, as well as something intrinsic, such as feelings of going nuts. The counselor and client can discuss these situations in the counseling sessions, and the client can also keep track of them as they occur in vivo by using notes. As each situation is identified, it is listed separately on a small index card.

Three possible types of hierarchies can be used in desensitization, depending on the parameters and nature of the client's problem: spatio-temporal, thematic, or personal. The *spatio-temporal* hierarchy consists of items that relate to physical or spatial dimensions, such as distance from a feared object, or time dimensions, such as time remaining before a feared or avoided situation (e.g., taking a test). Spatio-temporal hierarchies are particularly useful in reducing client anxiety about a particular stimulus object, event, or person.

Thematic hierarchies consist of items representing different parameters surrounding the emotion-provoking situation. For example, a client's fear of heights may be greater or less depending on the contextual cues surrounding the height situation and not just one distance from the ground. Or a client's social anxiety may vary with the type and nature of various interpersonal situations.

Personal hierarchies consist of items representing memories or uncomfortable ruminations about a specific person. Personal hierarchies can be quite useful in desensitizing a client to conditioned emotions produced either by a loss-related situation (e.g., loss of one's job) or dissolution of a relationship (e.g., by death, divorce, separation, etc.). Personal hierarchies can also be used to countercondition a client's avoidance behavior to a particular person who, perhaps because of negative interactions, has become aversive to the client. A typical personal hierarchy might begin with an item that has almost no effect on the client's anxiety and then move up a scale of anxiety stimuli to the point where the client typically reacts with high anxiety. For example, a client who experiences high anxiety over test taking might identify (with the counselor's help) a beginning point that is a month away from an exam and then progress to the point of walking into the examination room and receiving the exam. In addition to test anxiety, other possible sources of client anxiety include sensitivity to criticism, fear of losing a personal relationship, fear of looking stupid, fear of flying, and so on.

Regardless of which type of hierarchy is used, each usually consists of 10 to 20 different items. After each item is listed on a separate index card, the index cards are arranged by the client in order from the lowest or least anxiety-provoking to the highest or most anxiety-provoking. The ordering process is also facilitated by a particular scaling and spacing method. Although there are several possible scaling methods, the most commonly used is referred to as Subjective Units of Disturbance Scale (SUDS) (Wolpe & Lazarus, 1966). The scale ranges from 0 to 100. Zero represents absolute calm or no emotion; 100 represents panic or extreme emotion. The client is asked to specify a number between 0 and 100 that best represents the intensity of his or her reaction for each item. Effective hierarchies usually consist of items at all levels of the SUDS. If there are more than 10 SUDS between any two items, probably another item should be inserted.

After the hierarchy has been constructed and you have trained the client in muscle relaxation or some variation thereof, you are ready to begin the pairing process. This aspect of systematic desensitization can be summarized in the following steps adapted from Wolpe (1990):

1. You and your client discuss and agree on a signaling process that the client can use to let you know if and when anxiety begins to be felt. A common signaling system is to have the client raise an index finger if any anxiety (or other conditioned emotion) is experienced.

2. You then use the exercise to induce a state of relaxation for the client.

3. When your client is deeply relaxed (this will be apparent to you by details such as deeper and slower breathing, changes in body posture, etc.), you describe the first (least emotion-provoking) item on the hierarchy to the client and ask him or her to imagine that item. The first time, you present the item only briefly, for about 10 seconds, provided the client does not signal anxiety first. If the client remains relaxed, you instruct him or her to stop visualizing the scene and either to relax or to imagine a pleasant (or comforting) scene (e.g., a sandy beach in summer). Stay with this scene for about 30 seconds.

4. Return to the first anxiety hierarchy item, describe it again, and remain with it for about 30 seconds. This second presentation should include as much detailed description as you gave the first time.

5. If the client again indicates no anxiety, you have the option of repeating Steps 3 and 4, or moving to the second item in the hierarchy. Typically, an item may require from 3 to 10 repetitions before achieving a SUDS of 0. Scenes that have been desensitized in a prior session may need to be presented again in a subsequent session.

6. When your client signals anxiety present (by lifting an index finger), you immediately return to the relaxation process (Step 2) until the client is fully relaxed again. Then you return to the anxiety hierarchy at a lower level (one where the client experienced no anxiety) and begin the process again. Gradually you work back to the hierarchy level where anxiety was experienced. If anxiety is experienced again, repeat this process. Usually within two to three repetitions, the client is able to move through this level of the hierarchy without experiencing anxiety. If a client continues to experience anxiety in a given item, Cormier and Nurius (2003, p. 561) note there are at least three things a counselor can do to eliminate continued anxiety resulting from presentation of the same item: add a new, less anxiety-provoking item to the hierarchy; present the same or the previous item to the client again for a shorter time period; or assess if the client is revising or drifting from the scene during the imagery process.

There is one note of caution regarding the manner in which the counselor responds to a client who is indicating no anxiety. The tendency is to respond to the client's relaxed state by saying "Good" or some similar remark. The counselor's intent is to communicate to the client, "You are doing just what you should be doing." However, Rimm and Masters (1979) note that this could have just the opposite effect, reinforcing the client's not signaling anxiety, and thus disrupting the process. For this reason, it is better if the counselor gives no response as long as the client is not indicating the presence of anxiety.

Each new desensitization session begins with the last item successfully completed during the previous session and ends with a no-anxiety item. The pairing process is usually terminated in each session after successful completion of three to five hierarchy items, or after a duration of 20 to 30 minutes (10 to 15 minutes for children). Occasionally, however, a client may be able to concentrate for a longer period and complete more than five items successfully.

Because systematic desensitization may continue over several weeks, it is important that you keep accurate written notations about what you did and your client's success each session. Using a note card, write the date of the session, ending item number, and a brief description of the item, and indicate the duration of the last two presentations of the item (i.e., 30 seconds, 40 seconds). The counselor writes the scene, followed by how many presentations of the scene were given as well as the SUDS scores for each presentation. As items are successfully completed without anxiety within the counseling session, you may assume that your client will be able to confront them in real-life settings also without experiencing undue anxiety or discomfort. However, you should caution your client not to attempt to encounter the hierarchy situations in vivo until 75 to 80 percent of the hierarchy desensitization process has been completed successfully.

CASE ILLUSTRATION OF ANXIETY REDUCTION

The Case of Pam

Pam is a 10-year-old fourth-grader who has recently refused to go to school. According to her parents, about 1 month earlier, she got very upset at school and begged her teacher to send her home; her teacher referred her to the school nurse, who did so. In the last 2 weeks, Pam has become physically ill on school mornings and protests strongly when her parents insist that it is time to leave. Her teacher reports that Pam continues to have periods of being upset and of crying at school. Pam's mother took her to the family doctor, who could find no physical cause for her complaints. The parents are perplexed because Pam has always enjoyed school and seems relatively well adjusted in other areas of her life.

Pam was referred to the school counselor, whose assessment revealed that probably Pam became upset initially when a classmate teased her about the fact that she walks with a slight limp. Unfortunately, her feelings of anxiety and stress were terminated by her being sent home, rather than her being encouraged to stay at school and

to deal with the upsetting situation. Pam's reaction to the upsetting experience has remained in her awareness, and she has learned that by staying at home, she can avoid a repetition of the experience. The counselor explained to the parents how this may have occurred and, after determining that Pam's ability to engage in imagery would support this approach, suggests systematic desensitization as a successful treatment method. With the parents' signed approval, she began working with Pam, first discussing the procedure thoroughly, explaining that it is an imagination game that will help with fears. They began to identify the things Pam fears most at school. Together, they developed an anxiety hierarchy. Pam indicated that she became most upset as the time for school approaches, so a spatio-temporal hierarchy was constructed with time as the significant dimension. At this point, the counselor taught Pam how to relax using the relaxation method described earlier in this chapter. The hierarchy consisted of:

1. It's Friday night. School's over for a whole weekend, and you are thinking about the fun things you will do.
2. It's Saturday. You play most of the day but in the evening, you remember some homework your teacher gave you. It is a game that you think will be fun to do.
3. It's Sunday night. You are tired but had a lot of fun this weekend. It is time to get your books, pencils, and notebook together for school tomorrow morning.
4. It's Monday morning. You wake up feeling funny in your stomach.
5. Mom calls you for breakfast. You are thinking about school and remember the homework you did.
6. You eat cereal and a piece of toast. Mom checks you to see if you look okay. You do. It's almost time for the bus.
7. You stand at the front door. The bus turns the corner and you go down to the curb to be picked up.
8. The bus stops, and you get on. Your best friend waves you to the seat she has saved for you.
9. The bus arrives at school. You see your teacher standing on the sidewalk waiting for you. She gives you a big smile.
10. You walk with your teacher to your classroom as she tells you about the exciting project she has for you to do today.

The counselor led Pam through relaxation training and they began the desensitization process. During the first session, she explained the signaling system and then spent about 15 minutes helping Pam relax. Then she presented the first hierarchy item, "It's Friday night. School's over for a whole weekend . . . ." She reminded Pam to raise her index finger if or when she felt any discomfort or nervousness. Pam got through the first item with no problem. After two more repetitions to familiarize Pam with the process and increase her relaxed state, the counselor moved to the second item, "It's Saturday. You play most of the day but in the evening, you remember some homework your teacher gave you. . . ." Pam raised her index finger. The counselor immediately stopped the item and returned to the relaxation exercise, suggesting to Pam that she think about her cat, Toby. Pam relaxed quickly and the counselor returned to the first item, "It's Friday night. School's over for a whole weekend. . . ." This pattern continued until Pam could focus on the Saturday night homework item for 40 seconds without feeling any anxiety. The counselor terminated the counseling session at this point.

In the next counseling session, after making Pam feel comfortable and after talking about what she was doing, the counselor began the desensitization process with the second item, "It's Saturday. . . ." Pam experienced no anxiety. The process continued as before, returning to relaxation exercises and Pam thinking about her cat whenever she experienced tension, nervousness, or anxiety.

After nine sessions, Pam was able to go through the entire hierarchy without any anxiety, she no longer had any physical reactions to going to school in the morning, and her confidence was back. The counselor and teacher met twice to discuss how Pam's progress could be supported in the classroom. Pam felt she had successfully beaten her problem, and the case was concluded.

SELF-MANAGEMENT

Many people are legitimately concerned about the long-term effects of counseling. In an effort to promote enduring client changes, counselors have become more concerned with self-directed client change. This interest has led many counseling researchers and practitioners to explore the use of a variety of strategies called *self-control, self-regulation*, or *self-management*. The primary characteristic of these self-management strategies is that the client administers the strategy and directs the change efforts with minimal assistance from the counselor. These strategies are based on a participant model of therapy that emphasizes client responsibility. Self-management strategies are among the best strategies designed to strengthen client investment in the helping process. Self-management may eliminate the counselor as a middle person and ensure greater chances of success because the client invests so directly in the change process.

Using Self-Management Interventions

Self-management interventions are among the easiest and most effective tools to use with clients. But it is the counselor's responsibility to introduce and structure the interventions so that the client fully understands the assignment and the payoff. *Self-monitoring, self-reward*, and *self-contracting* are among the more frequently used interventions. All three of these activities allow the client to see progress even before the client is able to feel progress.

SELF-MONITORING.   Self-monitoring involves two processes: self-observation and recording. In *self-observation*, the client notices or discriminates aspects of his or her behavior. *Self-recording* involves using very specific procedures to keep a record of what the client is doing. Taken together, self-monitoring involves having your client count and/or regulate a target behavior—for example, an undesirable habit or a self-defeating thought or feeling. The process of self-monitoring seems to interfere with the target by breaking the stimulus-response association and drawing the behavior into consciousness or awareness where a choice or decision to enact the behavior can occur. Kanfer (1980) observes that "a person who is asked to observe and record his own behavior is helped immediately to become more aware of its occurrence" (p. 354). Such awareness helps clients to obtain more concrete information about their problem and to collect evidence of changes in the behavior pattern over time.

The initial step in setting up a self-monitoring intervention with a client is selection of the behavior to be monitored or changed. Usually, clients will achieve better results if they start by counting only one behavior. The type of behavior can also affect the degree and direction of change that occurs as a result of monitoring. Self-monitoring seems to increase the frequency of positive or desirable behaviors and to decrease the frequency of negative or undesirable behaviors. This effect is called *reactivity*. Self-monitoring of neutral (neither positive nor negative) behaviors results in inconsistent behavior change. For this reason, it is important to have clients monitor behaviors they value or care most about changing.

Deciding how to monitor the behavior depends on the circumstances of the client's environmental context and the nature of the behavior to be monitored. Generally, clients are asked to count either how often a behavior occurs or how long a particular condition lasts. If the counselor is interested in focusing on how often a behavior occurs, frequency counts are obviously appropriate. But if the counselor simply wants to reduce the amount of time dedicated to a particular behavior pattern, then recording the length of time spent talking on the telephone, studying, playing a computer game, or participating in any other activity is appropriate. Occasionally, clients may wish to record both the time and frequency of a behavior.

In some cases in which the target behavior occurs frequently or continuously, or when the onset and termination of the behavior is difficult to establish, the client might use an *interval method* of recording, which involves dividing the day into half-hour time intervals and then noting whether the behavior occurred in each time interval with a yes or no. This is often referred to as the all-or-nothing recording method. Where the observed behavior is qualitative (i.e., better or worse, warmer or colder, happier or sadder), a response scale may be used in which 0 represents one extreme and 7 represents the opposite extreme. The client is asked to rate the quality of his or her behavior somewhere between 0 and 7 at each interval. For example, the therapist might say to the client, "On a scale of 0 to 7, rate how confident you are feeling right now."

In the case illustration of Pam, the monitoring gave the client information about when she felt calm and when she felt anxious. Clients are helped to see that they are not anxious all of the time, and that often their anxiety is not as intense as they imagine it to be.

Clients will need some device to assist with recording. These can range from simple note cards, log sheets, and diaries for written recording, to more mechanical devices such as a golf score counter worn on the wrist, kitchen timer, or audio recording device. The device should be simple to use, convenient, portable, and economical.

The timing of self-monitoring can influence any change that is produced by this intervention. If the client wishes to decrease the frequency or duration of a monitored behavior (e.g., reduce the number of cigarettes smoked), it is more effective to record the event prior to lighting the cigarette. If the objective is to increase the frequency or duration of a monitored behavior (e.g., a positive self-statement), then the intervention is more effective if the client records the event after its occurrence.

Counting behaviors is the initial step in self-monitoring. The second and equally important step is charting or plotting the behavior counts over a period of time. This permits your client to see progress that might not otherwise be apparent. It also permits your client to set daily goals that are more attainable than the overall goal (successive approximation). Clients can take weekly cumulative counts of self-monitored behaviors and chart them on a simple line graph. After initial recording efforts are successful in initiating change, it is useful for clients to continue recording in order to maintain change. Often, clients' motivation to continue self-monitoring is enhanced if they reward their efforts for self-monitoring.

SELF-REWARD.   Self-reward involves intentionally giving oneself a reward following the occurrence of a desired response or behavior. Self-rewards seem to function in the same way as rewards that are external reinforcements. Watson and Tharp (2002) explain: "You are teaching yourself to discriminate between correct and incorrect performances. You are reminding yourself of your long-term goals and of your rules for getting there. You are learning self-awareness."

There are three major factors to consider when teaching clients how to use the self-reward intervention: (1) choosing the right reward, (2) knowing how to give the reward, and (3) knowing when to give the reward. Rewards can be objects, contact with other persons, activities, images and ideas, and positive self-talk. The most important reinforcers are those that maintain a new behavior once it is firmly established (Watson & Tharp, 2002).

Self-reward is a normal human behavior. You go shopping and see a new pair of exercise shoes and say to yourself, "I'm going to buy those and start exercising." The only problem is that the self-reward was not predetermined and it was given before the desired behavior. We have already noted that if you wish to increase a particular behavior, you should reward yourself *after* the behavior occurs. Thus, self-reward must be a planned strategy, systematically applied, and consistently practiced. That is unlikely to happen unless you have developed a plan for the self-reward intervention.

Specific types of self-rewards include verbal-symbolic (self-praise, such as thinking to yourself, "I really did that well"), imaginal (visualizing pleasant scenes, such as a new dress or a new suit you plan to buy), or material (tangible events or objects that you give yourself at the time of reinforcement).

The most effective self-rewards are perhaps similar to what Glasser and proponents of reality therapy term positive addictions—different from conventional addictions in that they bring both short- and long-term benefits, not just immediate gratification and delayed pain (Glasser, 1965). According to Glasser, a positive addiction is anything a person does regularly that is also noncompetitive, easy to do, and beneficial to him or her, and results in both self-improvement and self-acceptance.

Clients can be asked to create a so-called reward menu, which would vary from small to quite large rewards that they would value and like to receive. These rewards can be further defined as current reinforcers (something enjoyable that occurs on a daily basis, such as eating, reading, etc.) and potential reinforcers (something that could occur in the future that would be satisfying and enjoyable, such as going out to dinner with friends, taking a trip, etc.). Watson and Tharp (2002) have developed guidelines that can be used to help clients identify the things in their world that they find rewarding. They include questions such as the following: Have I identified appropriate rewards for my successes? What rewards do I already give myself and what conditions trigger the rewards? What existing activities would I hate to give up? What makes me feel really good? What kinds of presents would I most like to get? What are my favorite daydreams and fantasies?

The rewards clients select should be potent but not so valuable that they would not give them up in the event that the target behavior was not achieved. In other words, the reinforcer should be strong enough to make working for it worthwhile and, at the same time, not so indispensable that the client refuses to make it something that must be earned.

After identifying what the reward(s) will be, clients must be instructed on what must be done in order to give themselves a reward. The plan should be defined before starting the self-reward intervention rather than during the intervention. Clients should know, and it helps if it is written down, just what the desirable outcome will be for achieving a particular subgoal. This plan can be defined with the client's assistance. It is also important that clients know when they should administer a self-reward. It is perhaps more effective to encourage them to reward themselves for gradual progress toward the desired goal. Daily rewards for small steps are more effective, by and large, than one big reward that is given only when major progress is made. Watson and Tharp (2002) illustrate how this what/when schedule can be defined:

If the dieter arranges the reinforcement of, say, watching an enjoyable TV program immediately after (or even during) self-restraint, dieting is more likely to be observed than if he or she depends entirely on the long-range rewards of being slim someday. In other words, it is the TV program that right now competes with an extra bowl of spaghetti, not the dim dream of slimness in what, at the moment, may appear as a faraway future.

Immediate reinforcement is especially critical in cases in which the undesired behavior consists of consummatory or fear responses. The ice cream cone or piece of candy you eat right now is more reinforcing than the change in the scale next week or the drop in your clothing size next month. If clients select material rewards that aren't portable enough to be carried around for immediate reinforcement, they might consider the following three intermediate options as immediate rewards:

1. Tell a significant other about their behavior to elicit their encouragement. Social reinforcement can be very powerful in helping clients to find extra opportunities to be reinforced and also to ward off urges and temptations.

2. Assign points to each occurrence of the desired behavior; after accumulating a specified number of points, trade it in for a larger reinforcer. Points (sometimes called tokens) are useful because they make it possible to employ a variety of reinforcers and also make it easy to increase a behavior gradually.

3. Engage in imagined or verbal-symbolic rewards; see, hear, and feel what it is like to be 10 pounds slimmer, or praise yourself covertly for refusing that second helping (granted, this doesn't work for everyone).

SELF-CONTRACTING. Clients who are able to identify and be responsible for their behaviors often acknowledge that their current actions are resulting in some undesirable consequences. They can see how they would like the consequences to be different. They may or may not realize that in order to change those consequences, they must first modify the behaviors producing them. Behavior change of any kind can be slow. Therefore, getting clients to make behavior changes is not easy. You must first obtain the client's commitment to change.

The behavioral contract is a useful intervention for gaining a client's cooperation and commitment. Behavioral contracting is used by a growing number of theoretical approaches but has been popularized by behavioral and reality therapists. The contract specifies what actions the client agrees to take in order to reach the desired goal. Contracts provide important structure for clients. In addition to giving the client a "map" to follow and steps that are within the client's ability, contracts also extract a level of commitment from the client. The contract contains a description of the conditions surrounding the action steps: where the client will undertake such actions, how (in what manner) the client will carry out the actions, and when (by what time) the tasks will be completed. Because these contract terms are specified in writing and signed by the client, we refer to this intervention as self-contracting. The most effective contracts have terms that are completely acceptable to the client, are very specific, and reflect short-range goals that are feasible. Self-contracts often are more successful when they are paired with self-reward.

In some cases, a self-contract may also include sanctions that the client administers for failure to meet the contract terms. However, the rewards and sanctions should be balanced, and a self-contract that emphasizes positive terms is probably more effective. When clients do not fulfill terms of their self-contract, some theoretical orientations (i.e., Glasser's reality therapy) believe it is important for the counselor not to accept excuses but, at the same time, not to be critical or punitive.

Self-contracts are very useful in working with children and adolescents because the conditions are so concrete. When contracts are used with children, several additional guidelines are applicable, including the following seven:

1. The required behavior should be easy for the child to identify.

2. The total task should be divided into subtasks, and initial contracts should reward completion of each component or subtask. Other steps can be added later, after each successive target behavior is well established.

3. Smaller, more frequent rewards are more effective in maintaining the child's or adolescent's interest in working for change than larger, less frequently administered rewards.

4. In the case of a self-contract, rewards controlled by the child or teenager are generally more effective than those dispensed by adults. For example, a child who completes his workbook pages at school by lunchtime may dispense a variety of accessible rewards to and for himself, such as free time, visiting the library, drawing, and so on. This helps the child feel in control of his work.

5. Rewards follow rather than precede performance of the target behavior to be increased. The client must agree to complete the specified activity first before engaging in any part of the reward.

6. The client must view the contract as a fair one that, in an equitable way, balances the degree of work and energy expended and the resulting payoffs or consequences.

7. Children respond best to contracts that require daily efforts and that address larger issues such as acquiring friends, increasing school success, and other such global goals. However, the component parts of the contract must be specific and preferably behavioral in nature and allow for monitoring activities such as keeping a log, checklist, or scorecard.

Client Commitment to Self-Management

A critical problem in the effective use of any self-management intervention is having the client use the intervention regularly and consistently. Clients will be more likely to carry out self-management programs if certain conditions exist, including the following eight:

1. The use of the self-management program will provide enough advantages or positive consequences to be worth the cost to the client in terms of time and effort.

2. Clients believe in their capacity to change. Because beliefs create one's reality, the belief that change is possible helps clients try harder when they get stuck or are faced with an unforeseen difficulty in their change plans.

3. Clients' utilization of self-management processes reflects their own standards of performance, not the standards of the counselor or of significant others. One note of caution: Counselors sometimes suggest a goal, or society often seems to suggest a goal. Such borrowed goals work against self-management efforts if clients are merely learning how to behave in accordance with standards that are foreign to them.

4. Clients use personal reminders about their goals when tempted to stray from the intervention plan. A written list of self-reminders that clients can carry at all times may prove helpful in this respect.

5. If the client secretly harbors an escape plan ("I'll study every day except when my friend drops over" or "I'll diet except on Sundays"), this should be made explicit. Concealed escape plans are likely to wreak havoc on the best-conceived self-management programs. Some escape clauses may be particularly detrimental to change, particularly those that reactivate an irresistible craving. However, Watson and Tharp (2002) recommend that any plan "should clearly state all intended escapes, whether or not they are wise."

6. The self-management program is directed toward maintenance as well as initial acquisition of target behaviors. For this to occur, you must take into account the client's lifestyle.

> Self-management requires more than a temporary change in setting conditions or the acquisition of specific strategies. For therapeutic change to be maintained, the individual must be prepared, by virtue of his or her mode of information processing, the adequacy of active coping skills, and by dint of having selected a supportive social setting (friends, co-workers, spouse, etc.) to deal with unforeseen challenges, conflicts, periods of depression, and/or the periodic malfunctioning of "best laid plans." (Karoly, 1982, p. 22)

7. The client's use of the program may be strengthened by enlisting the support and assistance of other persons—so long as their roles are positive, not punishing. Peers or friends can aid the client in achieving goals through reinforcement of the client's regular use of the self-management strategies and reminders to resist temptations.

8. The counselor maintains some minimal contact with the client during the time the self-management program is being implemented. Counselor reinforcement is quite important in successful implementation of self-management efforts.

You can provide reinforcement easily through oral approval or by acknowledging progress. Have the client drop in or telephone regularly during the course of the self-management program. This enables you to provide immediate encouragement and, if necessary, to modify the program if it is flawed.

CASE ILLUSTRATION OF SELF-MANAGEMENT

The Case of Kareem

Kareem is a 14-year-old boy who has scored very high on ability tests but has performed consistently below his ability level in school. He admits that his poor grades are due, for the most part, to what he calls "not really trying." When asked by the counselor to define and give examples of this, Kareem noted that he rarely took homework home, or if he did, he didn't complete it. He also said that he rarely opened a book and often had not studied for tests. As a direct result of a series of events that occurred in his neighborhood, Kareem sought out the counselor for help in changing his ways. He has decided that he wants to go to college and was starting to realize that his bad grades would adversely affect this possibility unless he pulled them up. He was concerned because he did not know how to change what he referred to as bad study habits.

The counselor supported his newly found goals and explained some of the rationale and process of a strategy called self-management. She pointed out that Kareem, rather than herself, would be in charge of setting specific goals for his performance and monitoring his progress. She assured him that she would be there to help him start the process and to assist whenever he needed help. This appealed to Kareem, who stated that he is tired of having so many other people on his back about doing better in school.

Because Kareem's present base rate for studying was almost zero, the counselor initially discussed some realistic goals that he might want to set for himself as part of a self-contract. She helped him build in a self-monitoring system and a self-reward process. Kareem decided to set the following goals and action steps for his contract:

Goal: To improve my rate of homework assignment completion during the next nine-week grading period from 0 to 85 percent.

Action steps: To keep a daily record of assigned homework and to establish a time and place at home where I will work on homework every day. On Fridays, I will do Monday's homework. On Saturdays, I will be free from school work, but on Sundays, I will review my assignments and organize my books for the next school day.

In addition, he completed a reinforcement survey and selected eight potential rewards that he could use to reinforce his action steps. Kareem included a bonus clause in his self-contract, which specified an additional reward any week he exceeded the 85 percent level of homework completion. His self-contract is illustrated in Figure 10.1.

The counselor explained a self-monitoring system that Kareem could use to track his progress.

Name of Contractor: _____ Kareem L. _____

Date of Contract: _____ 2/5/08 _____

This I Will Do:

Goals of Contract: To improve my grades by improving my homework assignment completions from zero percent to 85 percent.

Action Steps:	1 a. I will keep a homework assignment book and will write down each homework assignment before leaving my desk after each class period.
	1 b. I will transfer my homework assignments from my book to my record poster before I become involved in any other activity at home.
	2 a. I will clear space in my room and move the old desk from the basement into the room as a working place.
	2 b. I will start my homework assignment no later than 4:00 P.M. each day and will not stop until it is completed (unless dinner interupts my plans, in which case I will return to homework until it is finished).
	3 a. I will indicate on my record poster which assignments I completed and I will record the percentage at the end of the week.
	3 b. I will bring my record poster to Miss Bancroft on Mondays at 7:45 A.M. and will review my progress before classes begin.
Rewards:	1. Watch the sports channel news at 11:00 P.M.
	2. Listen to my music between the end of school and 4:00 P.M.
	3. Play pool with the guys on Friday night.
	4. Go to the mall and take in a movie on Saturday night.
	5. Hang out.
	6. Buy a new CD.
	7. Talk to girls on the phone.
	8. Get a pizza.

Date contract will be reviewed: _____ 2/12/08 _____

Signatures: _____ Kareem L. (client) _____

_____ Miss Bancroft (counselor) _____

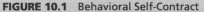

FIGURE 10.1 Behavioral Self-Contract

She suggested that he use a daily log to record completion of each homework assignment (a large poster board with each school day of the month and a thermometer-like graph to show the percentage of his homework that he completed). She also asked Kareem if he wanted to use any outside source to verify completion of assignments, but he indicated that he didn't need that. Finally, she and Kareem agreed to meet each Monday morning and he was to show her his monitoring chart (which he could roll up and store in his locker easily). Kareem's log for the first week is shown in Figure 10.2.

Scoreboard

Name: _____ Kareem L. _____

Behavior Record: 1. _____ Management of homework assignments _____

2. _____ Completion of homework assignments _____

Week of: February 5

Day	Assignments	Done	Reward
Monday	English (read)		
	Math (problems)	X	
	Biology (lab report)	X	Listen to music
	History (read)		
Tuesday	English (nothing—read Monday's)	X	
	Math (problems)		
	Biology (read)	X	Listen to music
	History (questions)	X	Watch sports news
Wednesday	English (read)	X	Listen to music
	Math (nothing)		
	Biology (questions)	X	Watch sports news
	History (read)	X	Call Clarice—talk
Thursday	English (study for quiz)	X	
	Math (problems)	X	Listen to music
	Biology (read)	X	Watch sports news
	History (questions)	X	Call Felicia
Friday	English (theme)		
	Math (study for test)	X	Listen to music
	Biology (read)	X	Watch sports news
	History (study for quiz)	X	

Amount completed: 15 out of 19 assignments

FIGURE 10.2 Assignment Record

Kareem found the self-management strategy to work. Several conditions contributed to this outcome: He was highly motivated; he did not want others to be monitoring him; he chose a reasonable goal and action steps; he liked the counselor; the counselor liked him and was clearly supportive of his goal, his motivation, and his plan; and the counselor followed up religiously on the Monday morning commitments.

CLIENT REACTIONS TO BEHAVIORAL INTERVENTIONS

Behavioral interventions are often very appealing to clients, particularly in the initial stages of counseling when clients are highly motivated and want something to be done about their situations. The specificity, concreteness, and emphasis on action that these interventions offer help clients to feel as if something important is being done on their behalf. Even nonbehavioral counselors sometimes use a behavioral intervention such as relaxation to capitalize on this phenomenon, which can increase the counselor's credibility with the client and the client's sense of trust that counseling can and will make a difference.

As the helping process continues, some of the clients' initial enchantment with the procedures may wear thin as they discover the different and often painful work of changing fixed and established behavior patterns. Successful use of behavioral interventions requires a significant investment of time, energy, and persistence from clients—daily practice, homework assignments, accurate record keeping, and so on.

To counteract any potential pitfalls or letdowns, counselors who rely heavily on behavioral interventions during the helping process must also generate involvement with the client through a positive relationship and commitment to action. When counselors use behavioral approaches, they must find ways to strengthen the client's compliance with the demands of the intervention. Compliance can be enhanced in a number of ways. Additional techniques for fostering compliance include creating a positive expectancy set, providing detailed instructions about the use and benefits of an intervention, having the client rehearse the intervention, and having the client visualize and explore beneficial aspects of change.

Summary

In this chapter, we have explored a variety of counseling interventions based on action-oriented helping approaches. These approaches focus on direct modification of a client's behavior and rely heavily on principles of learning to facilitate behavior change.

The modeling and rehearsal interventions we described are major components of skill training programs such as assertiveness training, job interview skills training, and social skills training. These interventions are most useful when clients have skill deficits or lack effective skills for selected situations.

Anxiety-reduction strategies such as muscle relaxation, sensory relaxation, and systematic desensitization are useful for dealing with the behavioral excess of fear, worry, and anxiety. Muscle relaxation is used as either a single strategy or as part of systematic desensitization.

Self-management intervention programs are growing in popularity and success. Clients are put in charge of their change program; the counselor acts as a facilitator of that process. Common components of a self-management program include self-monitoring, self-reward, and self-contracting.

Behavioral interventions are very appealing to many clients because they offer specificity, concreteness, and something that can be done by the client. A major problem with continued use is management of the appropriate level of client commitment to ensure success.

Exercises

I. Modeling

Listed below are four hypothetical clients who might derive benefit from a modeling intervention. Based on the description given about each client, select the model that might be most effective for the client.

A. The client is an African American male in a graduate program who is avoiding a required statistics course because of his fear of math.

   1. An older African American male who has already succeeded in statistics

   2. A white male who has overcome his fear of statistics

   3. An African American male of similar age who is also enrolled in a graduate program that requires statistics

B. The client is a young, white male who lost a leg in a car accident and is trying to learn to get around in a wheelchair without soliciting assistance from other people.

   1. A female who has been in a wheelchair since birth

2. A white male who survived a motorcycle crash
3. An older white male who is successfully employed

C. The client is a middle-age woman who is enrolled in a special treatment program for alcoholics.

1. Another middle-age woman who has successfully overcome alcoholism through a similar program
2. Another woman who is an active alcoholic
3. The woman's husband or a close relative

D. The client is a young woman who is institutionalized in a state hospital because she has refused to leave her house for 2 years and believes that people were after her.

1. Another institutionalized patient who is in the prerelease program
2. A staff psychiatrist
3. A female staff aide

II. Behavior Rehearsal

With a partner, try the process of behavior rehearsal. One of you should take the client's role, and the other can assume the role of helper. Have the client present a problem in which the desired behavior change is to acquire a skill or to extinguish a fear. The counselor should try the behavior rehearsal intervention to help the client meet this goal. Here are the tasks to remember to do:

A. Specify the target behavior(s).
B. Determine the situations in which the skills need to be used or the fear needs to be reduced.
C. Arrange these situations on a hierarchy, starting with the least difficult or least anxiety-producing situations and gradually moving up to situations of greater difficulty, complexity, or threat.
D. Beginning with the first situation on the hierarchy, have the client engage in covert rehearsal of the target response(s). Following this practice attempt, ask the client to analyze it.
E. Using the same situation, have the client engage in a role-play (overt) rehearsal. Give the client feedback about the strengths and limitations of this practice. Supplement your feedback with an audio or video recording analysis, as feasible.
F. Determine when the client has satisfactorily demonstrated the target skills or reduced anxiety within the interview rehearsals. Assign homework consisting of in vivo rehearsal of this one situation.
G. Repeat Steps D through F for the other situations on the hierarchy.

III. Relaxation

Using triads or small groups, practice providing muscle relaxation training for someone in the group. You can follow the instructions found on pages 000–000. After the procedure, obtain feedback both from your role-play "client" and from observers. Some of the items you may wish to solicit feedback about are the following:

A. Your voice—pitch, tempo, volume
B. The pacing or speed with which you took the person through the procedure
C. The clarity of your instructions

After you have practiced with this intervention and received feedback from another person, you may want to record the instructions on a CD and critique yourself.

IV. Systematic Desensitization

A. Match each of the client descriptions listed below with the type of hierarchy that would be most appropriate to use with that particular client. Be sure to give a rationale for your choice.
B. Pick one of the client descriptions from this list and develop a corresponding hypothetical hierarchy for the client. Consult with a colleague or instructor after your hierarchy is completed.

Type of Hierarchy
1. Spatio-temporal
2. Thematic
3. Personal

Client Descriptions
1. The client is very stressed after the recent dissolution of a 5-year relationship.
2. The client becomes increasingly anxious about a speech as the time of the speech draws near.
3. The client becomes anxious in situations that involve other people.
4. The client becomes more anxious as she gets farther away from her house.
5. The client is very upset after the death of her spouse 2 years ago.

V. Self-Management

This exercise is designed to help you modify some aspect of your helping behavior with the use of a self-management program.

A. Select and define a behavior you wish to increase or decrease that, when changed, will make you a better helper. The behavior may be an overt one, such as asking open questions instead of closed questions. Or the behavior may be covert, such as reducing the number of apprehensive thoughts about seeing clients or increasing some self-enhancing thoughts about your helping potential.

B. Record the occurrence of the behavior for a week or two to obtain a baseline measure; the baseline gives you the present level of the behavior before applying any self-management interventions.

C. After obtaining some baseline data, deliberately try to increase or decrease the behavior (depending on your goal) using self-monitoring. Remember, employ prebehavior monitoring to decrease a response and postbehavior monitoring to increase a response. Do this for about 2 weeks. Does the behavior change over time in the desired direction? If so, you may want to continue with self-monitoring for a few more weeks. Charting and posting the data will help you see visible progress.

D. Work out a self-reward plan or write a self-contract related to the behavior change you are seeking.

E. Continue to self-record the occurrence of the behavior during Step D; then compare these data with the data you gathered during baseline (Step B). What change occurs?

Discussion Questions

1. Behavioral approaches assume that much maladaptive behavior is acquired through learning. What is your reaction to this assumption?
2. In what ways does learning occur through counseling?
3. In using behavioral approaches with clients, to what extent do you think that you are treating real problems or merely symptoms?
4. In what counseling settings do you think behavioral interventions would be most useful?

MyCounselingLab Assignment

Go to the Video Resource Library on the MyCounselingLab site for your text and search for the following clips:

- **Family Confrontation** What behavior(s) is the counselor focusing on? How does he show the client that the behavior in question works against the client? What behavioral change is suggested or implied?

11

Systemic Interventions

PURPOSE OF THIS CHAPTER

The last three chapters have discussed counseling interventions that have an impact on feelings, thoughts, and actions. They would seem to imply that the problem lies within the client. While this perception may be correct, it is not entirely complete. What if the client's world is falling apart and this is the root cause of his or her situation? We know that sometimes a person's environment is the problem—whether social influences, gender or racial discrimination, employment dislocation, family, or peer issues are involved. Under such conditions, the counseling session must address the element that is not present in the session. Much that we have studied considers the individual client separate from his or her social environment. But, of course, that is not how humans exist. In this chapter, we will consider a theoretical alternative to the psychologically based interventions discussed in preceding chapters. We will examine a variety of counseling interventions that assume (1) human problems are not based in the individual, but rather in the system in which the individual functions; (2) change in any part of the system affects all parts of the system, and thus affects the individual who is experiencing the problem; and (3) systemic change must reflect not only the immediate social system in which it occurs, but also other systems—for example, gender, culture, race—as they contribute to the system's characteristics and values.

While the family systems approaches focus on the unit, for example, the couple or the family, the methods are also applicable to the individual as an extension of the unit. Thus, we will discuss how systems applications can be used in individual counseling sessions as we have discussed in the preceding chapters.

Considerations as You Read This Chapter

- Central to systemic thinking is the notion that behavior, including problem behavior, is rooted in systems. One criticism of this is that it removes any responsibility from the individual for his or her problems. Do you agree? How might this affect the individual's participation in counseling?

■ You will also note that the systemic counselor seems to be quite active and emphasizes change rather than insight. What advantages could you predict from this approach? What problems could you foresee?

■ To what problems in social units other than the family might these interventions be applied? How do you think the process would be different from that in which the family is the focus?

Systemic interventions are drawn from a variety of approaches that view the individual as part of a larger social context. Seen this way, the individual constantly interacts with that larger context, contributing and responding in ways that can best be comprehended by understanding the social context. Thus, the system's role becomes more meaningful and important, and the individual's role is diminished, when compared to most psychological views of human behavior. This way of viewing human functioning can be likened to ecological systems in which all elements are interrelated, and in which change at any level of those interrelated parts will lead to alteration of the whole system. One of the better ways of illustrating this is through the functioning of the family unit.

THERAPIES THAT STRESS THE IMPORTANCE OF SYSTEMS

Recent years have witnessed a maturing of the systemic therapy movement. Its roots date to the 1950s, when Gregory Bateson was first studying the relationship between schizophrenia and interpersonal functioning within the family. Stimulated by Bateson's early thinking, the next 20 years saw an explosion of new concepts on the functioning of family systems. These concepts began to crystallize into four recognizable schools of family therapy: the object relations school, which includes writers such as Framo (1982) and Zuk (1975); the family systems school, represented by Bowen (1978); the structural family therapy school, identified in the writings of Minuchin and Fishman (1981); and the strategic intervention school, which embraces a wide-ranging group of theorists and therapists. Strategic intervention gained recognition as a result of the work and writings of therapists associated with the Mental Research Institute (MRI) of Palo Alto. These therapists included Jackson (1961); Haley (1963, 1973, 1976, 1980); and Weakland, Fisch, Watzlawick, and Bodin (1974). Haley later established his own Family Therapy Institute in Washington, DC, where he and Cloe Madanes developed their particular variations of systemic thinking. The strategic intervention approach is also represented in other cultures, particularly in the work of the Milan systemic therapy school (Palazzoli, Cecchin, Prata, & Boscolo, 1978), which is also reflected in the work of the Ackerman Institute group of New York City (Hoffman, 1981). These groups reflect a theoretical continuum that extends from a highly psychoanalytic orientation (object relations) to an ecological basis (Foley, 1989).

In recent years, solution-focused and narrative therapies have emerged in the systemic therapy practice. As its name implies, solution-focused therapy emphasizes finding solutions rather than dealing with problems (deShazer, 1988, 1991, 1994). Narrative therapy involves exploring the stories "by which we circulate knowledge about ourselves and the world we inhabit" (Goldenberg & Goldenberg, 2008, p. 326). These stories reflect people's cultural perspectives as well as their realities. Principal contributors to narrative therapy have been

Michael White of Australia and David Epston of New Zealand (White & Epston, 1990; White, 1991; Epston, 1994; Epston & White, 1992). The movement has made significant inroads in the practice of family therapy in North America, too (Andrews, Clark, & Baird, 1998; Madigan, 1994).

The different schools all occupy prominent positions in the practice of marriage and family therapy in the United States and have a growing list of practitioners and advocates in Great Britain, Israel, Germany, and Finland. One might ask why the systemic approach has been particularly successful in moving into other cultures. One answer undoubtedly is that the philosophical underpinnings of this approach lend themselves to different cultural perspectives. Even in cultures as individualistic as the British or Finnish, an ecological perspective of human interaction seems to be more facilitative than some of the more individualistic approaches.

As with the interventions we discussed in earlier chapters, the interventions associated with the systemic model have received criticism from feminist therapists who believe that many of the family therapy models were developed without attention to the female experience and, as a result, contain covert gender bias (Goodrich, Rampage, Ellman, & Halstead, 1988; McGoldrick, Anderson, & Walsh, 1989). points to the way in which systems thinking can be gender-blind:

> The notion that all persons within a system contribute equally to problems ignores the reality of power differentials within the family and results in the minimalization or trivialization of acts of violence associated with battering, incest, and child abuse. By removing individual responsibility for behavior, these "neutral" systems also contribute to mother blaming. Family therapies have also contributed to the idealization of White, middle class family structures and may subtly reinforce stereotyped gender roles. Finally, terms such as enmeshment, fusion, and symbiosis are sometimes used to pathologize women's relational qualities and concepts such as complementarity and hierarchy encourage role differentiation along traditional lines. (p. 31)

Family therapy models that embrace systemic thinking have been criticized with respect to their lack of attention to the ethnicity of the family in treatment. Rigazio-DiGilio (1993) observed that "ethnicity is a filter through which families and individuals understand and interpret their symptoms, their attitude toward helpers, and their preferred treatment methods" (p. 338).

These criticisms may be more directed at what has been written about family therapy in the professional journals than by what is practiced in family therapy. Even if this is the case, it is important to recognize that the structure and social organization of families are strongly influenced by cultural and ethnic factors, thus producing wide-ranging variations among families in U.S. culture. What white middle-class U.S. families find acceptable as therapeutic interventions may alienate or completely miss the mark with many other U.S. families. For example, Berg and Jaya (1993, p. 32) note that U.S. children (presumably that middle-class white standard) seem to fight their way out of the family in order to emancipate or individuate themselves. By contrast, Asian American families view being excluded from the family as the worst possible punishment one can endure. Emancipation and individuation are alien concepts.

Hierarchy within the therapy relationship and the family system takes on a different meaning for African American families, however, many of which confront racism and oppression on a daily basis, again making their experience different from majority culture clients (Stevenson & Renard, 1993). As these authors note, an awareness and acknowledgment of the role and presence of racism and oppression is very important in working with African Americans because it has long been part of their system. Otherwise, the counselor may become an agent for illegitimate and abusive power in the hierarchy of the relationship and also may stimulate too many feelings of mistrust (Stevenson & Renard, 1993).

INTERPERSONAL SYSTEMS THINKING

In systemic thinking, families and other social systems have inherent structure, dictated by rules, roles, boundaries, and patterns of behavior. These structural qualities inform individual members on how they are to participate both in the family and in the culture outside the family.

Cohesive interpersonal systems develop a self-sustaining quality. The integral parts (members) of the system collectively seek to maintain the system, even when the system may be failing to meet the needs of an individual member. Thus the system's preservation becomes the dominant motive for functioning. This can be illustrated by the many ways families adapt to children's growing up and becoming adults.

The internal organization of the cohesive system is defined by systemic "rules." The term *systemic rule* is a euphemism for interactions between individual members that are so predictable that one might think a rule exists to govern the behavior. An example might be the manner in which the father reenters the family system each evening (no one is to disturb him until he has had time to read his paper or drink a beer) or the manner in which a particular child is disciplined (only the mother may discipline Billy). Such rules contribute to the family's drive to sustain the system. When rules are broken, the violator may be dealt with by the entire system or by a designated enforcer. For example, if the father is an incorrigible grouch, family rules will evolve that attempt to control those stimuli that will put him in a bad mood. Strong pressure will be exerted on maverick family members to keep them from breaking the rules that might lead to the father's bad temper.

Most individuals function within a network of systems embedded within systems. As you begin to conceptualize how and perhaps why the individual functions as he or she does, you must realize that more is involved than just the sociological family unit. Clearly, families also function within other systems. One of those systems is the family's cultural heritage, whether it be visibly obvious or apparent only through the family's ceremonial patterns. Szapocznik and Kurtines (1993) point out that this is particularly observable with the family that has a distinct cultural heritage, such as Hispanic or African American. Culture is not the only system in which families function. Socioeconomic status also contributes to functioning systems (e.g., families below the poverty level or those families that are in the upper middle class).

Dysfunctional systems tend to develop rigid boundaries. The psychological boundaries that define the system (separate the family system from other social units, such as neighbors) identify and sustain the family unit. Because dysfunctional families experience greater vulnerability, the systemic tendency is to become more rigid and resistant to change. Thus, the dysfunctional family finds change to be more difficult to accomplish than the family with more flexible boundaries. This can be particularly problematic when the dysfunctional system involves a cultural dimension in which family identity and solidarity are emphasized (e.g., the Italian American family), thus possibly magnifying the intensity of the problem.

The fact that family system rigidity is related to the family's level of dysfunction has caused theorists to search for more effective interventions. Thus, the structural and strategic approaches emerged. The first of these, *structural therapy*, has focused on redefining the system by altering interpersonal rules and boundaries in a behavioral manner. The second, *strategic therapy*, has developed cognitive interventions as a means of entering and altering family members' conceptualizations of the system and how it should function.

In this chapter, we will examine how many interventions are also adaptable and effective in achieving better individual communication, structural change, and strategic change. In addition, attention will be directed to systemic interventions that are associated with the newer family approaches.

These examples suggest that the family functions as an integral system embedded within other systems. When counseling is sought, the counselor must make the decision either to treat family members individually or to view the family system as the client. When treating the system, the counselor's conceptual approach must reflect an awareness of governing rules, structure, systems within systems, and other ecological factors. For this reason, systemic therapy has evolved by using traditional interventions in new ways or by developing new kinds of interventions that are more effective with system change.

The bulk of this book has addressed counseling interventions in an individual context. By increasing the number of individuals involved in any intervention, interpersonal dynamics (current or historical) become a significant dimension of the counseling process. This fact has led to the emergence of communications approaches. Even if you are working with a single client, however, systemic issues are operating. Consequently, it is entirely possible, and sometimes more appropriate, to use systemic interventions.

Assessing System Issues

In Chapter 5, we introduced the genogram as a tool used to assess issues involving couples and families. It also allows the counselor to assess individual client issues that may be derived from family-of-origin issues.

From a systems perspective, certain assumptions are made (there is fairly strong evidence that these assumptions are to be trusted). The first is that all family systems have some history of relationships that requires individual adaption and adjustment. It may be Uncle Willie who is in prison, Aunt Margaret who is a closet alcoholic, or brother Richard who is using drugs and failing college. From these conditions, family members make accommodations ranging from "We don't talk about Willie" to "Your brother is going to kill your Dad with grief. You better not do that to him." A second assumption is that adjustment patterns that develop in families *carry down to individual members*. In other words, the way I learned to deal with problems as a child, I still use as an adult. Consequently, information about family-of-origin relationships and conditions often reappears in a person's adult relationships.

The genogram may be used to map out the family's personal and private history of relationships (e.g. alcoholism, divorce, abortions, abuse, suicide) and to identify those distortions that families tend to make regarding how one functions in systems. While we will refer to the *family* system in this chapter, the material also applies to how individuals function in other systems, for example, work setting, peer group, and so on, too (McGoldrick, Gerson, and Petry, 2008).

ALTERING COMMUNICATION PATTERNS

Family or group dysfunctions may be approached from a variety of directions. Sometimes the underlying issue appears to be a fundamental misunderstanding among members. This misunderstanding may relate to members' expectations, roles in the system, or responsibilities. When communication appears either to have broken down or fails due to lack of communication skills, the counselor may use a variety of interventions to teach or develop insight and skills for family or group members to use. Most of the techniques used in communications family therapy consist of teaching rules of clear communication, analyzing and interpreting communication patterns, and manipulating interactions through a variety of strategic maneuvers.

COMMUNICATION SKILL BUILDING

Often, building communication skills begins with an introduction to basic rules of communication. These "rules" are really guidelines to sending and receiving clear and concise messages. Gestalt therapy, reality therapy, transactional analysis, and rational emotive therapy all emphasize these rules. In addition, programs such as the Minnesota Couples Communication Program have contributed to communication rules training. Effective communications rules are fairly simple. They include (1) speaking in the first person singular, (2) speaking for self, and (3) speaking directly to the person for whom the communication is intended.

These simple rules often prove to be rather difficult to master, particularly when they run counter to the individual's habitual or cultural patterns of communication. Consequently, the acquisition of a new pattern may require instruction, rehearsal, evaluation, and continued practice. (These elements of skill training are discussed in Chapter 10.) For example, some people develop a communication style in which the personal pronoun I is almost never used. In its place, the impersonal second person (you) or the collective (we or people) is used. This is illustrated by a brief dialogue between Bob and his wife, Janet.

JANET: Bob, are you going to cut the grass tomorrow?

BOB: You know people don't cut the grass on Sunday.

JANET: Well, I just thought it would be good to cut it before Monday.

BOB: Well, that's just not what one does on a Sunday.

The counselor might point out to Bob that when he uses such referents as *people* and *one*, he is speaking in terms that Miller, Wackman, Nunnally, and Miller (1989) refer to as *underresponsible*. This notion of responsible communication is the same as the gestaltist notion of *claiming ownership*. In other words, if Bob were to say, "You know I don't cut the grass on Sunday," he would be taking responsibility for the claim rather than attributing it to unknown "people."

Underresponsible communication is a style. It does not necessarily reflect an intention to avoid responsibility although it can. The counselor might work with Bob and Janet to increase Bob's awareness of both his style and the consequences of his style.

COUNSELOR: Bob, when you say, "People don't cut the grass on Sunday," aren't you also saying, "I don't cut the grass on Sunday?"

BOB: Right.

COUNSELOR: What would happen if you just said, "I don't want to cut the grass on Sunday"?

BOB: Nothing, I guess. Maybe Janet wouldn't understand why.

COUNSELOR: Could you tell her why if she didn't understand?

BOB: Yeah, I guess so.

COUNSELOR: Why don't you tell Janet why you don't want to cut the grass?

BOB: Okay. I don't want to cut the grass on Sunday because I don't think it looks good to the neighbors.

COUNSELOR: Janet, is it different when Bob says it that way?

JANET: Yes, I like it better when Bob tells me what he is thinking but I think it is silly to feel that way.

The other type of communication style is the indirect message. Janet answered the counselor's question and then added her opinion of Bob's view by saying, "I think it is silly to feel that way." By tacking this opinion onto her answer, she is actually communicating to Bob through the counselor. Speaking directly to the person for whom the communication is intended is responsible communication. When the message is made through another person (children, friends, neighbors), the communicator is, once again, using an underresponsible style. In this case, the counselor might turn to Janet and say:

COUNSELOR: Janet, you answered my question, and then you said something to me that Bob needed to hear.

JANET: What do you mean?

COUNSELOR: You told me your opinion of Bob's reason for not cutting the grass on Sunday. I think you really wanted Bob to hear your opinion. Is that right?

JANET: Well, yes, I guess so.

COUNSELOR: Then turn to Bob and tell him.

JANET: He already knows now. [Janet resists being responsible.]

COUNSELOR: I know, but this is just for practice.

JANET: I don't think you need to worry about what the neighbors think. They all work on Sunday.

At this point, the counselor interrupts the dialogue to review what was happening in the two communication styles and how underresponsible styles lead to ambiguity, confusion, and frustration. This is the teaching time and is as important as the rehearsal. During this time, the counselor can appraise each person's style, the consequences of that style, and its apparent effect on the other person. Sometimes the lesson is enhanced by asking the participants to exaggerate their underresponsible style (be even more underresponsible).

It should be noted here that these rules may not be as transferrable across cultures as professionals once thought. For example, the Native American culture views the person as part of a larger ecosystemic context and thus may not place the emphasis on individuals as these "rules" seem to imply. Other cultures also deemphasize individuality while raising the importance of the family, community, or society.

One particularly common communication problem that becomes evident in counseling has been labeled the distancer/pursuer system. This dynamic emerges over time when one partner pursues and the other distances or avoids communicating. Such communication styles are really personality characteristics of the players, one having learned (perhaps from his or her parent) that it is easier to hide or avoid than it is to confront, while the other has learned that it is more effective to approach or confront than to avoid. This systemic issue is illustrated in the following case described by Bernard and Hackney (1983).

CASE ILLUSTRATION OF DISTANCER/PURSUER

The Case of Sheila and Eric

Eric was attracted to Sheila because she was outgoing and fun. He was somewhat shy, so he admired this friendly quality in her. Sheila found Eric attractive because he was "the strong, silent type." She also liked his gentleness, which made him different from many of the men she had dated.

After a year of dating, they were married. They both felt they had found a mate who would complement them, someone who would bring out new things in themselves.

After a year, Sheila found herself edgy with Eric when they went to social gatherings. Although he wished to be friendly, he still acted aloof and distant. At home, they also seemed to have become "stuck" at an intermediate level of closeness. Eric didn't offer all of the information Sheila wanted. He didn't think to tell her about little details at work, funny things that happened. In an attempt to open him up, she would ask questions and more questions. Eric was not comfortable with what felt like an intrusion on his privacy. He wished Sheila were more like him. He was also beginning to feel that Sheila thought he was inadequate.

Ten years later, the scene looks quite different. Sheila is belligerent about her husband's quietness. "You never tell me anything. You don't want me in your world. What do you think it is like to live with a stranger?" Eric has become totally withdrawn. Sheila's role is to nag. Eric's role is to hide (Bernard & Hackney, 1983, pp. 52–53).

Eric and Sheila's communication difficulties are a product of personal qualities each brought into the marriage. They are complicated and intensified by the couple's lack of awareness of the systemic and personal issues that are involved. Sensitizing Eric and Sheila to the systemic issues will address part of the problem. This may be accomplished by pointing out the pattern and helping them see that it is not Eric's withdrawal or Sheila's demands but the interaction of their unique characteristics that contributes to the miscommunication.

Awareness should also be focused on interpersonal qualities because partial awareness of one's needs, motives, or intentions is a frequent source of miscommunication. Miller, Wackman, Nunnally, and Miller (1989, pp. 49–50) use an exercise they call the Awareness Wheel to help couples become aware of these interpersonal patterns. Each communicated message has five stages of development. The first stage is sensing, or receiving data into awareness (for example, awareness of discomfort). Stage two is thinking about that data (Why am I uncomfortable? What is the source?). The third stage, feeling, involves affective processing of the cognitive processes of stage two (How do I feel about being made uncomfortable by that?). In the fourth stage, intentions, the individual determines what should be done to respond to the thought and feeling stages (What do I want to change? How should things be?). In the final stage, the individual reaches the level of action (What am I going to do?). This is a circular sequence, with the action stage leading back into the sensing stage and beginning the process all over again. (It might help you to draw these stages in a circular pattern with arrows pointing from each stage to the next.)

This procedure can be used with couples as a means for analyzing each person's communication pattern. Typically, one or more stages are either weak or missing entirely from the process. The counselor can ask partners to select a topic and use the five stages to organize their messages. For example:

Sensing: I sense (observe) that you are irritated.

Thinking: This makes me wonder if I did something to make you mad.

Feeling: I'm nervous and uncomfortable with that thought.

Intending: I would like for you to be friendly and warm toward me.

Acting: I will ask you if I did something to upset you. If I did, I will apologize. If I didn't, I will ask what I could do to make your day more pleasant.

An insecure person might be highly sensitive (stage one) and unaware of the thinking or feeling stages. On the other hand, the spouse might be action oriented (stage five) but relatively unaware of stages one and three. In such an example, neither partner could communicate effectively until they were able to identify internal dimensions of their messages. First, one must know the message, and then it can be communicated.

Accurate and responsible communication is only half the goal of good communication patterns. If a message is clearly and responsibly sent but the receiver does not comprehend, then communication has failed. This may happen if the message is too threatening or if the receiver is preoccupied or otherwise blocked from perceiving the intent of the message. The person trying to communicate the message cannot know this without some feedback from the receiver. In other words, the communicator must know if the receiver (1) hears and (2) hears accurately what is being said. Miller et al. (1989) refer to this as a shared meaning, and they have developed a communication exercise for partners to use whenever they believe miscommunication is occurring. The shared-meaning exercise is a conversation in slow motion. The communicator is asked to phrase a communication (restricting it to not more than two or three parts). After stating the message, the communicator asks, "What did you hear me saying?" The receiver tries to repeat the elements of the communication and ask, "Is that what you meant to say?" If the message was perceived accurately, the communicator adds whatever is required to complete the message. If the message was perceived inaccurately, then the communicator corrects the misperception and proceeds.

Not all communication problems are caused by underresponsible patterns, of course. Very often, the problem has an interpersonal dimension that has developed over time. As a result of her past frustrations, a woman may have come to the conclusion that her partner does not care to communicate. This may cause her to assume a defensive stance when she needs to communicate. Whether or not her perception is accurate, by communicating defensively, she elicits a certain kind of response from her partner. This response, which is in part due to her approach, may give her further reason to think she is right. Such a sequence of events is obviously systemic. The counselor must recognize when poor communication is a systemic problem and develop an intervention that addresses the systemic issue rather than the communication issue. This can be done by observing how the couple interacts in the session, identifying patterns, and intervening in the pattern development. But if the problem is unique to the home environment, the best means for observation is to ask the couple to enact a typical encounter by role-playing.

Role-Playing

Role-play or role enactment has already been discussed in Chapters 8 and 10 as a useful intervention in individual counseling. It is also used in working with families or peer groups when a particular event or experience must be relived in order to be more real. Thus, the counselor may decide to ask a family member to enact a problematic encounter or to enact the role of another family member. This provides an immediate stimulus to which family members can react. It gives the counselor an opportunity to observe sequences and can lead to discussion of individual perceptions of the family system, individual differences, or conflicting loyalties.

Family members and couples may be surprised by the content that is provoked in role-plays. Often, they are able to see the other person's point of view more easily through an enactment than by having the person discuss viewpoints. Role-play also allows the counselor to intervene, ask why the scene develops as it does, and offer alternative patterns that the family or couple might try when family members become locked into a sequence of events.

Systemic Intervention Skills

Systemic Skills

Negotiating

Helping family members acknowledge issues and make compromises that serve the family.

Altering Family Structure

Recognizing and altering the rules and roles that govern family transactions.

Joining

Establishing a working relationship with each family member.

Circular Questioning

Soliciting perspectives from each family member.

Generating Interactions

Treating family systems in counseling allows the counselor to observe the system in action, a far better alternative to having a family member report on family interactions. To do this, sometimes the counselor must cause interactions to happen.

Recognizing Coalitions

Observing family coalitions that allow certain members of the system to organize in order to control, or to defend themselves from, certain family functions. Coalitions generally operate against the more productive functions of the family system, however.

Systemic Interventions

Family Sculpture

An exercise in which family members physically "arrange" one another (as on a stage) to illustrate relationships, boundaries, and other family dynamics.

Intensification

A way of increasing affect within or between relationships to cause the family to react to the situation.

Confrontation

An intervention that seeks to draw attention to details, responsibilities, or actions that affect the family system but that are being mutually denied or ignored by the system.

Reconstructing Boundaries

A way for the counselor to actively choreograph relationship arrangements to reconfigure how the system has organized itself.

Dealing With Triangulation

Recognizing and confronting coalitions or system efforts to manipulate one or more members of the system.

Reframing

A cognitive intervention that presents a situation, relationship, or action as a constructive alternative to the way in which family members have been viewing it.

Giving Directives

An instruction or assignment by the counselor for members of the family system to behave or react in a different way when a specific situation arises outside counseling.

Paradox

The presentation of contradictory conditions or actions that lead the client family to move beyond seemingly impossible situations.

Symptom Prescription

The application of paradoxical conditions that help or cause the system or family members to act at a different level of functioning.

Counseling Skills With Multiple Clients

The process of establishing a working relationship with multiple clients relies on many of the same skills as one-to-one counseling. With multiple clients, however, each participant must be drawn into the working alliance. From the systems perspective, rapport is established with each individual in the group as a first step. This process is referred to as *joining*. In addition, the counselor uses other systemic skills, including *circular questioning, generating interactions, recognizing coalitions, negotiation,* and *altering family structure.*

NEGOTIATING.   Families rarely enter counseling with agreement among members. In fact, this is often considered part of the problem, for example, "Bill just doesn't see it the way I do." It is important that the counselor defuse these disagreements by depersonalizing them. Pointing out a systemic rule that is interfering with communication rather than blaming the other person for being obstinate or resistant is one effective way of dealing with this issue. A second important area involves goal setting or the outcome of counseling. The counselor often must help individual members of the system compromise in their goals rather than extend the disagreement.

ALTERING FAMILY STRUCTURE.   System interactions are built around rules, roles, and habits. Often these behaviors are a source of the presenting problems. The counselor observes the family interact, looking for examples of ineffective communication patterns and then seeks to understand whether the pattern is driven by a family rule, a family role, or a ritualistic habit. It probably isn't enough to point out the issue because family member insight doesn't drive the pattern in the first place. Rather, the counselor might need to create some new rules or roles for the family member(s) in question and then require that the new rule or role is followed in the session until it becomes strong enough to compete with or replace the dysfunctional rule or role.

JOINING.   The process can be as simple as a personal exchange between each family or group member, or as complex as connecting individual responses to other members of the family (Minuchin & Fishman, 1981). The object is to establish a verbal exchange so that each member has a sense of personal recognition by the counselor. This is not the same, of course, as an empathic relationship.

CIRCULAR QUESTIONING.   Circular questioning is a systemic skill that comes from the Milan group of strategic therapists. The counselor selects an opening question, for example, "Do you think the group is having a problem?" and asks each member of the group the same question. It then can be followed with "What do you think the problem is?" again moving around the group in the same order. The object is to involve each member of the group in the process and to obtain each member's perspective. If a group member is unsure (or feels unsafe), the counselor moves to the next person. In other words, the exercise is not meant to be confrontational. Even though a group member does not participate, that person has been acknowledged as a member of the group and a potential participant in the solution.

GENERATING INTERACTIONS.   Bringing a group together, whether a family or a group of peers, allows the counselor to observe interactions between and among members, thereby adding significantly to the counselor's understanding of how the system functions. But merely gathering the group members together does not ensure that all members become participants. For that to happen, the counselor must generate or choreograph interactions among members. The most obvious example would be having each member react to a particular response by another member. For instance, because families tend to have a spokesperson who assumes responsibility for interpreting the family, the counselor might ask each family member to add to what the spokesperson has described. Or the counselor might describe a family scenario and ask each member to describe his or her role in that scenario.

RECOGNIZING COALITIONS.   Coalitions are alliances between two members of a group. They can be very apparent, as illustrated by two persons who actively agree with or support one another, or they can be subtle, recognized only by occasional eye contact or a nonverbal gesture. Generally, coalitions are formed and directed against a third family member (e.g., mother and child against father, two children against third child, etc.). Coalitions serve a function for family members. A coalition may provide support to someone who seems powerless, or it may serve to isolate a person. Some coalitions are both necessary and appropriate, however, for example, the coalition that parents form with each other to provide healthy support for children. Coalitions define boundaries and as such have powerful effects on family dynamics. It is important that group boundaries are recognized, acknowledged, and understood for their impacts. Thus, it is important that the counselor watch for and recognize the coalitions and boundary making that occur in groups and family systems and determine which boundaries are functional and which boundaries have negative effects.

Negotiation and Conflict Management

Many people find negotiation and decision making to be a time when communication is most likely to break down. In family counseling, negotiation is an ongoing process that involves both process issues and family issues. Consequently, the counseling setting provides an ideal opportunity for the counselor to observe family negotiation skills and to provide strategies the family can use to improve communication and negotiation. This approach also lends itself to situations in which culture is a contributing factor. Berg and Jaya (1993) note that there is a long Asian ritual that focuses on solving problems through negotiation rather than confrontation.

Notarius and Markman (1993) have developed a conflict management skills–training program for couples called Prevention and Relationship Enhancement Program (PREP) that can also be used with adolescent groups. This program was based on extensive longitudinal research of distressed couples over time. The authors note that the goal of PREP is not so much to enhance current relationship functioning as to prevent future distress. They have found that a couple's distress is greatly affected by adverse ways of handling conflict. Among the guidelines in PREP for negotiating and handling conflict effectively are the following five:

1. Difficult issues must be controlled.
2. Partners may call mutual time-outs as needed.
3. Conflicts that escalate need to be slowed down.
4. Conflicts need to be constructive.
5. Withdrawal of contact should be avoided and involvement maintained.

Marital conflict has been shown to correlate with poorer physical health (Gottman, 1993). Gottman (1991) has also conducted a series of studies (with Levenson) that examine the specific role of marital conflict in predicting marital dissatisfaction, separation, and divorce. His findings suggest that there are a series of events based around conflict that unfold in predictable ways. For example, conflict begins, and the husband becomes highly aroused and stonewalls his wife by withdrawing as a listener and subsequently by withdrawing emotionally. The husband's stonewalling is aversive to the wife; she becomes aroused but responds by trying to reengage the husband. Failing to do so, she becomes critical and contemptuous and also withdraws, increasing her husband's fear. Gottman notes, "The husband's withdrawal from tense marital interaction is an early precursor of the wife's complementary withdrawal. When both partners withdraw and are defensive, the marriage is on its way toward separation and divorce" (p. 5).

Gottman (1991) has found, however, that if tense marital conflict is offset by positive expressions of communication, such as "affection, humor, positive problem-solving, agreement, assent, empathy, and active non-defensive listening" (p. 5), arousal is reduced and the conflict is handled with better contact rather than withdrawal. Clearly, couples need substantial help in learning effective negotiation and conflict management skills. However, there remains a need for a third party (the counselor) who acts as a mediator. Berg and Jaya (1993) point out that family therapists are in an ideal position with Asian families to assume this role "because of their position of authority and their knowledge of family relationships and therapies that enhance 'face saving'" (p. 32). In addition, some family therapists have developed exercises to use with families for handling conflictual issues.

Gottman, Notarius, Gonso, and Markman (1976, pp. 62–63) have also developed an exercise that will help build negotiation skills. Despite its name, the family meeting activity can be used with a variety of systems or groups in addition to families. The exercise is divided into three parts: (1) gripe time, (2) agenda building, and (3) problem solving. The counselor should preface the exercise by explaining that all family members can have gripes and resentments and that these gripes are viewpoints rather than truths. They are the way the individual views the moment, the situation, or the relationship. They can change and, if ignored, they can get worse. It is important that each person's viewpoint be respected and aired. The counselor can help ensure each person's cooperation by introducing rules for griping (see Figure 11.1).

After all members have been allowed time to express their gripes (and this may require some encouragement from the counselor), the group moves into the second stage, agenda building. The purpose of agenda building is to evaluate the relative importance of gripes that have been expressed and select one or more that members believe should be remedied. The counselor is an active arbitrator during this process and thus helps members define specific dimensions of a particular gripe.

Having identified and defined a particular gripe, the group moves into the problem-solving stage. This is characterized by identification of positive behaviors that will address the complaint(s) and the writing of a contract that (1) specifies behaviors each member will change and (2) specifies incentives designed to increase the frequency of desired behaviors.

Do state clearly and specifically the gripes you have about other family members.	Don't try to define yourself by showing that the other person is wrong.
Do be honest and constructive when you gripe.	Don't sulk and withdraw.
Do listen and accept gripes as legitimate feelings.	Don't respond to gripes with a gripe of your own.
	Don't assume you know what the other person means; make sure you know.

FIGURE 11.1 Dos and Don'ts

ALTERING SYSTEM STRUCTURE

System structure refers to the patterns of interaction, the rules and roles that emerge to support these patterns, and the alliances that result from these rules and roles. All structure begins with family or group transactions that, when repeated, become patterns of behavior. As interaction patterns become well established, they begin to dictate how, when, and with whom family members will interact. For example, a young child falls, skins his knee, and runs to his mother for comfort. As this scene repeats itself again and again, a nurturing alliance forms between mother and child. Thus, the mother assumes a nurturant (role) posture, and the child learns to seek his mother when hurt (rule). The alliance between mother and child defines a subsystem within the family.

All families have subsystems that are determined by interaction patterns, rules, roles, and alliances. The spousal subsystem is the obvious beginning point. When the first child is born, two things happen. The spousal subsystem accommodates a new parental subsystem, and the mother-child and father-child subsystems emerge. Subsystems become differentiated from one another by boundaries. Additional children, grandparents, and other family relatives develop alliances within the larger family structure to the point that many subsystems emerge, with individuals occupying significant roles within more than one subsystem. There is a random as well as systematic dimension to the development of family structure. Consequently, families are often at a loss to explain how certain rules or subsystems become so powerful or how they could be changed.

Recognizing the powerful impact that structure has on family functioning, a group of family therapists began working with family structures. Significant among these therapists were Salvador Minuchin, Braulio Montalvo, and Jay Haley. They developed a scenario for working with the family based on five basic goals for the counseling process:

1. Joining (establishing rapport) with the family
2. Generating and observing interactions
3. Diagnosing the family structure
4. Identifying and modifying interactions
5. Reconstructing boundaries

These goals are applicable to groups, whether they are family units or other social units. The goals are accomplished through a variety of techniques and interventions: some require group cooperation and others are therapist manipulations.

JOINING WITH THE FAMILY. The first of these objectives, joining, refers to social identification with each family member. This is accomplished in a number of small but meaningful ways: addressing each member by name, shaking hands with each member (including even the smallest), touching the baby, and so forth. This individual and personal contact is seen as quite important to the later process of therapy because each family member has been given a personal acknowledgment by the therapist. Nichols and Schwartz (1994) note:

> It is particularly important to join powerful family members as well as angry ones. Special pains must be taken to accept the point of view of the father who thinks therapy is hooey, or of the angry teenager who feels likes a hunted criminal. It's also important to reconnect with such people at frequent intervals, particularly as things begin to heat up. (p. 229)

Joining does not mean that the counselor is catering to powerful family members. Rather, it means that the counselor acknowledges all family members, all of the time, even when a particular member's effect may be negative or overpowering.

GENERATING AND OBSERVING INTERACTIONS. After the family has been joined (in the first session and in subsequent sessions), the counselor turns to the task of setting up and observing family interactions. One of the real benefits of working with family units is that they allow the therapist the opportunity to observe them in realistic interactions (as opposed to the individual client who must report interactions). Some interactions are totally spontaneous sequences that emerge when the family is dealing with a current issue. Spontaneous interactions may not develop, so the counselor must help the family become involved in interactions that are representative. One of the first of these is the physical alignment the family displays at the beginning of each session.

RECOGNIZING PHYSICAL ALIGNMENTS. Prior to each session, the counselor arranges a sufficient number of chairs in a circle. As family members enter the room, they are encouraged to sit wherever they wish. The counselor observes closely who chooses to sit by whom, what kind of negotiation occurs when two members want the same chair, or who moves chairs (increasing or decreasing distance). This early expression of family dynamics is seen as a metaphor for the family's dysfunctioning system.

As the session progresses and subsystems become more apparent through interactions, the counselor may ask specific family members to exchange chairs, thus physically altering a boundary by separating subsystems. Or if the counselor senses that the family has excluded a member, he or she may physically move to sit beside that excluded member, again realigning the dynamics of the counseling scene. As counseling progresses in later sessions, family members become aware of this realignment activity and begin to realize that such alterations do change the dynamics of the family interaction.

FAMILY SCULPTURE. Family sculpture provides diagnostic insights and generates family awareness of perceptions, structure, and sequences. Perhaps a better label would be *family choreography* because the exercise calls for one family member to choreograph family members' involvement with one another in a typical scenario. It can be used to enact current family sequences or to reenact scenes from the past. Through family sculpture or choreography, family members are placed both in activities and spatial relationship to one another. As the director (the family member who is choreographing the scene) assigns, moves, or directs interactions, all family members respond both to the direction and to the director's perceptions of their interactive relationships.

In the following family therapy case of Bob and Jeannette, the therapist used family sculpting as a means to generate awareness of each spouse's perceptions of their problem. The situation that was selected for enactment was the end-of-day scene in which father and mother each arrived home from work.

CASE ILLUSTRATION OF FAMILY SCULPTURE

The Case of Bob and Jeannette

COUNSELOR: Bob, I'd like you to produce the scene at home when you and Jeannette arrive from work. We'll assume the kids are also home. Place each person in whatever is the typical activity they would be doing. Do this without discussion. Merely place them in a particular space, and tell them what they should be doing. Do you understand what I want you to do?

BOB: I'm not sure. Do I just say, "Jeannette, you yell at the kids" or something like that?

COUNSELOR: If that is what Jeannette typically does, yes. And then go on to tell the kids what they should be doing.

BOB: Okay. Jeannette, you are sitting in the living room with a martini. Tommy [7 years old], you are downstairs watching cartoons with Karen [9 years old]. Then Tommy, you and Karen come to the living room when I arrive home. [Bob acts as though he is coming in the front door of their house; both children rush up.] Now, I sit down with Mommy, and you start talking and demanding attention. Mommy and I will be trying to talk to each other while you try to talk to both of us. [Both children somewhat sheepishly begin talking about something. Bob and Jeannette try to begin a conversation but children won't let them complete the conversation.]

COUNSELOR: Okay. Now, what happens?

BOB: Well, if Jeannette and I try to ignore the kids, they end up in a fight. If we stop trying to talk to each other, I end up mad.

COUNSELOR: Okay, everyone. Act out that scene that Bob just described.

The family members begin to act out their parts. Just as Bob sits down and begins to talk to Jeannette, Tommy comes in to ask Mommy a question. Bob waits until Jeannette answers, at which time Tommy asks another question. Enter Karen, who proceeds to tell Mommy that Tommy ate all the potato chips. Jeannette responds, and it becomes obvious that Jeannette and the children are the focal unit. Bob, trying to look patient, asks the children to return to their activities so he and Mommy can talk. The children leave and Jeannette turns to Bob and tells him that the children need some parent time also after being away from them all day. Bob responds impatiently that he needs some spouse time and accuses her of not noticing that.

Diagnosing the Family Structure

In the discussion that followed this scene, Jeannette and Bob discussed their reactions. Jeannette was somewhat surprised that Bob wanted relationship time with her but was unable to have it because the kids were interrupting. She indicated that such interruptions didn't bother her as much as they apparently bothered Bob. Instead, she had been presuming that his reactions to her (this scene was a common one in their home) were merely reflecting a bad day at work. Bob, on the other hand, thought Jeannette understood his relationship needs but was opting to take care of the children. He assumed that her choice was in reaction to feeling guilty that she had been away from the kids all day. As they discussed their individual perceptions, each became aware of the other's needs, motivations, and misperceptions.

Throughout this type of interaction, the counselor also observes and looks for ways the couple might sabotage their negotiations. This process involves the recognition of dysfunctional sequences and the behaviors that maintain the sequences. It also includes recognition of boundaries and how they are creating or sustaining problematic behavior sequences. Diagnosing family interactions does not involve specific therapeutic interventions. However, you may want to point out the family boundaries and how they are operating in a particular interaction.

Identifying and Modifying Interactions

Having determined what sequences appear to be maintaining the dysfunctional interactions, the structural family counselor proceeds to bring the family's attention to the sequence. This calls for intensifying the interaction so family members cannot ignore or avoid the issue.

INTENSIFICATION. Intensification is a communication process through which the counselor draws the client's attention to a particular interaction, behavior, or event in such a way that client awareness is the inevitable outcome. Minuchin (1974, p. 310) provides the following example of intensification while working with the family of an anorexic girl. In the dialogue, Loretta, the daughter, has accused her mother of being too money conscious, and the mother responds:

MOTHER: Sophia [mother's sister, Loretta's aunt] tells me, "Don't do these things. You're killing yourself." Now you, Loretta, you tell me this, see? How many aspirin? I'll get them for you because when you get nervous, you stop eating. Right away, no food. Not get up from the bed. You don't want to see nobody. You don't want to talk to nobody. And Mama cries.
Therapist insists on conflict]

MINUCHIN: Is your mother saying that you are blackmailing them?

LORETTA: That's not. . . .
Therapist increases stress between mother and daughter]

MINUCHIN: That's what she's saying. She's saying that you are controlling her by having temper tantrums and not eating.

This style of intensifying conflict keeps family members to the task of resolving old issues rather than their typical style of brushing up against the issue and then retreating from it.

CONFRONTATION. Another way in which the counselor modifies interaction sequences is through confrontation and direction. In the following example, the parents are attempting to deal with a 3-year-old child who is having a tantrum. The counselor is observing and eventually intervenes.

MOTHER: Janice, please settle down or we are going to have to spank you. [Janice wails louder.]

FATHER: Janice, you heard what your mother said. [Mother places Janice on her lap and begins to soothe her. Janice continues to wail and resist. Father turns to the counselor and shrugs.]

COUNSELOR: Aren't you going to do anything? Are you just going to let her continue to disrupt us?

MOTHER: Well, do something.

FATHER: [To mother] Let me have her. [Mother hands Janice over to father.]

FATHER: Janice, stop now or you will have to go to the other room. [Janice doesn't stop.]

COUNSELOR: [To mother] Does he really mean that he will send her away until she stops?

MOTHER: I don't know.
[Father carries Janice to waiting room and returns. Janice wails for 5 minutes.]

MOTHER: Don't you think we should go check on her?

FATHER: I don't know.

COUNSELOR: She can't hurt herself out there.

FATHER: Right. She's just mad.

In this interaction, the counselor is forcing the parents to confront the issue. Mother attempts to intervene, and Father withdraws. The counselor turns to Father and challenges him to stay involved. Father becomes involved by threatening the child with removal, but neither follows through. At that point, the counselor increases the tension by asking Mother if Father intends to do what he threatened. This confronts Father, and he follows through. The parents then begin to waver as Janice turns up the intensity from the other room. The counselor assures them that their daughter is really all right, and they regain their resolve to win this battle of wills.

The process of identifying and modifying interactions is one way in which the counselor attempts to change the family structure by altering sequences of behavior. A second approach involves the manipulation of subsystem boundaries.

Reconstructing Boundaries

As the counselor works with families (or other systems), the concept of family identity becomes increasingly apparent. Families develop qualities that define their internal structure and interdependent characteristics. One family may be so cohesive that individual identities are relegated to a low priority, while the total family unit is elevated to the highest priority. In such a family, often referred to as enmeshed, group activities are emphasized over individual activities, the welfare of the family unit is emphasized over the individual, and the group will is more important. Minuchin (1974, p. 311) illustrated this by squeezing the teenage daughter's wrist and asking how many family members felt the pain. All but one raised their hands, and that person was apologetic for not feeling the pain (see page 000).

Family enmeshment is one end of the family organization continuum. The other end of the continuum is represented by the disengaged family. In disengagement, family members have little or no connection to one another. The family group identity is deemphasized, and individualization is held supreme. In the disengaged family, members' activities are planned without consultation or consideration of other family members. Group activity is rare.

Both enmeshment and disengagement are considered to be problematic in the family therapy literature. When cultural factors are taken into account, however, both arrangements might be considered normative for specific cultural groups. For example, in Asian American families, family identity and cohesiveness are highly valued by family members. It is considered both appropriate and healthy to deemphasize individuality and emphasize family agendas (Berg & Jaya, 1993).

Within the family system, boundaries function to differentiate between subsystems. They allow members to function in appropriate roles and to interact with other subsystems. But families can generate many different types of subsystems, and some subsystems exist to maintain a dysfunctional situation. For example, one parent may create an alliance with one or more children that effectively excludes the other parent from decision making or other family functions. In such situations, the counselor may wish to intervene in the system in ways that will reintegrate the excluded parent. This can be done through assignments, as discussed earlier in this chapter, in the section on family sculpture.

The use of assignments in the counseling setting to manipulate subsystem boundaries can resemble family sculpture in one respect. For example, if the counselor believes parents are failing to respect the sibling subsystem by interfering or invading the system, the counselor might invite the invading parents to join the counselor in an "adult observer" group because children "think differently these days than in our time and may have solutions [that] we couldn't even imagine" (Minuchin & Fishman, 1981, p. 149). By creating an adult observer group, the counselor has pulled the parents away from the sibling subsystem and assigned them the role of observer. Because one cannot be an effective observer and participant at the same time, the counselor has created a new boundary by separating parents from siblings.

The counselor also manipulates the spatial relationships that reflect boundaries between subsystems. It was noted earlier that the counselor may use the seating arrangements in the counseling room as a means of observing how subsystems operate. By moving family members to other chairs, thus altering the spatial arrangements, the counselor also alters the spatial expression of boundaries. Imagine a counseling scene in which the clients are a stepfamily composed of a mother, teenage son, and stepfather. The stepfamily has existed for about 12 months. During this time, the mother has created an obvious boundary between herself and her son on the one side, and the stepfather on the other. By moving the stepfather's chair in such a way that he now sits beside the stepson, the counselor has made a symbolic intervention into the family system. This intervention can be extended by asking the mother to become an observer of stepfather/stepson interactions, thus encouraging the stepfather and stepson interaction to happen, and removing the mother from active involvement.

By altering family structure, the objective is to interrupt habitual and dysfunctional sequences and patterns so that the family must create new patterns. With the counselor's help, these new patterns can be more functional and constructive for family relationships as well as individual needs.

Szapocznik and Kurtines (1993) observe that in structural family work, not only does an individual client need to be understood in the context of one's family, but the family also needs to be understood in the context of its culture. All three of these contexts overlap, as shown in Figure 11.2. In these authors' studies of Hispanic families, they found that understanding of the family dynamics was enhanced when the families were viewed not just from a Hispanic context but from a culturally pluralistic or diverse context. For example, they found that the conflict in these families resulted often from parents who had strong generational Hispanic cultural alliances, while the youth in the families rapidly had become acculturated or Americanized. The elders struggled for greater connectedness; the youth fought for greater freedom.

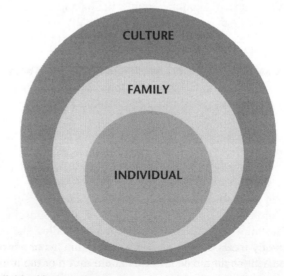

FIGURE 11.2 The Individual in Context

WORKING STRATEGICALLY WITH FAMILIES

The area of strategic family therapy includes a diversified group of family therapists, among whom are Cloe Madanes, Milton Erickson, Jay Haley, Maria Selvini Palazzoli, Paul Watzlawick, Lynn Hoffman, John Weakland, and Richard Fisch. With this variety of major contributors, one might expect the approach to be diffuse; in fact, strategic therapists have a significant core of agreement in their approaches.

Compared to the structural therapy approach, strategic therapists emphasize problem definition (including how the family perceives itself and its problems), brief or short-term therapy, interventions that focus on redefinition of the problem or perception, and interventions that affect sequences outside the session. It should also be said that strategic therapists often use structural interventions, just as structural therapists use strategic interventions.

The term *strategic therapy* was coined by Jay Haley in describing the work of Milton Erickson:

> [Erickson] assumed that deep down, patients knew what to do; they just didn't have access to that wisdom. One way to get access was to break out of habitual patterns of behavior or thinking, so Erickson developed many ways of getting people to simply do something different in the context of the old behavior, or to do the old behavior in a new context. (Nichols & Schwartz, 1994, p. 412)

Haley was one of the first to bring Erickson's work to the attention of professionals.

Another source of strategic thinking was the Brief Therapy Center, part of the Mental Research Institute of Palo Alto, California. Led by Don Jackson, this group came from a communications orientation to change and included Richard Fisch, Paul Watzlawick, and John Weakland, among others. They emphasized a close examination of how people tend to generate their problems and how families tend to generate unworkable solutions to those problems; when the solution does not work, the next solution tends to be more of the first solution.

You might note that, although many of the interventions used in strategic therapy tend to be cognitive in nature, they do not originate in the more traditional individual therapies, nor does the rationale for using them have a parallel in most individual cognitive approaches.

Defining the Problem

Because of the limit put on the number of counseling sessions, it is particularly important that the problem be well defined. In many ways, strategic family counselors mirror a behavioral approach in defining the family's problem. There are four guidelines the counselor would follow in defining the problem:

1. Each family member must contribute to the definition without becoming argumentative or defensive.
2. The problem must be stated in specific behavioral language.
3. If there is more than one problem, the most troublesome must be identified and made the target of counseling.
4. Unsuccessful attempts to solve the problem are described in detail.

Although each family member will see the problem from his or her own perspective, usually there is some agreement about the behavioral manifestation of the problem. For example, a father might see his teenage son's behavior as disrespectful, while the son experiences his father as overbearing. With the counselor's help, however, they might both be able to agree that they can define the problem as "the number of times they get into explosive arguments." Thus, the problem becomes the frequency of their arguments rather than each person's bad attitude. If the arguments tend to gravitate toward a specific theme—for example, the son getting home too late with the family car—then the problem would be defined as getting home too late. It is important not to rush this phase of counseling and to be willing to negotiate and renegotiate until one problem is identified as the goal of counseling.

It is imperative that the counselor collect information regarding attempted solutions that have failed. There are several reasons for doing this. First, a great amount can be learned about the family system by hearing the members describe their attempts to solve their problems. This information will be essential when attempting to identify an appropriate intervention for the family. Second, this discussion of failed solutions establishes the fact that the family does, indeed, have a problem that it has been unable to solve. Because most families continue to deny their problem even in counseling, this admission is important. Third, the process establishes that the counselor respects the efforts put forth by the family thus far. The counselor is saying, "I know you take your problem seriously and that you have already invested considerable energy in trying to solve it. I won't frustrate you by asking you to do what you have already tried without success." This part of the counseling process also gives the counselor another opportunity to watch the family operate and to determine the distribution of power in the family through such mechanisms as alliances within the family.

Setting Realistic Goals

It is not enough for the family and counselor to define the problem. The family must also agree on what degree of improvement will be considered a therapeutic success. The description of success must be as concrete and well defined as the description of the problem. Using our example of father and teenage son, it would not be appropriate to switch from "too many arguments" as the problem to "having a better relationship" as the measure of success (relationship quality not being of the same category as frequency). Rather, the goal might be "going from daily arguments to weekly arguments." Once the arguments were under control, it might be appropriate to work toward a positive goal such as "spending more leisure time together." The consequence of reducing the number of arguments added to spending more enjoyable time together might result in having a better relationship, but this cannot be measured and, therefore, is not considered an appropriate counseling goal.

Preparing for the Intervention

Although the ultimate goal of strategic family therapy is to prescribe an intervention that will cause change, the process leading to that objective is critical if strategic therapy is to work. Joining with each family member is very important, just as it is with structural family therapy. Indeed, family interactions in early sessions are closely scrutinized by the counselor. Typically, once a brief social interaction has been completed between the counselor and each family member, the counselor sets the stage for counseling to occur. This is similar to what a counselor does in individual counseling and includes informing clients of how audio or video recordings will be used, soliciting demographic data, having clients sign consent forms, and so on. An additional condition of strategic therapy that is not often part of individual counseling is an agreement that counseling will last a certain number of sessions, usually no more than 10. By definition, strategic therapy is brief therapy.

Directives for Change

The crux of strategic family therapy is the therapeutic directive, or intervention. Most strategic directives are paradoxical in nature; that is, they may seem to defy logic. The rationale behind the paradoxical directive is that most problems are more emotional than logical. Consequently, a solution that follows the typical laws of logic completely misses the point and simply will not work. Most attempted solutions in counseling are linear in nature; that is, they describe relationships that lead from a causal event to a responsive event. For example, if a child receives a weekend's punishment for misbehaving, the problem is presumed to have been addressed. But what if the child misbehaves again? The linear solution might be to punish the child similarly for an entire week. In this illustration, can it be said that the punishment had the desired effect? In this example, punishment was intended to produce good behavior in the future, a linear solution. These types of solutions are called more-of-the-same solutions, and they rarely work as intended. Paradoxical interventions attempt to come at the problem from a different perspective. In Chapter 9, we discussed paradoxical interventions as cognitive interventions. To return to the example of the child misbehaving, their effect is to change the child's frame of reference so that misbehavior appears to the child to be illogical or inappropriate rather than something that might lead to punishment.

Dealing With Triangulation

In addition to boundary issues, families can also configure themselves into alliances or alignments that interfere with the family's functioning. The best example is when family members triangulate one another (two or more "gang up" on a third member) to achieve specific outcomes while negotiating decisions that affect the family system. Triangulation can result in scapegoating, power plays, or system manipulation.

When the counselor recognizes that family members are triangulated, or even when family members are attempting to triangulate the counselor, the issue must be addressed. An example of efforts to triangulate the counselor would be if a family member attempted to get the counselor to take sides on a family disagreement. In this case, the counselor blocks the effort by not agreeing to take sides. The more difficult triangulation is one in which coalitions have been created by certain family members to achieve power, manipulate roles, or challenge rules. Family triangulation must be dealt with by confronting the issue. Minuchin would do this in the counseling session by moving his chair to sit beside the triangulated person, thus identifying himself (and his power as therapist) with the victim. Other ways in which triangulation is challenged include reframing family interpretations and giving directives that confront or alter family rules, roles, and boundaries.

SELECTING INTERVENTIONS

When using strategic interventions, the objective is to involve the manner in which the members of the family system conceptualize or rationalize the system relationships. We mentioned earlier that family systems develop rules of relationship, member roles to carry out those rules, and boundaries to protect or preserve those roles and rules. This process is not achieved in a deliberate, thought-out way. Rather, these conditions probably evolve in order to avoid undesirable consequences. Thus, the family's rules, roles, and boundaries are an attempt to organize the family in a functional way.

The result often goes far astray from the intention, however, and the family's solutions become the problem. When the counselor recognizes this, the appropriate therapeutic response is to help the family reconfigure its solutions along more realistic and rational lines. But family systems are reluctant to change even dysfunctional ways of responding. The strategic solution is to introduce cognitive interventions that literally lead the family into a different way of thinking. Examples of this intervention are (1) reframing, (2) giving directives, and (3) the paradoxical prescription.

Reframing

Reframing was introduced in Chapter 9 as the "gentle art of viewing or thinking about a situation differently." When working with families, each member brings a perspective of the family, and some of those perspectives will be candidates for change. Reframing offers a strategy for the counselor to use that allows the family member an opportunity to change perspective safely.

Giving Directives

In Chapter 10, we discussed the use of homework as a clinical intervention when individuals need to rehearse and strengthen a new behavior. The use of directives in systemic therapy is similar but the purpose is to change behavioral patterns in the system and thus produce new and more desirable outcomes between two or more people while giving the counselor an opportunity to observe how the participants react to changes.

Directives can be paradoxical in nature, and they can be guidelines for behavioral interactions. Goldenberg and Goldenberg (2008) describe the two ways that directives can be viewed:

> To the therapist, these are clever maneuvers designed to subtly gain control over the presenting symptoms and force families to attempt different solutions; to the family, these often appear to fly in the face of common sense but they nevertheless put themselves in the hands of the expert and follow instructions. Since second-order change is the goal, the therapist is attempting to circumvent family resistance to altering the interactive patterns that maintain the problematic behavior. (p. 236)

For example, if the presenting problem is that a young child is inclined toward temper tantrums when he does not get his way, a counselor directive might be, "The next time Mason begins to throw a tantrum, I want you both to quietly walk out of the room, and remain out of the room until Mason stops."

Paradoxical Prescriptions

When clients are making good progress, a common directive is to "expect a setback" or to "slow down." Such suggestions have the purpose of cautioning the client but also giving the client something to work against, thus ensuring further progress.

We are reminded of a former client who was attempting to redefine her life as separate from her overbearing parents. Although she was in graduate school and still somewhat dependent on her parents for financial support (loans), her parents continued to micromanage her life, calling almost daily to see "how she was doing." These daily phone calls had the effect of undermining her self-confidence and keeping her parents in control of her life. Her primary counseling goal was to get some emotional distance from her parents and to begin to build her own life as a responsible adult. The counselor suggested the following paradoxical prescription:

I'd like you to try an experiment with me. It will feel strange and risky to do. I want you to become overdependent on your parents for a while. Instead of waiting for them to call each day, I want you to call first with questions about how to deal with your life. Call more than once a day even. When your parents do call to give unsolicited advice, tell them how much you need their help; keep them on the phone and ask all of the detailed little questions you can think of. Try this for a month and I think you will find some dramatic changes taking place in your relationship with them.

The client was reluctant at first to accept this prescription. It seemed to take her life in exactly the wrong direction, but she finally agreed to try it. After a week, she reported that she had followed the prescription to the letter, but the only change was that her parents called her less because she was calling them more. After 2 weeks, she reported that her parents seemed to be backing off a little when she would call. They seemed more worried about her, however. After 3 weeks, she came to the session in a very positive frame of mind. Her parents had visited over the weekend and had explained that they were very concerned about her inability to assume adult responsibility. She must not keep relying on them for the kinds of decisions she should be making for herself and they were proposing that she enter counseling for help with this matter. For their part, they would pay for the counseling sessions, but they would not be available to help her make the mundane decisions of life and she must quit calling and asking for help. Their only request was that she call on Saturday mornings "just to catch up on the week." She ended by saying to the counselor, "Mission accomplished!"

Summary

As we have noted, systemic interventions do not originate in the traditional theories of counseling or personality. Instead, they derive from an ecological epistemology that many trained counselors find both unique and effective. The systemic orientation begins with a set of assumptions about human behavior that include (1) a self-sustaining quality known as homeostasis, (2) the tendency of dysfunctional systems to develop rigid boundaries, and (3) an internal system organization that is determined by systemic "rules" as defined by repeated behavioral interaction patterns.

Effective counseling with social systems begins by recognizing these conditions and then developing interventions that address the system character rather than individual psychological characteristics. The dominant approaches are represented by communication-oriented counseling, object rela-

tions, structurally oriented counseling, and strategic counseling. In almost all cases, systemic counselors feel free to draw on interventions from all three orientations and from individual therapy models, too.

Systemic counseling fits quite well into the five-stage model for the helping process. Particular emphasis is placed on assessment as well as intervention. A frequent admonition of the systemic counselor is that the problem cannot be treated until it has been accurately identified. Systems thinking has particular relevance in working with couples and families. Indeed, many family interventions make no sense unless you think of the family as an ecosystem that is self-reinforcing and self-sustaining. Therefore, we recommend that you become well informed in family systems approaches if you plan to work with families or use family interventions.

Exercises

I. Consider your family of origin. On a sheet of paper, write the names of your parents first. Then, as you add the names of siblings, place the names nearest

that parent with whom you think there was a primary identification. Draw lines connecting the subsystems you believe were operating in your family.

II. This is a two-part exercise. With a group of three to four class members, define yourselves as a family. Each person should assume a family member role: father, mother, oldest sibling, and so on. Given this "system," the family should discuss and make plans for a week-long vacation at the beach. After the plan has been finalized, step out of your roles and analyze the process and the system.

In the second part of the exercise, the family is to repeat the exercise, assuming the same roles. However, one family member in this second exercise is to be a dysfunctional member (exhibiting a marginal level of functioning). Given this condition, repeat the planning of the vacation. Once the plan has been finalized, step out of your roles once again and analyze the process and the system. How did a dysfunctional family member alter the system? How did the individual family member roles accommodate this change?

III. In the case of Sheila and Eric (page 000) the communication problem was identified as the product of personal qualities each brought into the marriage. Identify two or three individual goals of both Sheila and Eric that would have a positive effect on the communication problem.

Discussion Questions

1. In a small group of class members, discuss what you think would be the most difficult type of family problem on which to work. As you discuss the problem(s), consider whether you would choose to work with individuals or the total family in addressing the problem(s).

2. In this chapter, we compared the family's system to an ecological system. In what ways are the two similar? How is this illustrated by the so-called empty nest syndrome?

3. In a group of employees who have worked together in the same office area for 10 years, what kinds of systemic rules are likely to be developed? How easy would it be to alter those rules?

4. In this chapter, very little attention is given to soliciting input from members of the system regarding goal setting. Why wouldn't the counselor ask members of the system to help identify counseling goals?

MyCounselingLab Assignment

Go to the Video Resource Library on the MyCounselingLab site for your text and search for the following clips:

• **Family Therapy: Clarifying Specific Issues—Distancer and Pursuer**   In this clip, who is the pursuer and who is the distancer? How does the pursuer try to solve the problem? In what ways does the distancer react?

• **Family Therapy: Continuing to Clarify Specific Issues—Pursuer**   In this video clip, the counselor is the distancer of this dyad. How does the distancer describe his motivation to distance or avoid? What are his triggers that cause him to avoid communication?

• **Family Systems: Using Questions to Establish Family Systems**   What is the counselor looking for as he asks the client to describe the relationship? Describe the system that seems to be operating between the client and his wife.

• **Structural Family Therapy: Identifying Family Roles**   In this clip, what role does the mother assume? What role is Pam assuming? (*Hint:* Pam answers "I don't know" to the mother's questions. Her mother does not ask further when Pam says, "I don't know.")

• **Structural Family Therapy: Boundaries and Hierarchies**   In this clip, the counselor believes a boundary needs to be established between the mother and Pam. How does he try to establish that boundary? What is the boundary he wants to establish?

• **Family Therapy: Working With Culturally Diverse Families—Exploring Culture and Beliefs**   In this clip, the clients are Caucasian and yet the counselor asks about their cultural backgrounds. What does she uncover in this exploration? The one counselor seems to be educating the other counselor on how people with no visible cultural agendas still have cultural rules that they follow. How do these rules play out in the relationship between the husband and wife? What other important information came out of this discussion?

12

Termination and Follow-Up

PURPOSE OF THIS CHAPTER

Termination, the fifth and final stage of counseling, is the transition from assisted functioning to counseling-free functioning by the client. In this chapter, we discuss the dynamics that affect this transition, the counselor's role and responsibilities in seeing that this transition occurs, and the occasional necessity to make client referrals to other mental health professionals. It is important to keep in mind through each of the counseling stages that the ultimate goals of any counseling relationship are success and termination. How this is accomplished is the focus of this chapter.

Considerations as You Read This Chapter

- Beginnings and endings often prove problematic to people, particularly to sensitive persons. Sensitive persons are more aware of the importance of good beginnings. And they are particularly aware of the implications of ending relationships that have been productive, rewarding, and meaningful.

- Where do you fit in this picture? What have the beginnings and endings of relationships been like for you? Has it been your tendency to think of endings as a positive experience?

- Can you, as a counselor, put yourself in the client's world? How might termination be seen?

- What is the most constructive way for a client to view termination? How might you as a counselor enhance the client's ability to see termination in that constructive way?

In Chapter 3, we described termination as one of the five stages of counseling. This suggests that it functions as part of the therapeutic process and is not simply a significant moment in the counseling relationship. The dynamics of a termination are some indication of just how important the treatment of this stage can be. It has been described by writers as a "loss experience";

an "index of success"; a "recapitulation of the multiple preceding goodbyes in life"; a mixture of sadness and pleasure, pride and accomplishment; and a "transformative growth experience." Teyber and McClure (2011, p. 440) describe it as possibly "the first positive ending of a relationship (clients) have ever experienced." However one wishes to describe termination, the emotional dynamics of letting go, trusting gains, and facing future potential with only partially tested new skills present clients with multiple reactions.

The counselor also experiences pride and regret when a successful counseling relationship ends. Or if the relationship has been somewhat less than successful, the counselor probably feels unfinished or even unsure of the manner in which the counseling was conducted. In this chapter, we will consider termination as a therapeutic stage and will address issues such as who determines when termination should occur, problems in the termination process, and characteristics of successful termination.

THE TERMINATION STAGE

Termination is not so much an ending as it is a transition from one set of conditions to another. Pate (1982) has caught the spirit of this perspective, saying:

> When counseling is viewed as a process in which an essentially competent person is helped by another to solve problems of living, solving the problem leads to termination, not as a trauma, but as another step forward in client growth. (p. 188)

At some level, both the counselor and client know from the beginning of the counseling relationship that it will eventually end. But the knowledge that counseling ultimately will end provides no guidelines for making the decision. This raises the question, What are the determinants for when counseling should terminate? The answer to this question is based on both theoretical orientations and counselor-client interactions.

Theoretical Determinants of Termination

The counselor operates on a theoretical view of what counseling is meant to accomplish and how clients change through counseling. This theoretical viewpoint may be formalized (identified with a recognized counseling theory) or it may be idiosyncratic to the counselor's life view. The person-centered counselor might view termination as a decision to be made by the client. However, Pate (1982) observes that this position can be taken to the extreme:

> One point of view builds on the developmental nature of counseling and the goal of client self-actualization. Such a view might (wrongly) lead to the conclusion that a counseling relationship was always growth producing and thus ideally would continue. (p. 189)

A somewhat different position is reflected in family therapy practice. Madanes (1981) suggests, "After the presenting problems are solved, the therapist must be willing to disengage quickly, with the idea of keeping in touch occasionally with the family and to be available if problems arise" (p. 121).

Proponents of brief therapy take the position that counseling should be limited to a specified number of sessions (often 10 sessions). In this case, the counselor may contract with the client(s) in the initial session to terminate at a specific point in time.

In each of these examples, the question of when termination should occur may be answered by the counselor's theoretical stance. It should be noted, however, that many counselors do not feel bound to theoretical directives regarding termination. When theoretical determinants are not used, the counselor tends to rely on intuition or other variables.

Pragmatic Determinants of Termination

In practical terms, counseling ends when the client, the counselor, or the process indicates that termination is appropriate. Even in psychoanalysis, clients have input into the decisions:

> Often patients themselves bring up the matter of terminating by asking how much longer they will need to come. Sometimes they are more definite and may state, for instance, that they will not come back in the fall. This gives the analyst an opportunity to discuss a tentative time limit for winding up the analysis. (Lorand, 1982, p. 225)

But Teyber and McClure (2011) offer what is probably the most pragmatic answer to the question of when counseling should end:

> Therapists know that clients are ready to terminate when they have converging reports of client change from three different sources: (1) when clients report that they consistently feel better, can respond in more adaptive ways to old conflict situations, and find themselves capable of new responses that were not available to them before; (2) when clients can consistently respond to the therapist in new, more direct, egalitarian, and reality-based ways that do not enact their old interpersonal coping styles or maladaptive relational patterns; and (3) when clients' significant others give them feedback that they are different or make comments such as, "You never used to do that before." (p. 441)

When Clients Initiate Termination

Clients may elect to terminate for a number of reasons. They may feel that their goals have been accomplished. They may feel that the relationship (or the counselor) is not being helpful or may even be harmful. They may lack the financial means to continue. They may move to a new community or, if they are students, finish the school year. Whatever the client's reason for terminating, it should be emphasized that the counselor's legal and ethical responsibilities do not end with the client's decision. Ethical standards are quite clear on this. If your client initiates termination but you believe the client is not ready to terminate, you are ethically bound to "provide pretermination counseling and recommend other service providers when necessary" (American Counseling Association, 2005, Code of Ethics, Section A.11.d).Preparation for termination and possible referral are issues that must be addressed. These topics will be discussed in greater detail later in the chapter.

When the Counselor Terminates

Often, the counselor is the first person to introduce the notion that counseling is approaching termination. This decision may be based on the client's progress toward identified counseling goals, or the counselor may determine that his or her expertise does not match the client's needs.

When counseling has been predicated on a behavioral or other form of contract, progress toward the goals or conditions of the contract present a clear picture of when counseling should end. Although clients may be in the best position to experience counseling-based change, they are not always in the objective position needed to recognize change. Thus, the counselor may need to say to the client, "Do you realize that you have accomplished everything you set out to accomplish?" Ordinarily, the counselor can see this event approaching several sessions before. It is appropriate to introduce the notion of termination at that time, thereby allowing the client an opportunity to adjust to the transition. A fairly simple observation, such as, "I think we probably have about three or perhaps four more sessions and we will have finished our work," is enough to say. It provides an early warning, opens the door for discussion of progress and goal assessment, and focuses the client's attention on what life may be like after counseling.

Occasionally, as a case unfolds, the counselor may become aware that the demands of the client's problem call for skills or qualities the counselor does not possess. For example, after a few sessions a client may reveal that she is manifesting symptoms of bulimia. If the counselor is unacquainted with the treatment procedures for such a condition, the client should be referred to a professional who is recognized as competent with this problem. Or the client may present a dilemma that poses value conflicts for the counselor such that the counselor could not meet the client's needs without experiencing personal value conflicts. An example might be if a client discovers she is pregnant and wishes to consider an abortion. If the counselor's values will not allow her or him to include abortion as a possible solution, then the counselor might be unable to support an objective examination of this solution. In such cases, the counselor is ethically bound to refer the client to another professional who is able to do so. Obviously, this involves termination and transition to another counselor. (See the *ACA Code of Ethics, Section A.11.a* – Abandonment Prohibited; and *A.11.b* – Inability To Assist Clients.)

Premature Termination

Among the more demoralizing occurrences for inexperienced and seasoned counselors alike is premature termination. Very often, termination occurs almost before a working alliance can be formed. This can be a function of many different conditions. One important reason is client readiness. Smith, Subich, and Kalodner (1995) report that clients who are in a "precontemplation" or low potential for change stage are far more likely to terminate after only one session than those who initiate counseling at a contemplation stage. Other reasons for early or premature termination may be related to matching of gender, ethnic, or cultural factors (Lin, 1994; Kim, Lee, Chu, & Cho, 1989; Tata & Leong, 1994).

Sometimes counselors suggest that counseling terminate before an appropriate point has been reached. Because many clients rely heavily on the counselor to be the best judge of such matters, clients may go along with the counselor's recommendation, and the relationship may end prematurely. It has already been suggested that there are some legitimate reasons why the counselor may decide to terminate counseling and refer the client to another professional. Aside from these situations, three precipitating conditions can lead the counselor to initiate inappropriate premature termination:

1. The counselor experiences interpersonal discomfort.
2. The counselor fails to recognize and conceptualize the problem.
3. The counselor accurately conceptualizes the problem but becomes overwhelmed by it.

Personal discomfort may result from the counselor's fear of intimacy or inexperience with intense counseling relationships. With good supervisory assistance, this situation will remedy itself through continued counseling exposure and awareness. If the counselor's conceptual skills are weak or if the counselor's approach to all problems is to minimize the situation, then the result may be premature termination because of a failure to understand the client. This situation obviously calls for a careful reassessment of the counselor's decision to become a helper and whether additional training and supervision can remedy the situation. The third reason for premature termination is that the counselor accurately conceptualizes the client's problem but becomes overwhelmed by its complexity.

The special case of the counselor-in-training or the counselor who relocates should be acknowledged. In most cases, counselor trainees provide services in a practicum setting that conforms to university semester or quarter schedules. When counselor trainees know that their practicum will end at a certain date and the client will either be terminated or referred to another counselor, ethical practice dictates that the client be informed in the first session that a terminal date already exists. This allows the client a choice to enter into what might be brief counseling or potential long-term counseling with the condition of referral, or to seek another counselor who does not impose this terminal limitation on the counseling relationship.

The Termination Report

Whether counseling is brief or long term, a summary report of the process is appropriate and desirable for several reasons. Assuming that the client may have a need for future counseling, the termination report provides an accurate summation of the client's responsiveness to counseling and to specific types of interventions. Should the client request the counselor to provide information to other professionals (physician, psychiatrist, psychologist) or the legal system, the report provides a base for the preparation of that information.

The counseling case can usually be summarized in two or three typewritten pages and should include the counselor's name and address, date that counseling began and concluded, number of sessions, presenting problem(s), types of counseling interventions used and their effectiveness, client reaction to the counseling relationship over time, client reaction to termination, and the counselor's assessment of the client's success with counseling. The termination report is a confidential document and should not be released without the client's written permission (see Appendix B, Forms B-5 and B-8).

TERMINATION AS A PROCESS

The termination process involves several steps. The first is a careful assessment by the counselor and client of the progress that has been made and the extent to which goals have been achieved. Depending on the results of this assessment, the counselor will take one of two directions: termination or referral. Assuming termination is the appropriate choice, the counselor and client may proceed to discuss in depth the gains that have been made; how those gains might be affected by future situations; making plans for follow-up; and, finally, saying good-bye. Typically, the termination process is characterized by cognitive discussions interspersed with acknowledgment of emotional aspects of the relationship. When termination is appropriate, the process has a constructive, positive quality.

Assessing Progress

Quintana (1993) views the role of assessment during termination as

> [a] particularly critical opportunity for clients and therapists to update or transform their relationship to incorporate clients' growth. For this transformation to occur, clients need to acknowledge the steps they have taken toward more mature functioning. Perhaps most important to clients is for therapists to acknowledge and validate their sense of accomplishment. (p. 430)

This notion of transformation from the helping relationship to a more autonomous and normal lifestyle is related to the maintenance after counseling of those therapeutic gains that have been made. If the counseling agreement was based on specific goals identified by the client or if some form of counseling contract was established early in the process, then the assessment of change may take a rather formal character. Each goal that had been set becomes a topic to discuss, changes related to that goal are identified, perhaps environmental consequences that grow out of those changes are enumerated, and so forth. In this approach, there is a sense of structure as the counselor and client review the outcomes. When counseling has involved couples or families, the assessment becomes even more complex because each member's change is considered as well as systemic changes in patterns of interaction.

Summarizing Progress

It may seem redundant to suggest that the assessment of progress should be followed by some sort of summary of that progress by the counselor. The rationale for providing a summary is twofold. First, hearing one's progress from another person or perspective is quite different from hearing oneself describe progress. Most clients benefit from the counselor's statement even though it is not new information. As one client described it, "I knew I had made some gains, but it sure helps to hear you say it, too." Clients' efforts to internalize the counseling relationship are also enhanced when the counselor validates their accomplishments and encourages them to take credit for all of the steps they have taken toward their goals. The second reason for a summary is that the counselor can inject some cautions if some counseling gains need to be reinforced or monitored by the client. This is related to future client efforts to preserve or generalize the progress that has been achieved.

Generalizing Change

Having identified the changes that have occurred directly or indirectly through counseling, the counselor and client should turn to how those new behaviors, attitudes, or relationships can be generalized to the client's world. This step in the process calls on the client to extend beyond the immediate gains to potential future gains. The counselor might introduce this with questions such as these: In what other situations could you anticipate using these social skills you have acquired? If your husband should develop some new style of obnoxious behavior next month, how do you think you might handle it? The basic goal of the implementation step is to test the client's willingness and ability to adapt learned skills or new attitudes to situations other than those that provoked the original problem.

Planning for Follow-Up

Follow-up in counseling refers to the nature and amount of professional contact that occurs between the counselor and client after termination has occurred. Some counseling approaches place greater emphasis on follow-up than others. For example, some systemic family therapists take the position that a family therapist is like a family physician. Over the years, the family will encounter new crises and problems and will reenter counseling as these situations demand. Thus, counseling is viewed as a service that can extend, intermittently, over a portion of the client's lifetime. Other approaches, most notably those that emphasize self-actualization, view counseling as a developmental experience, the object of which is to facilitate the client's growth and capability of dealing with new problems more effectively. In this context, future returns to counseling are not expected although they are certainly not discouraged.

Follow-up also has an ethical aspect. Even when the counselor and client agree that sufficient progress has been made to warrant termination, it is appropriate for the counselor to (1) make his or her future services available and (2) explain to the client how future contact can be made. In so doing, the counselor has established a link between the client's present state and future needs. This link can also be an effective intervention for those clients who believe termination is appropriate but experience anxiety at the prospect. When this is the case, it may help if the counselor suggests a 3- or 6-month "checkup." Depending on the client's response to the suggestion, the counselor can even schedule an appointment or suggest that the client call to make an appointment if needed. This is an effective bridging intervention because it gives the client a sense of security and relationship continuation, even when counseling has terminated. The counselor might also suggest to the client that should the future appointment not seem necessary, a phone call to cancel the appointment would be appreciated. Our experience has been that clients are responsible about either keeping the appointment or canceling it. Even when they call to cancel, the telephone contact provides some follow-up information on how the client is coping.

If counseling outcomes include post-counseling activities that the client has decided to pursue, the counselor might want to follow up on the success of these goals. For example, if a client decides to make a career change that involves future job interviewing, the counselor might ask the client to keep him or her informed of progress, either through written or telephone contact.

THE REFERRAL PROCESS

Client referral is a special form of termination. Referral occurs when the counselor is unable to continue working with a particular client for a variety of reasons. For example, as the counselor is continuing the case assessment, it may become apparent that the client's problems are beyond the counselor's capabilities and referral to a counselor who has the necessary expertise is warranted (*ACA Code of Ethics*, Section A.11.b). Or the counselor may realize that personal or ethical values dictate that he or she should not continue working with a particular client. The referral involves a number of steps: (1) identifying the need to refer, (2) evaluating potential referral sources, (3) coordinating the transfer, and (4) preparing the client for the referral.

The Need to Refer

The most frequent reason for referral is that the client needs some specialized form of counseling. This does not mean that the client is seriously stressed although that can be the case for referral. It is more likely that the client needs a specific form of counseling that the counselor does not offer (e.g., career counseling or marital counseling). Because clients rarely are informed consumers of the various forms that counseling can take, counselors should be keenly attuned to specialized needs and their own ability to provide quality services.

Clients may also need or prefer special conditions for counseling. Those conditions might be related to gender, ethnicity, or culture. Even when the counselor recognizes the need, the task remains to help the client come to the same conclusion or referral will not be effective.

Clients may resist the first suggestions that a referral is appropriate. After all, having risked themselves by sharing their concerns or vulnerabilities, they probably would prefer not to have to go through the same process with yet another person. If you provide explanations that are complete, answer the client's questions clearly and thoroughly, and support the client's ambivalence, this resistance will ease.

Evaluating Potential Sources

It is important that counselors be familiar with potential referral sources in the community. Some communities publish a mental health services directory that lists public agencies and practitioners, services provided, fees, and how referral can be accomplished. Another source is the Internet. By doing a search for the terms *mental health counselor*, *marriage and family therapist*, *psychologist*, or *psychotherapist* for your city or county, you can obtain a list of licensed professionals and their areas of practice. Such lists or directories may provide little more than names and possible affiliations. For example, a listing under Marriage, Family, Child, and Individual counselors might read:

Psychotherapy/Counseling

Ralph T. Marcus, Ph.D.

Center for Psychotherapy

• Marriage Enrichment

• Divorce Bereavement

• Family Mediation

Conveniently located in the Meridian Center

Call for appointment: 555–5555

Just what can be learned from this listing? Dr. Marcus offers psychotherapy for marriages that may require enrichment, surviving divorce, and resolving family conflict issues. What is not known is (1) the kind of training Dr. Marcus received, (2) whether his doctorate was earned in psychology or a related mental health field or whether he is licensed as a psychologist, (3) his therapeutic orientation (individual versus family, theoretical base, etc.), or (4) his skill level or success rate with different types of problems. The best way to find answers to such questions is through exposure to different sources. Lacking that, the counselor might want to call Dr. Marcus and ask him such questions. After obtaining this information, the counselor should ask Dr. Marcus if he is accepting referrals and what referral procedures he prefers to follow. Over time, counselors can build up their own listings of referral sources based on direct experience. Such listings are by far the best resource when the need to refer a client arises.

Making referrals has legal ramifications. Because one can never know with certainty that a referral to a specific mental health provider will prove to be a positive experience for the client, it is probably best to provide the client with choices of referral sources. In that way, the client has the opportunity to choose a professional whose personal characteristics, values, and professional qualities are closest to the client's perceived needs. If the referring counselor provides only one potential referral professional to the client and that proves to be a problematic experience, the referring counselor may be held liable.

Coordinating the Transfer

Whenever a client is referred to another professional, the counselor hopes that the referral will occur successfully and without undue strain on the client. If the client is highly anxious or if the counselor thinks the client might not accept the referral, special attention should be devoted to the client's concerns. In addition, successful referrals require that the counselor make contact with the receiving professional and provide information that will facilitate the referral process.

Preparing the Client

Preparing the client for referral involves both details of the referral and the client's anxieties about the new relationship. It helps if the counselor has discussed the case with the receiving professional and can assure the client that painful details may not have to be repeated. It also helps if the counselor can tell the client some details about the potential new counselor(s), including personal characteristics, professional competency, and their receptiveness to the referral. Referral details may include helping the client identify what he or she should be looking for in a new counselor.

Communication With the Receiving Professional

Before any referral recommendation is made, you should establish whether potential receiving professionals are willing or able to accept the referral. This can be accomplished most effectively through telephone communications. Once the client has identified an acceptable receiving professional, the transfer of information about the case must be addressed. Usually, a receiving counselor will want a written case summary, in addition to the demographic information received by telephone. The termination report described earlier in this chapter will provide sufficient information to meet this requirement. Before sending any written material, however, you must obtain signed consent from the client to share this information. Most counseling centers use a standard consent form. Private practitioners should develop a statement form that gives the counselor power to transfer written information with the signed consent of the client to other specified professionals, agencies, or authorities.

BLOCKS TO TERMINATION

Counseling can be such an intimate and valued personal experience for both the counselor and client that the thought of ending the relationship may be most unappealing. From the counselor's perspective, helping a client who grows, overcomes obstacles, and accomplishes goals is an immensely rewarding experience. In addition, counselor-client relationships often assume a personal as well as a professional dimension. Counselors begin to like clients and appreciate their humanity and finer qualities. Thus, there can be some personal investment in maintaining the relationship. Clients often experience counselors in ways they wish could have happened in their family relationships. In this context, termination often means saying good-bye to a very good friend.

On the other hand, Quintana (1993) challenges the termination-as-crisis concept, suggesting that it is lacking in empirical support. He advocates an alternative definition of termination-as-development. This notion views termination as a transformation that encourages growth and development in the client "that is applicable across gender, ethnicity, and race" (p. 429).

Client Resistance to Termination

Much has been written in both the theoretical and experimental literature about the termination experience and its effect on clients. The theoretical notions of its impact appear to be in conflict with the empirical evidence. For example, according to psychoanalytic thinking, "the most desirable state of affairs is for the patient to slowly wean himself away, for him to eventually accept his limitations and be willing to relinquish the desires which cannot be realized" (Lorand, 1982, p. 225). In his review of the theoretical views of termination,

Quintana (1993, p. 427) describes how "clients are expected to react to termination with a plethora of neurotic affective, cognitive, interpersonal, and defensive reactions related to grief reactions [and] clients' reactions are . . . intense enough to overwhelm positive gains made earlier in therapy." On the other hand, Quintana describes the research on termination's effect on client reactions:

> The frequency and intensity of clients' reactions to termination do not reflect inherent crisis over loss. Results [of research by Marx & Gelso, 1987; Quintana & Holahan, 1992] suggest that only a small minority of clients experience a psychological crisis over the end of therapy, and the crisis seems to focus on the disappointing level of client outcome rather than specifically on loss. (1993, p. 427)

Whatever may be the more likely reaction, it is appropriate for the counselor to evaluate the client's degree of concern with the prospect of termination and respond therapeutically.

Counselor Resistance to Termination

It may be surprising that counselors often resist terminating with clients even though the client has reached a logical hiatus in the counseling process. Yet most counselor resistance is understandable. The counselor forms real human attachments to clients. In fact, it might be argued that counselor investment in the person of the client is a prerequisite to successful counseling. When this is part of the relationship, letting go has an emotional impact. Goodyear (1981) identifies eight conditions that can lead to the counselor's experience of loss when termination occurs:

1. When termination signals the end of the significant relationship
2. When termination arouses the counselor's anxieties about not having been more effective with the client
3. When termination arouses guilt in the counselor about not having been more effective with the client
4. When the counselor's professional self-concept is threatened by the client who leaves abruptly and angrily
5. When termination signals the end of a learning experience for the counselor (for example, the counselor may have been relying on the client to learn more about the dynamics of a disorder or about a particular subculture)
6. When termination signals the end of a particularly exciting experience of living vicariously through the adventures of the client
7. When termination becomes a symbolic recapitulation of other (especially unresolved) farewells in the counselor's life
8. When termination arouses in the counselor conflicts about his or her own individuation (p. 348)

The counselor trainee may have a supervisor who can point to any apparent resistance, but what does the professional counselor do? In the first place, most experienced counselors know, at some level of consciousness, when the relationship has grown quite important. This is a cue to the counselor that peer consultation or supervision would be both appropriate and desirable. The more human counselors tend to be, the more susceptible they are to personal intrusions in their professional practice. Having a colleague who can provide a level of objectivity through discussion and taped supervision is a valuable asset.

CASE ILLUSTRATION OF TERMINATION

The Case of Alex

In the following case, Alex is a 34-year-old stock-broker who has been unemployed for 14 months as a result of his firm's downsizing. He has tried to see this dilemma as an opportunity to move his career in new directions. However, he has decided to seek counseling at this time for two reasons. Although he had extensive outplacement counseling, he really doesn't know in what direction he would like to go with a new career and, in fact, has growing uncertainties about his potential. Added to this uncertainty, during the past few months Alex has grown increasingly bitter about being fired and how the outplacement was handled by his supervisor, whom he considered a close friend. The case was seen in a private psychotherapy group practice.

First Session

The first session began with the counselor orienting Alex to the conditions he could expect, including confidentiality, the necessity for the sessions to be recorded, and the fact that the counselor belonged to a consortium of mental health professionals who met periodically to provide and receive peer supervision. In addition, the counselor indicated that he practiced "short-term" psychotherapy, which meant that clients contract for 10 sessions. If, at the end of that time, the client had any remaining issues, the contract could be extended for an additional brief period of counseling.

COUNSELOR: Alex, one of the things we will be doing at each session is a review of your progress and how it is reflecting your goals. Because you have already had extensive career assessment, I would like your permission to request those results and they will become part of our weekly focus. So how would you like to begin this 10-week exploration?

ALEX: If you don't mind my saying so, I don't see how you can solve all my problems in 10 weeks.

COUNSELOR: You may be right, but of course, it won't be me doing it. It will be the two of us doing it.

ALEX: Still, I don't see how it can be done. I've been sweating this out for more than a year already.

COUNSELOR: Yes, and hopefully we can find some new and more efficient ways to look at your issues. But the first thing we need to address is which concern we should consider first: your future or your anger.

ALEX: Well, it's my future that brings me here.

COUNSELOR: Yes, but do you think your anger and your loss of confidence are having any effect on your ability to make sound decisions about your future?

Fourth Session

As the fourth session was about to end, the topic of termination was initiated by Alex. ALEX:

This was a really tiring session today.

COUNSELOR: Yes, we covered a lot of ground. I do think you are making some good progress.

ALEX: Yeah, I do feel better about things but that worries me, too.

COUNSELOR: What is it about a good feeling that makes you worry?

ALEX: Oh, it's not the good feeling. I'm just aware that things have been moving awfully fast and we only have 6 more sessions. I'm not sure I trust this idea of only 10 sessions and boom, you're fixed.

COUNSELOR: I don't think we said, "Boom, you're fixed," when we started. And we can renegotiate for a couple more sessions when the time comes. But let's not jump to conclusions too quickly now. Most of the time, when clients are feeling good about their progress for several weeks, the feeling can be trusted. I'm glad you raised the issue because we are almost halfway through our 10-week contract. We don't have to do anything about that except to be aware that we will be terminating one of these days.

The counselor took this opportunity to extend Alex's awareness of the termination process. In effect, this discussion became the starting point for the termination process. The seed of awareness was planted, and the client took that awareness with him at the end of the session. Three sessions later, the awareness had grown and matured.

Seventh Session

Nearing the end of this session, which had been a difficult but significant session, the counselor introduced the termination topic again with Alex.

COUNSELOR: Well, you've worked hard today, Alex. How are you feeling about your progress?

ALEX: To tell you the truth, I'm exhausted, Doc. But I feel pretty good about how things are going. I'm glad I have gotten over that anger I was feeling toward George. That was really getting in the way.

COUNSELOR: About a month ago, you mentioned that one of your fears was feeling too optimistic about your improvement. Do you still feel that way?

ALEX: When was that?

COUNSELOR: Oh, I was reviewing the tape of our fourth session and heard you say that you didn't trust that you could get your situation under control in only 10 sessions.

ALEX: Well, I still wonder about that. But I do feel like I'm a lot clearer on things now than I was then. I don't feel as shaky.

COUNSELOR: What about terminating soon. Do you feel shaky about that?

ALEX: [Laughing] Well, you still owe me 3 sessions. I'm not ready to terminate today. But, unless the bottom falls out, I don't think I will need another 10 sessions.

COUNSELOR: [Chuckling] No, if you had another 10 sessions, you'd probably begin to lose the ground you have gained.

ALEX: What do you mean? Do people lose ground if they stay in counseling too long?

COUNSELOR: I think so. There's a time to leave your parents; a time to leave your training; a time to leave a job; and, in our case, a time to leave counseling. If we don't make that break when it's time, then you could grow dependent and that would be self-defeating.

In this dialogue, the counselor is able to present the therapeutic effects of appropriate termination so that it is seen as a normal, developmental process, like growing up. That does not remove all of the client's fears, but it does place termination in a context that is anything but catastrophic. Quintana (1993) suggests that counselors can greatly facilitate the termination process by distinguishing between losing and outgrowing a valued relationship. He states:

> If therapy has been constructive . . . clients are likely to have outgrown much of their need for the formal structure of therapy at this time in their ongoing development. . . . [T]herapists should be careful not to imply that clients have outgrown their needs for therapy definitely . . . [because] future therapy should remain an option for clients as a way to support or catalyze their continued development. (p. 430)

Ninth Session

The counselor begins this session by introducing the topic of termination.

COUNSELOR: Well, Alex, this is our next-to-last session. How shall we use it?

ALEX: We could call it a tie and go into extra innings.

COUNSELOR: You're right, we could say that your weaknesses are still equal to your strengths.

ALEX: Well, I don't believe that and you don't either, I don't think.

COUNSELOR: No, I don't think that at all. In fact, I think your strengths are real and many of your weaknesses were imagined.

ALEX: Yeah, I am feeling that. But it's good to hear you say it, too. Maybe that's how I'd like to spend today.

COUNSELOR: What do you mean? Talking about your strengths?

ALEX: Yeah. I think I know what I want to do with my life. The graduate school idea seems right and I did have an interview at the university this week.

The counselor intentionally introduced termination at the beginning of the ninth session to allow Alex time to process his feelings about the imminent ending of the relationship. Alex might have dwelt on the insecurity of ending a meaningful relationship, he could have negotiated an extension at this time, or he could try to cement the gains he has realized through discussion and review. In this case, Alex chose the last alternative.

Tenth and Final Session

Alex began this session with the acknowledgment that it was the final session.

ALEX: Well, this is it.

COUNSELOR: What do you mean?

ALEX: This is the last time I'll be seeing you, I think.

COUNSELOR: I think so, too.

ALEX: It's been good. When we started, I really wasn't so sure this was going to work. But things are starting to pull together. Oh, by the way, George and I went out partying last Friday night. It was good to see him again. And I am filling out application forms for an MBA [masters of business administration] program.

COUNSELOR: That sounds good. Did George call you or did you call him?

ALEX: I called him. And it's neat. I think he's going to be able to help me with some contacts.
[Later in the session]

COUNSELOR: Before we finish today, I want you to know that I would like to hear from you in 6 months or so. Just a note telling me how things have been going would be fine. Would you do that?

Alex: Sure. What if I need a booster shot between now and then?

COUNSELOR: If that happens, you can call and set up an appointment.

In this final session, the counselor provided a bridge to aid the transition by asking Alex to get back in touch in 6 months with an informal progress report. This is as much for Alex's benefit as it is for the counselor because it says, "I'm not just dropping you from my appointment book and my consciousness. You will remain my client in absentia." Also, the counselor has provided a termination structure that allows Alex to make contact for future needs, should they arise. This would seem to be assumed, but clients often do not take this privilege for granted or are reluctant about such a move. In fact, an invitation to clients to return seems to result in greater levels of client satisfaction and lower levels of distress.

Summary

Often, termination is viewed as the moment when counselor and client conclude a successful counseling relationship. We have tried to dispel this notion and replace it with a broader definition of termination as a stage in the counseling process. As a stage, termination can be seen as the time when positive change is solidified and the transition to self-reliance is accomplished. Viewed in this way, termination can be as critical to successful counseling as are the assessment and the intervention stages.

When termination is an imminent possibility, the counselor and client should begin discussing the matter several sessions in advance. Many desirable consequences accrue from this discussion. The client becomes increasingly aware of new strengths and skills, the counselor is able to reinforce those gains, future demands and expectations can be considered, and fears and concerns can be assessed. The process addresses unfinished business and enhances a sense of completion. In all of this, the counselor has responsibility to see that the client's well-being is protected and preserved. When termination occurs through referral, the counselor has primary responsibility to see that the transfer to the receiving professional is handled smoothly and sensitively.

Successful termination must be seen as part of successful treatment. Without it, even the most impressive counseling gains are tempered in the client's perception, and future needs may be negatively affected.

Exercises

I. Class members divide into groups of three. Each group member assumes one of the following roles: counselor, client, or observer. The observer's responsibility is to record both the counselor's and client's behaviors during the exercise. Both the counselor and client should select a role from the following lists. Do not reveal your role to the other persons.

Counselor	Client
Resisting termination	Resisting termination
Encouraging termination	Requesting termination
Uncertain about termination	Uncertain about termination

Conduct a 10-minute counseling session simulation using the roles you selected. Following the session, discuss your reactions with one another. The person who observed the participants should provide feedback to each regarding the dynamics he or she observed.

II. In the following role-play, one person will be the counselor, the second will be the client, and the third will be an observer/recorder.

The client is being referred to a psychologist. The reason for the referral is that the counselor has realized that the client's problems are beyond his or her level of training and competence to treat. The client has seen the counselor for two sessions.

Allow 10 minutes for this role-play. Following the role-play, discuss among yourselves the dynamics of the interaction. What did you learn from this experience about its effect on the client? On the counselor? What interpersonal skills were required?

Discussion Questions

1. What are the pros and cons of early discussion about termination?
2. What types of clients are most in need of gradual introduction to the idea of termination? Why?
3. In this chapter, reference is made to premature termination. What are some of the conditions that might lead to premature termination? Can all be controlled by the counselor?
4. Discuss the idea of counselor resistance to termination. Do you possess any characteristics that might cause you to resist terminating a client?
5. Discuss the ways in which referral is similar to termination. How is referral different from termination, in terms of the counselor's responsibilities? What are the interpersonal dynamics of both referral and termination?

APPENDIX A

Integrative Practice Exercises

Learning to counsel is somewhat like learning any other complex task. It involves acquiring a set of skills, mastering a set of subtasks, and eventually putting everything together in some integrated fashion. Perhaps you can recall what the process of learning to drive a car was like for you. At first, the mere thought of being able to drive a car was probably an overwhelming idea. Now you drive and hardly pay any attention to the process because it is so familiar and has become such a part of you. In between the initial overwhelming idea of learning to drive and your current state of driving with relative comfort and ease, you practiced and mastered a variety of skills related to driving. You learned how to steer the car, use the accelerator, use the clutch, brake the car, and, while doing all of this, watch out for other drivers. And you learned all of this in a relatively short time period—although certainly not overnight.

Now it is time to try to put some counseling skills and strategies together for yourself—to take what you have learned in somewhat isolated fashion and integrate it in a meaningful way. The purpose of these exercises is to help you put the parts together in a conceptual framework that allows you to make even greater sense of the helping process for yourself. At the same time, it is important to realize that your ability to synthesize the tools and stages of counseling will necessarily stretch beyond the experience of these exercises, particularly if you are not yet in a field or job experience in which you can apply the tools with actual clients.

Although simulation such as role playing can be an invaluable way to learn under conditions of reduced threat, it is not a substitute for actual encounters and interactions with persons whose lives are distressed, whose emotions are conflicted, and who are sitting in front of you somewhat expectantly, relieved, and scared, all at the same time. As you accumulate actual counseling experience, your understanding and integration of the tools and stages of helping will continue to grow, just as you will also continue to grow and develop personally and professionally.

In this appendix, we present a variety of exercises designed to help you pull together the skills and strategies we have presented in this book into some meaningful whole. Additionally, we believe that completion of these activities will enable you to understand better the counseling process as it unfolds over an extended period of time with a client.

EXERCISE 1

In this exercise, we present three client cases. After reading each case, respond to the questions following the cases. In your responses, indicate issues that may arise in each of the five stages of the counseling process as well as your ideas for dealing with these issues effectively. You may wish to jot down your ideas in writing or use a partner or small group to help you brainstorm with this material.

Case 1. Sally is a college freshman at a large university; she is overwhelmed by the size of the university, having lived in a small town all her life. She is concerned about her "shyness" and feels it is preventing her from making friends. She reports being uncertain about how to "reach out" to people. She is concerned about her performance on tests; although she believes her study habits are adequate, she reports that she "blows" the tests because she gets so uptight about them.

Case 2. Mr. and Mrs. Yule have been married for two years. Both are in their sixties, and this is their second marriage; their previous spouses had died within the last 10 years. Mr. and Mrs. Yule are concerned that they "rushed into" this second relationship without adequate thought. They report that they argue constantly about everything. They feel they have forgotten how to talk to each other in a "civil" manner. Mrs. Yule states that she realizes her constant nagging upsets Mr. Yule; Mr. Yule discloses that his spending a lot of time with his male buddies irritates Mrs. Yule.

Case 3. Arthur is a third grader at Malcolm Elementary School. He is constantly "getting into trouble" for a number of things. Arthur admits that he starts a lot of fights with the other boys. He says he doesn't know why or how, but suddenly he is punching them. Only after these fights does he realize his anger got out of hand. Arthur realizes his behavior is causing some of the other kids to avoid him, yet he believes he would like their friendship. He is not sure how to handle his temper so that he doesn't lash out at his peers.

Rapport Relationship
1. List specific issues that may arise with this client in terms of establishing rapport and an effective helping relationship.
2. How might this particular client respond initially to the counselor?
3. How might this client respond to the counselor after several sessions?

Assessment of Problems
4. List what seem to be the major problem areas for this client. Consider the affective, behavioral, cognitive, and interpersonal dimensions.
5. What seem to be the client's main strengths, resources, and coping skills?
6. Can you identify any probable payoffs of the client's dysfunctional or problematic behavior?

Goal Setting
7. What might this client seek or expect from counseling?
8. What seem to be the ideal outcomes for this person?
9. How different might your choice of outcomes for this client be from the client's choice of outcomes? If the difference is great, what impact might this have on the helping process?

Intervention Strategies
10. Develop a list of possible intervention strategies that might be most useful in working with this particular client. Provide a rationale for your selection.
11. What theoretical approach underlies each of the intervention strategies on your list?
12. Would you *generally* favor using affective, cognitive, behavioral, or systemic strategies with this person? Why?

Termination and Follow Up
13. What are some indicators you would look for that suggest this client is ready to terminate counseling?
14. How would you help this client plan for transfer of learning from the counseling situation to the person's actual environment? What potential obstacles in his or her environment need to be anticipated?

3. How would you follow up on the progress of this client once the helping process is terminated?

EXERCISE 2

Select one of the three cases described in Exercise 1 to use for the purpose of conducting an extended series of role play counseling sessions. Enlist the help of a colleague or classmate who can meet with you regularly over the next five weeks. This person's task is to assume the role of the client from one of these cases and to "become" this client in the sessions with you. Your task is to meet with this person for five scheduled sessions during the next five weeks.

The first session should be directed toward establishing rapport and building an effective therapeutic relationship with this person. The second session should be an assessment interview and should reflect the content presented in Chapter 5. In the third session, try to help the client develop outcome goals, using the process and skills described in Chapter 6. In the fourth session, based on the assessed problem areas and defined goals, select one or two intervention strategies from Chapters 8 through 11 and implement these strategies with the client. Also in this session, begin to prepare the client for termination. In the fifth and last session, help the client summarize and evaluate the helping process and plan for changes in his or her environment. Terminate the counseling process and develop a follow up plan.

At a minimum, tape record each session—videotape if possible. After each interview, assess and rate your behavior using the corresponding part of the Counseling Strategies Checklist that follows. Your instructor or supervisor may also want to assess your performance. Your "client" can also provide you with informative feedback. Use this feedback and your ratings to determine which skills and parts of the helping process you have mastered and which areas need additional improvement and practice.

THE COUNSELING STRATEGIES CHECKLIST (CSC)

The CSC is divided into six parts: (I) The Process of Relating; (II) Assessment; (III) Goal Setting; (IV) Strategy Selection and Implementation; (V) Termination and Follow Up; and (VI) Individual Skills Summary. The first five parts correspond to each of the five stages of the counseling process. Each of these parts can be used to observe, evaluate, and rate sessions for each of these stages in the counseling process. For example, Part I, The Process of Relating, is used primarily to assess rapport and relationship building sessions. Part II, Assessment, is used to evaluate assessment interviews, and so on. Part VI, Individual Skills Summary, is a compilation of all the individual verbal and nonverbal skills associated with each of these stages of counseling. It can also be used following each corresponding type of session to determine the presence or absence of the skills associated with a particular stage of counseling.

Using the Counseling Strategies Checklist

Each item in the CSC is scored by circling the most appropriate response, either *Yes, No,* or *N.A. (not applicable).* The items are worded such that desirable responses are *Yes* and *N.A.* or *No* is an undesirable response.

After you have observed and rated each interview, sit down and review the ratings. Where noticeable deficiencies exist, you should identify a goal or goals that will remedy the problem. Beyond this, you should list two or three *action steps* that permit you to achieve this goal.

Part I: The Process of Relating

1. The counselor maintained eye contact with the client.
   Yes   No   N.A.

2. The counselor's facial expressions reflected the mood of the client.
   Yes   No   N.A.

3. The counselor demonstrated some variation in voice pitch when talking.
   Yes   No   N.A.

4. The counselor used intermittent one word vocalizations (e.g., mm hmm) to reinforce the client's demonstration of goal directed topics or behaviors.
   Yes   No   N.A.

5. The counselor made verbal comments that pursued the topic introduced by the client.
   Yes   No   N.A.

6. The subject of the counselor's verbal statements usually referred to the client, either by name or the second person pronoun *you*.
   Yes   No   N.A.

7. A clear and sensible progression of topics was evident in the counselor's verbal behavior; the counselor avoided rambling.
   Yes   No   N.A.

8. The counselor made statements that reflected the client's feelings.
   Yes   No   N.A.

9. The counselor verbally stated his or her desire and intent to understand.
   Yes   No   N.A.

10. Several times (at least twice), the counselor shared his or her own feelings with the client.
    Yes   No   N.A.

11. At least one time during the interview, the counselor provided specific feedback to the client.
    Yes   No   N.A.

12. The counselor encouraged the client to identify and discuss his or her feelings concerning the counselor and the interview.
    Yes   No   N.A.

13. The counselor voluntarily shared his or her feelings about the client and the counseling relationship.
    Yes   No   N.A.

14. The counselor expressed reactions about the client's strengths and/or potential.
    Yes   No   N.A.

15. The counselor made responses that reflected his or her liking and appreciation of the client.
    Yes   No   N.A.

Part II: Assessment

1. The counselor asked the client to provide basic demographic information about himself or herself.
   Yes   No   N.A.

2. The counselor asked the client to describe his or her current concerns and to provide some background information about the problems.
Yes   No   N.A.

3. The counselor asked the client to list and prioritize problems.
Yes   No   N.A.

4. For each identified problem, the counselor and client explored the
   a. Affective dimensions of the problem
   Yes   No   N.A.

   b. Cognitive dimensions of the problem
   Yes   No   N.A.

   c. Behavioral dimensions of the problem
   Yes   No   N.A.

   d. Interpersonal dimensions of the problem
   Yes   No   N.A.

   e. Intensity of the problem (frequency, duration, or severity)
   Yes   No   N.A.

   f. Antecedents of the problem
   Yes   No   N.A.

   g. Consequences and payoffs of the problem
   Yes   No   N.A.

5. The counselor and client discussed previous solutions the client had tried to resolve the problem.
Yes   No   N.A.

6. The counselor asked the client to identify possible strengths, resources, and coping skills the client could use to help resolve the problem.
Yes   No   N.A.

Part III: Goal Setting

1. The counselor asked the client to state how he or she would like to change his or her behavior (e.g., How would you like for things to be different?).
Yes   No   N.A.

2. The counselor and client decided together on counseling goals.
Yes   No   N.A.

3. The goals set in the interview were specific and observable.
Yes   No   N.A.

4. The counselor asked the client to state orally a commitment to work for goal achievement.
Yes   No   N.A.

5. If the client appeared resistant or unconcerned about achieving change, the counselor discussed this with the client.
Yes   No   N.A.

6. The counselor asked the client to specify at least one action step he or she might take toward his or her goal.
Yes   No   N.A.

7. The counselor suggested alternatives available to the client.
Yes   No   N.A.

8. The counselor helped the client to develop action steps for goal attainment.
Yes   No   N.A.

9. Action steps designated by counselor and client were specific and realistic in scope.
Yes   No   N.A.

10. The counselor provided an opportunity within the interview for the client to practice or rehearse the action step.
Yes   No   N.A.

11. The counselor provided feedback to the client concerning the execution of the action step.
Yes   No   N.A.

12. The counselor encouraged the client to observe and evaluate the progress and outcomes of action steps taken outside the interview.
Yes   No   N.A.

Part IV: Strategy Selection and Implementation

1. The counselor suggested some possible strategies to the client based on the client's stated goals.
Yes   No   N.A.

2. The counselor provided information about the elements, time, advantages, and disadvantages of each strategy.
Yes   No   N.A.

3. The counselor involved the client in the choice of strategies to be used.
Yes   No   N.A.

4. The counselor suggested a possible sequence of strategies to be used when more than one strategy was selected.
Yes   No   N.A.

5. The counselor provided a rationale about each strategy to the client.
Yes   No   N.A.

6. The counselor provided detailed instructions about how to use the selected strategy.
Yes   No   N.A.

7. The counselor verified if the client understood how the selected strategy would be implemented.
Yes   No   N.A.

Part V: Termination and Follow Up

1. The counselor and client engaged in some evaluation or assessment of the client's attainment of the desired goals.
Yes   No   N.A.

2. The counselor and client summarized the client's progress throughout the helping process.
Yes   No   N.A.

3. The counselor identified client indicators and behaviors suggesting termination was appropriate.
Yes   No   N.A.

4. The counselor and client discussed ways for the client to apply or transfer the learnings from the helping interviews to the client's environment.
   Yes   No   N.A.

5. The counselor and client identified possible obstacles or stumbling blocks the client might encounter after termination and discussed possible ways for the client to handle these.
   Yes   No   N.A.

6. The counselor discussed some kind of follow up plan to the client.
   Yes   No   N.A.

Part VI: Individual Skills Summary

Instructions: Check (✓) any of the skills that were utilized by the counselor in the observed interview. Use the space under Comments to record your qualitative assessment of the use of this skill. For example, how appropriately and effectively was it used?

SKILLS OF COUNSELING	COMMENTS

Rapport Relationship
Nonverbal attending
Verbal attending
Paraphrase
Reflection
Self disclosure
Immediacy
Pacing

Assessment
Questions
  Open
  Closed
  Clarifying

Goal Setting
Confrontation
Ability potential
Instructions

Strategy Implementation
Information giving
Modeling
Rehearsal/Practice
Feedback

Termination
Summarization

APPENDIX B

Forms and Guides for Use in Counseling Practice

Appendix B-1

Case #: _____

Date: _____

Referred by: _____ Phone: _____

Client Intake Form

Name: _____ SS#: _____

Address: _____ DOB: _____

_____ Sex: M   F

Phone: (H) _____ (W) _____

(C) _____

Employer: _____ Length of employment: _____

Reason for seeking counseling:

_____

_____

_____

_____

Medications:

_____
Date
_____

Previous counseling?   Yes   No   How long? _____

Name of counselor: _____

In case of emergency:

Person to contact: _____ Relation: _____

Address: _____

_____

Phone: (H) _____ (W) _____

(C) _____

To be signed by client:

I give permission for _____ (counselor) to contact the
above person in the event of an emergency.

_____   _____
        Client's signature   Date

Case #: _____

Date: _____

Referred by: _____   Phone: _____

Extended Client Intake Form
(To be completed by counselor)

Name: _____   SS#: _____

Address: _____   DOB: _____

_____   Sex: M   F

Phone: (H) _____   (C) _____   (W) _____

Employer: _____   Position: _____

How long? _____   Highest educational level: _____

Previous employment history:

_____

_____

Presenting problem(s):

_____

_____

_____

In case of emergency:

Person to contact: _____   Relation: _____

Address: _____

_____

Phone: (H) _____   (C) _____   (W) _____

Allergies? _____

Medical insurance?   Yes   No   Policy #: _____

Name of provider: _____

Family history: Single   Married   Divorced   Remarried   Children? _____

Names/ages of children: _____

Currently on medications?   Yes   No

Med/Dose: _____   How long: _____   Dr.: _____

Med/Dose: _____   How long: _____   Dr.: _____

Med/Dose: _____   How long: _____   Dr.: _____

Appendix B-2

Physical/somatic complaints: Yes   No

Sleeping: _____   Nightmares, sweats: _____

Headache: _____   Stomach: _____

Heart palpitation: _____   Weight: _____

Blood pressure: _____   Panic attacks: _____

Shortness of breath: _____   Appetite: _____

Use of alcohol or drugs to relieve stress?   Yes   No

Frequency: _____

Initial Assessment of Client Stability

	Excellent	Above Average	Average	Below Average	Poor
Attention span	_____	_____	_____	_____	_____
Self-image	_____	_____	_____	_____	_____
Physical appearance	_____	_____	_____	_____	_____
Verbal acuity	_____	_____	_____	_____	_____
Affective functioning	_____	_____	_____	_____	_____
Cognitive functioning	_____	_____	_____	_____	_____
Interpersonal functioning	_____	_____	_____	_____	_____

Descriptors of Initial Client Presentation

Aggressive	_____	Personable	_____	Assertive	_____	Engaging	_____
Dependent	_____	Depressed	_____	Shy	_____	Preoccupied	_____
Avoiding	_____	Friendly	_____	Social	_____	Withdrawn	_____
Motivated	_____	Distracted	_____	Impulsive	_____	Argumentative	_____

Factors that are operating in client's favor:

_____

_____

_____

Factors that are operating to client's disadvantage:

_____

_____

_____

(continued)

Counselor characteristics that would facilitate client progress:

_____

_____

_____

Counselor characteristics that would impede client progress:

_____

_____

_____

Date: _____   Intake counselor: _____

Disposition:

Client assigned to: _____   Date: _____

Counseling Progress Notes—Continuing Sessions

Counselor: _____   Date: _____

Supervisor: _____   Client*: _____
                                          *First name only or case number.

What were your objectives (goals) for this session?

Describe the dynamics in the session (your reactions to the client and the interactions between you and the client).

Summarize the key issues discussed during the session. Indicate who (you or client) initiated each issue to be discussed.

Describe relevant cultural or developmental information revealed in the session as it relates to the session content or to the client's history.

To what extent were your objectives (goals) for this session achieved?

Explain changes (or expansion of your conceptualization of the client's problem[s]).

(continued)

Explain changes (or expansions) of your treatment plan for this client.

Explain any changes to your diagnostic impressions (*DSM-IV-TR* code/axis).

What are your objectives for the next session?

Question(s) you would like answered by your supervisor:

_____   _____
       Counselor's signature   Supervisor's signature

Appendix B-4

Outpatient Treatment Plan (OTP)

Counselor: _____

Client: _____ Birthdate: _____ Age: _____ Sex: M   F

SS#: _____ Phone: (W) _____ (H) _____

(C) _____

A. Initial Assessment: Date: _____

Presenting problem:

_____

_____

Precipitating events:

_____

_____

Relevant medical history:

_____

_____

Presenting mental state evaluation (circle appropriate):

Appearance	*Judgment*	*Stability*	*Intelligence*	*Memory*
Appropriate	Intact	Stable	High	Intact
Inappropriate	Impaired	Variable	Average	Impaired
Not Assessed	Not Assessed	Unstable	Low	Not Assessed

B. Diagnostic Assessment: (*DSM-IV-TR*)

Axis I: _____

Axis II: _____

Axis III: _____

Axis IV: _____

Axis V: _____

Brief summary:

_____

_____

_____

(continued)

C. Treatment Plan

Type of treatment: Insight/Affective   Systemic/Interpersonal   Cognitive/Behavioral

Goal #1: _____

Time frame: _____

Success indicator: _____

Subgoal A: _____

Intervention strategy: _____

Time frame: _____

Alternate intervention/strategy: _____

Subgoal B: _____

Intervention strategy: _____

Time frame: _____

Alternate intervention/strategy: _____

Subgoal C: _____

Intervention strategy: _____

Time frame: _____

Alternate intervention/strategy: _____

Goal #2: _____

Time frame: _____

Success indicator: _____

Subgoal A: _____

Intervention strategy: _____

Time frame: _____

Alternate intervention/strategy: _____

Subgoal B: _____

Intervention strategy: _____

Time frame: _____

Alternate intervention/strategy: _____

Subgoal C: _____

Intervention strategy: _____

Time frame: _____

Alternate intervention/strategy: _____

D. Treatment Update #1   Date: _____

| Goals (see above) | Progress | Comments |

Goals (see above)   Progress   Comments

Goal #1   1   2   3   4   5 (Achieved)   _____

  Subgoal A: 1   2   3   4   5   _____

  Subgoal B: 1   2   3   4   5   _____

  Subgoal C: 1   2   3   4   5   _____

Goal #2   1   2   3   4   5 (Achieved)   _____

  Subgoal A: 1   2   3   4   5   _____

  Subgoal B: 1   2   3   4   5   _____

  Subgoal C: 1   2   3   4   5   _____

E. Treatment Update #2   Date: _____

Goals (see above)   Progress   Comments

Goal #1   1   2   3   4   5 (Achieved)   _____

  Subgoal A: 1   2   3   4   5   _____

  Subgoal B: 1   2   3   4   5   _____

  Subgoal C: 1   2   3   4   5   _____

Goal #2   1   2   3   4   5 (Achieved)   _____

  Subgoal A: 1   2   3   4   5   _____

  Subgoal B: 1   2   3   4   5   _____

  Subgoal C: 1   2   3   4   5   _____

F. Termination Report: Date: _____

Goals (see above)   Success Criterion Met   Termination Reason

                  Yes   Partial   No   Comment   ____ Goals met

1. _____   ___   ___   ___   _____   ____ Client
                                                                          terminated

2. _____   ___   ___   ___   _____   ____ Client
                                                                           moved

3. _____   ___   ___   ___   _____   ____ Ineffective
                                                                           treatment

Counselor signature: _____   Date: _____

Supervisor signature: _____   Date: _____

Appendix B-5

Consent to Release Confidential Information

I, _____, (_____)
                      (Client's name)   (Social Security number)

of _____
                                      (Client's address)

authorize _____
                  (Name of counselor and agency/organization making the disclosure)

to disclose to _____
                     (Name of person and agency/organization receiving the disclosure)

the following information:*

_____

_____

_____

_____

*(including counseling/psychotherapy records related to emotional illness, and including diagnoses and interventions used in the treatment of diagnosed illnesses)

for the purpose of:

_____
                          (Purpose of information to be released)

_____

_____

_____

I also understand that I may revoke this consent at any time except to the extent that action has already been taken in reliance on it, and that, in any event, this consent expires automatically as described below:

Specific date upon which this consent expires: _____

Executed this _____ day of _____, 20 _____.

_____
                                  Client's signature

_____
              (Parent, guardian, or authorized representative's signature)

Permission to Audio- or Videotape Counseling Interviews

I hereby give permission to _____,

(Counselor's name)

representing _____,

(Training institution or agency)

to make audio- and/or videotape recordings of our counseling interviews.
I understand that these tapes will be used only for the purpose of providing
clinical supervision to the counselor-in-training in the above institution/agency.
These tapes may be heard or viewed only by professional training staff of the
above institution/agency, and professional staff from the agency/school from
which I am receiving services. This permission may also include consultation
with other mental health professionals, if that seems professionally appropriate.
If any other use of the tape(s) is desired by the training institution, I must first
be asked for permission and must give that consent separate from this agreement.

_____   _____

(Signature of client)   (Signature of witness)

_____   _____

(Date)   (Date)

If the client is a minor (under 18 years), his or her parent or legal guardian must also
sign this agreement.

_____   _____

(Parent or legal guardian)   (Date)

Audio- or Videotape Critique Form

Counselor: _____ Date: _____

Placement: _____

Client*:_____ Sex: _____ Session #: _____
*First name only or case number.

Counseling format: Individual _____ Group _____ Family _____ Other _____

Please respond to the following questions for each audio- or videotape of counseling session(s). This form is primarily for training purposes and should not be viewed as an assessment.

Client's presenting problem(s):

_____

_____

Your theoretical conceptualization of the problem(s):

_____

_____

Counseling goals/objectives for this session? Explain your rationale for focusing on each.

_____

_____

Identify verbal or behavioral interventions that facilitated the session:

_____

_____

Identify any verbal or behavioral interventions that detracted from the session:

_____

_____

If you could do the session over again, what would you do differently?

_____

_____

Termination Summary Report

Counselor: _____   Date: _____

Supervisor: _____   Client*: _____
                                                *First name only or case number.

Initial reason for seeking counseling:

_____

_____

_____

Number of sessions: _____, beginning on_____ and concluding on
                                                  (date)
_____.
    (date)

Treatment plan called for the following:

_____

_____

_____

The following aspects of the treatment were accomplished:

_____

_____

_____

Counseling was terminated for the following reason(s):

_____

_____

_____

Client's status in the final session:

_____

_____

_____

Referral was made to: _____

_____   _____
        Counselor's signature   Supervisor's signature

Evaluation of Counselor Trainee Skills*

1 = needs improvement; 2 = adequate; 3 = good; 4 = student strength;
5 = exceeds expectations

Student _____

Semester _____   Instructor _____

Relationship/Attending Skills

1. Listens carefully and communicates an understanding of the client.	1	2	3	4	5
2. Is genuine and warm with client.	1	2	3	4	5
3. Is immediate with the client.	1	2	3	4	5
4. Is respectful of, and validates, the client.	1	2	3	4	5
5. Is appropriate regarding the cultural context of the client.	1	2	3	4	5
6. Is appropriate regarding the developmental context of the client.	1	2	3	4	5
7. Uses interpersonal strengths appropriately, including humor and self-disclosure.	1	2	3	4	5
8. Is comfortable with a variety of feelings and/or issues shared by the client.	1	2	3	4	5
9. Provides support to the client when appropriate.	1	2	3	4	5
10. Challenges the client when appropriate.	1	2	3	4	5
11. Tracks the main issues presented by the client.	1	2	3	4	5

Assessment Skills

12. Is able to organize session data into meaningful frameworks.	1	2	3	4	5
13. Appreciates cultural and/or developmental issues that may affect assessment.	1	2	3	4	5
14. Is able to recognize normative from problematic behavior during assessment.	1	2	3	4	5
15. Can assist the client in considering different components and sequences that make up and sustain problems.	1	2	3	4	5
16. Is able to identify cognitive components of client issues.	1	2	3	4	5

*Developed by Janine M. Bernard, Ph.D., NCC, LPC, 1998.

Appendix B-9

17. Is able to identify affective components of client issues.	1	2	3	4	5
18. Is able to identify behavioral components of client issues.	1	2	3	4	5
19. Is able to identify systemic components of client issues.	1	2	3	4	5
20. Identifies appropriate process goals.	1	2	3	4	5
21. Can assist client in translating problems into realistic outcome goals.	1	2	3	4	5
22. Can assess one's own performance in counseling.	1	2	3	4	5

Intervention Skills

23. Maintains an appropriate pace during sessions.	1	2	3	4	5
24. Uses questions skillfully.	1	2	3	4	5
25. Uses nondirective interventions skillfully.	1	2	3	4	5
26. Can direct the session in a meaningful manner.	1	2	3	4	5
27. Can deliver appropriate confrontations.	1	2	3	4	5
28. Can demonstrate an appropriate use of affective interventions.	1	2	3	4	5
29. Can demonstrate an appropriate use of cognitive interventions.	1	2	3	4	5
30. Can demonstrate an appropriate use of behavioral interventions.	1	2	3	4	5
31. Can demonstrate an appropriate use of systemic interventions.	1	2	3	4	5
32. Is able to work effectively with multiple clients.	1	2	3	4	5

Professional Skills

33. Is aware of personal issues (countertransference/ parallel processes) that might impact counseling.	1	2	3	4	5
34. Demonstrates openness to and use of supervision.	1	2	3	4	5
35. Appreciates own limits without overreacting to them.	1	2	3	4	5

Additional Aspects of Prepracticum

36. Participation in class discussions	1	2	3	4	5
37. Written assignments	1	2	3	4	5
38. Performance in role of observer	1	2	3	4	5
39. Ability to demonstrate empathy for different life situations through simulations as client	1	2	3	4	5

(continued)

Counselor-trainee's areas of strength:

_____

_____

_____

_____

Counselor-trainee's areas requiring additional work:

_____

_____

_____

_____

Final grade: _____   Ready to begin practicum: Yes _____   No _____

_____   _____   _____

      (Student)   (Instructor)   (Date)

APPENDIX C

Ethics and Professional Practice Websites

American Association of Marriage and Family Therapy (AAMFT)
http://www.aamft.org/imis15/content/legal_ethics/code_of_ethics.aspx

American Association of Pastoral Counselors (AAPC)
http://aapc.org/content/ethics

American Counseling Association (ACA)
http://www.counseling.org/Resources/CodeOfEthics/TP/Home/CT2.aspx

American Mental Health Counseling Association (AMHCA)
*https://www.amhca.org/assets/news/AMHCA_Code_of_Ethics_2010_w_pagination_
cxd_51110.pdf*

American Psychological Association (APA)
http://apa.org/ethics/code/index.aspx

American School Counselor Association (ASCA)
http://asca2.timberlakepublishing.com//files/EthicalStandards2010.pdf

Canadian Psychological Association (CPA)
*http://www.cpa.ca/cpasite/userfiles/Documents/Canadian%20Code%20of%20Ethics%20
for%20Psycho.pdf*

Commission on Rehabilitation Counselor Certification (CRCC)
http://www.crccertification.com/pages/crc_ccrc_code_of_ethics/10.php

National Association of Social Workers (NASW)
http://www.socialworkers.org/pubs/code/code.asp

National Board for Certified Counselors (NBCC)
http://nbcc.org/AssetManagerFiles/ethics/nbcc-codeofethics.pdf

REFERENCES

American Counseling Association. (1997). Minutes of the September 1997 governing council meeting. Alexandria, VA.

American Counseling Association. (2005). *ACA Code of Ethics.* Alexandria, VA: ACA Press.

American Heritage Dictionary of the English Language (4th ed.). (2006). Boston: Houghton Mifflin.

American Psychiatric Association. (2007). *Diagnostic and statistical manual of mental disorders—TR* (4th ed.). Washington, DC: American Psychiatric Press.

Andrews, J., Clark, D., & Baird, F. (1998). Therapeutic letter-writing: Creating relational case notes. *The Family Journal: Counseling and Therapy for Couples and Families, 5,* 149–158.

Argyle, M., Henderson, M., Bond, M., Iizuka, Y., & Contarelo, A. (1986). Cross-cultural variations in relationship rules. *International Journal of Psychology, 21,* 287–315.

Atkinson, D. R., Casas, A., & Abreu, J. (1992). Acculturation, ethnicity, and cultural sensitivity. *Journal of Counseling Psychology, 39*(4), 515–520.

Atkinson, D. R., & Hackett, G. (1998). *Counseling Diverse Populations.* Boston: McGraw-Hill.

Atkinson, D. R., Morten, G., & Sue, D. W. (1989). *Counseling American Minorities: A Cross-Cultural Perspective* (3rd ed.). Dubuque, IA: William C. Brown.

Baker, S. B., Thomas, R. N., & Munson, W. W. (1983). Effects of cognitive restructuring and structured group discussion as primary prevention strategies. *School Counselor, 31,* 26–33.

Bandura, A. (1969). *Principles of behavior modification.* Englewood Cliffs, NJ: Prentice Hall.

Bandura, A. (1977). *Social learning theory.* Englewood Cliffs, NJ: Prentice Hall.

Bandura, A. (1988). Self-efficacy conception of anxiety. *Anxiety Research, 1,* 77–88.

Bandura, A., Grusec, J. E., & Menlove, F. L. (1966). Observational learning as a function of symbolization and incentive set. *Child Development, 37,* 499–506.

Barnland, D. C. (1975). Communication styles in two cultures: Japan and the United States. In A. Kendron, R. M. Harris, & M. R. Key (Eds.), *Organization of*

behavior in face-to-face interaction (pp. 427–456). The Hague: Mouton.

Beck, A. T. (1976). *Cognitive therapy and the emotional disorders.* New York: International Universities Press.

Beck, J. S. (1995). *Cognitive therapy: Basics and beyond.* New York: Guilford.

Berg, I., & Jaya, A. (1993). Different and same: Family therapy with Asian-American families. *Journal of Marital and Family Therapy, 19,* 31–38.

Bernard, J. M., & Hackney, H. (1983). *Untying the knot: A guide to civilized divorce.* Minneapolis: Winston.

Berne, E. (1964). *Games people play.* New York: Grove.

Bettelheim, B. (1976). *The uses of enchantment: The meaning and importance of fairy tales.* New York: Knopf.

Birdwhistell, R. (1970). *Kinesics and context: Essays on body motion communications.* Philadelphia: University of Pennsylvania Press.

Bishop, D. R. (1995). Religious values and cross-cultural issues. In M. T. Burke & J. G. Miranti (Eds.), *Counseling: The spiritual dimension* (pp. 59–71). Alexandria, VA: ACA Press.

Bowen, M. (1978). *Family therapy in clinical practice.* New York: Jason Aronson.

Carkhuff, R. R., & Berenson, B. G. (1967). *Beyond counseling and therapy* (2nd ed.). New York: Holt, Rinehart and Winston.

Carli, L. L. (1989). Gender differences in interaction style and influence. *Journal of Personality and Social Psychology, 56,* 565–576.

Chandler, C. K., Holden, J. M., & Kolander, C. A. (1995). Counseling for spiritual wellness: Theory and practice. In M. T. Burke & J. G. Miranti (Eds.), *Counseling: The spiritual dimension* (p. 58). Alexandria, VA: ACA Press.

Cheatham, H. et al. (2002). Multicultural counseling and therapy I: Metatheory—Taking theory into practice. In A. E. Ivey, M. D'Andrea, M. B. Ivey, & L. Simek-Morgan (Eds.), *Theories of counseling and psychotherapy: A multicultural perspective* (5th ed.). Boston: Allyn & Bacon.

Cheek, D. (1976). *Assertive black ... puzzled white.* San Luis Obispo, CA: Impact.

Chung, R. C. Y., & Bemak, F. (2002). The relationship of culture and empathy in cross-cultural counseling. *Journal of Counseling and Development, 80,* 154–159.

Collins, B. G., & Collins, T. M. (2005). *Crisis and trauma: Developmental-ecological intervention.* Boston: Lahaska Press.

Combs, A. (1986). What makes a good helper. *Person-Centered Review, 1*(1), 51–61.

Corey, G. (2011). *Issues and ethics in the helping professions* (8th ed.). Pacific Grove, CA: Brooks/Cole.

Cormier, S., & Hackney, H. (2012). *Counseling strategies and interventions* (8th ed.). Boston: Allyn & Bacon.

Cormier, S., & Nurius, P. S. (2003). *Interviewing and change strategies for helpers* (5th ed.). Pacific Grove, CA: Brooks/Cole.

Cormier, S., Nurius, P. S., & Osborn, C.J. (2009). *Interviewing and change strategies for helpers fundamental skills and cognitive behavioral interventions* (6th ed.). Pacific Grove CA: Brooks/Cole.

Cowan, E. W., & Presbury, J. H. (2000). Meeting client resistance and reactance with reverence. *Journal of Counseling and Development, 78,* 411–419.

Cross, W. E., Jr. (1971). The negro-to-black conversion experience: Towards a psychology of Black liberation. *Black World, 20,* 13–27.

deShazer, S. (1988). *Clues, investigating solutions in brief therapy.* New York: Norton.

deShazer, S. (1991). *Putting differences to work.* New York: Norton.

deShazer. S. (1994). *Words were originally magic.* New York: Norton.

Dixon, D. N., & Glover, J. A. (1984). *Counseling: A problem-solving approach.* New York: Wiley.

Donley, R. J., Horan, J. J., & DeShong, R. L. (1990). The effect of several self-disclosure permutations on counseling process and outcome. *Journal of Counseling and Development, 67,* 408–412.

Dowd, E. T., & Milne, C. R. (1986). Paradoxical interventions in counseling psychology. *The Counseling Psychologist, 14,* 237–282.

Drummond, R. J., & Jones, K. D. (2010). *Assessment procedures for counselors and helping professionals* (7th ed.). Upper Saddle River, NJ: Pearson/Prentice Hall.

Egan, G. (2010). *The skilled helper* (9th ed.). Pacific Grove, CA: Brooks/Cole.

Ekman, P. (1973). Cross-cultural studies of facial expression. In P. Ekman (Ed.), *Darwin and facial expression.* New York: Academic Press.

Ekman, P. (1993). Facial expression and emotion. *American Psychologist, 48,* 384–392.

Ekman, P., & Friesen, W. V. (1967). Head and body cues in the judgment of emotion: A reformulation. *Perceptual and Motor Skills, 24,* 711–724.

Ekman, P., & Freisen, W. V. (1969). Nonverbal leakage and clues to deception. *Psychiatry, 32,* 88–106.

Ellis, A., & Wilde, J. (2002). *Case studies in rational emotive behavior therapy with children and adolescents.* Upper Saddle River, NJ: Merrill/Prentice Hall.

Enns, C. B. (1993). Twenty years of feminist counseling and therapy: From naming biases to implementing multifaceted practice. *The Counseling Psychologist, 21,* 3–87.

Epston, D. (1994). Extending the conversation. *The Family Networker, 18*(6), 30–37, 62–63.

Epston, D., & White, M. (1992). *Experience, contradiction, narrative, and imagination: Selected papers of David Epston and Michael White.* Adelaide, Australia: Dulwich Center Publications.

Foley, V. D. (1989). Family therapy. In R. J. Corsini & D. Wedding (Eds.), *Current psychotherapies* (4th ed.). Itasca, IL: F. E. Peacock.

Framo, J. (1982). *Family interaction: A dialogue between family therapists and family researchers.* New York: Springer.

Gazda, G. M. et al. (1984). *Human relations development: A manual for educators* (3rd ed.). Boston: Allyn & Bacon.

Gelso, C. J., & Carter, J. A. (1994). Components of the psychotherapy relationship: Their interaction and unfolding during treatment. *Journal of Counseling Psychology, 41*(3), 296–306.

Gendlin, E. T. (1969). Focusing. *Psychotherapy: Theory, Research and Practice, 6,* 14–15.

Gilmore, S. (1973). *The counselor-in-training.* Englewood Cliffs, NJ: Prentice Hall.

Giordano, J., McGoldrick, M., & Klages, J. G. (2005). In M. McGoldrick, J. Giordano, & N. Garcia-Preto (Eds.), *Ethnicity and family therapy* (3rd ed., pp. 616–628). New York: Guilford.

Gladding, S. T. (2007). *Counseling: A comprehensive profession* (5th ed.). Columbus, OH: Merrill.

Gladstein, G. (1983). Understanding empathy: Integrating counseling, development and social psychology perspectives. *Journal of Counseling Psychology, 30,* 467–482.

Glasser, W. (1965). *Reality therapy.* New York: Harper & Row.

Goldenberg, I., & Goldenberg, H. (2008). *Family therapy: An overview* (7th ed.). Pacific Grove, CA: Brooks/Cole.

Goodrich, T. J., Rampage, C., Ellman, B., & Halstead, K. (1988). *Feminist family therapy.* New York: Norton.

Goodyear, R. K. (1981). Termination as a loss experience for the counselor. *Personnel and Guidance Journal, 59,* 347–350.

Gordon, R. L. (1969). *Interviewing strategy, techniques, and tactics.* Homewood, IL: Dorsey.

Gottman, J. (1991). Predicting the longitudinal course of marriages. *Journal of Marital and Family Therapy, 17,* 3–7.

Gottman, J. (1993). A theory of marital dissolution and stability. *Journal of Family Psychology, 7,* 57–75.

Gottman, J. M., Notarius, C., Gonso, J., & Markman, H. (1976). *A couple's guide to communication.* Champaign, IL: Research Press.

Greenberg, L. S. (1979). Resolving splits: Use of the two chair technique. *Psychotherapy: Theory, Research and Practice, 16,* 316–324.

Gudykunst, W. B., & Ting-Toomey, S. (1988). *Culture and interpersonal communication.* Newbury Park, CA: Sage.

Hackney, H. (1974). Facial gestures and subject expression of feelings. *Journal of Counseling Psychology, 21,* 173–178.

Hackney, H. (1978). The evolution of empathy. *The Personnel and Guidance Journal, 55,* 35–39.

Haley, J. (1963). *Strategies of psychotherapy.* New York: Grune & Stratton.

Haley, J. (1973). *Uncommon therapy.* New York: Norton.

Haley, J. (1976). *Problem-solving therapy.* New York: McGraw-Hill.

Haley, J. (1980). *Leaving home.* New York: McGraw-Hill.

Hall, W. S., Cross, W. E., & Freedle, R. (1972). Stages in the development of Black awareness: An exploratory investigation. In R. L. Jones (Ed.), *Black psychology.* New York: Harper & Row.

Halstead, R. W., Brooks, D. K., Goldberg, A., & Fish, L. S. (1990). Counselor and client perceptions of the working alliance. *Journal of Mental Health Counseling, 12,* 208–221.

Helms, J. E. (1990). *Black and white racial identity.* Westport, CT: Praeger.

Helms, J. E., & Cook, D. A. (1999). *Using race and culture in counseling and psychotherapy: Theory and process.* Boston: Allyn & Bacon.

Hill, C. E. (2009). *Helping skills: Facilitating exploration, insight and action* (3rd ed.). Washington, DC: APA Press.

Hinterkopf, E. (1998). *Integrating spirituality in counseling.* Alexandria, VA: ACA Press.

Hoffman, L. (1981). *Foundations of family therapy.* Cambridge, MA: Harvard University Press.

Holdstock, T. L., & Rogers, C. R. (1977). Person-centered theory. In R. J. Corsini (Ed.), *Current personality theories* (pp. 125–151). Itasca, IL: F. E. Peacock.

Hosford, R., & deVisser, L. (1974). *Behavioral approaches to counseling: An introduction.* Washington, DC: American Personnel and Guidance Association Press.

Iberg, J. R. (1981). Focusing. In R. J. Corsini (Ed.), *Handbook of innovative psychotherapy.* New York: Wiley.

Ivey, A. E. (1994). *Intentional interviewing and counseling* (3rd ed.). Pacific Grove, CA: Brooks/Cole.

Ivey, A. E., D'Andrea, M., Ivey, M. B., & Simek-Morgan, L. (2007). *Theories of counseling and psychotherapy: A multicultural perspective* (6th ed.). Boston: Allyn & Bacon.

Ivey, A. E., Ivey, M. B., & Zalaquett, C. P. (2010). *Intentional interviewing and counseling: Facilitating client development in a multicultural society* (7th ed.). Pacific Grove, CA: Brooks/Cole.

Jackson, B. (1975). Black identity development. *Journal of Education Diversity, 2,* 19–25.

Jackson, D. D. (1961). Interactional psychotherapy. In M. T. Stein (Ed.), *Contemporary psychotherapies.* New York: Free Press.

Jacobson, E. (1939). Variation of blood pressure with skeletal muscle tension and relaxation. *Annual of Internal Medicine, 2,* 152.

James, R. K., & Gilliland, B. E. (2005). *Crisis intervention strategies* (5th ed.). Pacific Grove, CA: Brooks/Cole.

Jessop, A. L. (1979). *Nurse-patient communication: A skills approach.* North Amherst, MA: Microtraining Associates.

Johnson, D. W. (1993). *Reaching out: Interpersonal effectiveness and self-actualization* (3rd ed.). Boston: Allyn & Bacon.

Kanfer, F. H. (1980). Self-management methods. In F. H. Kanfer & A. P. Goldstein (Eds.), *Helping people change* (pp. 309–355). New York: Pergamon.

Karoly, P. (1982). Perspectives on self-management and behavior change. In P. Karoly & F. A. Kanfer (Eds.), *Self-management and behavior change.* New York: Pergamon.

Kasdin, A. E. (1973). Covert modeling and the reduction of avoidance behavior. *Journal of Abnormal Psychology, 81,* 89–95.

Kim, S. C., Lee, S. U., Chu, K. H., & Cho, K. J. (1989). Korean-Americans and mental health: Clinical experiences of Korean-American mental health services. *Asian American Psychological Association Journal, 13,* 18–27.

Klopf, D. W., Thompson, C. A., Ishii, S., & Sallinen-Kuparinen, A. (1991). Non-verbal immediacy differences among Japanese, Finnish, and American university students. *Perceptual and Motor Skills, 73,* 209–210.

Knapp, M. (1978). *Nonverbal communication in human interaction* (2nd ed.). New York: Holt, Rinehart and Winston.

Knox, S., Hess, S. A., Petersen, D. A., & Hill, C. A. (1997). A qualitative analysis of client perceptions of the effects of helpful therapist self-disclosure in long-term therapy. *Journal of Counseling Psychology, 44*(3), 274–283.

Kottler, J. A. (1991). *The compleat therapist.* San Francisco: Jossey-Bass.

Kurilla, V. (1998). Multicultural counseling perspectives: Culture specificity and implications in family therapy. *The Family Journal, 6*(3), 207–211.

Laidlaw, T., Malmo, C., & Associates. (1990). *Healing voices: Feminist approaches to therapy with women.* San Francisco: Jossey-Bass.

Lazarus, A. A. (1966). Behavioral rehearsal vs. non-directive therapy vs. advice in effecting behavior change. *Behavior Research and Therapy, 4,* 209–212.

Lin, J. C. H. (1994). Americans stay in psychotherapy? *Journal of Counseling Psychology, 41,* 288–291.

Lombana, J. H. (1989). Counseling persons with disabilities: Summary and projections. *Journal of Counseling and Development, 68,* 177–179.

Lorand, S. (1982). *Techniques of psychoanalytic therapy.* New York: St. Martin's Press.

Madanes, C. (1981). *Strategic family therapy.* San Francisco: Jossey-Bass.

Madigan, S. (1994). Body politics. *The Family Therapy Networker, 18*(6), 18.

Mahoney, M. J. (1988). Constructive metatheory: II. Implications for psychotherapy. *International Journal of Personal Construct Psychology, 1,* 299–316.

Marx, J. A., & Gelso, C. J. (1987). Termination of individual counseling in a university counseling center. *Journal of Counseling Psychology, 34,* 3–9.

McGoldrick, M., Anderson, C., & Walsh, F. (Eds.). (1989). *Women in families: A framework for family therapy.* New York: Norton.

McGoldrick, M., Gerson, R., & Petry, S. (2008). *Genograms: Assessment and intervention* (3rd ed.). New York: Norton.

McMullin, R. E., & Giles, T. R. (1981). *Cognitive-behavior therapy: A restructuring approach.* New York: Grune & Stratton.

Meador, B. D., & Rogers, C. R. (1984). Person-centered therapy. In R. J. Corsini (Ed.), *Current psychotherapies* (3rd ed., pp. 142–195). Itasca, IL: F. E. Peacock.

Meichenbaum, D. (1971). Examination of model characteristics in reducing avoidance behavior. *Journal of Personality and Social Psychology, 17,* 298–307.

Meichenbaum, D. (1977). *Cognitive-behavior modification: An integrative approach.* New York: Plenum.

Meichenbaum, D. (1985). *Stress-inoculation training.* New York: Pergamon.

Miller, S., Wackman, D. B., Nunnally, E. W., & Miller, P. (1989). *Connecting.* Minneapolis: Interpersonal Communication Programs.

Minuchin, S. (1974). *Families and family therapy.* Cambridge, MA: Harvard University Press.

Minuchin, S., & Fishman, H. C. (1981). *Family therapy techniques.* Cambridge, MA: Harvard University Press.

Morgan, O. J. (2000). Counseling and spirituality. In H. Hackney, *Practice issues for the beginning counselor.* Boston: Allyn & Bacon.

Moursund, J., & Kenny, M. C. (2002). *The process of counseling and psychotherapy* (4th ed.). Englewood Cliffs, NJ: Prentice Hall.

Nelson, M. L. (1993). A current perspective on gender differences: Implications for research in counseling. *Journal of Counseling Psychology, 40*(2), 200–209.

Nelson, M. L. (2002). An assessment-based model for counseling strategy selection. *Journal of Counseling and Development, 80,* 416–421.

Neukrug, E. (2007). *The world of the counselor* (3rd ed.). Pacific Grove, CA: Brooks/Cole.

Neukrug, E. S., & Schwitzer, A. M. (2006). *Skills and tools for today's counselors and psychotherapists.* Pacific Grove, CA: Thomson/Brooks/Cole.

Nichols, M. P., & Schwartz, R. C. (1994). *Family therapy: Concepts and methods* (3rd ed.). Boston: Allyn & Bacon.

Notarius, C., & Markman, H. (1993). *We can work it out.* New York: Putnam.

Okun, B. F., & Kantrowitz, R. E. (2008). *Effective helping: Interviewing and counseling techniques* (7th ed.). Pacific Grove, CA: Brooks/Cole.

Ozer, E. M., & Bandura, A. (1990). Mechanisms governing empowerment effects: A self-efficacy analysis. *Journal of Personality and Social Psychology, 88,* 472–486.

Palazzoli, M., Cecchin, G., Prata, G., & Boscolo, L. (1978). *Paradox and counterparadox.* New York: Jason Aronson.

Pate, R. H. (1982). Termination: End or beginning? In W. H. Van Hoose & M. R. Worth (Eds.), *Counseling adults: A developmental approach.* Pacific Grove, CA: Brooks/Cole.

Pearce, S. S. (1996). *Flash of insight: Metaphor and narrative in therapy.* Boston: Allyn & Bacon.

Pederson, P. B. (1991). Multiculturalism as a generic approach to counseling. *Journal of Counseling and Development, 70,* 6–12.

Perry, M. A., & Furukawa, M. J. (1980). Modeling methods. In F. H. Kanfer & A. P. Goldstein (Eds.), *Helping people change* (pp. 131–171). New York: Pergamon.

Powell, J. (1996). Spiritual values clarification. In F. H. McClure & E. Teyber (Eds.), *Child and adolescent therapy.* Ft. Worth, TX: Harcourt Brace.

Quintana, S. M. (1993). Expanded and updated conceptualization of termination: Implications for short-term individual psychotherapy. *Professional Psychology, 24,* 426–432.

Quintana, S. M., & Holahan, W. (1992). Termination in short-term counseling: Comparison of successful and unsuccessful cases. *Journal of Counseling Psychology, 39,* 299–305.

Reps, P. (1981). *Zen flesh, zen bones.* Garden City, NY: Doubleday.

Richards, P. S., & Bergin, A. E. (1997). *A spiritual strategy for counseling and psychotherapy.* Washington, DC: American Psychological Association.

Ridley, C. R., Mendoza, D. W., & Kanitz, B. E. (1994). Multicultural training: Reexamination, operationalization, and integration. *The Counseling Psychologist, 22,* 227–289.

Rigazio-DiGilio, S. (1993). Family counseling and therapy. In A. Ivey, M. B. Ivey, & L. Simek-Morgan (Eds.), *Counseling and psychotherapy: A multicultural perspective.* Boston: Allyn & Bacon.

Rimm, D. C., & Masters, J. C. (1979). *Behavior therapy: Techniques and empirical findings* (2nd ed.). New York: Academic Press.

Rogers, C. R. (1957). The necessary and sufficient conditions of therapeutic personality change. *Journal of Consulting Psychology, 21,* 95–103.

Rogers, C. R. (1989). A client-centered/person-centered approach to therapy. In H. Kirschenbaum (Ed.), *The Carl Rogers reader* (pp. 135–152). Boston: Houghton Mifflin.

Rogers, C. R., & Rablen, R. A. (1958). *A scale of process in psychotherapy.* Unpublished manuscript, University of Wisconsin. (Available in mimeo from Center for Studies of the Person, La Jolla, CA.)

Rosenthal, T., & Steffek, B. (1991). Modeling methods. In F. H. Kanfer & A. P. Goldstein (Eds.), *Helping people change* (4th ed., pp. 70–121). New York: Pergamon.

Sage, G. P. (1991). Counseling American Indian adults. In C. C. Lee & B. L. Richardson (Eds.), *Multicultural issues in counseling: New approaches to diversity.* Alexandria, VA: ACA Press.

Seligman, L. (2004). *Diagnosis and treatment planning in counseling* (3rd ed.). New York: Plenum.

Seligman, L. (2009). *Conceptual skills for mental health professionals.* Upper Saddle River, NJ: Pearson Merrill.

Sexton, T. L., Whiston, S. C., Bleuer, J. C., & Walz, G. R. (1997). *Integrating outcome research into counseling practice and training.* Alexandria, VA: ACA Press.

Smith, K. L., Subich, L. M., & Kalodner, C. (1995). The transtheoretical model's stages and processes of change and their relation to premature termination. *Journal of Counseling Psychology, 42,* 34–39.

Smith, M. L., & Glass, G. V. (1977). Meta-analysis of psychotherapy outcome studies. *American Psychologist, 32,* 752–760.

Steenbarger, B. N. (1993). A multicontextual model of counseling: Bridging brevity and diversity. *Journal of Counseling and Development, 72,* 8–15.

Stevenson, H. C., & Renard, G. (1993). Trusting ole' wise owls: Therapeutic use of cultural strengths in African-American families. *Professional Psychology: Research and Practice, 24,* 433–442.

Sue, D. W. (1992). Derald Wing Sue on multicultural issues: An interview. *Microtraining Newsletter,* 6.

Sue, D. W., & Sue, D. (1990). *Counseling the culturally different: Theory and practice* (2nd ed.). New York: Wiley.

Sue, D. W., & Sue, D. (2008). *Counseling the culturally different: Theory and practice* (5th ed.). New York: Wiley.

Sussman, N. M., & Rosenfeld, H. M. (1982). Influence of culture, language, and sex on conversational distance. *Journal of Personality and Social Psychology, 42,* 66–74.

Szapocznik, J., & Kurtines, W. M. (1993). Family psychology and cultural diversity: Opportunities for theory, research and application. *American Psychologist, 48,* 400–407.

Tata, S. P., & Leong, F. T. L. (1994). Individualism-collectivism, social-network orientation, and acculturation as predictors of attitudes toward seeking professional psychological help among Chinese Americans. *Journal of Counseling Psychology, 41,* 280–287.

Taussig, I. M. (1987). Comparative responses of Mexican-Americans and Anglo-Americans to early goal-setting in public mental health clinics. *Journal of Counseling Psychology, 34,* 214–217.

Tepper, D. T., & Haase, R. F. (1978). Verbal and nonverbal communications of facilitative conditions. *Journal of Counseling Psychology, 25,* 35–44.

Teyber, E. & McClure, F. H. (2011). *Interpersonal process in therapy: An integrative model* (6th ed.). Pacific Grove, CA: Brooks/Cole.

Thomas, A. J. (1998). Understanding culture and worldview in family systems: Use of the multicultural genogram. *The Family Journal, 6*(1), 24–32.

Tomine, S. I. (1991). Counseling Japanese Americans: From internment to reparation. In C. C. Lee & B. L. Richardson (Eds.), *Multicultural issues in counseling: New approaches to diversity.* Alexandria, VA: ACA Press.

Tran, N. C. (1981, May 11–12). Counseling Vietnamese women in transition. *Helping Indochinese Families in Transition Conference* (compiled proceedings). University of Nebraska, Lincoln.

Watson, D. L., & Tharp, R. G. (2002). *Self-directed change: Self-modification for personal adjustment* (8th ed.). Pacific Grove, CA: Brooks/Cole.

Weakland, J., Fisch, R., Watzlawick, P., & Bodin, A. (1974). Brief therapy: Focused problem resolution. *Family Process, 13,* 141–168.

Welch, I. D., & Gonzalez, D. M. (1999). *The process of counseling and psychotherapy: Matters of skill.* Pacific Grove, CA: Brooks/Cole.

White, M. (1991). Deconstruction and therapy. *Dulwich Centre Newsletter, 3,* 21–40.

White, M., & Epston, D. (1990). *Narrative means to therapeutic ends.* New York: Norton.

White, P. E., & Franzoni, J. B. (1990). A multidimensional analysis of the mental health of graduate counselors in training. *Counselor Education and Supervision, 29,* 258–267.

Wilks, D. (2003). A historical review of counseling theory development in relation to definitions of free will and determinism. *Journal of Counseling and Development, 81,* 278–284. Alexandria, VA: American Counseling Association.

Wittmer, J. M., & Sweeney, T. J. (1995). A holistic model for wellness and prevention over the life span. In M. T. Burke & J. G. Miranti (Eds.), *Counseling: The spiritual dimension* (pp. 19–39). Alexandria, VA: ACA Press.

Wolpe, J. (1958). *Psychotherapy by reciprocal inhibition.* Stanford, CA: Stanford University Press.

Wolpe, J. (1982). *The practice of behavior therapy* (3rd ed.). New York: Pergamon.

Wolpe, J. (1990). *The practice of behavior therapy* (4th ed.). New York: Pergamon.

Wolpe, J., & Lazarus, A. A. (1966). *Behavior therapy techniques.* New York: Pergamon.

Wrenn, C. G. (1962). The culturally encapsulated counselor. *Harvard Educational Review, 32,* 444–449.

Young, M. E. (2009). *Learning the art of helping* (4th ed.). Upper Saddle River, NJ: Prentice Hall.

Zimmer, J. M., & Anderson, S. (1968). Dimensions of positive regard and empathy. *Journal of Counseling Psychology, 15,* 417–426.

Zimmer, J. M., & Park, P. (1967). Factor analysis of counselor communications. *Journal of Counseling Psychology, 14,* 198–203.

Zimmer, J. M., Wightman, L., & McArthur, D. I. (1970). *Categories of counselor behavior as defined from cross-validated factorial descriptions.* Final Report, Project No. 9-A-003. Washington, DC: U.S. Department of Health, Education, and Welfare, Office of Education, Bureau of Research.

Zuk, G. (1975). *Process and practice in family therapy.* Haverford, PA: Psychiatry and Behavioral Science Books.

INDEX